KARMIC
CONNECTIONS

The Birthchart, Karma and Relationships

by

Judy Hall

Published in 2001 by
The Wessex Astrologer
PO Box 2751
Bournemouth
BH6 3ZJ
England

www.wessexastrologer.com

ISBN 1902405102

Printed and Bound by Biddles Ltd,
Kings Lynn and Guildford

A catalogue record for this book is available at the British Library

DEDICATION

This book is dedicated to Justin Adam Carson. A cherished friend and an accomplished teacher of loving relationships and much else besides. Enjoy the great adventure!

ACKNOWLEDGEMENTS

As always I would like to thank the people who have contributed their stories to this book and all the clients from whom I learn so much about relationships. David Lawson and Peter Crowsley are the only people I can name, but much love to you all and may your relationships flourish.

Whosoever has never arrived at pondering on these four things:
What is above?
What is below?
What was before the world?
What will be after it?
It would be better that he had never been born.

Babylonian Talmud, Haguigah ll6
(translated from Spanish by Robert Jacobs)

Other books by Judy Hall:

Art of Psychic Protection Findhorn Press and Samuel Weiser 1996
Deja Who: A New Look at Past Lives Findhorn Press 1998
The Hades Moon Samuel Weiser 1998
Hands Across Time: The Soulmate Enigma Findhorn Press 1998
Holistic Menopause Findhorn Press 1996
The Illustrated Guide to Astrology Godsfield Press 1999
The Illustrated Guide to Crystals Godsfield Press 2001
The Illustrated Guide to Divination Godsfield press 2000
Patterns of the Past The Wessex Astrologer 2001
Principles of Past Life Therapy Thorsons 1996
Principles of Past Life Protection Thorsons 1999
The Way of Reincarnation Thorsons 2001
The Way of Karma Thorsons 2002
What's Your Future? Penguin/Carroll & Brown 2000
The Zodiac Pack: A Visual Approach to Astrology Findhorn Press 1996

Other books by The Wessex Astrologer:

Astrolocality Astrology Martin Davis
The Consultation Chart Wanda Sellar
The Essentials of Vedic Astrology Komilla Sutton
The Lunar Nodes Komilla Sutton
You're not a person - just a birthchart Paul F. Newman

The No Nonsense Guides to Astrology
         Aspects Sally Davis/Bethea Jenner
         Elements and Modes Sally Davis
         Progressions Lesley Griffiths
         Transits Paul F. Newman

CONTENTS

INTRODUCTION: THE GODDESS OF LOVE

It is no longer a warmth hidden in my veins: it's Venus entire and whole fastening on her prey.

Jean Racine 'Phedre' (1677)

Relationships are productive, challenging and sometimes painful. They are one of the most profound ways our souls learn and grow. Few important relationships begin in the present life, and even fewer are the result of a chance meeting. Astrologically speaking, relationships are ruled by Venus, a most capricious mistress. Her family, as portrayed in Greek myth, throw an interesting light on relationships in general, and her love life provides a useful counterpoint to overly romantic visions of 'happy ever after'. Given her character and history, Venus is a surprising choice for the astrological Goddess of Love - unless the ancients were trying to communicate to future generations something of the hidden nature of this most misunderstood of human emotions and the dark entanglements that underlie relationships. Up close, the planet itself is not at all attractive, despite its beauty from afar. As one astronomer pointed out: 'If you venture onto the surface of Venus, you will be fried, poisoned, suffocated and corroded'.

The nature of the planet can tell us a great deal about how relationships function. A scientist has put forward the theory that the crust of Venus is liable to disintegrate and fall into the molten and sulphurous centre – in exactly the same way 'love' can reach out and break through the barriers people build around themselves, pulling them down into the irrational, instinctual self where karmic patterns reside. Here are met the darker qualities of love: devouring possessiveness, jealousy, rapacious lust, envy, hatred, vengeance, covetousness and deep, unstoppable desire.

In myth, the goddess of desire, Venus had an adulterous affair with her brother Mars, god of war and libido. As a result, five children were born: Eros (Love), Anteros (Reciprocal Love), Harmonia (Harmony), and Deimus and Phobus. The latter two translate as Terror and Fear, not the first thing one normally associates with love.

Nevertheless, in a karmic astrologer's postbag, all too often Fear and Terror accompany Love in the quest for connubial Harmony. Most people hope to find Reciprocal Love in their relationships, but many are disappointed not just once but across lifetimes.

Venus's birth was hardly a promising beginning. The god Uranus was castrated by his son Saturn and his genitals flung into the sea. Some sources say that it was from this bloodstained foam that Aphrodite the beautiful arose (Venus' Greek name). Even her paternity is in question, certain myths citing Uranus as her father, others Jupiter - making Uranus her great-grandfather. She came from a highly dysfunctional family: Grandfather Saturn (god of Time and the Lord of Karma) had the habit of swallowing his children whole and had had to be tricked into regurgitating them by Jupiter, a lineage breaker who had escaped this fate. The entire family were more like characters from a soap opera than divine beings - they reflected all the flaws and foibles of humanity and played out all the variations of so-called love that can be found today.

Venus was charmingly packaged. She was said to exude an aura of seduction, which no man could resist. She was 'mistress of gracious laughter, sweet deceits, the charms and delights of love.' The *Homeric Hymns* tell us that only three people were able to resist her: her sisters Artemis (Huntress and Moon goddess) and Athena (goddess of Wisdom), and her aunt Hestia (goddess of the Hearth who sanctified any place where she was invoked). Hestia was a sister of Jupiter, and had been swallowed by her father. When she was returned to life, Hestia took up her power and refused to yield it to any man.

These women are all described as virgin goddesses. The old meaning of virgin was 'whole and intact'. These were goddesses who did not need a man to make them feel complete and who were not, supposedly, vulnerable to the temptations of Venusian-style love – although this did not preclude them from indulging in love affairs. This in itself can teach us a great deal about the nature and purpose of relationships. Everyone else around Venus succumbed to the charms and machinations of the goddess of love:

> 'She who awakens a pleasant yearning in gods, she who subdues the race of mortal men, and the birds of Zeus, and all the many animals that the land nourishes and the sea nourishes... None of the blessed gods, no mortal man, no one else can ever escape Aphrodite [Venus]. She even leads astray the mind of Zeus [Jupiter] himself, the lover of

lightning, the greatest of all... And when she wants to, she can deceive that sage heart of his easily and make even him mate with mortal women'.[1]

Venus certainly had her darker side. She instilled into mortal men unparalleled lust and desire, and into women incestuous desires and 'monstrous and bestial passions'. It is said that her son Eros, the Cupid who randomly fired the darts of love, may well have been the result of Venus' incestuous liaison with Jupiter, rather than with Mars. The extended family's dynamics were confused, illicit and amoral, each generation compulsively living out the dramas of earlier generations but, of course, as gods they did not die and so the generations interwove their dysfunctional sagas.

Venus was forcibly married to Hephaestus, the ugliest of the gods. The union did not prosper and she took a series of lovers, some with dire consequences for humankind. Having literally caught her *inflagrante delicto* with Mars, her husband Hephaestus (who had woven a steel net for the trap) demanded heavy penalties as retribution for the affair. After the divorce, her uncle Neptune romantically offered to restore her virtue through marriage. He may have been under the illusion that he could tame this wild woman, but she turned him down flat. Venus's subsequent steamy love affairs were full of dark passion and eroticism. Although mortal men who made love with a goddess were said to lose their potency, Venus nevertheless seduced more than one. She was part of an eternal triangle with Persephone, goddess of the Underworld and wife to Pluto. Both loved the handsome hunter, Adonis. When he was killed and his soul went to Hades where Persephone ruled, Aphrodite was grief-stricken and begged Jupiter to return him to the upper world. Eventually a time-share bargain was struck whereby he spent part of the year with each of the goddesses. The Trojan War came about because of Venus's interference in the affairs of men, although some of the mortal relationships in which she intervened were idyllic – for a while.

'She is Venus when she smiles'

As Ben Jonson pointed out in the seventeenth century, all women are Venus and take on her role in the great play of life. Her potent allure, encapsulated in woman, is feared by men who are, at the same time, passionately enamoured of her. In many cultures, women are blamed for this paradox - they have to be veiled and hidden from sight so that men may be safe from overwhelming temptation, but both men and women carry Venus' sexual heritage and respond to her erotic promptings. When modern man looks to his feminine side, it is with Venus he is engaging.

Many of the characters playing supporting roles in Venus's story can be found in present day astrological connections. The karma Venus created passed down through the generations and we will meet the archetypal images she portrays over and over again as we explore the nature of karmic relationships.

Note: I am always aware when I look at relationships just how biased my sample is. Few people consult me about relationships that are working well but literally hundreds of people need help with their difficulties. Consequently what we look at in this book will be heavily weighted towards the problem areas and why these arise. To redress the balance, you will also find suggestions for healing some of the causes of relationship karma.

Some of the astrological material and case histories used in this book have already appeared in *The Karmic Journey* (now revised and updated as *Patterns of the Past*) which deals with personal karma. I have chosen to retain these case histories because they are still as relevant - and ubiquitous - as they were when I selected them over fifteen years ago. People still say to me: 'I see you used my story but you got the astrology slightly wrong, the aspects were different'. I didn't use their story; I used a story which applied to many people. It was one I had seen over and over again, with slight variations, when working with karmic relationships. The decade that has passed since I wrote *The Karmic Journey* has confirmed how universal the stories are. The minor differences in the actual aspects are irrelevant; it is the fact that the planets concerned make a contact that is important.

1

KARMA AND RELATIONSHIPS

No major human relationship is the result of chance.[1]

Gina Cerminara

Karma shows itself in relationships. The people you meet, the expect-ations you have, the circumstances in which you relate, the kind of marriage or other association that you find yourself in, all reflect previous liaisons. You are the sum total of all your experiences, and much it will come about through relationships.

If you have experienced 'good' and positive relationships in the past, you will find relationships beneficial and life enhancing, but 'bad' experiences will be traumatising and maybe even soul destroying. It is these difficult past relationships that create the most ingrained karma and which need healing. As Chuck Spezzano says: 'Relationships are the juice of life. If you do not experience them as an elixir, then they have probably become a poison'.[2]

Many people ask why they have to experience difficult relationships. Mavis Klein once explained that pain in our intimate relationships challenges the fixity of our personality and joy in our intimate relationships is the fulfilment of our ideal self. In other words, relationships are the way we grow and evolve into what we must be. And, as Thomas Moore puts it:

> The intimacy we pledge at the wedding is an invitation to open the Pandora's box of soul's graces and perversities. Marriage digs deep into the stuff of the soul. Lifelong, intense, socially potent relationships don't exist without touching the deepest, rawest reservoirs of soul. Few experiences in life reach such remote and uncultivated regions of the heart, unearthing material that is both incredibly fertile and frighteningly primordial.[3]

The threads of a relationship can often be traced back through several lives. Most significant others have been with you before, many times. The roles may be different this time, but the connection is there.

Karma is a continuous process by which we meet what we have previously created: it is not necessarily 'bad'. All karma is actually neutral, it is how we perceive and react to it that makes it seem like we have 'bad karma', and few people take the time to consider their 'good karma':

> 'Karma' is a Sanskrit word meaning work or action. It is an on-going process. Something is set in motion and has repercussions. This can occur on many levels and in ways that are subtle or gross, immediate or long term. Karma arises not only out of action but out of thoughts, attitudes and desires. It is the sum total of all that the soul has experienced in its cycle of incarnations – although in Buddhism, for instance, there is no notion of a separate soul moving from life to life but rather karmic seeds and potentials passing from moment to moment. The concept of karma is usually associated with rebirth, but this is not necessarily so. The past is the past, whether it belongs to another life or to the present one. Actions have consequences and time has little relevance in the working out of karma.[4]

Relationship karma occurs in all parts of life: in friendships, business partnerships, teacher and pupil, employer and employee, healer and patient, next-door neighbours, casual meetings or marriage partners, and almost every other human interaction. Relationships provide fertile soil in which to work on soul purpose for the present life. The soul is that part of a human being that is divine and eternal, it is what passes from life to life: our immortality. Indeed, it is more true to say that a human being is a soul who is on a spiritual journey and who, for the moment, has incarnated on earth to meet its karma and continue its evolution.

For much of its incarnation on earth the soul has to contend not only with ingrained patterns from the past but also with the ego which is part of the personality taken on for the present life. The ego develops early in life and may well incorporate reactions to past life buttons that are pushed as it develops throughout childhood. The ego has concepts that define the incarnated soul as separate and *other*. It is identified with external things and roles rather than the inner being of the soul. Egos have their own agendas and strategies for getting their needs met which may conflict with the soul's desire to grow and evolve. Egos also have a habit of setting up future karma.

Karma means action, what goes around, comes around. The causes of present life experiences usually lie in the past, whenever that may have been. Old attitudes and actions create a picture of which only a small part can be glimpsed in any one lifetime. Relationship karma has many angles and manifestations and can operate in all types of interconnection: families, love affairs, friendships and business ventures. Souls have a wide variety of reasons for entering into relationship again, not all of them based on love. Anger and resentment are powerful generators of karma, as are unfinished business and an inability to let go. Karmic connections can be formed with anyone, not just family or lovers. Strong links forged over several incarnations, or at soul level, can bring people together to carry out a specific task, deal with unfinished business or duties, or repay debts and obligations. One soul may act as a catalyst for another. The intention may be to meet fleetingly or to spend a lifetime together.

Inappropriate and yet powerfully intense sexual attraction is often the first indication of an earlier karmic connection - and is one of the pitfalls of the search for a soulmate. Such a connection occurs at the base chakra level: in the sexual organs. This is where past life contact is experienced and it feels as though a wave of lust travels from one person to the other as the chakra opens with irresistible force. If that is immediately acted upon and the people concerned fall on each other to discharge the energy in passionate sexual activity rather than asking: 'What does this mean? Is it simply a signal that we have known each other before or are we meant to take it further?' there can be problems. People find themselves embroiled in the most unlikely and impossible of situations, especially where ages and gender have changed since that last life contact. If they are the only one of the two experiencing the sexual charge, they may also end up embarrassed or feeling rejected when the other person does not respond.

Sexual attraction can come about too when one soul has been working on its spiritual development and has stimulated the powerful kundalini force that normally lies passive at the base of the spine. It can also occur because someone is a perfect hook for collective projections of the 'ideal man' or 'woman of my dreams'. When this is uncontrolled, the person will have sexual magnetism, a certain *frisson* surrounds them. Unless they are very careful, they may end up creating considerable relationship karma with any and every woman or man who responds to this powerful emanation of sexual energy.

There are times when this sexual charge signals that the souls are meant to be together. I always use my own experience as an example of this. When I met my present partner, it was at an ancient temple site on Rhodos. We stood together under an old olive tree on the night of the full moon - which was transiting his Sun and my Moon along with Pluto. Without even touching each other, we simultaneously experienced a rush of energy, a kind of cosmic orgasm. We have explosive Uranus interaspects across our charts and this was an extremely physical - and yet spiritual - manifestation of that energy. It certainly caught our attention. Several psychics have described a life we had together at that particular temple site thousands of years ago - and said that we were destined to be together again as we had spiritual work to do. One result was a 'cosmic child', a book we wrote together about menopause (also known as the moon of pause).

Certain aspects of karma are purely personal. A soul meets its own expectations of love through association with other people, although the expectations need not necessarily have arisen with those people. It could all have been created through different contacts somewhere in the past. Other aspects of relationship karma are specific to the two, or more, people concerned. They have unfinished business from previous lives together. However, some people get together to work on karmic issues that have nothing to do with each other in a personal sense, they simply share the same themes and take the opportunity to work on them. In this way, progress can be made before confronting the person with whom the karma arose.

TYPES OF RELATIONSHIP KARMA

Personal Karma
What each individual created and is dealing with. It is carried forward and brought into a relationship along with the issues between the people concerned (see below).
Astrological Indicators: The birth chart (see *Patterns of the Past*) and synastry.

Group or Racial Karma
This is carried by a specific group, which may be a family, a group of friends, or a soul group. It can also be a country, tribe or race of people. Most people who become involved in group karma will have incarnated into that group before, but this is not always so.

Astrological Indicators: The eleventh or twelfth house, or the fourth/ tenth house axis for families.

Collective Karma

This arises from all that has gone before, and it is the karma of the human race. Although positive collective karma is generated too, it is the negative karma that creates problems for future generations. No one person is responsible for it but individuals may well have been part of its manifestation in other lives. Certain people incarnate with the intention of taking on part of this collective karma and clearing it for the wider whole.

Astrological Indicators: Twelfth house, Moon in Capricorn, planets in Pisces, Neptune-Chiron interaspects.

Cosmic Karma

The spiritual karma of humankind, which can override all other karmas. Cosmic karma includes the need for each individual to evolve and to recognise, and take responsibility for, their part in the whole. With specific regard to relationships, cosmic karma is concerned with the development of unconditional love and entering into true relationship.

Astrological Indicators: Beyond the birthchart.

Retributive Karma

The classic 'eye for an eye, tooth for a tooth' which boomerangs back. If the soul has failed to grasp a lesson, it gets back what it put out. If it was unloving, it will experience not being loved; if it has been an abuser, it becomes abused; if it manipulated, it is manipulated; if it was overly dominant, it may be dominated; if it abandoned, it could be rejected. The person a soul treated badly may come back in the role of abuser but equally the soul may find it has to care for that person, possibly in difficult circumstances. If someone in a past life had had an affair which caused great hurt to another person, in the present life that situation could be reversed. In other words, what you have done to others comes back to you.

Astrological Indicators: Extremely challenging aspects, interaspects and planetary placements especially of Venus, emphasis on the fifth, seventh, eighth and twelfth houses.

Recompense Karma
Recompense karma also comes back, but positively. It is a reward or recognition for the things that the soul got right in the past, or for the sacrifices it made in order to help others. If, for example, someone put a relationship on hold to care for someone who was ill, then that person could well come back as a good friend or lover in the present incarnation.
Astrological Indicators: Helpful planetary placements and smooth, harmonious aspects and interaspects.

Redemptive Karma
Some people incarnate to help others or to do something for the world. High Tibetan Lamas, for instance, could well have reached a state of enlightenment and had the opportunity to move off the wheel of rebirth several lives ago, but they come back to help others reach the same state. Other people take on tasks that help to clear collective karma.
Astrological Indicators: Emphasis on Chiron, Neptune or the twelfth house or Pisces. Clearing collective karma: twelfth house North Node.

Merit Karma
This is a reward for all the things the soul got right in previous lives, all the lessons learned, all the insights put into practice, all the beneficial relationships enjoyed. It is money in the karmic piggy bank and may attract positive relationships.
Astrological Indicators: Easy aspects or specific beneficial planetary placements, especially second house Venus.

Attitudinal Karma
This has usually been present during several lives. An intransigent attitude, ingrained behaviour or an intractable or habitual emotional stance often manifests at the physical level during the present incarnation. So, for example, believing there would 'never be enough love', could attract difficult relationships that could shut down the heart.
Astrological Indicators: Outer planet to inner planet aspects, especially fixed squares, Venus in Leo/Virgo/Scorpio/Capricorn and/or the sixth house.

The Karmic Treadmill
Destructive patterns that have not been outgrown are like a karmic treadmill. The same old thing goes round and round. Relationships can provide many examples.
Astrological Indicators: Difficult aspects and interaspects, and a preponderance of planets in fixed signs.

Symbolic Karma
Not all karma is immediately obvious and symbolic karma can take some unravelling. The present life condition symbolises what was done in the past or how the person felt. For example, the American past life reader, Edgar Cayce, maintained that epilepsy in the present life indicated the possibility of sexual excess in a previous life.
Astrological Indicators: Aspects to specific and relevant planets.

Communication Karma
How the soul communicated itself in the past leads to communication karma, especially in families and partnerships. The soul may have spoken out intemperately, or held back from speaking at all. It may have spoken truly from the heart, or been economical with the truth especially in emotional matters. It may have felt one way but said something different. It may have criticised, betrayed or slandered the other soul. In relationships where this karma exists, there is often difficulty in communicating thoughts, feelings and beliefs and misunderstandings may arise.
Astrological Indicators: Aspects to Mercury and house placement: especially fifth, seventh and eleventh; Chiron in third or ninth or Gemini.

'Sins of Omission and Commission'
'Things that have been done that ought not to have been done, and the things that have not been done that should have been done'. If a soul has always behaved in a certain way, or consistently refused to take action, or to learn a lesson, then the karma comes around and around until the soul gets the message.
Astrological Indicators: fixed aspects or many sextiles.

Ideological Karma
Attachment to a belief can create ideological karma, as can imposing beliefs on other people. The beliefs may be religious, philosophical or purely secular.

Astrological Indicators: Ninth house placements, especially Pluto and Chiron.

Karma of Hypocrisy

Having said one thing, or done things a certain way, and yet believed something different gives rise to the karma of hypocrisy. As does the 'anything for a quiet life' approach. Hypocrisy arises from a lack of spiritual conviction and inner truth, or a betrayal of truth. A life then arises when that inner foundation has to be regained and reparation may need to be made.

Astrological Indicators: Mercury its aspects and placement.

Karma of Mockery

Mocking other people's afflictions, thoughts, beliefs or actions, gives rise to this karma. It stems from not valuing the path that another person travels. The person who mocks often finds him or herself living out in the present life the circumstances he or she so despised. So, for instance, someone who mocked others for falling in love easily could find his or herself helplessly afflicted by uncontrollable, and probably unattainable, passion for someone else. The incarnating soul may also find itself in close relationship with the person it mocked in the past.

Astrological Indicators: Mercury, its placements and aspects especially Gemini and Scorpio placements.

Pacts and Promises

Pacts and promises made in a past life can strongly affect the present, whether they involve another person or are purely personal. A promise to always be there for someone could result in relationship karma. A former vow of celibacy could strongly affect sexual life in the present incarnation.

Astrological Indicators: Depends on the vow. For example, celibacy: Saturn in the eighth house or Scorpio, difficult Mars or Venus aspects.

Karma-in-suspension

As not all karma can be dealt with at once, some of it remains in suspension to be dealt with at some other time - which may or may not occur during the present life.

Astrological Indicators: Wide aspects that decrease by progression.

Karma-in-the-making

What goes on at the present time creates future karma. Remembering that each thought, deed, action and belief you have creates what you become is a way to bring positive karma into your next life.

Astrological Indicators: Cardinal squares and one way interaspects between charts.

Relationship Karma

This has many aspects and most of the above karmas can operate in addition to themes that we will meet as we explore karmic relationships (see Chapter 2). Relationship karma often includes an element of retributive karma. Someone who in the past was unfaithful, had many affairs, or who was fickle in love may find themselves with a partner who, in the present life, acts in this way. Someone who found it difficult to open up to love may long for a partner, and yet not find one.

Astrological Indicators: fifth, seventh and eighth houses, outer planet aspects to Venus, and interaspects.

Karmic Mutation

Not all relationships improve as they mature. In some the interplay changes subtly and yet the underlying dynamics are the same. For example, a relationship which was violent and abusive in its early manifestations may appear on the surface to be kinder, yet below the surface cruelty may still be present manifesting on a more psychological level. Sarcasm, endless put-downs, indifference, self-centredness, infidelity, and the like are all mutations of the previous abuse. The couple may be drawn together by hate and a desire for revenge, or they may truly believe that this is 'love'. Until the karma is neutralized and the underlying attitude changes, they will be drawn back together time and again. The mutation of roles may be many and varied, but the challenge remains the same.

Not all marriages or contacts are between people who have had exactly the same relationship in other lives. In my experience, it is possible that the parties were married before, but it is equally likely - confirmed over and over again by regression work - that the relationship could also have been as parent and child, siblings, friends and acquaintances, bitter enemies, employer-employee, master and slave, and so on. Children may incarnate into families where their parents are people to whom they have been married in the past.

What is clear, however, is that the issues being worked on are rarely new. It is perfectly possible to share a life with somebody one has never met before, yet with whom one has certain karmic issues in common. It is sometimes easier to work on these things at a more objective distance, and the incarnation may be a preparation for working with the person with whom the karma arose in a future incarnation. Even if the relationship is a sequel to the past, it may be that the couple are trying out a different way of doing things, learning new responses, maybe even changing roles or gender. They could be exploring interdependence after lifetimes of dependence or extreme independence. Many karmic issues are expressed in relationship and these issues will also mutate as the souls mature.

Gender

It is clear from regression and soul work that the soul is neutral and genderless. A soul will only be male or female according to the lessons and needs of an incarnation. Souls change gender through the physical bodies they inhabit when they take on an incarnation, and experiences from when the soul was in the opposite sex body are then internalised as the anima or animus. A soul may carry a sense of being male or female into the between-life state at the end of an incarnation. Certain souls will tend more towards a particular gender, and others to the opposite gender so they may feel masculine or feminine in the between-life state, especially on those planes of existence that are close to the earth. As the soul leaves earth behind and sheds the various subtle bodies, gender identity drops away.

In this book I have called the incarnating soul 'it' to avoid the use of 'he or she' and 'him or herself' too frequently. I have tended to refer to the partners in a relationship as 'he and she' but this is not intended as a bias towards heterosexual relationships. It is quite clear from regression work that same sex relationships are as natural to the soul as opposite sex ones, gender being a continuum that stretches from 'mighty male' to 'effeminate man' and continuing on from 'strong female' to 'passive woman'. It passes through many stages in between. Equally, sexual attraction and orientation is not black and white, it passes through many shades of grey. What matters to the soul is the karma it has with the person with whom it is in relationship, the experiences it undergoes, and the patterns that are working out. Emotional expectations are the same for both sexes and can be experienced in liaisons with either a man or a woman.

Projection and attraction work exactly the same way whichever sex is carrying them.

Similarly, if a child has a particular emotional imprint, it can be experienced through a parent of either sex. This can happen despite a tendency for a pattern signified by the Moon to relate to the mother and the Sun to the father, Mars to the male and Venus to the female. If there is no biological mother or father around, then the soul will play out the story with someone who is an appropriate hook because of their own in-built emotional pathology, no matter what sex. There may be a subtle tendency, which increases as the child moves into maturity, solidifying into a trait that is played out in adulthood. Relationships are just as complex an intermingling of masculine and feminine, anima and animus, god and goddess, as they are in an individual.

Time

From over twenty-five years of working with regression and other lives, I do not personally believe in linear time where the past is somewhere back in one direction and the future at the opposite extreme. To me, time is much more flexible than this and can perhaps best be described as a spiral or wheel (see Figure 1). Lives that still

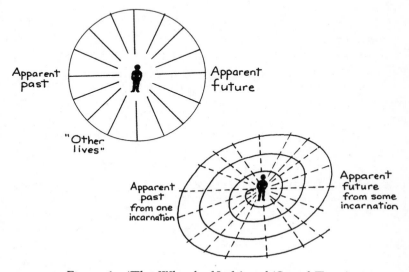

Figure 1 - 'The Wheel of Life' and 'Spiral Time'

hold an emotional charge, or which have unfinished business, are closer to the present life because they still have an impact no matter when they occurred in historical time. However, to make sense of our experience here on earth, we need to use the concepts of past, present and future so I refer to 'past' as well as 'other' or 'previous' lives.

THE BIRTHCHART AND RELATIONSHIP KARMA

A birthchart maps out a soul's expectations and its karma around love. (The soul's general karma is discussed in *Patterns of the Past*, the companion volume to this book, and individual expectations around love appear in the next chapter of this book.) Deeply held beliefs are described in the chart, themes are laid out, and intentions stated. Different facets of the past may conflict as the chart pulls together karmic experiences from two or more lives for resolution. A soul may choose, for example, to confront all its beliefs around love. In one or more lives the belief may have built up that love hurts (Chiron-Venus) and yet the soul may also carry, from other lives, the belief that perfect love (Neptune-Venus) is possible. At the same time, the soul may feel it does not deserve love (Saturn-Venus) and fear that there will never be enough love (Pluto-Venus). Throw in the deep fear of intimacy that Uranus-Venus has developed, and the soul may well decide: 'I don't need relationships at all'. And yet, this is the soul that may find itself in some extremely intense relationship scenarios as it struggles to resolve the different messages from the past. Overcoming such challenges brings about enormous soul growth.

Some houses in the birthchart such as the twelfth are particularly karmic, as are certain planetary contacts, while other houses relate specifically to love and relationships. Karma with lovers may be delineated by fifth house planets, karma with partners by seventh or eight house placements, those with friends by the eleventh house, those with enemies by the twelfth house and so on.

One of the greatest barriers to true and intimate relationships is that people do not take responsibility for their own feelings, and may blame others for how they themselves feel. They act as though they are responsible for how other people feel, and expect other people to take care of their feelings. Certain signs and aspects take on the responsibility for others, and assign blame, more easily. Water signs find it difficult at times to distinguish between their own feelings and those of other people, but the soul with the Sun in Pisces suffers particularly from a kind of existential guilt. It often feels responsible for the whole world and its feelings and yet longs for someone to take care of itself. The soul with the Sun in Cancer, on the other hand, being rather more prone to self pity, tends to look to other people to make it feel good - and blames them when it does not. Libra is another sign which feels intensely responsible for other people and will do all in its power not to upset someone else or cause conflict. The Sun placed in a water sign house may signify that the soul has hidden guilt and feelings of responsibility. Aries is normally an independent and self-sufficient sign, but place the Sun in Aries in the seventh house of relationship and the Libra shadow may make itself felt. Such indications are subtle and can point the way to a deeper understanding of a soul's relationship dynamics than the superficial placement of the planets.

The karma embodied in an association can be studied through the synastry between the charts of the two partners, and from composite and relationship charts (these are based on the midpoints created between two charts when calculated in various ways) which illustrate how and why the association functions. In synastry, the outer planet contacts to the partner's inner planets, angles and nodes (the interaspects), signify the lessons to be worked on. The degree of difficulty is likely to be expressed by the type of aspect. These same lessons will be reiterated through several interaspects, and by aspects within the relationship and composite charts, illuminating the underlying karmic theme of the liaison. If the karma is personal to the two people concerned the interaspects will repeat 'each-way'. If it is not personal there will be a one-way aspect (See Chapter 5).

Either partner can take on the role of the outer planet within the relationship. For example, if one partner has Uranus in the seventh house conjunct the other partner's Sun, and that partner has Uranus in aspect to Venus which in turn is involved in the synastry through a Venus aspect to the first partner's Uranus, then the underlying themes are freedom versus commitment and a difficulty in being truly intimate. One partner may now be ready for close relationship, the other may not yet have reached this stage. This theme will have played out through several lives. At some point in the relationship one of the partners has to decide whether to stay in the relationship or to move out of it, unless an interaction has evolved which allows for both space and intimacy.

Aspects and Orbs

Whilst minor aspects may play their part in relationship astrology, karma is most immediately visible in the major aspects and in that most karmic of aspects, the inconjunct or quincunx, 150°. For the major aspects and the quincunx I use an orb of 8°. Of the minor aspects, I pay attention to the other inconjunct, the 30° semi-sextile which shows karma that tends to be projected onto, and lived out through, other people. I also look at the quintile 72° if it occurs in an aspect between the major love planet Venus and one of the outer planets. As this aspect is one of fate or destiny it may show an evolutionary potential to reconcile or transform the karmic expectations embodied in the contact.

It is only when trying to track down extremely subtle indications of karmic attitudes or expectations that are clear from what a client says that I go to more obscure aspects. For example, if the inner planet is moving towards (applying to) the outer planet, these aspects can become more strongly operative by progression as the client reaches the relevant age. And they can also signify 'karma in suspension' which becomes operative during a lifetime but is not immediately obvious at birth.

Transits and Progressions

I have frequently noted that major partnerships or events within a relationship correspond to either a planet in the natal or composite chart being triggered by a transit, or to a planet moving into orb through secondary progression. In Chapter 9 for instance, Tyrrell classically went into a relationship that taught him a great deal about projection and delusions on a Neptune transit to his Venus - although at first he thought he had met his ideal woman. In fact he had, but he was just not aware that the shadow side of an Aquarian Venus is remote, detached and unable to commit to a deep relationship, so when the living embodiment of his ideal displayed these characteristics, he felt 'gutted'. Although he understood about projection, he did not at that time know about the astrology involved.

This is so typical of a Neptune transit. Neptune can also bring out inherent deception - both self-delusion and that perpetrated by someone else. I know a woman who met and married 'Prince Charming' on the transit of Neptune to her Moon. Six months later, when the transit was finally over, she felt as though 'someone had snapped their fingers and brought me out of hypnosis. I just couldn't believe what I had done.' The charming man turned out to be a complete con man, Neptune in disguise.

Another transit that feels fatal and fated is Pluto to Venus. It attracts someone from the past, someone with whom the soul has many issues to work on and deep emotional karma. It is immediately intense and powerful - the souls pick up well into the patterns of the past that they had left off before. It often feels as though the soul lays eyes on someone and 'that's it, I'm in love'. But it quickly becomes apparent that they are dealing with emotional baggage from the past.

Few people can escape meeting their relationship karma under transits like these. I know one man who did - or thought he did. For several months, astrologers and psychics were constantly telling him: 'This is it. This is when you go into a relationship. You just won't be able to help it. You'll walk through the door and she'll be there.' Not that he sought such advice, far from it, as this was the last thing he wanted to hear but, somehow, he kept bumping into it. Just about every major planet was aspecting his Venus including a Pluto conjunction. So determined was he that he would not go into a relationship that he virtually barricaded himself in his house for six months. He emerged triumphant: 'There I've made it, I did not go into relationship.' What he did do during that time, however, was get to know himself much better. The relationship was with himself.

Progressions work to bring an issue into focus. If an aspect is wide the issue may not surface until adulthood when the progression closes the gap. It does not mean that the issues are not there, they almost invariably are, but it takes that long to get a handle on them. So, again, Tyrrell in Chapter 9 speaks of his 'horrendous' mothering issues and his battle with the dark feminine. It took many years and training as a therapist to understand how this was related to his relationship to his mother. It came into focus each time the swiftly-moving Moon progressed to a close aspect to Pluto. He worked through many of the issues in his relationships with women and then began to deal with their source: his actual relationship to his mother.

Soul Groups

Souls tend to travel in groups, loosely related not at a biological level but through a similarity of *essence*. A soul group is an interwoven web of spiritual connections who have travelled together across time (see Figure 2).

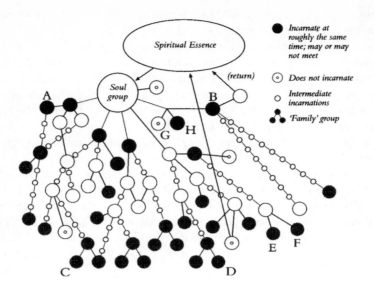

Figure 2 - The Soul's Journey into Matter

Whilst the exact process of how a soul group forms differs according to the source of the teaching, there is a surprising congruence in ancient wisdom from all over the world in the belief that the soul is divine. According to the western mystery tradition, a soul group breaks off from the pool of spiritual essence in which all souls originate. At this stage, the individual souls are undifferentiated, floating in Neptunian oneness. The group may remain like this, learning on the spiritual planes for aeons of time, or it may pass down through the various planes of being until the souls are able to incarnate on to the earth, establishing Saturnian boundaries as it does so. On the way, the group may break down into individual souls or into smaller groups of souls. Even what appears to be an individual soul in one incarnation may break down further in subsequent incarnations and can have several incarnations at once (rather like the Buddhist notion of *skandas*, 'fragments' that carry karma after death and move from life to life.) It is unusual for the whole of a group to incarnate at any one time, but it does happen. More usually, some souls remain close to the earth to act as guides for those who have incarnated.

The metaphysical truth of the oneness of life - and the

possibility of shared soul or consciousness substance - is now being supported by a surprising source: astro-physics. Scientists have found that material which may have begun life as a single star that imploded and scattered its carbon and nitrogen elements is now spread throughout the universe forming the basic building blocks of life. Everyone on earth has some of this material incorporated into their physical body, but much of the material is not in incarnation and is still scattered throughout space. From the scientific point of view, it is the substance that links the universe together. This can pass into and out of incarnation very easily and is similar to the Buddhist notion of mind or consciousness existing independently of the body and yet being embodied from time to time.

In Figure 2, souls A and B will undoubtedly recognise each other and may well feel 'this is my soulmate'. If E and F meet, they may feel like soulmates also. G and H are 'soul companions', one soul incarnated on earth and the other remaining in the spiritual realms as a guide. C and D, however, have travelled a long way from the original soul group splitting off point. If they have had difficult experiences together in other lives, they may feel more like powerful enemies than soulmates. (Love and hate being two sides of the same coin). Soul D will be part of a 'soul family', which may or may not be part of the biological family into which the soul incarnates in the present life.

Souls from the same soul group often feel like soulmates when they encounter each other on the earth, but this is not necessarily so. It all depends on how individuated the souls have become, and how far they have travelled from their origins. If a soul has had many earth incarnations without rejoining the soul group, then that soul feels separate and isolated (typically an Aries phenomenon.) If a soul has had few incarnations, or frequently returned to the group, then the soul will feel much more a part of the whole - and may well feel torn from its roots when in incarnation (classically a Pisces or Neptune experience).

People from within a soul group take on many roles, and some of them may seem destructive when viewed without a knowledge of the spiritual purpose behind the contact. As one of my clients put it: 'Your soulmate is the person who is here to teach you the hardest lesson.' She was referring to the fact that many people have found, through regression to other lives or to the between-life state, that people who they thought were their worst enemy were actually part of their soul group. Out of love for them, these souls took on a role that seemed cruel, abusive or cold so that the person would have the opportunity of experiencing whatever it was they had come to experience. This is because karma is a learning process. It is not a question of punishment and retribution, although restitution and reparation may be called for. Rather, karma is an on-going process of evolution. A soul may need to know what it feels like to be the abuser and the abused, the betrayer and the betrayed and so on. Or the soul may simply be repeating an old pattern - stuck on a karmic treadmill - and so a member of the soul group enters into an association which is such a strong manifestation of the old pattern that the soul simply has to change or chooses to exercise grace.

The state of grace says that the soul can step out of the old pattern and find a new way to interact. Grace is not an escape clause but it can be used to release the soul from impossible, stuck situations. Insights into the reasons behind relationships can be gained from the synastry between charts, but there are times when regression to other lives - or a knowledge of those lives - is the only way to be freed from old patterns. Astrology is a useful tool when looking at karmic relationships, but healing at a deeper level may be called for. When I wrote *The Karmic Journey* in the mid-eighties, there were few competent past life healers around, now there is a proliferation. The residues of relationship karma that has accrued over many lifetimes need to be shed as we enter a new astrological age and therapies such as past life reframing and body-based approaches such as process acupressure can be extremely useful.

People from the Past
Meetings with people from the past can be wonderful. They can also be devastating. Instant antipathy or fear can be traced back to previous interaction, and a chart for the moment of meeting can be illuminating if a chart is not available for the other person, as can the transits involved. Many years ago, before I had come to consciously believe in past lives, I had an appointment with a local solicitor. As soon as I entered his office I felt cold and could not stop shaking, I was literally terrified of him. I was even affected by his voice on the telephone and always referred to him as 'The Inquisitor'. No one else could understand this as he was a mild, ineffectual little man. Several years later he cropped up in a regression to a former life in which he had appeared in a minor role as a member of the

Inquisition. From that time on he did not affect me at all, I was able to see him as he was in the present incarnation.

At the time of our first meeting transiting Saturn was conjunct my natal Mars, activating its difficult position between Uranus and Saturn. The encounter brought out my inner powerlessness and old fear. At the time of the regression, transiting Neptune was on my Mercury, opposing Uranus. I was released from the past through the spiritual knowledge and insight offered by Neptune.

Equally difficult to handle can be an irresistible attraction to an inappropriate person. A middle-aged woman (Sun-Venus in Pisces opposing Neptune, and Moon-Mars in Aries) was overcome by totally inexplicable but very strong feelings of lust towards the teenage son of one of her friends, a situation which she found extremely embarrassing. In a regression she went back to ancient times when they had made a sacred marriage. The tie had been strongly sexual but he had died at a young age. She had been left feeling cheated, frustrated and resentful as the sacred marriage had included the vow to be faithful to him for life and she had therefore had to remain celibate. In the present life she had never found the sexual fulfilment she was seeking. The synastry between the charts included his Aries Sun conjunct her Moon-Mars, signifying a strong sexual attraction. His Pluto was also conjunct her Neptune and opposed her Sun-Venus, indicating an old symbiotic interplay with the frustrations and resentments (Pluto) from their time together, plus the 'desire for what could not be' (Neptune) in the present life.

Viewing the relationship as an old contact coming forward into the present can help the participants to handle this type of attraction constructively. It often arises out of a 'sacred marriage' having been made way back in the mists of time and not dissolved before moving on into other incarnations. The sacred marriage was a linking together on all the levels of being, but on the physical level it is often the feeling of lust or sexual desire which is most likely to break through from the past. Once this has happened, however, the deeper links are able to manifest, providing an opportunity for unconditional love with spiritual sustenance and support to grow. The specific purpose of such a contact may be to act as a catalyst for hidden knowledge or abilities. As these emerge from the past they can contribute to the incarnating soul's growth in the present life.

There is a similarity with contacts which are based on a

different type of former interaction. Once the soul has learnt to detach itself from the past, that past, together with whatever feelings it involved, can be released and a new energy can manifest. Some of the deepest spiritual ties have unpromising beginnings but an examination of the charts will help to clarify the situation and pinpoint the lessons to be learnt from the relationship.

For instance, a client was concerned about a teacher with whom she was studying the spiritual aspects of yoga. From time to time, despite her seeming friendliness, the client was aware of 'a glint of hatred' in her teacher's eyes and this held her back from a fully relationship. The client regressed back to a life in which they had both been sisters. The teacher/sister had been extremely jealous and killed her over a man she had been promised to but whom the sister wanted. Once she had become attuned to this old trauma, the woman was able to forgive. Although she never told her teacher of the regression, the situation between them improved dramatically and they became close friends and spiritual companions. Her Sun-Pluto-Mars conjunction was in the twelfth house of enemies and the interaspects between the charts included a Neptune-Mars opposition. Having forgiven her sister/teacher unconditionally, the client was able to trust her teaching and to grow spiritually.

2

KINDRED SPIRITS

When a couple are genuinely related to each other, they are willing
to enter into the whole spectrum of human life together.[1]

Robert A. Johnston

Most relationships have their agenda set outside the present lifetime.
They may be planned in the between-life state before incarnation,
but this is not necessarily so. There may simply be unfinished business
from the past. It is clear from regression to the between-life state
that whilst some souls plan incarnations most carefully, others are
drawn back into relationships by forces operating outside their
control. These forces may be personal or shared by two or more people
and include individual expectations, ingrained patterns, attraction
to specific situations, mutual desires or craving, or repetition of an
old interaction.

Repetition creates a karmic treadmill, but this is not necessarily
negative. It is simply an ingrained habit, situation or type of interplay,
that no longer serves the soul's growth - which is why some seemingly
idyllic relationships have to end. Whilst there are karmic associations
that are life enhancing, productive and positive, others can be
destructive and depleting. Things are not always what they seem
and the soul may need to pass out of incarnation before all the
ramifications of a relationship are understood.

At a personal level, your soul may have an agenda you are
totally unaware of. This is particularly so when it comes to qualities
that need to be developed, and emotions and attitudes that have to
be explored or let go. If you have incarnated as a woman with the
desire to learn about tolerance and patience, for instance, that
impossible man you are married to may be just the thing you need.
Love it or hate it, he is giving you the opportunity to develop exactly
those qualities. There's no point trying to change him if you are the
one for whom the lesson is intended; the quicker you learn, the sooner

he can be set free to explore a new way of being. You could well have planned things in advance and will, when you return to the between-life state, thank him for being such a good teacher.

Nevertheless, there are factors that can hold you in nonproductive, repetitive situations. If a vow has been made in the past to 'always be with you', for instance, then the soul finds itself pulled to the person to whom that promise was made. But! Without careful planning, the soul may well find itself the parent or child of that person, or find true love only to discover that the beloved is already married or that there is a vast age different or some other barrier exists to relationship. Even when careful planning has taken place, the souls forget as they come back into incarnation and it may take many years for the intention behind the connection to surface again.

At a joint soul level, not all love relationships are intended to be happy-ever-after fairy tales. A couple may have been together for many lifetimes and have decided that the time has come to pursue new contacts, and yet they get pulled back together either by habit or by a strong physical attraction. One half of such a couple may be helping the other to learn some difficult lessons such as independence and assertion. From the superficial view, the relationship may appear to be destructive although at a soul level it is beneficial.

Many people travel with their soul group, coming back into incarnation with the same people around them although the roles may change from incarnation to incarnation. Such soul groups may comprise a family but this is not necessarily so. Soul groups can tend to play out the certain scenarios over and over again, although the major players may take different stances. So a present life husband and wife could have been parent and child, master and servant or other combinations of dominant and submissive roles in previous lives. Elements of these roles are inevitably drawn into, and reflected within, the present life interaction. However, it is not necessary for there to have been a previous, personal connection between the people involved in a relationship. A soul may have had a repeating pattern of destructive relationships through several lives and is pulled back into the same old scenarios, where the actors in the drama can change or remain the same. It is rather like a long-running play that may use understudies from time to time, or find a new co-star, but the script hardly changes.

It is rarely possible to know, from the perspective of the earth, all the reasons that lie behind a relationship, although major themes do emerge, together with certain astrological indicators. Some of these indicators occur in the personal chart and others in the synastry between the charts of two people in relationship.

REASONS FOR INCARNATING TOGETHER

The major reasons for two or more people coming back into relationship together are:

> Spiritual bonds
> Previous relationship(s) carried over
> A soulmate connection
> Unfinished business
> Habit or inertia
> Dependence and symbiosis
> Lessons to be learned
> Attitudes to be transformed
> Debt or duty
> Attachment to mutual unhappiness or happiness
> Vows or promises
> Love or hatred
> The desire for revenge
> Specific tasks
> Catalyst
> Positive Service
> Enmeshment
> Guilt
> Holding onto the heart

These reasons may overlap and a relationship can include elements of several themes being played out.

Spiritual bonds

People incarnating together will often either originate from the same soul group or have built up powerful spiritual connections over many lifetimes. Some may have been specifically trained to connect at a soul level, such as making a 'mystic marriage' in which they were joined at the physical, emotional, mental and spiritual levels; or through several incarnations together as monks or nuns within a religion where the emphasis was on spiritual unity. Spiritual bonds can underpin relationships that flourish within the most difficult circumstances and may support a couple through many incarnations. These often feel like soulmate connections.

Astrological Indicators: Neptune to personal planet repeating interaspects and strong nodal connections by the personal planets and/or Neptune, reversed nodal connections.

Previous relationship

A previous relationship which has carried over may play itself out again and again, pulling the two people back into incarnation together in the process. This is particularly so when a pattern of dependency or abuse has developed but it can occur in families and marriages as well as other interactions. Such a relationship can be experienced as good or bad depending on how it is played out and the pattern behind it.

Astrological Indicators: Personal planet to outer planet repeating interaspects, nodal connections and relevant house placements.

Soulmate connection

Soulmates feel as though they are made for each other, often to the extent of being two halves making a whole. Two people may well be soulmates, although this does not necessarily mean they are destined for a sexual relationship this time around. Soulmate connections can occur between parents and children as well as friends and mentors.

Astrological Indicators: Repeating each-way Sun/Moon/Venus connection to the Nodes or Neptune.

Unfinished business

Unfinished business is one of the most powerful factors in returning to earth together. If a lesson or task is incomplete, or not yet begun, or if a pattern has been strongly established and not broken, then the souls are pulled back time after time to resolve or fulfil matters. One soul may have to learn forgiveness, or to let go, to be independent, or to assert its own needs and so on. The other soul provides the opportunity for this to occur. Unfinished business may also be positive, the souls will have an on-going plan or purpose they are in the process of completing or they may be evolving together towards a specific aim.

Astrological Indicators: Repeating outer planet to inner planet interaspects, reversed nodal placements, Sun-South Node or Moon-North Node connections.

Habit or inertia
If the souls have not been moving forward, growing and evolving together or separately, then habit or inertia has set in. They may return together simply because it has always been that way. Habit may also show itself in how one person treats the other - as a slave, for example. The habit may not be personal to the two people concerned. The present incarnation may be an opportunity to change.
Astrological Indicators: Saturn, Chiron and/or Pluto interaspects to the personal planets. Inertia may be signified by a strong Taurus or fixed sign emphasis.

Dependence and symbiosis
If one person is used to relying on, or feeding off, another person they may return time and again in the same mode. 'Psychic vampirism', where one person draws energy off the other, is often found in relationships and the partner whose energy is sapped may be trying to break away. People caught in a symbiotic partnership often feel they will die if the relationship comes to an end and they may need to learn that this is not so.
Astrological Indicators: Pluto and Neptune interaspects to the personal planets, together with strong Taurus, Cancer, Libra and Pisces emphasis, element imbalances and incompatibilities across the charts.

Lessons to be learned
Many souls plan in the between-life state scenarios: the lessons to be learnt, the qualities to be cultivated and the skills enhanced. One soul may act as teacher or mentor to the other, or be the victim or perpetrator through whom the other soul experiences whatever is required for soul growth.
Astrological Indicators: Saturn and the Nodes to personal planet contacts, reversed nodal connections.

Attitudes to be transformed
The attitudes may be personal ones which change through the association, or repeating patterns that show themselves within a relationship. For example, a person who has always felt superior to the other may be in a relationship in which the other person takes an inferior part until the attitude is transformed. On the other hand, a soul may need to undergo a lifetime where it feels inferior, simply

to understand what it is like and to overcome previous arrogance.
Astrological Indicators: Natal aspects and interaspects according to
the attitude.

Debt or duty
One soul may feel that it owes a debt or duty to another. This may
arise from promises made, either in another life or in the between-
life state, or from events which have taken place. One of the souls
may have saved the other's life, for instance, made a sacrifice, or
performed a service in the past.
Astrological Indicators: Saturn and Neptune repeating interaspects
with the personal planets or Nodes.

Attachment to mutual happiness or unhappiness
Two souls may be held together by an attachment of one or both of
the parties to the status quo, or to the desire of one party to make
the other party happy - or miserable. This attachment can be to
unhappiness just as much as happiness. If, for example, a couple are
unhappy, one of the parties may feel 'if I can't be happy, he can't
either', or 'if I can't have him, no one else will' and therefore refuse
to divorce. The depth of the attachment pulls the couple back
repeatedly until detachment is reached. This is really an underlying
issue of control and cannot be solved until the dominant partner
surrenders control of the other person's life into their own hands, or
the submissive partner assertively takes back that control.
Astrological Indicators: Pisces and Cancer Moons are frequently
involved. Jupiter or Saturn interaspects.

Vows or promises
Pacts, vows and promises hold people together across lives. These
may be intentional or unintentional - saying such things as 'of course
I'll always be there for you' can create a powerful bond, as can vows
of fealty or obedience. They can occur between lovers, parent and
child, or strangers.
Astrological Indicators: Saturn, Neptune, Chiron repeating
interaspects to the personal planets, or these outer planets falling in
the other person's eighth house.

Love or hatred
The love and hatred in this interaction is not necessarily personal,
although it can be. One person may feel great love and loyalty for

someone he, or she, deems to be far beyond them on the social scale and similarly the hatred may be on a collective level - for a race for instance. At the personal level however, love holds many couples together and this may be constructive or destructive depending on whether it aids their mutual evolution or holds it back. Not everything that masquerades as love is a positive experience, it can be smothering or symbiotic for instance. Similarly, hatred may actually be the spur that helps a soul to grow. Nevertheless, hatred does create an exceedingly strong bond between two people and the lesson involved may be forgiveness and letting go.

Astrological Indicators: Powerful Neptune or Pluto contacts in synastry.

The desire for revenge

The desire to be avenged or to get even with someone can pull two people back strongly into incarnation. But the attitude may be transferred onto someone other than the original perpetrator if there is a resonance in the circumstances, attitudes, etc. Here again, the soul is challenged to forgive and move on, or to do something constructive to transform the karma embedded within the situation.

Astrological Indicators: Pluto contacts, especially with Mars, or Mars/ Pluto in Taurus or Scorpio in the natal chart or in synastry.

Specific tasks

Two or more souls may incarnate having agreed to take on a specific task together. This can range from creating the latest weapon of mass destruction to finding a cure for a rare disease. It is often concerned with healing or transforming earth life, for better or worse. Once the task is completed, the two souls may go their separate ways. Many people who incarnate with a task tend to forget as they become immersed in the incarnation. Meeting the other person again may be misconstrued as an opportunity for sexual contact as the attraction, or reaction, can be powerful.

Astrological Indicators: Nodal connections, planets falling in specific houses on the other chart - Saturn in Virgo in the sixth, for instance; and interaspects particularly with Jupiter involved.

Catalyst

One soul may incarnate to be the catalyst for another's growth or to bring about change. From outside, this may appear to be through destructive as well as constructive events or attitudes. For instance,

if someone has always been clinging and dependent, the soul acting as a catalyst might leave the relationship abruptly, forcing the other soul to use his or her own inner resources to deal with the crisis.
Astrological Indicators: Strong Uranus and Aquarius emphasis in the synastry.

Positive Service

Positive service can occur in friendships, families, love relationships or work situations. One person takes on the responsibility of caring for another or performs a task specifically to help the soul growth of the other. (This is the positive manifestation of service. Inappropriate service can occur if the parties become stuck in the helping or enabling scenario). Positive service may also include the opportunity to develop unconditional love - sometimes through one soul playing an extremely difficult role.
Astrological Indicators: An emphasis on Virgo/Pisces, the Nodes, the sixth house, Chiron, Saturn and Capricorn in either the natal chart or in the synastry.

Enmeshment

Enmeshment is a situation where two souls are strongly intertwined due to karmic experiences. The souls incarnate together again and again in an effort to clear the situation. Enmeshment occurs:

- where relationship karma is unfulfilled or unresolved
- if the obligations to a soul for whom one is responsible (as in parent and child) are not fulfilled
- where too much responsibility is taken for someone else
- where someone who seeks their freedom is held onto
- when someone else is blamed for the soul's own limitations or inability to move forward
- in situations where old promises remain

To hold others culpable for the limitations a soul puts on itself creates a situation where the souls are drawn back time and again as one struggles to become free from the other. One soul may have to learn to stop blaming the other and take responsibility for itself. Another scenario which invites karmic enmeshment is where one person feeds off the other: psychic vampirism. Symbiotic, dependent relationships and situations such as master/slave or marriage where one person owns the other body and soul also create the same problem. The lesson is to let go, *even when it is passing for love*.

Enmeshment can occur when a soul takes on too much responsibility for another, especially for their well being or their feelings. But equally, if one soul has failed to take *appropriate* responsibility for another - as in a situation where a child is abandoned, for instance - then releasing the enmeshment may first involve appropriate parenting or care. This may possibly be to the extent of caring for someone for an entire life if they are ill or disabled. At the right time, the soul must then be allowed the freedom to make its own journey. Letting go is an enormous karmic challenge.

Astrological Indicators: An emphasis on water signs, particularly Pisces (especially Sun-Moon connections), Neptune to the Sun, Moon or Venus, Pluto-Venus interaspects, nodal connections.

Guilt

Guilt is one of the strongest factors involved in drawing people back together who would perhaps be better served by letting go and moving on. Quite often the guilt is out of all proportion to what provoked it in the first place, but guilt grows and may be stoked by the other person as a form of manipulation. Unnecessary guilt can also fuel relationships. The challenge is to forgive and forget, to let go.

Astrological Indicators: An emphasis on Neptune and Pisces.

Holding Onto The Heart

Popular songs from all ages include lines like: 'That kiss you stole held my heart and soul'. The heart has always been associated with love and we speak of a broken-hearted lover. However, it is clear from regression to other lives - and to earlier events in the present one - that 'giving away the heart' or 'someone taking a piece of my heart' are all too common experiences. This may be done intentionally or, seemingly, by accident or as a game. If the event took place in another life and was not resolved, it brings the two parties together again so that the heart can be reclaimed (see Chapter 9).

Astrological Indicators: An emphasis on Leo, Sun falling in the fifth or twelfth house in the other chart, Pluto to the personal planet interaspects, a Sun-Chiron connection.

RELATIONSHIP THEMES

There are certain ubiquitous themes and roles that recur time and again in relationships. Issues such as power ploys, dependence and collusion versus interdependence or independence; parent and child sagas, or victim/martyr/saviour scenarios play themselves out through generations and across lifetimes. Karmic relationships fall into two distinct types: those where there has been previous personal interaction between the parties concerned and so the agenda has been created by the two people in the relationship; and those where the leitmotiv did not arise between the two people in the past but formed part of their separate, individual or collective experiences. Major themes and roles being played out within relationships include:

- Unconditional love
- Freedom/commitment
- Parent/Child
- Power
- Victim/Martyr/Rescuer/Saviour
- Dependence/collusion v. unconditional love
- Betrayer/betrayed/scapegoat
- Seducer/seduced
- Debts/obligations/guilt
- Fear/Antipathy
- Reparation
- Mutual Growth

Unconditional Love
Unconditional love is an opportunity to love another person, warts and all. It means accepting someone as they are, without forcing change but at the same time learning not to be trampled on, taken advantage of, colluded with or abused. In unconditional love scenarios, the pearl at the heart of the other person, their potential, is often glimpsed by one soul who is tempted to put pressure on to facilitate transformation. The challenge is to leave the possibility open, but not force it. In loving and accepting the person *as they are*, that soul may learn, perhaps for the first time, that they are okay.

Notwithstanding, boundaries have to be set. Souls who are practising unconditional love must 'stand in their own hoop', remaining empowered and undisturbed by another person's behaviour, distancing themselves if necessary. The tendency to allow the other person to do their worst under the illusion that this is unconditional love, confuses love with abuse. Part of the challenge may be to simply allow the other person some space. It may also be to practise 'tough love' where what is unacceptable is pointed out and standards of behaviour are set. Of course there is a fine line between setting boundaries with unconditional love and putting out the subtle, or not-so-subtle message: 'You are only okay if you do what I say.'

Astrological Indicators: Neptune interaspects with the personal planets or the Nodes.

Freedom/Commitment Dilemmas

A 'can't live with, can't live without' scenario may be played out over many lifetimes, as may issues around intimacy and commitment. One soul finds it difficult to commit to the relationship, or the time may have come to give the other person freedom. Often the past involvement was passionate, intense, and sporadic; the present lesson may to let go, or to definitely commit. If a dedicated relationship is entered into, then sufficient space has to be allowed for each person to be his or her self.

Astrological Indicators: Uranus aspects to Sun in natal chart or interaspects in synastry and to the Moon or Venus. Aquarius falling in the seventh house or by synastry; Venus or the Moon in Aquarius, or Aquarius in the seventh in the natal chart.

Power

The abuse and misuse of power can span generations and many lifetimes. Issues of power-over versus empowerment underlie many different relationships and may manifest extremely subtly indeed. During the course of incarnations the power can have swung between the two people concerned, or one person may always have held the power. Power issues arise within families and in employment situations as well as love relationships. Being powerless has as many karmic connotations as does having power over other people. As Thomas Moore says:

> 'Getting stuck in one's powerlessness is a way of avoiding having power. In a person identifying with victimization, power doesn't go away: it is present instead in a raw form that appears as plain emotionalism or displays of anger and aggression, empty threats, scorn, curses and so on.'[2]

The challenge is for both partners to become *empowered*: standing in their own power and having control over their own destiny, joint or separate.

Astrological Indicators: Pluto aspects and interaspects.

Parent/Child

These roles rarely have anything to do with the biological connection or family relationship. Appropriate or inappropriate acting out of these roles is perpetuated and may be carried over from other incarnations. For example, the wife who calls her husband 'Daddy', the child who has to parent his or her parent, or the secretary who has to 'mother' her boss may have been in a parental relationship before or may be acting out present life needs and expectations.

Astrological Indicators: Sun or Moon natal aspects or interaspects to Pluto/Saturn or these planets falling in the fourth, tenth, seventh or twelfth houses either in the natal chart or in synastry.

Victim/Martyr/Rescuer/Persecutor/Scapegoat

A victim needs a persecutor, a rescuer needs someone to rescue, martyrs have a built-in need to suffer and so attract a persecutor. Within these scenarios, a soul may set out to rescue someone and could quickly become the victim or martyr - and even a persecutor. Victim and martyr roles are extremely depleting. If someone weak is continually being rescued they will never find the ability to stand on their own feet.

Abuse of power, particularly in covert ways, and projection onto others are fundamental to this kind of interplay. A child may be picked on by the rest of the family and coerced into acting as a scapegoat for the family, who thereby do not have to deal with their own issues. These roles are particularly common in families or relationships that feature addictions of one kind or another. One person becomes the helper - and often feels stronger than the other person or may feel put upon and weak, a classic victim. Co-dependent and abusive relationships revolve around this pattern. One person is regarded as superior or inferior to the other, or is identified as 'the cause of the problem'. These roles often pass down through families perpetuating the pattern through the generations.

Astrological Indicators: Neptune or Pluto interaspects to personal planets or falling in the seventh house, an emphasis on Pisces in the charts.

Enmeshment/Dependence and Collusion

Enmeshment and dependence often masquerade as helping or being helped. 'Helplessness', 'helping' or 'enabling' scenarios keep one person weaker than the other and create dependence which may reflect past life symbiosis. They also serve to make one person in the relationship feel useful and needed. The two people concerned may collude with one another to maintain the roles - or switch roles from time to time. These are particularly common scenarios within addictive interconnections of all kinds. The patterns are an opportunity to practice unconditional love and mutual support, creating interdependence instead of dependence.

Astrological Indicators: Neptune-Pluto interaspects to personal planets, or Neptune/Pisces falling in the seventh house in personal chart or in synastry.

Enabler/Enabled

An enabler creates a situation where the other person either flourishes, the positive expression of the theme, or where the other person is kept helpless. One person puts all the energy and effort into the relationship and is the power behind the throne. Often found in so-called soulmate relationships, and common in addictive interactions, one person may have a vested interest in keeping the other person locked in dependency, even though, to the outside world, they may appear to be the successful partner. The two people concerned feel that they cannot survive without each other. The enabler feels 'he or she needs me', the enabled feels: 'I can't live (or do this) without him/her'.

Astrological Indicators: Sun-Moon contacts to Jupiter, or Neptune; Pisces featuring strongly in both charts.

Betrayer/Betrayed

So many promises made, so few kept, but the parties are pulled together time and again by the hope that things will be different this time. This scenario may arise between adults or parents and child where support is suddenly withdrawn or wherever hurtful acts occur. The theme is obvious where a husband or wife takes a lover against the other party's expressed desire for faithfulness, but it is less so when a child is ignored when a new baby is born. That child could carry forward into adult relationships the tendency to dump someone before he or she can be dumped as there is a basic lack of trust due to that early betrayal - which no doubt picks up on betrayals in other lifetimes. Some people are deeply ingrained in the betrayer pattern and are challenged to find the ability to keep a promise or to express commitment and fidelity in the present incarnation.

Astrological Indicators: Chiron or Neptune aspects and interaspects to Venus-Mars, Pisces, Pluto in Scorpio.

Seducer/Seduced

This theme is often, but not necessarily, based on a previous sexual relationship coming forward into the present to make one person vulnerable to subtle enthralment by another. It does not always operate as sexual seduction. It can occur at an emotional or intellectual level where ideas or emotions are too enticing to be resisted. Seduction also occurs in families and may be a misuse of a soulmate connection. A child is inveigled into becoming the ally of one parent against the other, for example. Seduction is also common in guru/pupil relationships where one person seems to know more than the other and where abuses of power may also take place.

Astrological Indicators: Neptune/Pluto to Venus/Mercury/Mars interaspects; emphasis on Scorpio or Pisces; planets falling in the other person's fifth, seventh or eighth houses.

Dominance and Submission

Power and control issues can literally be a replay of old master/slave roles, or may encompass power trips of all kinds. The domination may be the result of a domineering or authoritarian personality making itself felt but the underlying causes may be much more subtle - masochism and sadism manifest in obscure ways and things are not always as they appear on the surface. Someone who is meek and mild may in fact be extremely domineering in their own way and skilled at pushing buttons that elicit a violent response. If the scenario is played out unconsciously, then considerable violence - physical, mental or emotional - may be part of the script. This is particularly so if the person being dominated has an unconscious need for, and provokes a partner into, subjugation.

It is now accepted that abused children often grow up to be abusers, and that some people crave violence because they confuse this with love - which is why the victims of marital abuse so often find it impossible to leave the situation. Participants in these dramas crave the security of what is known and familiar even though to outsiders the relationship may appear to be extremely abusive. The healing of such relationships may need role play or role reversal - which may come about over several lives. Domination issues may also surface when formerly submissive partners start to assert their independence, and when projections of power are withdrawn. Relationships which cannot change at this point may need to end. *Astrological Indicators:* Saturn/Uranus/Pluto-Mars aspects or interaspects (physical abuse or aggression); Saturn/Pluto/Neptune/ Uranus to Venus aspects or interaspects (emotional); or Mercury (mental), Neptune-Mars (spiritual); Mars or Pluto in Scorpio/ Capricorn/Taurus; a preponderance of negative or positive signs in one chart or an elemental imbalance such as more than four planets in water signs.

Debts, Duties, Obligations, Guilt

Many souls incarnate feeling that they have a debt to repay or a duty or obligation to another person. This theme can manifest positively when one person intends to help another fulfil their potential or learn a specific lesson, but it can lead to guilt pervading the relationship and to manipulative behaviour by the other person. *Astrological Indicators:* Saturn or Neptune interaspects to personal planets.

Fear or Antipathy

Feelings of fear or antipathy may be carried over from the past and may indicate a previous personal involvement, or a generalised fear that is triggered by a present life action. *Astrological Indicators:* Saturn and/or Pluto aspects to personal planets

Reparation

Guilt can be a powerful force driving karmic interaction. One soul may feel it simply has to make reparation to another for things that occurred in the past. Nevertheless, reparation can be a positive experience. If someone put their life on hold to provide an opportunity for another soul to grow, that other person may want to make reparation in the present life by encouraging the other to fulfil potential or to evolve spiritually. Similarly, if someone has been in any way harmed in the past, the soul who was responsible may feel that it is now appropriate to make reparation. Making reparation does not have to be a heavy issue and the soul may find that forgiveness rather than reparation is required, or indeed that there is no need to do anything at all except move on. *Astrological Indicators:* Neptune and Chiron interaspects to the personal planets or the Nodes.

Mutual Growth

Many interactions stem from a genuine commitment to mutual growth, often based on a soul group connection. The souls want to evolve and are prepared to aid each other in this process, and the theme may have encompassed many lives. Children who are disabled in some way may be offering their parents, or siblings the chance to grow or to change attitudes or to develop qualities in the same way as the children themselves evolve through the experience. Other souls may have a target of spiritual growth, supporting this in each other. Many mentors evolve through sharing their knowledge unselfishly with those they aid.

Astrological Indicators: Jupiter with the Sun interaspects, aspects to the Nodes, Saturn to the personal planets, planets in mutual reception across the charts, and reversed nodal connections.

All of these expectations and themes play their part in bringing people together. The personal expectation brought into incarnation also powerfully affects the kind of relationships experienced throughout life from the cradle to the grave (see Chapter 3).

THE STAGES OF RELATIONSHIP

The development of a relationship falls into clearly defined stages, during which certain issues will be come up and various states of mind will be encountered. Many people have identified these phases and the headings below are based on the work of Chuck Spezzano[3] who feels that everyone will invariably go through all of these stages sequentially as a relationship progresses. In my experience, however, it is possible for a relationship to pick up at any point where it left off in a past life, or to repeat the stages from the beginning. It is also possible to work through the stages in a different order although for most people the progression is from stage one to stage five.

Stage 1 - Romance

Planets operating: Venus, Neptune, Jupiter- and Pluto if the meeting feels 'fated' and compulsive.

This is the stage where potential becomes visible and there is promise of a wonderful relationship to come. The couple have fallen in love - possibly with each other and most definitely with the idea of being in love. A romantic relationship fulfils the soul's need to be special to someone. It is a time when the ideal man or woman is projected onto the prospective partner, and may, or may not, be fulfilled. In this phase it is 'sameness' that is perceived, similarities to the ideal of the other, or behaviour and looks that feel familiar.

Stage 2 - Power Struggle
Planets operating: Pluto, Saturn, Uranus, Mars.
This is the time when past life tensions, power struggles and ego conflicts surface. It is also the phase where differences become apparent as fears arise and each partner struggles to get their needs met. For some partners, that fear is of stepping into their own power. They prefer to remain powerless and open to victimization because it is known and familiar - and therefore safe. For other partners, the fear is of giving away their power in an equal relationship. Yet other fears include that of intimacy and trust, or commitment.

Within Power Struggle there are different steps. With The Shadow, the worst case scenario from past experience, childhood and split-off parts of the self, is introjected into the relationship. It triggers Saturn issues around the personal shadow and negative expectations. The partner may be demonised - or demoralised - as each person in the relationship struggles to get their needs met and to feel in control. The challenge here is to forgive and integrate all the qualities of the split-off self that are perceived in the partner into oneself.

The Independence and Dependence phase is where the partners learn to balance out the conflicts. At this stage each partner will take on a role - which can switch - and play that out for a time as they negotiate to have emotional needs and expectations met. If the soul can value the partner more than the need to have its own way, then healing takes place and the relationship progresses.

In the Positive and Negative step each partner usually plays out one of these roles, which are simply different ways of seeing and interacting with the world as with the astrological polarities. 'Positive' goes for the bigger picture and solves problems, whilst 'negative' identifies problems and attends to the details. If the two can work together in partnership, they are complementary styles and lead to a successful relationship.

Stage 3 - The Dead Zone
Planets operating: Saturn, Chiron, Uranus, Neptune, Pluto.
The Dead Zone is that plateau most relationships hit when the

excitement and initial challenge have gone and boredom sets in. It is where many past life issues will be replayed and potentially worked through to resolution. The soul's ingrained expectations will arise as will deep-seated needs that demand satisfaction.

The Dead Zone can be characterized by a sense of being trapped: one soul struggles to be free (Uranus) whilst the other holds on (Saturn or Pluto) or tries to merge (Neptune). There can also be withdrawal due to the fear of being close, so one partner holds back and the other partner either tries to give them the space they need or presses forward to fill the space as they withdraw. When this occurs, the soul who is holding back either feels abandoned as the partner withdraws, or feels overwhelmed if the partner advances: all the fears seem to be coming true.

In the Dead Zone Neptunian fusion can take place. Chuck Spezzano defines fusion as 'counterfeit bonding'. It is characterized by diffuse boundaries and co-dependency. One person being swallowed up by the other is a more Plutonian style of fusion. For a time fusion may feel very comfortable- the souls believe, falsely as it turns out, that they have achieved exactly what they set out to find: union and togetherness. When they recognise consciously or unconsciously that the partnership is without heart, then the problems begin again and the soul will use various strategies to feel comfortable once more. Partners caught up in fusion may become heroic givers out of guilt, or act out the needy demanding role which causes the other partner to fear being swallowed alive. One partner may go into self-destruct mode or create an illness in an attempt to get the attention and care he or she so desires, or to break free from the situation.

This is also the plateau where over-compensation for perceived failures takes place. The ego is at work here. It will be 'over-good' as it tries to cover feelings of inadequacy or self-hatred. It may cause a soul to sacrifice itself to compensate for what it believes must be a lack of love. Whilst the partner may not fully recognise what is going on, at a subtle level the soul will pick up on the lack of congruency between inner feelings and outer behaviour. This forms a block to continuing relationship until the two can align and become authentic.

Partners can also play on the other's weaknesses and create Chironic pain or wound as retaliation for perceived hurt. Perhaps not surprisingly, Saturn also takes a hand in the Dead Zone and ingrained patterns make themselves felt. People play out roles or take on burdens - or stay in a relationship because of duty. They may replay childhood trauma or unfinished parental business with a partner. They could also do the right things for all the wrong reasons. For example, to make themselves feel better rather than coming from the heart, or to be thought good and caring rather than genuinely expressing compassion. If the souls can successful negotiate the pitfalls and traps of the Dead Zone, then the relationship can continue into a more positive phase.

Stage 4 - Partnership

Planets operating: The positive face of the outer planets according to the synastry.

By the time the partners get to this stage they have become comfortable with each other. They will probably have incarnated together many times and taken on a number of different relationship roles. They now truly recognise each other and value what they see. Two people have become one, not in the sense of merging into each other but in the reality of having created a relationship that functions creatively and well. But it does not do to get complacent. The souls have an impetus towards growth and deep issues may arise which need healing so that the souls can move on into what Chuck Spezzano calls:

Stage 5 - Leadership

Planets operating: The highest vibration of the natal, composite and relationship charts and the synastry between the couple.

At this stage a couple have moved to the highest manifestation of their astrological union. Chuck Spezzano has a specific concept around leadership but I find this term difficult and prefer to call this the 'Spiritual Relationship' stage. This is where the day to day struggles have dropped away. It is transformational, inspirational and intimate. The souls know each other very well indeed and offer support at all levels. They honour and respect each other's individuality and yet are closely bonded. This is where sexual alchemy begins to subtly transform the partners and their soul energy in the spiritual dimension. They commence the journey of reunification with the divine. At this stage, where the souls totally trust and have limitless compassion for each other, deep soul fractures can be brought to the surface for healing. These are the chronic problems that have dogged the soul for many lifetimes. When these are released, spiritual peace is achieved.

Beyond the Leadership Stage are what Chuck Spezzano refers to as 'Vision, mastery, tantra and union'. These are stages which take place at the level of the spirit rather than the psyche or the ego. Souls have to have cleared 'all their stuff' around relationships and be practising truly unconditional love to enter these levels of partnership. When they do, they step off the wheel of relationship karma and into an entirely different space.

3

INDIVIDUAL EXPECTATIONS

Once again,
Love the limb-loosener sweeps me away
Bitter-sweet monster - there is no defence against it

Sappho (c.600 B.C.)

When I first studied natal astrology, my urgent question was: 'How did that arise?' It may no sense to me that the child was a blank slate on which a chart was somehow impressed. It was at a time when psychological astrology was just getting into its stride and planets were being taught as archetypal energies operating within the psyche. This instinctively felt right to me and I began to understand that the soul chose the chart because it *fitted*. But I wanted to know what made a particular soul resonate to that specific archetype in the first place. When I discovered reincarnation and past lives, everything fell into place. Karmic astrology supplied the 'why' of a chart. Having spent the past twenty-five years applying this understanding to more than a thousand charts, my original insights have been reinforced over and over again, and new revelations have expanded that understanding further.

I came to realise that what the incarnating soul experienced in relationships in other lives creates automatic reactions and expectations about how a relationship will be, and may inculcate deep fears around love because the past is extrapolated into the present. Remember Venus's children, Terror and Fear, whom we met in the Introduction? They so often form part of the soul's total experience. However, ingrained expectations can be reprogrammed so that the soul responds in a new way instead of reacting as it has done for lifetimes. It is a matter of learning to recognise the trigger, catching the moment when the expectation kicks in, and then creating a fresh response. In the process, souls usually find that they get caught up in the old scenarios, but are able to get out of them much quicker. Eventually, they are able to spot them coming and make a conscious decision not to go down that route again. Then, a fresh pattern or possibility opens up. When this happens, a new type of partner will be attracted and a different part of the chart - with its karmic potential - will come into play.

Karma related to an individual's approach to, and expectations around relationships shows in the natal chart through the placement of planets in houses, the position of house rulers, and most especially through the aspects planets make to each other - in particular outer-to-personal planet contacts. That is to say, the relationship the planets make to each other describes the soul's karmic experience. In this respect, even so-called easy aspects such as sextiles and trines can delineate a residue of unresolved karma and therefore the karma can apply to any contact between the two planets. On the whole the easy aspects tend to manifest as slightly less intense or difficult experiences, but much depends on the stage of consciousness reached by the incarnating soul. How much does it see itself as at the mercy of fate and how much awareness has it of its own inner dynamics? When the soul recognises it is creating its own reality, the aspects are likely to manifest as more internally centred experiences leading to psychological and spiritual changes that create a new response, rather than re-running the same old reaction.

Not all experiences that relate back to old habits are negative, although it can often feel that way. The soul may pick up on some positive attributes along the way. Reconnection to old skills or abilities is important to the soul's evolution, and lifetimes or situations may be set up in which the soul re-accesses qualities which have been temporarily overlaid or mislaid. It may sometimes be necessary for the soul to reconnect to a particular feeling or experience before it can be owned or released, if this is appropriate. In such a case the experience may be intense, but it may also be short-lived as acceptance brings release, integration and change. It must of course be borne in mind that the planets and their aspects represent the part of the psyche which derives from the past-life experience, and although the word 'soul' has been used to describe the principle which carries these patterns, it should perhaps more properly read 'the part of the soul'. Another part of the soul may carry a much more positive or negative charge and the two segments of the soul must come to an accommodation.

The nature of the planets indicates the type of karma and the emotional expectations involved. Saturn, who is the Lord of Karma, for instance, particularly when in difficult aspect to the Sun, Moon or Venus, can describe deeply ingrained, long-standing fears and lack of self-worth. There is a sense of being unlovable which combined with consequent inner helplessness may manifest as extremely tight outward control. Unmet dependency needs may leave an aching emptiness which the child, and later on the adult, tries to satisfy through a comfort-object or dependent symbiotic liaisons. Power issues and manipulation are a feature of Pluto contacts and it may be a lifetime task to regain power handed over to a dominant parental or other authority figure, for example. People with strong Plutonian characteristics often confuse love with compulsion or neediness and assume that someone who has an intense need for them, or for whom they have a desperate need, must therefore love them.

VENUS: RELATIONSHIP EXPECTATIONS

In relationships, people are initially attracted to each other for what seem to be totally irrational reasons: 'I just saw the back of his head and knew I was going to marry him', 'There was something about her I was immediately attracted to', 'He was the kind of man I'd always shied away from and yet the moment he spoke, I was hooked.' Some of these reasons will be karmic: the souls have recognised each other at an unconscious level. Other reasons, however, have more to do with Venus. There are crucial factors that people unconsciously look for in relationships: someone who fills in a missing piece and someone who affirms who they are. This affirmation happens at a subliminal level and is very subtle; it is a matter of body language and hidden signals rather than overt validation. If someone mirrors our body language, we will find them *sympatico*. If they look like someone we know (even from a past life), or subconsciously remind us of ourselves, then they will feel 'good' or 'bad' according to our associations with the person they remind us of.

This is an unconscious process and we rarely realise it is going on. If the other person has totally opposite signals or mismatching body language, we may instantly feel that they dislike us or that they are hostile. The unconscious mind interprets these signals and body language according to its inbuilt patterning. Body language is an important part of Venus. This planet represents how we present ourselves to the world, and the lens through which we perceive how other people present themselves. If what we are looking for matches with what we perceive, then Venus feels comfortable - and amorous. If not, the darker qualities of Venus may make themselves known.

As we saw in the introduction, the goddess Venus had many sides to her character, all of which will be apparent in relationships. Traditionally, in addition to being connected with love, Venus is sensuality: the capacity to enjoy gratification of the senses and to give or respond to pleasure. This planet also indicates whether the incarnating soul believes that it deserves happiness, especially in relationships. The characteristics of the sign in which Venus is placed colour how a person approaches love. These characteristics will inevitably make themselves known as they describe innate factors in the soul. Looking at Venus from the karmic perspective suggests this is something that was laid down before the soul was born. The present life experience may adjust or subtly modify the ingrained response, but the tendency will be to go back to what is known and familiar.

Traditionally Venus in a man's chart describes the kind of woman to whom he will be attracted. This may be a projection of his idealised feminine self (or anima) which he needs to own within himself rather than seeking it in the outer world in another person. If he is unable to own these qualities, the ideal woman quickly turns into a virago who threatens to devour him. A man can also be attracted to a particular type of woman because he has had relationships with someone similar in another life, or because he himself has been that way when inhabiting a body of a different gender. If a man is orientated towards his own sex, then his partner will carry the projection of the idealised female, and may well act out the shadow characteristics.

In a woman's chart Venus shows her approach to her femininity and how much she values herself as a woman. The way a woman presents herself to the world, the body language she uses and how comfortable she feels with herself, also arises out of her past experiences of being a woman.

No matter where Venus is placed, if a woman ignores her Venusian urgings a deep dark eroticism can emerge that puts out the unconscious and unspoken yet clearly visible message: 'Come and get me, I'm yours'. This can create great confusion, not least in the woman concerned - particularly so if the planet is unaspected.

Unaspected or singleton planets indicate a place where a past life persona is likely to break through and show itself - much to the surprise of the person concerned who feels 'this is not me'. It is, but it is me from another life. (If Venus is unaspected in a man's chart then he will usually draw to himself a partner who acts out a Venusian role from his past.)

A woman born with Venus in Virgo, for instance, is likely to have the chastity and purity ethic deeply ingrained. Whilst she is naturally sensual (Virgo being an earth sign) those ethics can interfere with her expression of the innate voluptuousness and fecundity expressed by the ancient symbol for Virgo: the corn maiden. So if the 'old Venus' is triggered by meeting a partner from her past, the magnets are switched on and the body responds powerfully. The head may be left wondering how it all happened - Virgo being prone to analysis and self-criticism. If the head wins, Venus remains frustrated as the soul may rationalise the abandoned feelings by saying: 'Well he probably wouldn't have been good enough anyway', a perfectionist message from the past also carried by Venus in Virgo.

The unclouded core experiences of Venus in the signs are pinpointed in the following short interpretations. All or any may be hidden behind emotional expectations that have built up through several lives, which will be delineated by outer planet aspects to Venus.

Venus in Aries or the First House

Men: The soul is attracted to strong, independent women (or men), who may have a masculine edge to their femininity. The man with this placement will expect his partner to fend for her or himself, to take the initiative and to make sexual advances. Past relationships may well have been volatile. The shadow side of his ideal woman is egocentric, selfish, self-absorbed and unable to share intimacy.

Women: This soul has learned how to assert itself sexually. The woman with this placement goes all out for what she wants. She is confident within her body, enjoying using it and displaying her sexuality proudly. Her challenge is to recognise that her partner has needs too.

Venus in Taurus or the Second House

Men: The soul with this placement is attracted to good looking, sensual and yet practical women or men who have an earth mother quality about them and who offer secure relationship prospects. The shadow side of the picture can be a possessive, bossy partner whose suppressed anger occasionally breaks out with dire consequences, or a hedonistic, big spender who makes the home as opulent as possible in order to give her or himself much needed security.

Women: This is a woman who has learnt to enjoy her sexuality and takes pleasure seriously. She needs a secure relationship in which to flower but feels completely at home in her body. Her challenge is to overcome inherent jealousy and possessiveness.

Venus in Gemini or the Third House

Men: A man with this placement has a natural tendency to flirt and philander. He is attracted to many women - or men - all of whom combine brains with beauty. He wants a vivacious partner who will entertain him and who is inventive enough to stave off the sexual boredom to which he is prone. His ideal woman shadow may be uncommitted and shrewish-tongued or flighty and uncommitted.

Women: The woman with this placement has a need to present herself intelligently. She may well go in for sophisticated glamour as an antidote to sexual insecurity. Her challenge is to overcome a tendency towards superficial emotional encounters - something in her fears emotional intensity and she may well have trauma in her past.

Venus in Cancer or Fourth House

Men: Nurturing, mothering and glamour appeal to the man with Venus in Cancer. He wants someone who intuitively understands the feelings he keeps hidden, and may fall for a sensitive partner only to find that he or she expresses the clinging shadow qualities of moodiness, unpredictability and possessiveness.

Women: The soul with this placement has a powerful urge to nurture her partner. In the past her role will have been to do with mothering and caring for others. Now she needs to feel needed and much of her behaviour will be geared towards eliciting this response. Her body language rarely gives away her true feelings. Her innate over-emotionality may need to be tempered with rationality.

Venus in Leo or the Fifth House

Men: The man with this placement seeks a partner to be proud of and show off as well as someone to love. He or she must have beauty, intelligence and playfulness - a sex kitten or a trophy wife. The ideal

woman shadow may well be vain and too demanding of attention.
Women: Venus in Leo tends to flaunt sexuality and femininity. This is a woman who needs to be admired and to give free rein to her sexual appetites. She is happy with her body, values her femininity and wants the world to know this. Her challenge is to curb the emotional games to which she is prone.

Venus in Virgo or the Sixth House

Men: A man with Venus in Virgo is seeking an almost impossible combination: the perfect Love goddess who yet remains virginal and untouchable. On the one hand he wants to release earthy sexuality, on the other he needs his partner to remain chaste. The shadow side of his ideal is prudish, critical and cold or promiscuous and detached.
Women: the woman with Venus in Virgo enjoys her body and her femininity, until that little voice that says: 'impure' kicks in. In the past she has been taught to dislike her physical self and to keep her sexuality strictly under control. She valued virginity, waiting for the right man. Now her challenge is to allow her innate sensuality to flower without guilt.

Venus in Libra or the Seventh House

Men: A man with this placement expects his lover to be his other half. This is a placement that has had a soulmate in the past, and expects one in the present incarnation. Nothing less will do. The partner has to be stylish, pleasing to look at and pliable. The shadow is vain, shallow, critical, vacillating - and judgmental.
Women: A woman with Venus in Libra is made for pleasure. She is at home in her body, values her femininity and refined sensitivity. Her only problem is that she may be too absorbed in pleasing her partner to attend to her own needs. Her challenge is to avoid losing herself in a partnership.

Venus in Scorpio in the Eighth House

Men: Men who have this deep, dark and powerful placement have been through the emotional mill in the past and are pre-programmed to seek intensity in their relationships. The ideal woman is a hypnotic anima figure who pulls the man down into the depths of himself. Glamour, sexual magnetism and eroticism are the lure. The reward can be great, but the shadow side brings all Venus's darker qualities to the fore.

Women: Glamour used to mean to cast a spell and Venus in Scorpio women work sexual magic. Those with this placement of Venus often have a special magnetism about them. Their use of their body to allure and enchant may be unconscious but it is powerful nonetheless. They value their sexuality and the pleasure it can bring, but may fear it too. Sexually timid Sun-signs may be overwhelmed by the intense passion. The challenge of this placement is to integrate the darkly erotic side of Venus into healthy relationships.

Venus in Sagittarius or the Ninth House

Men: Men with Venus in Sagittarius are looking for a hetaera: a charming, intelligent companion who can entertain as well as provide sexual divertissement. This man has had problems with intimacy in other lives and prefers to skirt around emotional issues. The ideal woman may metamorphose into an uncommitted, promiscuous flirt who constantly moves on.

Women: The woman with this placement enjoys her body and her fiery femininity, and has probably been a courtesan in earlier times. She values sexual freedom and is the perennial flirt. Her challenge is to be committed in relationship.

Venus in Capricorn or the Tenth House

Men: Cool and contained, the man with Venus in Capricorn is nevertheless drawn to strong, passionate yet feminine women - or men. This complex placement may have internal conflicts - celibacy, duty or restraint may have been a feature of past relationships. If these issues are not addressed, the ideal woman may manifest the hard shadow qualities of control, coldness and judgmentalism.

Women: This is a woman who is comfortable in her body and usually enjoys her sexuality, although she may not show it outwardly. In which case, there could be a past life programme running that says sex is sinful. Control is important to the woman with this placement. When she does cast constraint to the winds, her passion is strong but it will be in the privacy of her bedroom. Appearance is important to her and she wants to look good, but this is in an organised, businesslike fashion. She is the ultimate power-dresser. The challenge is to loosen up, to allow other people in emotionally and to trust enough to love and be loved.

Venus in Aquarius or the Eleventh House

Men: Venus in Aquarius men like their partners to be a little different. This is a quirky placement that wants to experiment and so the ideal woman is not averse to sexual risks. On the other hand, Aquarius has difficulty with intimacy and may prefer someone who is available only in fantasy. Shadow qualities include distance and detachment, or mood swings, and this man may find himself with an unstable partner who is unable to enter into a close, committed relationship.

Women: This is an independent woman who values herself but may be unsure of her sexuality, especially its orientation. She may prefer to be asexual, having taken a vow of celibacy in the past, or finds it easier to relate to other women. The challenge for this placement is to enter into close intimate relationship with oneself and others.

Venus in Pisces or the Twelfth House

Men: To men with Venus in Pisces, all women are ideal or idealised. Those who idealise women may well enter into homosexual rather than heterosexual relationship. This is a natural deceiver, someone who draws people through sympathetic emanations, and the man with this placement may confuse fantasy with reality. This placement is prone to finding itself in a relationship that was never intended, and then has difficulty extricating itself so the ideal woman may turn out to be nothing of the sort. The shadow carries a powerful victim orientation.

Women: Venus in Pisces defines herself through other people. If others find her attractive, and she may well be stunningly beautiful, then she is at home in her body and revels in her femininity. If others reject her, then she assumes there must be something wrong with her. Her challenge is to find her own inner value and worth.

'As it Has Been, So Will it Be'

As we have seen, the incarnating soul's emotional experience in previous lives colours its relationships in the present. Everyone goes into relationships carrying the weight of the past, projecting old experiences into what might be - unless they have come to recognise the inbuilt reaction and changed it into a more positive response. Old experience is mapped out in the aspects between Venus and the transpersonal planets. An emphasis on a particular sign or the placement of a planet such as Venus in a sign *if supported by other factors* may be enough to indicate the underlying message.

It is necessary, however, to examine all the aspects and placements in the chart in order to ascertain underlying emotional themes which may be in conflict with one another, and which affect how the soul enters into relationship. The Moon square Saturn in Capricorn, or the Moon in Capricorn, and Mercury or Venus in Virgo, for instance, all carry constriction on expressing emotion. The soul will not find it easy to show, or discuss, strong feelings except in the privacy of the bedroom. On the other hand, a North Node-Sun conjunction in Cancer in the same chart would have a deep need to explore and express the emotions, but may do this through nurturing rather than passion. The different energies represented by the planets and their aspects are experienced as warring factions within the psyche which battle for domination. The incarnating soul's behaviour at any one time depends upon which faction is in ascendancy over the others, but the overall behaviour patterns will present all the underlying themes.

The soul attracts relationships and situations that mirror the expectations around love carried forward from other lives. Outer planet to Venus aspects in the natal chart, along with the Venus sign placement, particularly indicate these expectations and suggest how they will manifest. We create what is familiar and known. If our relationships in the past have been painful, we attract pain in an effort to exorcise it. If we have experienced positive loving, we expect to repeat the experience. Childhood experiences strengthen and reiterate these karmic patterns, which are then carried forward into adult relationships. Most adults unconsciously expect love to make up for any lack of love not only in childhood but in other lives, and suppose that a partner will 'make my life better'. However, as Ben Renshaw explains:

> 'A relationship can encourage you to be fulfilled, but it cannot make you fulfilled. No relationship can match your expectations because that is not the purpose of a relationship... Ending the myth that a relationship is going to be the solution to your life's problems removes the unrealistic expectations and conditions that often undermine the relationship itself.'[1]

It is not only in love relationships that karmic expectations intervene. If there has been a tendency in the past to project power onto other people, the soul may attract a powerful mentor or employer who holds the power. Work-related issues are really those of personal relationship in a different setting.

Negative Expectations Around Love

·	Love is all there is/all consuming	Emphasis on Venus, Cancer, Libra, Pisces
·	Love has to be perfect	Neptune-Venus, Venus in Virgo or Pisces
·	If it isn't hurting, it isn't love	Chiron-Saturn to Venus, Venus in Scorpio
·	Love hurts	Chiron-Venus aspects
·	Love leads to heartbreak	Saturn or Chiron-Venus aspects, Venus in Leo
·	I don't deserve love	Saturn-Venus aspects, Venus in Virgo or Capricorn
·	I don't need love	Uranus-Venus aspects, Venus in Aquarius
·	There will never be enough love	Pluto-Venus aspects, Venus in Scorpio
·	Love is a power trip	Pluto-Venus (or Mars) aspects Venus in Scorpio or Capricorn
·	Sexual love is sinful	Neptune or Saturn to Venus, Venus in Pisces or Virgo
·	Need equals love	Pluto-Venus, Neptune-Venus, Venus in Pisces, Cancer, Libra or Scorpio
·	Love is manipulative	Pluto-Venus, Neptune-Venus, Venus in Pisces, Cancer, Gemini, Scorpio
·	Love will be taken away	Venus-Pluto
·	Love costs	Jupiter-Venus, Saturn-Venus
·	A partner will save me	Neptune-Venus, Venus in Pisces or Libra
·	My partner is responsible for/ will take care of my needs and feelings	Saturn, Neptune, Pluto to Venus, Venus in Aries, Cancer, Libra, Scorpio, Pisces

Positive Expectations Around Love

·	I grow through relationships	Jupiter-Venus aspects, Venus in Libra or Sagittarius, Venus in the seventh house

51

· Love heals	Chiron-Venus, Venus in Pisces
· Love sets you free	Uranus-Venus, Venus in Sagittarius or fifth house
· The more you love, the more it comes back	Pluto-Venus
· I deserve love	Jupiter-Venus, Saturn-Venus, Venus in Taurus, Libra
· Love knows no boundaries	Neptune-Venus, Uranus-Venus, Venus in Sagittarius, Aquarius, Pisces
· There is an abundance of love	Jupiter-Venus, Pluto-Venus, Venus in Taurus, Leo and second house.[2]

Any aspect between the outer planets and Venus (including wide orb contacts) can carry beliefs as shown above, as can planets placed in houses ruled by the significator, or planets in mutual reception (each planet falling in the sign that the other rules). As a general rule, the stronger the aspect or the more indications there are, the more ingrained the expectation will be.

Jupiter in aspect to Venus
(or Venus in Sagittarius, Jupiter in Taurus, Libra or seventh house)
With Jupiter in aspect to Venus the incarnating soul's experience of relationships has been growth enhancing and positive. It is a point of expansion - and of possibly going over the top as with all Jupiter contacts. Such a positive experience can mitigate the effect of more difficult relationships. Even when there is a preponderance of heavier aspects to Venus, Jupiter allows the soul to return to the memory of a time when relationships worked. It knows how to do them, even though that knowing may have been obscured in the meantime.

So, for instance, Patricia whose story is told in Chiron in aspect to Venus, finally left a relationship that had caused her great pain but was still optimistic about the possibility of a future relationship. She knew that there was someone out there for her with whom she could have the fulfilling spiritual and emotional contact she needed. Her Venus formed the point of a finger of fate to Mars sextile Jupiter (which has learned in the past to manifest what she needed). When her grieving process was completed and the healing had come about, she would draw to herself exactly the right man for her next stage of soul evolution.

Chiron in aspect to Venus
(or Chiron in Taurus or Libra, or ruler of the seventh house)

The soul with an aspect between Chiron and Venus has been hurt in love, many times. The past experience of relationship has been painful, traumatising and debilitating. Pain has been created through and despite love. This wounding can occur on a physical, emotional, mental and even spiritual level. The soul may have come to believe 'if it isn't hurting, it isn't love' or, simply, that 'love hurts.'

Chiron-Venus can operate in any relationship. This is the soul that may act out, or take on, scapegoating within the family or within a group. It is the child, for instance, onto whom all the family dysfunction is projected. The identified patient who is blamed and marked out as bad so that the rest of the family do not have to deal with their own issues. As a result, the soul with Venus-Chiron may have stopped trying to have relationships and chooses to withdraw to lick the wounds, and to have time to heal in a celibate state. On the other hand, a soul with this placement may try to hurt before they get hurt, dropping partners before there is any commitment. This soul may need experience of gentle loving to heal and could well go into passionless relationships. Or the soul may attract difficult and painful experiences and say: 'There, I knew I would be hurt'. Whilst this is rarely a conscious choice made in-between lives, it is nevertheless what the soul expects. Chiron-Venus aspects can also signify an almost Neptunian level of idealisation where one partner has such high ideals or expectations that the relationship cannot possibly live up to it and so wounding occurs again.

Many people, especially those with this aspect, believe that difficult relationship experiences are part of their spiritual evolution, particularly when the experience *appears* to be that of soulmates with a very deep love for each other. Chiron may have the built-in expectation that love, and relationships, are a struggle to which the person has to find a magic key through the development of spiritual awareness and by becoming sufficiently loving. However, regression to other lives might reveal that the experience that love hurts is more closely linked to their past experience than they suspected. They may discover that an old belief is being graphically lived-out. There are times when such expectations manifest physically as well as at an emotional level.

The soul with this aspect attracts people who have been involved in its emotional wounds in the past, and/or those who have the capacity to aid healing. If the soul is still at an unaware level of spiritual evolution, it will seem that 'they are wounding me again and again'. But if the soul has reached a level of understanding, then it interprets events as an opportunity to learn how to heal the emotional wounds of the past. Relationships often occur with members of the soul group and the soul may, at times, take on another's emotional pain to a greater or lesser degree as an act of redemptive karma.

Patricia is a woman who is deeply committed to her own spiritual growth as well as to helping others. She wanted to explore the blocks in her relationship with her partner, John, with whom she felt an exceptionally deep and old connection, with great love at a soul level. John had ceased sexual contact with her after seven years in relationship, despite continuing to live together for many more years. She felt their first meeting in the present life was a reconnection and that they had a life-task to undertake together. She explained that there was a powerful attraction between them right from the start, but that at first she had refused to make love because she was married. However, John did not give up easily and he called round to see her carrying a box of her favourite chocolates. They ended up on the lounge floor:

> 'There was not a lot of foreplay. It was too forceful for me to enjoy it as I was menopausal and very dry. By the end of the weekend, I was quite sore! It wasn't gentle sex, it had an urgency.'[3]

Patricia, a Libra, was in the throes of her Uranus opposition at the time and she quickly left her husband and went to live with John. The sex did improve a little but their basic rhythms never really meshed and, eventually, at the time of Patricia's Chiron return, John began to look elsewhere for sexual satisfaction, which caused Patricia great anguish. The Chiron return is a period when issues, especially karmic wounds, surface for resolution. Patricia has an almost exact square from Venus in Scorpio to Chiron conjunct Pluto in Leo. The expectation that love hurts manifested physically that first time they met, and emotionally throughout the relationship, but this wasn't the first time they had had sexual problems. In regression she reported:

> 'I see a gargoyle. It is a church. I am wearing a white Guinevere-type dress, low cut, long sleeves, long skirt. I have a headdress with flowing

net on its top. John is coming. [Joyfully:] It's our wedding; we walk down the aisle together towards the priest.'

Then suddenly she was in a bedroom, her body language that of a shy young girl:

'I can't turn my head. I don't want to look. He comes and leads me to the bed. It's a big four-poster in a large room with two windows with heavy damask drapes. It has panelling and a fireplace. I'm feeling very panicked. I don't want to look…. Aaargh…'

In the regression, piercing, heart-rending screams shook her. She put her fist in her mouth and bit on it. Later she explained that there had been no foreplay at all. She had bitten on her fist to quell the pain so as not to upset him. Both of them had been innocent and, not knowing what to do, he had penetrated her without warning. Love, most definitely, hurt.

'He's withdrawn, I'm bleeding. He's gone to the chair in the corner near the window. He's sobbing, head in his hands. I go to kneel in front of him and take his hands. We love each other so much. We make a vow never to make love again. After this we sleep in separate rooms. There is great love between us, but we don't express it physically.'

This was a situation that did not change throughout a long life together and which manifested again in the present incarnation. Unfortunately, John was unable to accept her regression as truth and, although she rescinded her part of that vow, he did not see the need. The relationship could not improve whilst that vow was there and eventually they parted at Patricia's instigation. She then had to deal with the pain of letting go of what she had felt was a life task for her and John. She went back to the time before she incarnated to reframe any vow she had made in this regard, concentrating instead on setting out her own, achievable, life purpose.

Resolution: The challenge for Venus-Chiron is to find a relationship that heals the old belief that love hurts, and shows the soul how to find fulfilling love once again. This challenge occurs between children and their parents as well as between lovers. The healing relationship comes from a supportive partner who is there regardless of what happens, the old cleaving together in sickness and in health, for richer, for poorer. Karmic injuries such as a broken heart may need to be repaired, or a part of the soul - or the heart - retrieved from the place where it took refuge from the pain (see Chapter 9).

Saturn in aspect to Venus
(or Venus in Capricorn or Pisces)

With Saturn in aspect to Venus past life relationships have been heavy, dutiful, restricting and cold. A considerable age difference may have been a feature or a noticeable lack of affection. Due to previous experiences of emotional inhibition, lack or loss of love and family disapproval, the soul with this aspect incarnates with an inherent sense of being unlovable, unworthy or not deserving love. As the incarnating soul does not believe it can be loved, its internal message is 'I don't deserve love'. It may also feel deeply vulnerable to pain through the emotions and so, to avoid the risk of experiencing pain yet again, defends itself in advance by remaining emotionally uninvolved, holding partners at arm's length, or by leaving before it is rejected.

This aspect is also prone to looking for approval rather than congruency in relationships. In congruent relationships the inner and outer agendas and behaviour of both parties are consistent and run parallel. In non-congruent relationships, the hidden agenda may well be geared to one, usually unconscious, objective, and the outward behaviour to another. If this occurs in both partners, the resulting mixed messages lead to enormous confusion. Gaining approval is important to the soul with Saturn in aspect to Venus and this need is often reiterated and strengthened in early life experiences where the soul is only valued when he or she conforms to parental expectations. If the soul feels it has approval, either in the parental or in adult interactions, then it is able to enter into intimate relationship and open up to a partner. If it does not, it falls into a passive mode and remains closed.

Many past relationships for the Saturn-Venus combination will have been cold and unloving: centring around a trade-off of some kind, which may be repeated in the present life. Jacqueline Kennedy Onassis, for instance, had Venus in the emotionally superficial sign of Gemini in the eighth house opposite Saturn. She did not expect joy in her relationships and may well have traded love for an inheritance of wealth in the past. It has been suggested that she married John F. Kennedy for the power and prestige his family and his political ambitions could offer. Having achieved the position of first lady, she had to endure his philandering in return - and the grief of losing two babies. After the death of her first husband she married one of the world's wealthiest men, Aristotle Onassis, a man much older than her, a classic Saturn manifestation. His enormous wealth fuelled her spending addiction. Her social standing gave him entry to a world he had previously been denied. His continued liaison with his long-time mistress Maria Callas could well have caused Jacqueline grief, and the couple were living separate lives by the time Onassis died but that was what, deep down, she expected.

The soul with this aspect tends to attract 'bad' or cold relationships, or to choose a partner who finds it impossible to love, thus confirming the expectation. Such partners will almost inevitably have been through emotional trauma and inhibitions of their own or may be repeating a role that they have taken on in the past - the karmic treadmill and retributive karma being a feature of Saturn-Venus contacts.

This soul tends to incarnate into a family which supports its perception of being unlovable. It expects and often receives emotional deprivation and conditional loving. The child may experience being the outsider in the family, or is born to replace a sibling who has died but, of course, one child can never replace another. The child is loved for being good and doing as it is told and so on. As a result, the child may retreat into being good in order to obtain what passes for love. As with Chiron-Venus, this is an aspect which indicates that the soul may well settle for safe relationships.

The soul with Venus-Saturn contacts often falls into, or repeats, a pattern of departing before the other person can leave, rejecting before it is abandoned, or behaving appallingly badly as though to drive the other person away. This is because, deep down, the soul believes that if that other person can love them, that other person can't be worth much themselves. If the other soul can put up with this and still maintain unconditional love, it can offer the incarnating Venus-Saturn soul the opportunity of changing the ingrained pattern.

With Saturn-Venus contacts there may also be a prior life scenario where the soul behaved badly within a relationship and therefore unconsciously feels that punishment is deserved or that reparation is required. Such a soul may feel that lack of love is the appropriate punishment, or that more and more effort should be put into a situation where there is no love, because that would mean restitution is being made. Healing comes when the soul is able to stop punishing itself.

This aspect may indicate someone who feels that they have a debt or duty to another person which goes beyond the normal limits of Saturnine duty. However, this may be more a matter of psychology than karmic debt. This is a soul who easily shoulders burdens or takes on a caretaker role because this has become a habit over several previous lives. Such a burden may be seen as making restitution or reparation for earlier acts, or as a punishment from God. With an overly developed sense of responsibility, this soul feels safe and good when overloaded. Part of the current life lesson may be to let someone else take up the responsibility.

Much of Saturn-Venus's sense of being unworthy of love arises out of selling itself in the past. Saturn-Venus has close links with prostitution - literal and metaphorical. This is not necessarily related to standing on a street corner and selling one's body to a stranger, although it may be. At times the prostitution is entered into because of low self esteem but the soul is equally likely to be forced into such circumstances by necessity. Prostitution may include selling one's soul in a loveless marriage for the sake of security, in order to put food on the table for children, or to keep body and soul together, but it can be much wider than this. A woman subtly prostitutes herself to a man if she gains power or position from the relationship. A man prostitutes himself to a woman if she takes his protection in return for sexual favours.

However, much earlier in the world's history, prostitution was sacred. woman was the link between the goddess and man, and divine energy poured through the body of the sacred prostitute. More than one woman with a Venus-Saturn aspect has regressed to a time when it was the custom for a woman to go the temple and offer herself to the first man that passed, or to any man that would have her. This was an offering of her virginity to the goddess. In some orgiastic religious rites such as those to Dionysius or Hathor, men and women came together as part of the religious celebrations. In later scenarios, wedding fairs would be arranged when the available young women were looked over by the young men. Unfortunately, it was sometimes the case that the woman (in regression) was not chosen. This left her with an indelible feeling of 'I'm not worth loving' - especially in those cultures where it was a condition that the offering should have been made before marriage. Healing could only come about when the woman was able to release the old experience, recognise herself as an expression of divinity, and then love herself.

Repressed sexuality may also feature in the past. A vow of celibacy could be intruding into the present relationship, and may need revoking. Attitudes may have been ingrained by a mother who despised sex, or from an earlier life where sexual contact was regarded as impure or sinful. Convents and religion in general have a habit of imprinting a notion that sex, and the body, is sinful. God in this view is something utterly other, set apart. 'He' demands absolute obedience and punishes any transgression, especially those on a sexual level. Healing for this comes, once again, in recognising the body and soul as part of the divine instead of feeling cut off and isolated from the source of love.

At a more aware level, this aspect may indicate someone who has, or will, take on a situation where the soul is a foil for a person learning a difficult lesson. The soul may be offering someone else the opportunity to learn to love, or to develop tolerance and other qualities.

A soul with these planets in trine may find that the experience has subtly shifted. Towards the end of the last life, or in the between-life state, there was a recognition that the soul did deserve love and so the soul set itself the task to love itself. Putting that into practice however may take a whole lifetime.

Resolution: The challenge for this aspect is to first learn to love yourself, and then to allow someone else to love you. There may be a need to forgive oneself for the past, letting it go. The soul may have to overcome deep inner programming that it is wrong to love yourself and positive affirmations can be extremely useful in retraining the mind. Looking oneself in the eye, saying firmly: 'I am lovable, I deserve love and I will value myself more deeply as time goes on' may feel strange initially, but it helps this aspect to make a huge shift. After all, if a soul cannot love itself, who else can?

Uranus in aspect to Venus
(or Venus in Aquarius, Uranus in Libra or Taurus, or seventh or eighth house)

Commitment and intimacy have been extremely difficult issues for this soul in the past and, as a result, the soul has internalised the message: 'I don't need love'. The soul is afraid to get close to someone and, at its extreme manifestation, may prefer to be a loner rather than risk love.

Previous relationship experiences for the soul with Uranus in aspect to Venus may have been erratic, chaotic and unpredictable. They will certainly have been different in some way and the soul may well have been accused of deviance from the norm. Separations and sudden endings will have featured strongly and there may well have been political marriages or marriages of convenience in which love had no place. As a result, the soul with this aspect subconsciously believes that it doesn't need love - and may shun or fear it.

At one extreme, Uranus-Venus is the commitment phobic who avoids intimacy at all costs, at the other it is the soul who stands hopelessly isolated, not having a clue as to how to be intimate with other people. In between is a spectrum with varying degrees of difficulty in sharing feelings and closeness. In the past, the soul incarnating with this aspect may have settled for celibacy rather than relationship or may have split off sex from love so that the mind and the emotions were detached from what was happening in the body. Learning to be intimate and to share thoughts and feelings can be a process that takes several lifetimes, and which may be tried out at first through friendships rather than sexual relations. Gradually the soul learns to trust and move beyond fear into a closeness that is an expression of soul love.

The detachment with which Uranus in aspect to Venus can approach love is indicated in the writer Charlotte Bronte's prosaic advice to her friend Ellen Nussey:

> 'No young lady should fall in love till the offer has been made, accepted - the marriage ceremony performed and the first half year of wedded life has passed away - a woman may then begin to love, but with great precaution - very coolly'.[4]

(This attitude was compounded by a wide semi-square to Saturn conjunct the Moon in Aquarius in the eighth house on her chart - time dowsed). Charlotte Bronte turned down three suitors because they 'could not know her'. She eventually married her father's curate, whom she had known for some years but had resisted his advances. She died, when pregnant, less than a year later. Given the complex nature of the aspects to her Venus, it may well be that she did not believe she deserved happiness or thought that she did not need love and this was her unconscious way of opting out. All her repressed passion went into her books in keeping with her ninth house Venus (time of birth dowsed).

In her twenties Charlotte had conceived a compulsive love for a married man whom she met when studying abroad (she had a

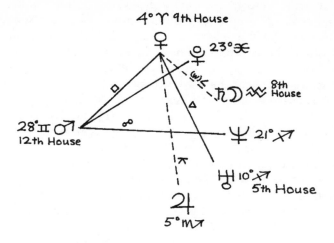

Figure 3 - Charlotte Bronte Aspects to Venus
(Time of birth was dowsed)

very wide Venus-Pluto conjunction). He taught her language and literature. The love affair was mainly carried on through correspondence from Charlotte after her return home: Uranus-Venus likes its relationships to be conducted at a safe distance. The object of her affection rejected her, at the instigation of his wife who did not believe it proper that he should maintain such an emotionally intense relationship with a pupil. The affair exactly mirrors the dilemmas in Charlotte's chart. Having given in to the unexpected and overwhelming love she conceived for this man, and been rejected, she then believed herself not worthy of love. Charlotte had Uranus in impetuous Sagittarius and Venus in passionate Aries, but the chilly detachment of the Moon in Aquarius brought out the innate caution of the Uranus-Venus with Saturn contact. Once the affair was ended, all her repressed passion was channelled into erotic daydreams and her emotionally intense writing. As is often the case with Uranus-Venus contacts, Charlotte hid behind a male pseudonym as the Victorian public were not ready to accept such writing as coming from a respectable woman who still lived in her father's parsonage.

That Charlotte also had a wide Pluto-Venus conjunction can be detected as she goes on to say in her letter to Ellen Nussey: 'If she ever loves so much that a harsh word or a cold look from her husband cuts her to the heart - she is a fool. If she ever loves so much that her husband's will is her law - and that she has got into a habit of watching his looks, in order that she may anticipate his wishes, she will soon be a neglected fool'. Charlotte's expectations of love - and her chart are summed up: 'It is a solemn [Moon-Saturn] and strange [Uranus] and perilous [Pluto] thing for a woman to become a wife'.

The man Charlotte married finally won her hand by promising to look after her father for the rest of his life. Saturn-Venus has many ways of prostituting itself and this was one manifestation. However, her marriage was a passionate and happy one - she did after all have Venus in Aries, interrupted prematurely by her death. In this she was repeating a family pattern. Her mother had died in pregnancy when Charlotte was young - something Charlotte's close Saturn-Moon conjunction in Aquarius no doubt expected. She was then raised by an aunt who had no love for her. Charlotte carried many internalised messages, not the least was that she neither needed love nor was she worthy of it.[5]

With this aspect the soul may never have opened its heart to another person, or may have left its heart in another's keeping and is unable to enter into relationships until the heart is retrieved (see Chapter 9). It could well attract relationships that are conducted at a distance - physical or metaphorical - as the soul feels more comfortable this way. The person with this aspect often gives off a subtle air of unavailability that deters other people from attempting to get close.

Such a stance can be healed, however, and some relationships are intended to heal the messages behind Venus. The Victorian poet Elizabeth Barrett Browning had a Uranus-Saturn conjunction in Libra tightly inconjunct Venus in Pisces, and Neptune trine Venus (see Figure 4a). A reclusive opium addict who suffered from ill health most of her life, Elizabeth hardly left her room for twenty five years. Her tyrannical father would not allow any of his children to marry. Her poems were her only emotional outlet. No matter how much she may have longed for romantic love - and a Sun in Pisces woman with Venus in Pisces trine Neptune has a powerful fantasy life - her father was determined such dreams would not come to fruition. He enforced Elizabeth's Venus-Uranus expectation that she did not need

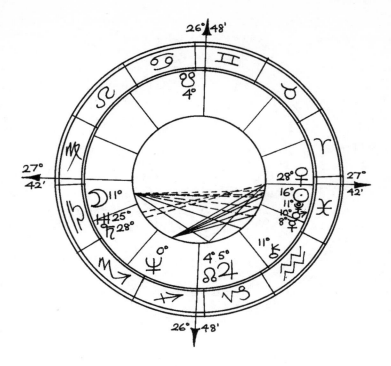

Figure 4a Elizabeth Barrett-Browning

love. Her Saturn-Venus also carried with it the feeling that she did not deserve love, no matter how she may have longed for it, and the Saturnine barrier her father erected protected her, as did her mother's emotional distance. However, Uranus also held the potential for a sudden and unexpected event to free her both from the tyranny of her father and her emotional expectations.

At almost forty, Elizabeth was a much-respected poet. Robert Browning, who was to be the Uranian catalyst who changed her life, was a younger poet just coming into prominence. Elizabeth mentioned Browning in her poem *Lady Geraldine's Courtship*: 'Or, from Browning, some "Pomegranate" which if cut deep down the middle, shows a heart within blood-tinctured of a veined humanity.'

As his picture was beside her bed, we can surmise that Browning was the focus of some of that Neptunian fantasy and one of her friends later insisted that Elizabeth was in love with the handsome poet long before they set eyes on each other. When Robert

63

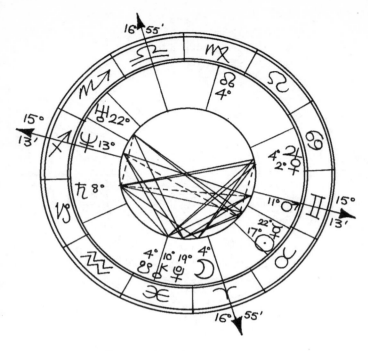

Figure 4b Robert Browning

wrote to her, ostensibly about the poem, he declared his love for her - before they had even met. His letter said: 'I do... love these verse with all my heart and I love you too'. Whilst this is typical of the flowery style of Victorian prose, it is still a very direct statement. Elizabeth immediately wrote to a friend: 'I had a letter from Browning the poet last night, which threw me into ecstasies'. This was all her unfulfilled romantic Neptune-Venus contact needed. Over the next twenty months they wrote each other 574 letters. When they finally managed to meet some five months after the initial contact, Elizabeth found her 'ideal man fleshed out'. His visit deeply unsettled her. She could not sleep and could not get him out of her mind - classic symptoms of love but alien to someone whose emotional life had been so repressed to that point. Nevertheless, in keeping with her Venus inconjunct Saturn, she told Browning repeatedly that she was not worthy of his love, she was a jinx and made everything she touched turn to evil and had a duty to prevent him sacrificing himself.[6]

Robert, however, who had his Saturn opposition to Venus enlivened by a conjunction of Jupiter to Venus in Gemini in the seventh house, immediately declared, yet again, his love 'from his soul' and quite independently of whether she loved him or not. As Elizabeth's biographer Margaret Forster says:

'He acted with the wisdom which had come from learning to understand her character. Patiently, he stressed that she would be doing him the honour. He was poor stuff; she was a prize. Bit by bit he struggled to erode that huge mountain of pessimism which oppressed her. He would not allow his love to be pushed away into a dark corner, to be hidden in case it vanished, but displayed it repeatedly so that she would become familiar with it and learn to trust it.' The synastry between them (see Chapter 5) is indicative of a reunion of old lovers with a freedom-commitment dilemma to work out and, with Venus falling in the seventh house in both the composite and the relationship charts, it was clear they were destined to meet.'[7]

Uranus can be a powerful catalyst. Within months, Elizabeth was out and about. She shed the worst effects of her illness (which, with Mercury, Mars, Pluto and the Sun in Pisces in the sixth house was probably largely psychosomatic following the drowning of her brother), defied her father (taking back the Pluto-Sun projection of power), married secretly and travelled to Italy with her new husband, where she bore a son. It was the first love relationship for either of them in their in present lives. They spent the next seventeen years together, during which time Robert wrote little poetry although Elizabeth was prolific, writing some of her best known work. When Elizabeth died, Browning told a friend: 'My heart lies buried in Florence' (Elizabeth's burial place). Browning did not remarry, remaining a widower for twenty-eight years. His Saturn-Venus opposition, having made its commitment, was faithful to the end.

With Uranus-Venus Elizabeth was looking for space to be herself and Robert gave her this. In *Sonnets from the Portuguese* she said: 'If thou must love me, let it be for naught. Except for love's sake only... that evermore thou mayst love on, through love's eternity.' And asks:

How do I love thee? Let me count the ways.
I love thee to the depth and breadth and height
My soul can reach, when feeling out of sight! - and
For the ends of Being and ideal Grace.

I love thee to the level of every day's
Most quiet need, by sun and candlelight.
I love thee freely, as men strive for Right.
I love thee purely, as they turn from Praise.
I love thee with the passion put to use
In my old griefs, and with my childhood's faith.
I love thee with a love I seemed to lose
With my lost saints - I love thee with the breath,
Smiles, tears, of all my life! - and, if God choose,
I shall but love thee better after death.

Nevertheless, despite the happiness of the marriage, Elizabeth had an intense relationship with another woman. Her early emotional life had been traumatic, her beloved brother drowned and she was plagued with depression even after her marriage. Her desire to contact her brother took her to Spiritualism - of which Robert strongly disapproved.

Sophie Eckley declared herself Elizabeth's sister 'in the spiritual world', she was a soul sister who idolised and idealised Elizabeth, with whom she shared a deep interest in the spirit world. Sophie was a powerful medium herself, however their friendship went far beyond this. Their love for each other is declared in their letters, a love which on Sophie's side was both deceptive and obsessive. Elizabeth eventually found it necessary to break free, after which her relationship with Browning was strengthened.

The Venus-Uranus aspect can indicate ambiguity and ambivalence around sexuality and gender. It often shows up in lesbian relationships. It may indicate that the soul has changed gender between lives or that a soul has had many incarnations as the opposite sex. It is quite common for people with this aspect to feel that they are in the wrong body. At the extreme, transsexuality or transvesticism may result as the soul struggles to come to terms with the change of gender. On the other hand, a soul may fight against the role that society commonly allots to the gender they happen to have taken on for the present lifetime. Several women have said that, whilst they believed they were the right gender for what they needed to experience now, they knew that once they returned to the between-life state they would revert to being more predominantly male rather than female - the soul being neutral and genderless. In the present life, these women were assertive and powerful and saw no reason why they should not be treated exactly as men were. One, for instance, was a female fire officer who pioneered the acceptance of women into the fire service. But, as she said, this did not prevent her from being utterly feminine in her sexual relationships. Some of these women, however, have found it more comfortable to relate to other women.

Venus-Uranus (or Mars-Uranus) aspects also show up in charts, usually with eighth house involvement, where the soul has taken on a lesbian or homosexual lifetime to learn a different approach to sexuality and explore different facets of relationships. It may also occur where the soul is repeating an old pattern of relating to a same-sex partner. Bi-sexuality is common. The task is to move beyond gender restrictions and into open relationship with oneself and others.

For the writer George Sand, the unconventionality of Uranus-Venus showed up a little differently. She wrote under a masculine name but her chaotic love life was 'all woman'. Despite her somewhat ugly appearance, she was extremely attractive to men. She had magnetic Uranus in Libra in the seventh house, sextile Venus in Leo. Her conventional marriage (she also had Saturn in the seventh) was soon replaced by a Bohemian life style in which she had many lovers. She said: 'Everything is propitious to lovers. They are the spoilt children of Providence.'

Resolution: Allowing oneself to be loved is an enormous challenge for this combination, as is getting close to someone else. But it is in this opening to another person that the healing takes place and trust develops. Finding open and true intimacy with another person, and allowing sufficient space for the union to grow whilst each soul retains its own individuality is essential. This is not an aspect where one and one are halves that make a whole. One and one make a relationship, neither symbiotic nor exclusive.

Neptune in aspect to Venus
(Neptune in Libra or Pisces, Venus in Pisces)
With Neptune in aspect to Venus the incarnating soul has had previous relationships which may have been regarded as perfect but which could equally well have been a beautiful illusion - Neptune is predictably evasive when it comes to dealing with the reality of relationship situations. The soul with a Neptune attunement seeks romance but may have felt deeply guilty about sexuality in former

lives. Neptune, more than any other planet, is into 'what might have been' scenarios. Unfulfilled longings have such power that, on looking back, the soul's imagined, or fantasised, relationships become fact even though they never actually took place in the flesh - which can lie behind many so-called soulmate meetings in the present life. With this aspect, the soul can easily split off love and carnality, and may have preferred celibate yearnings to the actuality of connubial bliss or erotic pleasure no matter how much it deluded itself. This soul has internalised the message that love has to be perfect, sexless and blissful, not an easy combination within a relationship.

People with Neptune-Venus often find sexual activity vaguely dissatisfying, or experience a curious lethargy afterwards. Elisabeth Haich, a wise woman who wrote *Initiation*[8] explained that people with a potential for spiritual union at a soul level - what she calls 'paradisical union' - often confuse the desire for that with sexual intercourse. As the sex is at the physical level, it does not satisfy the spiritual desire and results in fatigue or dissatisfaction.

The soul with Neptune in aspect to Venus is seeking a soulmate. There is a deep yearning to return to the unity with the divine that the soul knew before. Venus in aspect to Neptune idealises the feminine and has romantic notions of love. The soul incarnates with impossibly high expectation around love, seeking nothing less than perfection. People with this aspect may clutch at any relationship that feels like 'my other half.' Confusions, delusions and deceptions are common with this combination. The soul may attract someone with whom there is unfinished business - that relationship that never did get consummated for instance. But equally unfulfilled yearnings can draw souls back together when one soul has no intention of entering into relationship with the other - the challenge for the incarnating soul being to recognise the illusion for what it is.

Prone to living in a fantasy, thinking it could be perfect when it cannot, or that the other person wants a relationship when they do not, are some of the manifestations of Venus-Neptune. This aspect finds it terribly difficult to let go of whatever the current delusion might be. This illusion can last way beyond one lifetime. It can take the soul several lives to realise that the soulmate it is so attached to is nothing of the sort. As the combination feels incomplete without someone to love, anyone is better than no one at all or so it feels. As a result, this combination frequently gets drawn into abusive, collusive and dependent relationships of all kinds. Addictive relationships are common. The illusion is that: 'I can help him/her', 'I can make him/her better', 'I can change this', 'he or she needs me' and so on. Neptune has both victim and martyr tendencies as well as playing the saviour, so the soul with this combination often finds itself a victim of love. Neptune-Venus may confuse need with love. If someone is clinging, needy, and seems unable to function on their own, the Neptune-Venus attuned soul may mistake the consequent dependency for love. This is particularly so where Venus is placed in the water signs, although Libra too can jump to the same unwarranted conclusion.

The soul with this aspect has a challenge to love unconditionally, but all too often the point is missed. Unconditional love does not involve allowing someone else to walk all over you, to abuse and misuse you. It is not about accepting lies and deceptions, nor about colluding with someone to keep them dependent. Neither is it concerned with sacrificing yourself for someone else or making them better. Unconditional love means loving another person, as they are, and yet boundaries and limits can be set. It is about you being in your space and being okay about the other person being in theirs, no matter what that might involve them in. It may require you to say that you find something unacceptable, and so you remove yourself from the situation. It does not involve demanding that the other person change. So often this aspect can see the pearl in the heart of other person, recognising what the other person could be, but healing or transformation for the other person does not come about through being forced to confront this pearl. It comes through being accepted for who and what they are, *as they are now* not as they could be 'if only...' Thus the possibility for change is opened, but it is manipulative love (not unconditional love) if loving is done on the basis of what could be.

Neptune-Venus is an aspect of idealised femininity. The tendency, particularly for males with this aspect, is to place first the mother and later the desired sexual object, cunningly disguised as 'the beloved', on to a pedestal. Women may do the same to the men they love. This 'perfect being' is idealised and worshipped, literally idolised. When the all-too-human feet of clay become apparent, the idealised object falls off the pedestal and shatters, creating enormous disillusionment. And yet the soul goes into the next relationship still seeking that perfection, only to be disappointed time and again.

Such a desired sexual object or beloved may be totally inappropriate. One client expressed this as 'a tendency to put any old slag on to a pedestal and refuse to let her get off no matter what she does'. The women he chose to worship were almost always incapable of a close and loving relationship, which safely prevented him from having to enter into actual relationship and thereby soil the memory of mother and the female sex which his past-life and childhood training had taught him to regard as sacred, non-sexual beings.

Similarly, a young woman was quite happy to have promiscuous relationships with men she did not love (twelfth house Neptune inconjunct seventh house Venus), but not to have sex with the man she loved and married 'because it would spoil everything'. She had been brought up by a mother who herself had an unavailable fantasy lover, who she said was her spiritual soulmate, and yet the mother was married to a man with whom she had sex to procreate. The child had absorbed the mother's romantic yearning for an idealised, platonic love totally devoid of sexual contact, a yearning which reflected her own pattern. This was eventually traced back to a previous Cathari existence during which she had renounced sex.

With the Venus-Neptune contact the soul may carry over the memory of a romantic, blissful relationship from the past. If the contact also involves the Moon, the soul may carry over a memory of a time when it had a particularly ecstatic relationship with the present-life mother, possibly as lover or beloved. If there has been no disillusionment and separation from the mother in childhood, the soul carries this unrealistic expectation of perfection and merging into marriage or other relationships - and is usually deeply disappointed.

The soul with Venus-Neptune yearns for the romantic, mystical union which masquerades under the name of love. It is, of course, difficult to have a physical relationship with a fantasy goddess, and great disillusionment is felt whenever the idolised object behaves in any way which is not perfect. Such an unrealistic vision of woman - by both men and women - may have been carried over for many incarnations and throughout several different types of experience. Just as the nun became the Bride of Christ, so monks and priests, needing a focus for their sublimated sexual energies, entered into relationship with 'Mary, the Mother of God' or the virginal 'Madonna', both of whom epitomise perfection and idealised love.

Prince Charles has a close Neptune-Venus conjunction in

Libra, the sign of relationship, sextile Pluto in Leo. Through his marriage to the fairy tale Princess Diana, he projected out to the world an idealised illusion of Neptunian bliss. His position as future King of England demanded that his Princess had to be virginal, perfect and untouchable, the unsullied mother of his children (a Madonna figure). What was not apparent at first was just how deceptive this picture was. Although Diana had Venus in earthy Taurus, it was square to Uranus. She was not comfortable in her body and possibly carried forward a vow of celibacy - she remembered a life as a nun in a former incarnation. Like Charles, his long-time mistress, Camilla Parker Bowles has Neptune in Libra on the I.C., the root of the chart. Her Neptune is trine Venus in secretive Cancer in the hidden, karmic twelfth house - an ideal placement for a mistress. She may well have played the same role in the past for there is certainly a family link. Her great-great-grandmother, Alice Keppell, and Charles' great-great-grandfather, Edward VII, were long-term lovers and Camilla is supposed to have alluded to this when she and Charles first met, suggesting that they carry on where the 'greats' left off.

It is said that Charles and Camilla will not be able to marry because, as prospective head of the Church of England, Charles should not marry a divorced woman nor, as a divorced man, re-marry at all. (Although Diana's death leaves a typical Neptunian constitutional conundrum around that one.) That Charles has Neptune-Venus at the base of his chart could easily point to the fact that he is living out a family saga. One of his ancestors, also heir to the throne, made a morganatic marriage to a woman who could never be queen. Charles' great-uncle abdicated his throne because he, famously, would not rule without the woman he loved by his side.

Neptune-Venus has a strong Madonna-Whore dichotomy. This paradox is a fundamental part of the Venus-Neptune conundrum. The question is 'How can I be sexual and sacred at the same time?' The past life patterns are that in several lives libido was repressed and the soul kept the body pure in the pursuit of spirituality. In different lives sexuality would be explored fully but not spirituality. Men often split off one or more parts of the Venus-Neptune dilemma and project it onto their women. One woman takes on one role, another the opposite role - and these roles can reverse. So, although to the eyes of the outside world Diana ultimately played out the 'whore' through her public affairs, reversing the public's previous perception of her as a Madonna, it was Camilla with whom the graphically Scorpionic Charles was sexually compatible. Whatever reason she may have had for not marrying her Prince Charming when they first met, it was with her that his Scorpio loyalty and libido lay.

The Madonna-Whore dichotomy often arises through previous lives in which spirituality and sexuality were either intertwined or split off. A soul incarnating into a female body prior to the Christian faith may have belonged to a religion which honoured sex and sexuality as an expression of the creative life force, or she may have kept herself chaste as a priestess of the goddess. After the arrival of the Christian faith, she may have been in a blessed sexual relationship or celibate as a nun. In Buddhism she could have taken the tantric path or the asexual one. In one view, divine union sees sex as sacred, but in another the body is only holy as long as it is inviolable. The great misogynist, St Paul, declared that celibacy was the ideal - although 'it was better to marry than burn'. Sex, in his view, was infinitely inferior to chastity.

Romantic Neptunian notions of love were also present in the Troubadour chivalrous or poetic relationships expressing Courtly Love, in which a woman was loved devotedly but never physically, there being a total divide between sacred spiritual love and profane sexual love. The conflicts may also have manifested in the type of marriage in which the woman is seen as pure and untouchable, and prostitutes or mistresses are utilised to take care of the partner's physical needs. Or again in the relationship which is never consummated for one reason or another, or in the happy-ever-after fairy stories or the old style Mills and Boon novels. The challenge in the present life is to integrate spirituality with sexuality.

Difficulties may be encountered when the soul has been involved in an ancient mystical marriage and incarnates expecting to be joined in relationship on all the levels of being (see Chapter 10). Unless the soul consciously and carefully chooses its partner, with full awareness of all the underlying shadows and projections, it is open to disillusionment. However, if the soul does meet its spiritual match then the relationship becomes a way to achieve union with the divine, and as such a valuable pathway for spiritual growth.

I once counselled a man who had the Sun conjunct Venus in Pisces quincunx Neptune in Libra. He had a longstanding desire for a soulmate with whom he could continue his spiritual evolution. He had met a woman, briefly, with whom he felt a strong soul contact

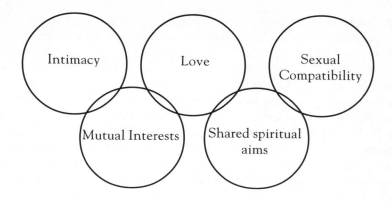

Figure 5: The Five Golden Rings: a typical example

but she lived on the other side of the world. However, his marriage had ended and his mind kept returning to this woman who was powerful, stunningly beautiful and highly spiritual. She was Venus restored to life: a real goddess figure. She appeared to be exactly what his Venus was looking for but he was aware that it could be an illusion - the synastry between them was full of Neptunian interaspects with all the personal planets, and there were no Saturn aspects to ground the relationship into everyday reality. Trained in psychology and conscious of past life influences, he was aware of the projections and mirroring that could occur in 'perfect' relationships.

He sat down and did a Five Golden Rings exercise. He listed all the qualities he wanted in his relationship, each facet that was essential to him from sexual to spiritual harmony, and many practical points too. Choosing five words to epitomise what he wanted, he put them into five interlocking golden rings. Shortly afterwards a lecture tour took him to the city where this woman lived and they met up again. She soon joined him on his side of the world and the relationship remains everything, and more, that he had hoped for. They have consciously made a mystical marriage in the present, following an initiatory process they believe came from a past life together. Each is convinced that they have found their soul partner.

Resolution: The illusions and deceptions of Neptune are healed and transformed into unconditional love through realistic partnerships that bring the souls into divine harmony. But the ultimate task for the soul with this aspect is union with the divine part of the soul, recognising oneself as a divine being and expressing that love out to the world.

Pluto in aspect to Venus
(or Venus in Scorpio, Pluto in Libra)

As with all Pluto aspects, there is little to indicate on the surface the powerful libido and emotional purgatory of the soul with Venus aspected by Pluto. Indeed, the person themselves may have little indication. This is a deeply subconscious contact full of repression, compulsive working and reworking of the dynamic, and a hidden desire to manipulate events so that the person feels comfortable. For this soul, past life relationships have shown the darker side of Venus. Obsession, compulsion, rejection, power struggles, trauma, abuse, fear, dark eroticism and symbiosis will all have featured strongly. The challenge has been to transmute this energy through the alchemy of the heart into a powerful creative force.

The soul with Pluto in aspect to Venus who has not found the key to emotional transformation has a deep, dark and needy abyss inside that believes there will never be enough love. In the past, the emotional deprivation has been so strong that the soul has developed an insatiable desire for love. No mere mortal, no matter how wonderful a human being, can possibly supply enough love to fill up the tenebrous depths of a Pluto-Venus black hole. This desperate fear of lack of love is accompanied by a need for intense emotional closeness - which sometimes amounts to a sex addiction. This is the soul that has experienced emotional traumas of all kinds. The soul is insatiably greedy for emotional nourishment, sucking in all that it can find and yet it is never enough. Sex is often confused with love. Relationships will have been predatory, symbiotic and demanding. The past pattern is to have manipulated, manoeuvred and demanded; using emotional blackmail, and clinging to whatever passed for love whether it be abusive, collusive, dependent, symbiotic or indifferent. The great fear for this soul is 'If I let this go, there might never be love again.' This is manifested out to the world, where it can be clearly seen by others, and yet the person is usually unaware of it. The incarnating soul's challenge is to eliminate the negative emotions and transmute its whole approach to love.

One client of mine, a professional astrologer with an out-of-sign Venus-Pluto conjunction across Cancer-Leo, laughed nervously when I talked about the Pluto-Venus black hole and said: 'To me, woman is a black hole. I literally experience the vagina in this way and fear as well as crave sexual contact. It is my drug.' This is the *vagina dentate*, the vagina with teeth that swallows men whole. It was described in ancient Egypt thus:

> The goddess who guards the second pylon
> is treacherous and her ways are devious.
> Lady of the Flame, whore of the universe,
> with the mouth of a lioness,
> your vagina swallows men up
> they are lost in your milky dugs[9]

As I said in *The Hades Moon*:

> It is the place out of which man emerged; he spends his life separating from this. It is the place of primal fear, the lunar birth canal to the other world. At this gate, we must confront the apparent duality of the dark goddess: that what grants life, and individuality, can also take it away. We must recognise that one is the shadow face of the other, that, without one, we could not have the other. [10]

The Duat is the Egyptian otherworld that solar consciousness must traverse each night, fighting its demons to be born anew. Many commentators equate this traverse with the soul's journey through the subconscious mind. The second hour in the Duat is the hour of magic and transformation and the place where the past can be stripped away. But it is also the place where man must confront his atavistic and primeval fears. It is little wonder that the French refer to orgasm as the little death. This is the dangerous moment when the rampant, untamed eroticism of Venus must be confronted. Men with Pluto-Venus could use tantric sex to transform the sexual creative force into spiritual energy, bringing about a fundamental transformation.

At the same time as needing intense emotional closeness, the soul with this aspect can fear it greatly, expecting to be swallowed up by the relationship. The Scorpionic poet Sylvia Plath had Pluto exactly sextile Venus in Virgo. She said:

> 'It came over me... the sudden shock and knowledge that although this is the one man in the world for me, although I am using every fiber of my being to love him, even so, I am true to the essence of myself, ... and will live with him through sorrow and pain, singing all the way, even in anguish.'

And yet, a little later, she wrote

> 'we have mystically become one [Neptune in the seventh]...we share
> ourselves perhaps more intensely at every moment..'

The couple eventually divorced and Sylvia Plath finally committed suicide after several failed attempts spread throughout her life.

A soul with this aspect is likely to attract a person with whom there has been an obsessive, compulsive relationship - or where an obsession has arisen that has pulled the souls back together. Unfinished business includes power struggles, abuse and abandonment, but little of this shows when a couple first gets together. In typical Plutonian fashion the dynamics lurk beneath the façade of a perfectly normal relationship and only themselves known at a later date.

The soul with Pluto-Venus has developed the habit of watching 'the beloved' closely. An antenna is developed that is always out there seeking to make contact, wanting to know what is going on with the other. The fear of losing love leads the soul to try to anticipate needs and wishes, and fulfil them. There is an anxiety attached to 'where is he or she?' which goes beyond normal boundaries. It is partly manipulation and control, but it is also the desire to *make things right*, to propitiate and cajole. To be in control. There is an enormous fear of losing the partner, either to death or to another woman or man. The list of fears is endless, the foreboding a bottomless pit because this is what the soul has known in the past.

Loss, death and transformation are all keynotes of Pluto. Stephen Arroyo speaks of Pluto-Venus in connection with a repeating pattern where a fiance or lover dies or disappears[11] and this has been backed up by my clients' experiences, both in the present life and in other lives. I have found that it also extends to the loss of husband or children as well as lovers. It is a theme that often runs in families, the aspect weaving down through the generations (and this is particularly so when the contact also includes the Moon, see *The Hades Moon*). One of my clients, who had Venus in Scorpio square Pluto in Leo, lost not one but two sons. This double loss depleted her energy so much that it seemed unlikely that she would live to complete her life task. It is characteristic of the loss that Venus-Pluto so fears. The loss may be physical, through death or the relationship ending, or it may be that affection dies. The grief and pain are the same whatever the direct cause, and hooks into all the old pain and grief that lie behind this aspect. The soul is challenged to let go of the grief as well as finding a new way of relating, moving away from the old absorbed, symbiotic and manipulative pattern.

People with Pluto-Venus aspects have a tendency to confuse need with love. If an urge is insatiable, devouring, overwhelming and intense, then, in their eyes, it must equate to love. So, if someone with a sex addiction uses their body to satisfy that addiction, it would be confused with love because the soul would register the intensity of the physical or emotional compulsion rather than the lack of profound feeling. In the same way, if the soul with Venus-Pluto conceived an obsession with someone - as often happens - they assume this has to be love. After all, they need that person desperately. They do not see that they are trying to fill their own need rather than moving out to share themselves equally in relationship with someone else.

The manipulative, needy aspect of this contact can make itself known through any kind of relationship. It is common between friends, employer and employee, mentor and pupil, or in a counselling situation. Indeed, many counsellors are drawn to the work exactly because they have a Pluto-Venus contact which they see mirrored in their clients. Some project their issues onto their clients, but for counsellors who are self-aware Venus-Pluto can give enormous insight into what clients are going through. It is also extremely common to find this aspect in people who seek counselling.

As I said in *The Karmic Journey*, clients who phone or write 'just to see how you are getting on with my reading', or who are exceptionally friendly and subtly demanding of my attention at workshops, invariably have a Venus-Pluto connection. Even when they have read what I have to say about the contact, they still put covert pressure on, ringing to see how I'm getting on with the reading. Their own needs are so overwhelming, that they feel they must be given priority. This is an aspect that is used to using friendliness, charm and covert manipulation to achieve what it wants. As Stephen Arroyo put it: 'this placement is prone to use one's attractiveness or friendliness to gain power, money, or simply to inflate one's ego.[12] Pluto-Venus makes itself felt strongly within friendships. All the intensity and obsession hovers just below the surface, together with a certain manipulative quality.

When I heard a letter from the American poet Emily

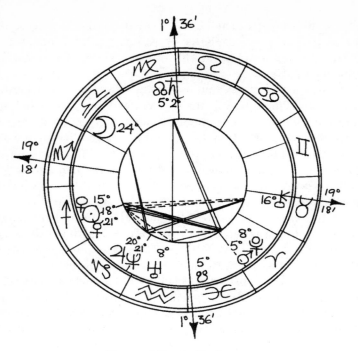

Figure 6 Emily Dickinson

Dickinson read out on the radio my first thought was that she must have Pluto-Venus in aspect. It turned out that she did, although it was a wide trine from Venus conjunct the Sun and Mercury in Sagittarius to Pluto conjunct Mars in Aries, together with a 1° orb inconjunct from Venus to Chiron. (see Figure 6).

The letter in question was to her childhood friend Abiah Root and the Pluto-Venus 'black hole' is all too obvious:

> When I am most happy there is a sting in every enjoyment...There is an aching void in my heart which I am convinced the world never can fill. .. I continually hear Christ saying to me Daughter give me thine heart... You [Abiah] are earning control and firmness. Christ Jesus will love you more. I'm afraid he don't love me *any!*.. [13]

Here she is describing being offered a cure for her aching void, but is unable to accept. Perhaps because she gave away her heart in the past, she is loath to do so again. Giving away the heart to a divine figure, such as Christ, has the same karmic consequences as giving the heart to a human figure (see Chapter 9). So long as Christ is seen as something separate and apart, she would be handing over her power. What she could have done was to fill her heart from this source of divine love which would have healed the black hole (something which developed later in her life). Even better would have been to make a mystic marriage with the divine part of herself.

One of Emily's greatest male friends, whom she met when she was twenty-five and exchanged letters with on spiritual topics, was a somewhat romantic figure, the Reverent Charles Wadsworth. An eloquent preacher, he had known great sorrow and was given to deep introspection, and was therefore a fitting hook for the projection of Emily's Plutonian emotional angst. He may also have been the man she fell in love with, for there is no doubt that Emily fell in love around this time, but with whom it is not known.

Emily's father was a major figure in her life and his domineering and possessive nature may have been the reason she gave up the possibility of an outside relationship. But nothing human could fill her Pluto-Venus black hole, which was so insatiably greedy for love. As one commentator on her poems says: 'Although sexual love is not directly specified in these poems, it is difficult to imagine that the sequence of need, partial gratification, anxiety, renunciation that constitutes the emotional essence of them could refer as readily to any other experience.'

After her father's death Emily again fell in love, this time with one of his friends, a Judge. But although they exchanged tender letters that show that he reciprocated her feelings, he died without the relationship developing further - her karmic expectation was that love would hurt and she would lose a loved one. Her life reflected that expectation. All Emily's repressed passions went into her mystical verse:

> He fumbles at your soul
> As players at the keys
> Before they drop full music on.
> He stuns you by degrees.
> Prepares your brittle nature
> For the ethereal blow
> By fainter hammers further heard,
> Then nearer, then so flow
> Your breath has time to straighten,
> Your brain to bubble cool,
> Deals one imperial thunderbolt
> That scalps your naked soul.
> (*He Fumbles at Your Soul*)

What the soul with a Pluto-Venus aspect wants above all is to be in control of the process of love and yet paradoxically to surrender to its all-embracing force. The hidden expectation is that love will overwhelm, consume with its intensity. The fear is that the soul will be swallowed up and taken down into the Plutonian underworld and obliterated.

This is perhaps why so many souls with Venus-Pluto contacts find themselves in abusive, addictive or symbiotic relationships. They attract exactly what they fear so much, but the destructive side of the experience is often projected out onto their partner. An alcoholic or drug addict is more prone than most to facing death and the Plutonian underworld, and yet to the partner of an addict it can feel like they are the ones who will die from the situation.

So often, there is so much projection going on within the relationship it is impossible to see exactly what is happening. An alcoholic is devious, manipulative and controlling yes, but so is the spouse who tries so hard to control his or her drinking. Power is such a Plutonian issue and addictive relationships are imbued with power struggles and control bids. A great deal of unconscious enabling goes on within such partnerships, as does taking on the role of protecting someone from the consequences of their actions - in other words, not letting them face their karma. The lessons epitomised in addictive relationships and in the Pluto-Venus connection are set out in an Al-Anon handout aimed at abrogating the controlling nature of the alcoholic partnership:

Letting Go
To 'Let go' does not mean to stop caring, it means I can't do it for someone else.
To 'Let go' is not to cut myself off, it's the realisation I cannot control another.
To 'Let go' is not to enable but to allow learning from natural consequences
To 'Let go' is to admit powerlessness, which means the outcome is not in my hands.
To 'Let go' is not to care for, but to care about.
To 'Let go' is not to fix, but to be supportive.
To 'Let go' is not to be in the middle arranging all the outcomes but to allow others to effect their destinies.
To 'Let go' is not to be protective, it's to permit another to face reality.

To 'Let go' is not to adjust everything to my desires, but to take each day as it comes and cherish myself in it.
To 'Let go' is not to regret the past, but to grow and live for the future.
To 'Let go' is to fear less and love more.

It is through the pathway of loving more and loving unconditionally without strings (see Neptune-Venus), and giving love without expectation or demanding it be returned, that the soul who is attuned to Venus-Pluto can grow beyond the 'black hole' and learn the true power of love.

Pluto-Venus naturally attracts to itself a companion who mirrors the issues involved. An American woman consulted me whose husband had started looking for intense, passionate friendships with other women. She had moved from the East to West Coast of America to be with him and was afraid that if he left her she would be isolated and alone. He was her only source of Love. He had had an affair shortly after they married but had assured her that he wanted to remain with her. She was his comfort object and he relied closely upon her, particularly in social settings where her more adventurous and gregarious nature made her the natural leader.

She said that sex between them had never been good and that he had always ogled attractive women, behaving in public in a way she felt was inappropriate. She needed and expected her partner to be faithful, both publicly and privately, but whenever she complained, he accused her of being jealous and possessive. She gradually came to believe this was her fault and that if she could become loving enough, the situation would change.

Venus-Pluto squares featured strongly in both charts, and both partners having Venus in Scorpio emphasized the Plutonian aspect to the combination. However, the planets were not conjunct and made only one wide, one-way interaspect so this was nothing personal to the two of them; karma did not accrue from other lifetimes, they were merely working on the same issues. This emotionally abusive relationship masqueraded under 'A Very Deep Love' and, in true Plutonian fashion, the partnership was symbiotic with him drawing strongly on her energy. She, on the other hand, could not imagine life without him no matter how uncomfortable it was. Recognising her problem, she began to work on finding love within herself. She used meditation and flower essences, and took herself to a support group for abused women. Eventually, she found the courage to leave.

He was devastated at being 'abandoned'. He finally had to face his feelings.

Resolution: The healing for Venus-Pluto comes both in letting go and when the person no longer looks 'out there' for love. The lesson for the soul with this aspect is to that no human can fill that bottomless pit; the soul has to turn to a connection with the divine. In deepest meditation, the soul can touch a point which is all loving. This is divine love, which never runs out, and drawing in love from that source fills the soul. With the hole filled, the soul can give out pure love, which attracts it back in turn. (Not that it should be done with that intention as that would be manipulative – a return to the old pattern.) With this connection to divine love in place, loving becomes a natural part of life. The soul can breathe in love, and breathe it out again knowing it will always be replenished. This is a most healing experience for all concerned.

INGRAINED EMOTIONS: THE MOON

Venus is not the only planet involved in emotional reactions and deep-seated needs. The Moon represents a deeply ingrained, instinctual response to life that has arisen over many lifetimes. It is also strongly related to family matters and to the past. As Haydn Paul puts it: 'Challenging Moon aspects indicate that the ghosts of the past, family traditions, and established patterns, are unduly powerful and are preventing change.'[14]

How a soul fundamentally reacts or responds emotionally is described by the placement of the Moon in a sign. The Moon sign can conflict with the Sun-sign and is usually more powerful, especially in relationships. For instance, a soul with the Sun in Libra has a deep need for relationship and usually does all it can to compromise, adapt and adjust to meet the needs of others. But place an independent Aries or Sagittarius Moon into the equation and the soul will, once it has tried its best, quickly let go and move onto another relationship. A clinging, possessive Taurus, Cancer, Scorpio or Pisces Moon would hang in there long after all hope of a fulfilling relationship had passed.

Moon in Aries
The soul incarnating with the Moon in Aries has a powerful desire to have its needs met, instantly. Those needs are immediate,

overwhelming and inherently self-centred. The Aries Moon finds the notion of emotional sharing difficult and illustrates the insensitive person who demands his or her own way. This is a placement that cannot tolerate frustration, and much outward behaviour is unconsciously created by hidden sexual or comfort needs. Due to past life experiences, this independent soul often puts out the unspoken message that it doesn't need anyone, so that there is an isolation and separation from other people and close relationships may be a difficult area. The potential, however, is to become aware not only of one's own needs but those of other people also.

Moon in Taurus

This Moon has one of the most deeply ingrained patterns of behaviour of all the signs. Emotions can be toxic as the past is held onto - firmly. This soul can put aside its emotional needs if they conflict with its basic desire for security. The Moon in Taurus dislikes change of any kind. Home, family and work are where this soul finds security - and the person with this placement will often lose parts of itself that do not fit rather than make necessary changes in its emotional environment. This is a soul with both a powerful sex drive and deep sensual yearnings, and if these can be satisfied relationships are usually a bonding for life. This Moon has the potential to develop a deep, unshakeable inner security.

The Moon in Gemini

The soul incarnating with the Moon in Gemini has a deep desire to communicate and, on the surface, appears to talk about needs and emotions quite openly. The problem comes with actually feeling those feelings - they can quickly be verbalised or rationalised out of existence. As this is such a changeable sign, emotions tend to be facile and superficial, and the person gives out double messages. Way back in the past, the soul has had traumatic emotional experiences it prefers to forget. It eschews real intimacy, as being too scary and its emotional fickleness and infidelities can be a defence against a close relationship which, in other lives, has created pain. However, this Moon has the potential to be able to recognise not only its own emotional needs but to clarify those of other people also.

Moon in Cancer

Deeply possessive, the soul with this Moon clings to the past. This is a highly sensitive - and sensitised - soul. As a Moon-ruled sign,

Cancer is extremely emotional and vulnerable but does not want to display this openly. The Moon in Cancer tends to be defensive and overly protective. Events in the past may have given this soul good reason to be afraid of loss, and its natural instinct to nurture can create a situation where it will not let go. This Moon is prone to manipulation for similar reasons. Of all the signs, this is the one most affected by unconscious emotional needs and childhood conditioning, but the conditioning may go much further back into the past. It is essential that this soul takes time to process its emotions - then it will be capable of deeply nurturing both itself and others.

Moon in Leo

The soul with the Moon in Leo has been working on opening the heart in the past, and may find itself in the present life challenged to keep an open heart within relationships. Another challenge this Moon faces is the conflict between arrogance and humility. This is the Moon of power, and power struggles will have featured in past relationships, as did emotional games. Leo has a strong need to be special and as a sign it craves adulation and attention. With the Moon placed here, this is the repeat of an old pattern of grasping at specialness to overcome feelings of mediocrity. Events in the past may have led the soul to deeply doubt itself. Given sufficient ego-massage, the soul bathes everyone around in sunny warmth. Denied it, a drama queen can emerge who demands attention. The soul with this Moon usually has overweening pride - and will stand on its dignity if emotionally challenged. This is a soul that takes offence easily. Partners need to be aware of this. Leo can be playful but hates to be made to look a fool. Nevertheless, this Moon signifies a generous spirit and a soul who has the capacity to become empowered from the heart and thereby find its own validation.

Moon in Virgo

The soul with the Moon in Virgo has been strongly identified in the past with service. Previous events can have created an unconfident soul who served out of the need to be thought good enough. Now the need to is to be of service without servitude or servility. This soul has a strong perfectionist streak and high standards which are imposed both on itself and on partners. If these standards are not met, then the critical side of Virgo comes into play. This heavily developed critical faculty is often applied to sexual desires. The Moon in Virgo is more likely than most to have taken an earlier vow of celibacy and to regard purity as goodness and sexuality as bad. The soul is challenged to integrate sexuality with spirituality, allowing the earthy sensual nature of Virgo to flower. This soul has the potential to accept itself, and others, as perfect now.

Moon in Libra

As with Virgo, Libra has a deep desire for perfection, especially in relationships. This placement indicates a soul who has been intimately involved in partnerships throughout many lifetimes, and who may have come to rely on a partner for validation and a sense of completion of itself. More than any other sign, Libra is looking for 'my other half' and this soul is deeply involved in the search for a soulmate. It is not comfortable alone and sees its own self-worth reflected through how other people respond emotionally. In the past the soul with this Moon has adapted, compromised and adjusted its own needs to meet those of another. These unmet needs burst out from time to time, demanding attention, and the challenge is for the soul to find a creative compromise that meets the needs of all concerned. The potential for the Libra Moon is to reach a point of emotional equilibrium that creates wholeness.

Moon in Scorpio

The soul with this Moon sign has experienced an enormous amount of emotional trauma and drama in the past. It brings forward resentment, jealousy and other painful emotions for catharsis. Fears of rejection, betrayal, abandonment and persecution run deep - the soul has come to expect this because it has experienced it so intensely in the past. This soul is deeply in touch with its own darkness, and that of others. Expressed unconsciously, it draws to itself all that it fears, and enters into compulsive and obsessive relationships - until it becomes aware that things can change. When the destructive side of this Moon is played out, relationships may explore all the taboo areas of life. When the constructive side is allowed to surface, there is an emotional powerhouse that transforms previous experience. With such a deeply intuitive Moon, and sensitive antenna, this soul can see under the surface of a partner and know what is really going on - which can be disconcerting for the partner. Only with complete honesty can such a relationship function, but if it does the emotional rewards are considerable.

Moon in Sagittarius

The soul with the Moon in Sagittarius has a strong urge towards emotional freedom. It is a Moon that finds it hard to trust - or else trusts too easily and then finds that the trust is misplaced. In the past this soul may have been tied into tight, possessive relationships. Now it wants space. If excessive emotional demands are made, this soul's instinctual urge is to move on - and for 'excessive' you can usually read 'any'. Pressurised to commit, the insouciant Sag Moon quits. But given sufficient space, this Moon develops an inner emotional freedom that ultimately allows the soul to commit. In the meantime, the Sagittarius Moon happily discusses feelings and relationships - indeed it is fascinated by these subjects.

Moon in Capricorn

A Capricorn Moon indicates a deep mistrust of relationships and a blockage around expressing feelings that has built up over several lifetimes. The soul with this placement represses emotions and tries to keep strict control. It is often believed to be unemotional but this is not so. The emotions are there but the soul is simply too afraid to allow them to the surface, or just does not know how to express them spontaneously. In the past there will have been an enormous pressure to be respectable and to conform to social norms; now the soul wants to break out, but is afraid that this is unacceptable. All the old rules are still there, internalised and rebelled against, but in command nonetheless. This is a Moon placement that can indicate a particularly inhibited or difficult childhood, with burdens shouldered early. There would have been little emotional closeness with parents - a preoccupation with wealth or status often means that one or both parents is rarely there for the child and this results in enormous pressure to succeed. The potential for the soul with this placement is to develop personal autonomy and a deep-rooted sense of personal worth.

Moon in Aquarius

Intimacy is a huge issue for the soul with the Moon in Aquarius. Aquarius can relate to the mass of humanity - in the way that a scientist observes an experiment in the laboratory. But one-to-one relationships are difficult for this placement. Traditionally, Aquarius is an unemotional sign. But the soul with the Moon in Aquarius is detached from emotions that run very deep indeed. The problem is that the soul is not in touch with them, which can lead to erratic emotional responses and sudden outbursts. The past may have contained traumatic emotional events and so the soul cut off, to protect itself. Now, these emotional currents create a reaction that the soul is unaware of and pull emotional events towards the soul for resolution. The challenge is to be in touch with the emotions once again. Until this occurs, the soul inhabits a cold and lonely place whenever any emotional pressure or challenge makes itself known. The potential is to find the kind of emotional detachment that allows one's self to stand in the centre of the emotions, feeling the feelings but not being overwhelmed by them. When this stage is reached, the soul then has the challenge to express universal love to all.

Moon in Pisces

Everything is emotion for this placement. The soul flows here and there as the emotional current takes it, with no direction and no discrimination. The soul with this Moon has a far memory of how it felt to be in blissful union with the divine - and wants to recreate that in a current relationship. It is seeking a soulmate, but anyone who comes into the Pisces' Moon's orbit is sucked into the fantasy of the perfect relationship. So, relationships tend to be messy for this soul. One affair is rarely ended before another begins. Lies, evasions and deceptions are common with resultant karma. Past life scenarios inevitably include victim-martyr-saviour-rescuer roles. Emotional contacts are on a subtle, unseen level, but extremely strong nonetheless. For this soul to disentangle emotional ties is a priority, but one that is rarely addressed. This is a highly sensitive and intuitive Moon with the potential for empathetic relationship with another.

LUST AND LIBIDO: MARS

Mars symbolises virility and passion, lust and potency. How well Mars is aspected by the outer planets, and the sign and element in which this planet is placed, indicate whether the soul has learned to be sexually expressive in the past, with libido flowing spontaneously, or whether passion has been repressed and contained. Where Mars is placed in a sign that shows a free expression of libido and yet has restrictive aspects such as Saturn, the underlying freedom has to be regained. If Mars is placed in a sign that indicates a repressed libido, then outer planet aspects may throw light on how libido came to be suppressed.

Mars in Fire Signs

The soul with Mars in a fire sign has a volcanic sexual past and a strong libido. Passion is hot and spontaneous, and may arise out of the blue. This is the element of immediate gratification. There is little foreplay with this placement. Mars sees what it wants, and goes for it. The soul may need to temper the immediacy of its own sexual needs so that it can enter into a sharing relationship with another.

Mars in Water Signs

Passion runs strong in the water signs, but it is more diffuse. Mars in this element prefers to be the pursued rather than the pursuer. Libido gives way to emotional needs. Fantasy may become an emotional escape. Water signs like to lead up to things gradually, savouring the emotion of the moment. Some souls with Mars in the water element have become adept at hiding their passion (Scorpio), others approach circuitously (Cancer), and those with Mars in Pisces almost inevitably confuse love with lust.

Mars in Earth Signs

The soul with Mars in the earth element takes a pragmatic approach to sex. Libido is strong, sex a basic urge to be filled regularly. This placement has rarely had problems expressing its desire in the past, although Mars in Virgo can be prissy and restrained if the intellect intervenes.

Mars in Air Signs

For Mars in the air element, sex takes place in the head. The rational is preferred to an irrational outburst of unrestrained passion. There is an active fantasy life - which is sometimes retreated into instead of the real thing. This soul is turned on by ideas and libido can be sublimated into other outlets. Mars in Libra is one of the least assertive placements, and the soul may find itself overwhelmed by someone else's passion and have difficulty in saying no.

SEXUAL DIS-EASE

There are certain outer planet aspects to Mars that indicate ingrained physical responses to past life events - a type of symbolic or organic karma, but the soul may also have an emotional response that creates sexual dis-ease.

Figure 7a Mars-Saturn

Saturn in aspect to Mars

My first astrology tutor, Robert Tully, always drew Mars aspected by Saturn with a droop in its arrow (Figure 7a) because he found it had a strong correlation with impotence and erection difficulties. This is a very physical manifestation of blocked libido. The sexual urge can no longer trigger the necessary physiological response. In my experience this is usually linked to past life problems with aggressive sexual acts or with blocked will or assertion. Women with Saturn-Mars aspects may be anorgasmic. Their inability to reach orgasm may be due to repressed anger or to traumatic sexual acts leaving a lasting legacy. (Saturn-Venus contacts can also be frigid or non-orgasmic because in its heart of hearts the soul with this aspect believes itself to be incapable of responding to love.) Prostitution, rape or repressed sexuality may be a contributory past life factor to the present-life sexual difficulty in both Mars and Venus aspected by Saturn.

Uranus in aspect to Mars

With Uranus to Mars aspects, there is a mind component to the sexual dis-ease. Premature ejaculation is often indicated by Uranus aspects to Mars or the Sun (or by Aries) particularly in the eighth house. It may be linked to a past-life persona who was always in a

Figure 7b Mars-Uranus

hurry, rushing here there and everywhere and never taking time to finish anything. It may also connect to guilty or sinful encounters during which it was felt, usually for religious or moral reasons, that what was happening was 'wrong', and, therefore, something to be got over with as quickly as possible.

Uranus-Mars may also relate to stolen sexual experiences where discovery may have been imminent, often a feature of teenage sex in the present life. One man regressed to 'screwing the maid in the linen cupboard at every opportunity, but we had to watch out for the old girl (wife/housekeeper?) coming so it had to be quick. On one occasion she caught me with my trousers down and gave me hell and sacked the poor girl'. In the present life his sexual experiences had started with furtive fumbles in his bedroom which his mother may have walked in on at any point. It immediately triggered off the past-life reaction.

Uranus-Mars tends to like its sex a little different from the norm. This may indicate bi-sexuality, sexual games, kinky sex, and so on. The libido here has often been subverted into other channels when the natural outlet was blocked. A quick look down the 'Alternative Lifestyles' section of the personal columns of some national newspapers reveals the wide variety of Uranian sexual activity - much of which will be based on incidents from the past that have become powerfully linked to sexual satisfaction, although they may not have begun that way. Uranus-Mars may also delineate a component to sexuality that is away from the norm and which explores a different facet. Transvesticism and transsexuality may be indicated, both of which could have their roots in another life or in childhood.

Neptune-Mars

Neptune-Mars is heavily into escapism and fantasy, and frequently dislikes the messy reality of sexual activity. Pretence forms a large

Figure 7c Mars-Neptune

part of this soul's approach to sexuality and in the past the soul may have deluded itself about libido and sexual motivation. Drink or drugs, dressing up, living out fantasy scenarios and the like absolve the soul from the need to enter into direct relationship. Such escapism may come from previous life sexual encounters which were only made bearable by the ability to 'float away' into a more pleasurable scenario, or from the guilt to which Neptune is so prone.

I have only ever met one person who admitted to being a nymphomaniac; she happened to also be a dipsomaniac. She had Neptune conjunct Mars and Venus and always swore that her condition was the direct result of having been 'unwillingly locked up in a convent with a load of bloody women in a past life!' It left her with an overwhelming but rarely completely satisfied need for sexual encounters that went beyond physical orgasm - something she could easily achieve alone. Her partner once compared it to living with a black widow spider: 'She wants to consume me and become imbued with my life-force at a soul level'. When the fantasy failed, she drank to forget.

Pluto in aspect to Mars
When Pluto aspects Mars the libido has become blocked and subverted into taboo channels. Sexual difficulties connected with violence or cruelty may arise from past-life causes when linked to Pluto-Mars aspects, and/or to abuse as a child in the present or a past life. This may lead to subtle incidents of sado-masochism or to abusive sexual or emotional relationships in the present life. Whilst much of this will be acted out by other people and will *appear* as though it has nothing to do with the soul, with Pluto things are rarely what they seem to be on the surface. Somewhere deep within each one of us, the darkest face of Pluto lurks. This is the God of the Underworld who abducted the young and innocent Persephone and who transmogrified her into the Queen of the Underworld. In other

Figure 7d Mars-Pluto

words, she took a trip into her own inner shadow world, and embraced there what she saw. She faced her Plutonian shadow and integrated it, with all its possibilities of violence and aggression transmuted into the creative force.

Pluto has difficulty in letting go, in opening itself up to another person, and the soul with a strong Pluto placement may experience sexual difficulties linked into old power, manipulation or abuse issues whereby it fears that the sexual partner will, in its most vulnerable moment, have control over it. In women this can result in difficulty in relaxing enough to achieve orgasm. Strong Pluto aspects - particularly to Mars - can also indicate the masochist who is pre-programmed by past life experiences to find pleasure in pain. In men these difficulties may be expressed as a preference for masturbation - which may include the use of a female in order to achieve orgasm but not to share feelings. It may also be the sadist who receives his pleasure by inflicting pain, or the man who uses his sexual power to achieve mastery and who cannot fully allow himself to join with his partner on the inner level. He therefore always remains vaguely dissatisfied, but blames his partner. In both sexes Plutonian difficulties in attuning and opening to another can lead to restless promiscuity as the person seeks fulfilment through a series of partners instead of looking within for the release which would heal the difficulty.

A man with a Pluto-Mars contact remembered dozens of incarnations, all of them as a man. He said that he 'just loved incarnating back into a physical body'. He denied he had ever been female. When regressed back to being a woman in ancient Greece, however, he relived a mass rape, after which he had sworn that he would never return again as a woman. In the present life he had been 'interfered with' by a man within the family as a young child, and had difficulty in achieving a normal sexual relationship with a woman as he inwardly craved and fantasised violence but was afraid to live it out. His sexual dis-ease could possibly have been healed had he found a partner with whom it was safe to act some out of his fantasies.

As the former monk Thomas Moore has pointed out when discussing the sado-masochism embodied in the work of the Marquis de Sade and its connection with the lives of people who might never consider themselves in any way epitomising his dark fiction:

'Everyone has his or her own master of the dungeon who inflicts his special kind of pain: loneliness, unrequited love, jealousy, envy, grief.

We speak easily of self-torture, but dreams make it clear... that the inner figure who tortures has a face or several faces. If we knew the 'persons' behind those faces, we might understand the telos of torture and the necessity of the Sadeian libertine who haunts the psyche. Often we overlook the libertine within because we assume that the torment is coming from the world, from another person, from some past trauma, or from some social ill. But this is nothing more than sophisticated scapegoating. If a person is suffering, then there is someone turning the screws, someone whose job it is to tend the chamber of horrors'.[15]

Anyone with a Pluto-Mars aspect in their chart knows that inner chamber all too well and that the torturer is really hidden within themselves.

Power struggles are always a feature of Plutonian karma but the addition of Mars adds another layer of danger or aggression, and a further impetuous to dark desire. And yet the soul will often repress this and project it to be acted out by another. The soul does not want to own such strong sexual power, and if it does act it out, then it tends to do so compulsively as an addict or victim rather than as a potent creative force. As Thomas Moore explains:

'By treating sex as a biological instinct and strong persistent desire as addiction, we lose touch with the soul of sex and desire: their poetic resonances, and the meaningfulness they carry... Our usual imageless language for sex and desire serves to protect us from their potency.' [16]

His solution to the 'dark eros' of Pluto-Mars is to:

'prepare yourself for a lifetime of struggle with the dark passions, knowing that the crucible of evil desires offers concoctions that have soul... we can trust that whatever appears will not arise from the sentimentalization of experience – the result of a denial of darkness. What appears will have a fullness that is denied us when our psychology is devoted only to the positive virtues...'[17]

He is not here advocating acting out 'evil desires' but is saying that by the use of ritual and imagination rather than repression, and by acceptance and integration of these dark qualities within oneself, the energy behind Pluto-Mars can be released and given positive expression.

A surprising number of people with Pluto-Mars aspects have come to expect violence and need the adrenaline rush which fear and violence present to them. A friend took in a girl who had a violent husband. In the middle of the night she was shaking and begging to be hit as only violence could end her withdrawal symptoms. She went back to her husband the next day. Such a case needs psychotherapy and supervised withdrawal to handle the ravages of Plutonian violence and to own and integrate the darkness within.

BLOCKAGES AND REPRESSIONS: SATURN

Aspects of Saturn to the personal planets indicate old patterns of constriction and repression: a long-standing sense of inadequacy and a deeply ingrained fear of not being good enough which colour how the incarnating soul reacts, especially in early relationships. The soul may have resolved these issues in another life, but carries the memory trace, but is more likely to be actively confronting these factors in the present life through interaction with another person. Aspects by Saturn to the Sun or Moon indicate an archetypal expectation around parenting based on previous experience. This expectation may or may not be epitomised by the present life parent. It may be later in life that the parenting expectation gets projected onto a convenient hook such as an employer or partner. If the Saturnine expectations are confirmed by the parent, no matter in how small a measure, they are reinforced and become part of the present life. Easy aspects such as the trine or sextile may indicate that the soul has begun to change the pattern, but hard aspects such as a fixed square, point to a deeply ingrained expectation. If the expectation is reinforced in the present lifetime, or is supported by other planetary aspects or placements, then the soul takes these deeply entrenched patterns into new relationships.

Saturn in aspect to the Sun
(or Sun in Capricorn and Saturn in Leo)
An aspect of Saturn to the Sun is indicative of an inner lack of self-esteem arising out of a fundamental block on the soul's sense of self-worth and value. This frequently manifests in the present life through an early experience of emotional coldness from, or loss, of a parent, usually the father - an experience which is a rerun of the events of previous lives. The soul may incarnate to elderly parents, or suffer the isolation of an only child, and there may be loss of a sibling that emphasises the aloneness. A family ambience of grief or deprivation is common. The soul may find itself valued only if it conforms to the demands of a parent - individuality being positively discouraged. This

soul lacks confidence and is unable to express emotional warmth as it has not had the vital experience of receiving unconditional love and affection - unless positive Jupiter to the Sun aspects have outweighed Saturn (an unusual occurrence). The lack of validity of one's selfhood connected to the old pattern gives the message: 'I have no value, I might as well not exist.' The soul's energies are channelled into inner defences against deep feelings of vulnerability and into its outward need to succeed, to prove to the world that: 'I am here, I do exist, I have worth and substance.' At some point in its journey this soul has to meet its shadow and integrate into itself all that it has denied for so long.

This soul, as with Saturn-Moon, is challenged to parent itself, or to find a transpersonal, divine parent that gives unconditional and loving support. It often chooses a parent with whom there has been personal karma that has to be resolved.

The soul with this aspect also takes into adult relationships the inner fear and emotional coldness or inhibitions that arise out of not being good enough. It needs experience of a close, warm, loving relationship to thaw the barriers and blockages that have built up in the past. However, it may attract to itself the same characters in the drama as previously - but, this time, the potential is there for a different outcome.

Saturn-Moon
(or Moon in Capricorn, Gemini, or Virgo and Saturn in Cancer or Capricorn)

The difficulty here tends to lie in obtaining nurturing and affection from the mother. The soul incarnates expecting coldness and emotional distance. The past life pattern is such that, whenever in the present life the mother does not respond as quickly or as well as the baby would like, the soul says to itself: 'There, I knew I would get bad mothering'. This need only occur on one or two occasions for the old pattern to be triggered and relived through childhood and beyond. As with Saturn-Sun, the child is usually valued more for what he or she achieves rather than who he or she innately is.

The incarnating soul with this aspect lacks self-esteem and a sense of self-worth. Because of its past, it makes the assumption that it is unworthy, and experiences a deep constraint in relation to feelings or emotions. The past-life pattern is one of emotional isolation - and difficulty. The soul is cut off from the emotional nourishment of a family because it does not know how to receive it, and the family into which it incarnates may well also not know how to give it. This soul yearns for love like a small child, but is frequently unable to make the contact or feel the warmth needed for mutual interaction. It often settles for a safe relationship rather than risk exposing its vulnerability.

The soul with this aspect may not fit into the family as a result of having had poor, or no, previous life contact with family members. Liz Greene [18] points out that this aspect has to learn that the security of family ties is an illusory one, the only security being within oneself. The soul with this aspect must, therefore, learn to parent itself and to recognise that: 'The bond that links your true family is not one of blood, but of respect and joy in each others life. Rarely do members of one family grow up under the same roof.'[19] As with Saturn-Sun aspects, people who have either or both of these contacts benefit greatly from recognising that they have chosen to incarnate with these childhood experiences so that they can heal the old patterns and find a new level of parenting within themselves.

It is typical of this and other Saturn aspects that the incarnating soul may experience the loss of a sibling or grandparent either just before or after birth so that the mother is unavailable to the child because of her grief. This loss interferes with future relationships as the soul subconsciously still carries that grief by proxy as it were, and is inhibited from reaching out to another person because of the lack of love from the mother.

Saturn-Mercury
(or Mercury in Capricorn and Saturn in Gemini or Virgo)

Saturn in aspect to Mercury incarnates with a fundamental difficulty in communicating itself to others. The soul may reflect fixed patterns of thought inculcated in the past. It can find communication within a relationship difficult and may incarnate into the kind of family in which children are 'seen and not heard' and in which great emphasis and value is laid on intelligence and ability, rather than on who the child *is*; or in which individual expression is discouraged or forced into a channel unnatural for that soul.

The soul must learn to communicate itself out to the world and to express its own unique self in its interconnection with others, as a way of valuing both who it is and what it has to say. It is often around the time of the first Saturn Return, or even later, that the soul discovers that it can communicate, and has something of value to offer in a partnership.

Saturn-Venus see p. 56

Saturn-Mars
(or Mars in Capricorn and Saturn in Aries or Scorpio)
Saturn in aspect to Mars experiences a fundamental block on its will, often incarnating into a strongly repressive, controlling family with no room for individuality or personal choice. The soul's underlying feelings are helplessness, powerlessness and frustration, with an inability to follow its own pathway. A child with such a placement might experience violence, physical or verbal, from one or other parent. This experience then intensifies its inability to assert itself in any way, and ultimately will push the soul into lessons centred around aggression, assertion and the use of the will: most but not all of which will come about through a partner.

INDIVIDUALITY: URANUS

Souls attuned to the vibration of Uranus incarnate with a need for space, recognition of their own unique individuality, and with lessons to learn concerning commitment. Early relationships may therefore be difficult for the soul with a strong Uranus attunement unless it has specifically chosen Uranian, Aquarian, or Air/Fire parents who are able to tolerate this need to be different.

Aspects to Uranus are often seen in the charts of children who have emotional difficulties caused by a reluctance to fully incarnate. The lesson the incarnating soul may have to learn is one of individuality and separation, following too many experiences of symbiotic interaction (Uranus in Taurus or Cancer, Libra, Pisces, for example). On the other hand, it may need to learn how to interact with others, taking account of individual difference and yet recognising a deeper level of interconnectedness (Uranus in Libra or Pisces or in aspect to Neptune). Its lesson may also involve separation from the father (aspects to the Sun) or mother (aspects to the Moon) or the beloved (aspects to Venus), which may be linked either to the particular soul who has incarnated as parent or beloved, or to the archetypal collective energies that manifest as Father, Mother or The Loved One.

Uranus-Venus see p. 59.

REALITY OR FANTASY: NEPTUNE

The old relationship pattern for Neptune is to have idealised, idolised, colluded, and sometimes deceived, rarely seeing itself or the person to whom it was relating clearly. The soul attuned to Neptune has a yearning to return to the more spiritually based relationships available in other realms, and can therefore be wide open to deception and disillusionment, both its own and that of another. At the first hint of a possibility of regaining that lost union, it sacrifices its individuality and willingly merges into the other. This is the planet of romantic love, based on cultural illusions and stereotypes and unrealistic expectations of eternal fidelity from a one-and-only soulmate. It is also the planet of fantasy and illusion, and of 'non-relationship' that exists only in the mind of one person. In its highest form Neptune represents a deep soul connection and unconditional love - love which just *is* - asking and expecting nothing. But unfortunately Neptune is also a master of disguise and all too often subtle control and assimilation of the beloved lie at the heart of the Neptunian masquerade of love.

Neptune-Sun (or Sun in Pisces)

With the Sun in aspect to Neptune there tends to be idealisation of the father, who may be seen as a god-like figure, and/or of a significant male, who may be weak and an inappropriate object of adulation. In such a case it could be that the relationship is an old one and the attachment goes back to happier times.

It may also be that the earlier relationship was a sexual one and that the closeness from that time has manifested in an inappropriate way in the present interplay. This is clearly seen in the child who is sexually abused and yet perceives nothing wrong, or in the child who has to enter into collusion with the father to keep the secret of their closeness. This is a different kind of abuse from that based on fear, which is linked to Saturn and Pluto. In the case of Neptunian abuse the child longs, on an inner level, for a psychic closeness with the father which does not involve physical penetration. The relationship can, however, be emotionally or mentally incestuous and still be damaging in the sense that the child does not develop its own individuality. When the relationship with the father is finally severed, the child will seek the same closeness and merging into any partner, however unsuitable. He or she may fall into a pattern of addiction and/or relationships with weak partners who need to be rescued and saved, and whom he or she believes is 'my very own', with ultimate consequent disillusionment.

Neptune-Sun contacts may also project this need for closeness on to a godlike figure and seek to merge into the divine. A woman with first house Neptune in Virgo conjunct the South Node sextile the Sun in Cancer was particularly aware as a child of having a spiritual vocation. She later entered a contemplative Order and made the mystical marriage as a Bride of Christ. She remained in the convent for twenty years, but became increasingly conscious (through the demands of her North Node) that she should move into a physical rather than spiritual relationship. Sacrifice and sublimation were no longer an appropriate life pattern for her. She left the convent and married a man she knew from a past life: 'I recognised him from the back immediately and knew we were destined to marry.' She had the Moon in Virgo and found it difficult to enter fully into her emotional and physical levels of being. Her strong Pisces and Neptune energies still yearned for a more mystical contact and she also entered into a relationship with a guru god-figure who was always with her, much to the discomfort of her husband. With her strong Pisces energy she was able to handle with perfect ease the ambiguity of two such partnerships. Perhaps in so doing some of the idealisation and unrealistic expectations which might otherwise have been projected on to her husband were channelled into a more constructive, spiritual outlet.

Neptune-Moon

When Neptune aspects the Moon, the idealisation and illusions centre around mother and femininity, or around female relationships for a male. A much-loved mother may be more like a fantasy figure than a real person. One man I knew had Neptune-Moon across the fourth-tenth house cusp, with the Moon in Pisces. As a child he only saw his mother once a day. He would be bathed, dressed specially and taken down to see her for half an hour before her supper. She would be dressed for dinner in all her finery and he wasn't allowed to touch her. The rest of the day he spent with Nanny. When his father died in his early teens, his mother returned home to France whilst he was left with his aristocratic grandparents. He rarely saw her, but still believed that she was 'the most wonderful woman on earth'. No woman ever matched up to his romantic expectations. This idealised feminine is extremely difficult for anyone to live up to and disillusionment inevitably sets in. When Moon-Neptune occurs in a woman's chart, she may split off her sexuality, as with Neptune-Venus contacts, as she tries to attain a state of inner holiness rather than wholeness.

Neptune-Venus see p. 67.

POWER: PLUTO

The karmic lessons for Pluto centre around power, symbiosis and separation, together with long-held feelings of guilt, resentment and rage. There will be underlying issues of rejection and abandonment. As Susan Forward points out: 'Parental love is the only kind of love in which the ultimate goal *must* be separation.'[20] However, for many incarnating souls who are attuned to Pluto, insidious strangulation by a psychic umbilical cord pervades relationships far into adulthood. The roles of Mother or Father take on archetypal dominance and authority, acquiring the willing or unwilling projection of power from the child who must later struggle to regain it for itself. When such a projection of power is withdrawn within either the parental or an adult relationship, enormous struggles ensue as the person who is the 'hook' is usually comfortable with the authoritarian role and finds it difficult to relinquish this in favour of a more equable division of power. When the soul tries to break free, the parent or partner may resort to emotional blackmail to retain control. People with natal Pluto aspects are particularly susceptible to this ploy - until they become aware of the situation and switch off the automatic reaction so that they can make a free choice.

Pluto-Sun (or Sun in Scorpio)

Aspects of Pluto to the Sun involve overt power struggles with the image, if not the actuality, of Father in order that the incarnating soul may regain its lost power. The tendency for many lifetimes will have been to be disempowered through contact with an authoritarian man who held the power. A client, a twin, (Sun in Gemini inconjunct Neptune and square Pluto) was most concerned about her fear and dislike of her father. She described a 'creepy feeling' about him and was sure that he had abused her as a very young child. Now in her twenties she was still experiencing interference from him in the form of a strong mental power over her and deliberate participation in her dreams. Her twin did not experience difficulties to the same extent and she had married and become the powerful partner. This is a classic scenario for twins. One lives out the dominant side of the archetype and the other the submissive side of a karmic aspect such as Pluto-Sun. It was suggested that both girls should work on cutting the ties with the father, and with taking back their own power from him. This was particularly applicable to the one who first consulted me, as there were strong past-life links to him, but each twin would benefit form this work. Tie cutting does not cut off any unconditional, soul love that exists. It removes the emotional expectations, projections and 'oughts, shoulds and if-onlys' that develop throughout the course of a life or lives. Shortly afterwards my client moved out of the family home, something she had found impossible to do prior to this despite her problems with her father.

This aspect is particularly difficult for women, who have traditionally handed over all their authority to a man: first father, later husband. They may well find themselves in families where powerful, authoritarian fathers still demand absolute obedience, with the consequent enfeebling of the soul's ability to exert itself, and risk of abuse of the child. Repressed rage and anger then fester into resentment; an energy carried over into so-called adult relationships which may in turn be abusive or parasitic.

The Pluto-Sun aspect can also indicate difficulties for a male in handling his power and his potency. The chart shown here (Figure 8) is that of a man who sued, in the English Courts, for restitution of conjugal rights. His split-off first house Pluto in Cancer opposing seventh house Sun in Capricorn indicates power issues manifesting through a relationship. In spite of winning his case, he did not win his power struggle as he discovered that, although she had been ordered by a judge to do so, his wife was not going to resume marital relations willingly.

He incarnated with various karmic patterns which led him to anticipate a power struggle. Outwardly he was confident, but his confidence failed to result in fulfilling relationships. The message contained in his out-of-element Grand Trine of Chiron-Jupiter-Neptune-Saturn-Moon, and the Neptune opposition to Venus, is a mixed one. His Moon conjuncts Saturn indicating a poor self-image, constriction on emotions, and expectation of inadequate nurturing. His Moon is in Sagittarius and, as his wife pointed out, he may have won control over her body, but her mind and her Self did not have to be involved in the sexual transaction. His Moon-Saturn opposes

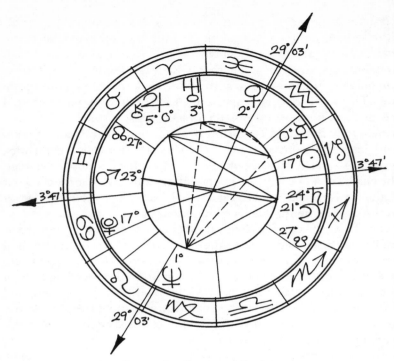

Figure 8 - Conjugal Rights

twelfth house Mars, indicating a will conflict which leaves him feeling inwardly powerless, as well as with anxiety about his own potency and adequacy in sexual relationships which he took to a judge (Saturn) for confirmation of his authority (Capricorn Sun opposing Pluto). He also has a Neptune-Venus fourth-tenth house opposition, which led him to both idealise and deceive women, particularly his mother. The split pattern of the chart showed up clearly in his behaviour both as a child and an adult. He incarnated into the typical English upper-middle-class home where he reigned as tyrant in the nursery. Cared for by a nanny, he was shown briefly, suitably sanitised, to his adored and adoring mother before supper. She was totally deceived by his little-boy charm, never believing the stories his sisters, and later his wife, told about his temper and autocratic behaviour. He was sent off to a boarding preparatory school at the age of seven, in conformity with his in-built expectation; there he encountered the usual bullying problems but quickly became the bully himself. An example of Sun-Pluto preying on the weak.

After his marriage finally ended he used his charm to live off women, virtually hypnotising them into complying (Neptune-Venus) and he duped several extremely intelligent women using flattery and promises he had no intention of keeping. One of these women later commented that, looking back, she had no idea why she had been so infatuated as 'he was a once-a-week man and useless in bed!'. Neptune and Pluto are both subtle seducers that fascinate and coerce their prey. But, when the light of consciousness shines upon them, transformation is possible.

Pluto- Moon (or Moon in Scorpio)

The power struggles involved in Pluto aspects to the Moon are more subtle and covert, but no less damaging, and are linked to ancient traumatic experiences which programme the incarnating soul to expect emotional issues such as rage and resentment, abandonment, rejection, and guilt. These are carried over first into childhood and then adult relationships. Pluto has great difficulty in letting go and stores up resentments and hurts which can well up from the depths of the unconscious with a force which has nothing to do with the present-life trigger event. In particular these negative emotional expectations are linked to karma around mothering and being mothered - an experience which the Pluto-Moon soul anticipates as life-threatening and devouring. The most appropriate symbol for the Moon-Pluto mother is that of the Indian goddess Kali who holds the power of life and death.[21]

The challenge with a Pluto-Moon aspect is to be creative, although not necessarily on a biological level. Many women with this pattern are expected to conform to what their mothers have always done or to live out the unlived life of a deeply frustrated mother and, although they may inwardly feel deeply rebellious, some comply. A considerable number of them, aged around thirty-five to forty, ask for readings as they have to face making a decision on whether to have children or not 'before it is too late'. For some of these women, a partner enters into the equation but many who follow this biological imperative become single mothers:

> Too often women get caught in a restrictive, single vision... Instead of admitting everything into her totality - waiting, accepting, ripening, transforming and being transformed - a woman will literally conceive and bear a child.[22]

Moon-Pluto women have to break free from the past and from their mothers, or from archetypal expectations of women. Pluto signifies that it is hard to let go - on many levels, but especially of the past. It has issues such as guilt to confront - particularly if Neptune aspects are also involved. This guilt is usually all-embracing, non-specific, and cannot be pinned to anything in particular. When analysed, this guilt is found to be partly related to the mother in the present life and partly to the soul's interaction with the mothering energies and emotions in past lives. The positive side of the Pluto-Moon contact is a healing of those old wounds in the psyche and a release of the inner creative energy to make dynamic, life enhancing partnerships.

It is not only women whom the Pluto-Moon energies affect. This combination represents the devouring mother in all her awesome power, who swallows her boy-child whole rather than allow him to separate from her. Roger Waters (Mercury and Moon quincunx Pluto, and Moon square Saturn) articulates the underlying fear of the Moon-Pluto aspect in the Pink Floyd song '*Mother*', in which he perceptively points out that mothers have a habit of making their children's worst nightmares come true. This, not unnaturally, has a powerful effect on men's relationships. Susan Forward links the misogynist, the man who hates and abuses women, to this devouring mother figure:

> The mother who validates her son's striving for independence and encourages him to separate from her when he needs to, gives him some very important tools with which to deal with life. 'When the mother is willing to let her son establish his own identity, by permitting him to take risks on his own and by allowing him to make mistakes, yet being there for him should he need her, she helps to build a man who is confident about himself and his abilities. The suffocating mother, on the other hand, restrains and constricts her son's development by over-controlling him and by making him feel inadequate and helpless.'[23]

A scenario that inevitably carries over into his adult relationships. As many women find to their cost, the Pluto Moon man carries all his mothering issues into each and any relationship with women - and at times with other men. It is perhaps the most often projected expectation: all women are perceived as devouring, and yet paradoxically such men and the women they interact with need each other.

It is this symbiotic dependence in infancy, and beyond, which ultimately forces the incarnating soil to face up to the separation issues and the prospect of abandonment which so terrify it. If these issues are not confronted in childhood, they can arise on the death or loss of a parent, partner or child, propelling the soul back to explore roots either in helpless infancy, or beyond, into the previous incarnations which have contributed to this desperate fear of letting go. Relationships bear the full brunt of this unrecognised theme and projections are rife. Partners almost always carry an unconsciously assigned role, particularly if the aspect occurs in the man's natal chart and as interaspects across the chart. Ancient scenarios can be acted out time and time again. Fears of abandonment pervade even the apparently healthiest of relationships when this issue is unresolved. When the Moon-Pluto emotional dynamic has been healed, it brings powerful transformation into relationships, offering new possibilities of creative partnership.

Pluto-Venus see p. 73.

4

THE RELATIONSHIP HOUSES

If we do not know what port we are steering for, no wind is favourable.

Seneca

The houses in the birthchart show *where* karma manifests itself. The house placement of a planet indicates the area of life in which the soul will expect to meet the karma attached to that planet. In the relationship houses, the karma will make itself known through the specific relationship linked to that house - parental, sibling, partnership and so on. (Note: if the time of birth is unknown or uncertain, placing the Sun on the first house cusp gives a useful symbolic indication of where the karma will manifest and works better than a noon chart.)

The natal chart is divided into 12 sections which may or may not be equal, depending on the house system used. The numbers are read anti-clockwise from the left as shown below. I personally use Placidus house cusps because I feel that by using one of the 'unequal' house systems, the size and strength of a given house can indicate something about the karma of previous lives.

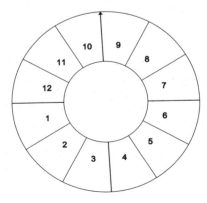

Sibling Karma: The Third House

The third house gives an indication of karma with siblings and can illustrate the type of former interaction relating to that karma. It may also show how well the child fits into its role in the family. Both Uranus and Pluto in this house may, for different reasons, make the soul feel suffocated within the family and express a need for freedom and space to offset past experiences of symbiosis, for instance.

The Sun

The Sun in the third house signifies that in a previous incarnation the soul may have been the father of its present-life parent or sibling. The child may find itself parenting a parent, or acting as a surrogate mother or father to its siblings in a replay of old roles. Unresolved authority issues coming forward from old interaction, can create difficulties within the family. It may also be that the incarnating soul has to recognise itself as separate from the family and claim its individuality.

The Moon

Similarly, with the third house Moon the soul may have been the mother in the past or may find itself mothering its siblings or a parent. It may also have unfinished emotional business with the soul who is now its sibling. This was apparent in the third house Moon of a young woman who found it exceedingly difficult to image cutting the ties with her brother. The ties she perceived were sexual and emotional ones, coming forward from past lives. It was necessary to first explore that old involvement and to recognise what had been unresolved before the present-life negative conditioning, in the shape of inappropriate ties with her sibling, could be cut.

Mercury

Mercury in the third house indicates either karma with a sibling who is now repeating the same family interaction, or karma around how the family have communicated in the past - and, of course, both could be present at the same time. The two may be linked, in that the sibling may have been injured by unwise gossip or slander in the past, or may have been forced into a career or lifestyle which it did not seek. This is seen in the case of those old family patterns in which one son was destined to inherit the estate, another to join the army, and another to enter the Church, and so on.

Venus

Venus generally indicates a good prior interaction with siblings which was both loving and harmonious, although this can depend on the sign placement. In Gemini or Libra, for example, the past contact may have been that of good friends; but when Venus is in Scorpio or in aspect to Pluto there is always the possibility of old jealousies. Similarly, emotional games coming forward from the past can pertain to a Leo placement. It should also be remembered that a thwarted Venus can wage a war of attrition for past emotional pain from behind a façade of niceness, and that when this happens the history of the relationship may need to be explored before a conclusion is reached.

Mars

Mars in the third house invokes the possibility of violent encounters between the present-life siblings in the past, with karma related to aggression and assertion featuring prominently in the past and present interplay. This is the placement of sibling rivalry and may indicate two souls who have previously been at war with one another in some way. The child with this placement may have to learn to assert and stand up for itself within the family as a preparation for more assertive interaction with the outside -world.

Jupiter

Jupiter can indicate that in the previous interaction siblings were priests or priestesses, linked in spiritual brotherhood, pupil and teacher or master and apprentice, and that they may have an innate trust in the rightness of the family connection. On the less positive side, there may be karma related to the squandering of an inheritance or assets, as in the case of two business partners reincarnating together again in order to work out unfinished business concerning the misuse of company funds, for example.

Saturn

When Saturn is in the third house there is almost always an issue around one sibling having had control over another. This may be, metaphorically or actually, a master and slave, prisoner and gaoler, or teacher and pupil type of interaction, or an elder and younger brother conflict being re-enacted. The child may experience the family as cold and unwelcoming or unloving, undergoing alienation from, or rejection by, its siblings by virtue of age, its interests, etc.

This placement may also indicate a child who becomes, or has been, responsible for its brothers or sisters, as in the case when a parent dies and the elder child brings up the rest of the family. The incarnating soul may carry the burden of, or actually be, a chronically sick sibling. This placement is often connected to a karmic theme of responsibility and self-image, which manifests within the family and is then carried over into interplay with the outside world. It may also be connected to an old vow or promise to look after the sibling - something which the soul may or may not have intended to operate in the present life. Siblings with whom there is this kind of unconscious connection may become a heavy burden on a soul.

Chiron

With Chiron in the third house, the soul's expectation is of encountering a wounded sibling or being wounded by a sibling. This may, or may not, be retributive karma from contact in another life. The child or the sibling may also become the scapegoat at the feet of whom all the families troubles are laid – or who takes on the family karma to release it.

For a woman with Chiron in Virgo in the third house, the initial wounding was the birth of a brother, on whom his mother doted. Her relationship with her mother had always been difficult and it was made much worse by the neglect she suffered when her brother was born. By the time her brother reached puberty, he had developed epilepsy in reaction to the overpowering and over-protective love he was receiving from his mother and to hidden undercurrents in the family. His uncontrolled twitching mirrored the hastily smothered, explosive outbursts to which his mother was prone as she projected all her angst out onto the daughter, the family scapegoat. (She did not dare show this anger to her husband, whose extra-marital affairs were the unacknowledged cause.) The brother's epilepsy became a deep dark family secret. It was never openly spoken about and the woman was not allowed to bring friends home in case they witnessed a seizure, which isolated her still further.

This was a family pattern. Her grandmother had a brother who lived in the attic of the family home. The only time the woman had heard him referred to was when her father mentioned that 'Uncle Ernie' had been 'very peculiar' but her mother cut him off sharply. The woman's way of dealing with the family secret as an adult was to bring it out into the open, but the family resisted this strongly - she also had Neptune in the third and already felt alienated from them. Her attempts to heal the family dynamic led to more isolation, however, but made her aware of her own inner strength. She found consolation in a spiritual family of friends who were members of her soul group.

Uranus

As with all things Uranian, this placement may have something unexpected or *different* in the past interaction. Uranus often signifies the loner or outsider who finds it difficult to fit in the family, although there may have been a previous connection between siblings. It can be that there was a good friendship or membership of a 'brotherhood' of some kind, or that the sibling souls have been caught up in revolution together. It may also be that they have been trying to cut loose from each other for several lifetimes - Uranus being the catalyst that could set them free.

Neptune

With Neptune in the third the soul almost inevitably feels like an outsider in the family, or has a sense of being swamped and trying to keep its head above the emotional currents that threaten to suck it down into oblivion. This is the alienated soul, to such an extent that clients with this placement often ask which planet is their real home and when will they be allowed to return 'home'. They rarely feel that they have any connection with the family into which they have incarnated. I once did a workshop in which we were divided into groups who had particular outer planets in the third house. There were eight of us with third house Neptune. Six of us had believed as children, even against all the evidence, that we must have been adopted because we simply did not fit into the family group.

In such a case the elements predominating in the chart are often incompatible with those of the rest of the family. For example, a child with strong Air and Fire feels totally alienated from 'Watery' parents and siblings. The third house Neptune may also have issues of deception and delusion with brothers and sisters. Compatible elements within the family would make for more harmonious functioning, which can help to overcome other difficulties.

If the soul does have a sense a connection with a sibling, it is often to feel guilty or responsible in some way. People express this as owing a debt, having to look after the sibling - something which almost inevitable stems from a previous life. Unlike Saturn, there is usually a strong soul connection which makes the debt much less onerous. If a sacrifice is called for, it is given willingly.

Pluto
Pluto in the third house invariably involves a power struggle with a sibling which may be overt or covert, and which reflects the past interaction. The soul with this placement may also experience rejection by the family or participate in a symbiotic interconnection which must be severed before the incarnating soul can find its own place in life. The roots of Plutonian karma are inevitably deep and difficult to ascertain, going back far into the past and frequently involving death or destruction, domination and manipulation and emotional blackmail as an underlying theme.

PARENTAL KARMA: THE FOURTH -TENTH HOUSE AXIS
Planets in the natal tenth and fourth houses show both good and bad, positive and negative contacts with the parents in the past, and the type of parenting the incarnating soul expects to receive. Either house can equate to either parent, although the tenth house tends to indicate the mother when she is dominant within the family and represents the main source of interaction with the outside world for the child. Planets located in these houses can be linked both to a past-life parental interplay, and to the present experience. Once again, the manifestation of karma is subtle and complex and many factors need to be taken into account.

The Sun or Moon
When the Sun or Moon falls in the fourth or tenth house it is likely that the parent represented by that planet has been in the same relationship to the child before. That is, the Sun indicates that the father has been the father previously, and the Moon that the mother has been the mother before. The sign on the cusp indicates the old pattern. For example, if the Sun is in Capricorn, the parent may have been strongly authoritarian in the past life, and now has the opportunity to encourage the child's autonomy and self-responsibility. It is also possible that the parent may be taking on the opposite sex role to the one it has played before - indicated by the Moon in Capricorn or Sun in Cancer, for example. This can lead to confusion over the role taken, as when the mother is the dominant parent, or

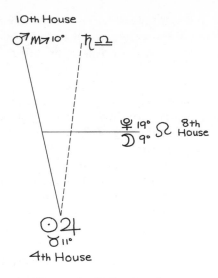

Figure 9 - Fathering Issues

there is a role-swap in which the parent takes on a function not usually associated with his or her sex. A baby born with fourth house Sun in Cancer to a Sun in Cancer father and mother, was brought up by his father whilst his mother ran a restaurant business. His father gave up a successful career as a concert musician because he wanted to experience bringing up his child. His mother needed a wider experience of nurturing.

With the Sun in the parental axis, the incarnating soul may also have to resolve karma carried over from a time when a parent was in a different relationship, but the same kind of issues arose. This is illustrated in the following past-life dream of Claire, a client with the Sun and Jupiter in the fourth house opposition Mars in the tenth house forming a T-square to the Moon (see Figure 9). With the Sun also squaring Pluto, there was a projection of her own power on to her father, and Saturn inconjunct to the Sun showed that she expected 'cold' fathering.

At the time the dream took place the T-square had been triggered by transiting Pluto, bringing to the surface old emotional trauma. The T-square suggested conflict and difficulties between the archetypal parental energies, but also supportive parenting from the fourth house Jupiter. Claire was used to working with dreams and recognised this as a past life:

'Eighteenth-century Europe - I'm married to a man who in this present lifetime is my father. He is a rather weak character who inherited much wealth. He finds it hard to express his love towards me and I ridicule him [eighth house Pluto trine Mercury]. I'm a vivacious, proud woman [South Node, Pluto and the Moon in Leo] who loves high society - I spend his money recklessly [Jupiter in Taurus] and take a string of young lovers, which I flaunt in front of him [eighth house Pluto square to tenth house Mars].

A few months after this dream I spend Easter with my family. My father sees me to the bus stop - he has been very withdrawn all weekend which has irritated me and I rather reluctantly say goodbye to him. In return, he gives me a look of misery and hatred [Sun inconjunct Saturn] which touches a chord deep inside and I spend the whole bus journey in total fury. At home, I alternate between floods of tears and fury, and the next morning create a row at my local gym which nearly gets me banned! [Tenth house Mars projecting its rage out to the world.] I realise that I have to sort this out and ring him - ready to tell him that if he ever looks at me like that again, I'll never see him again.'

This was a typical experience of projection. What Claire saw in her father was to do with her own pathology. It had little to do with what was actually going on with him:

'However, I find that he was completely unaware of his actions [tenth house Neptune] and in fact was withdrawn after spending a week in hospital - his first stay in his life.

I realise that I had read meaning into the situation [in other words, projected] - I had recognised this particular look back to childhood, but now I could see it was beyond this. It wasn't comfortable for me to recognise the pattern of this past life within my present life. I had had affairs with men younger than myself - relationships of little value [Sun inconjunct Saturn] which only lasted a few months [seventh house Uranus] and I have always expected my father to bail me out whenever I got into trouble financially [fourth house Sun square Pluto, eighth house South Node]. When I was able to thank him for all his financial support [fourth house Jupiter] and to share with him my experiences with men, my resentment and my judgmental attitude to his relationships with women disappeared. Acceptance on both sides has brought us closer, but at the same time there is now space between us.'

Her karmic lesson, defined by fourth house Jupiter in Taurus, the Taurean Sun square Pluto and the reversed nodal connection of second house Aquarius North Node to her father's South Node, was to contact her own inner resources of security and power. She had been utilising the personal manipulative power of the eighth house Leo South Node conjunct Pluto to gain support and sustenance from her father and it was now time to move into an era of self-sufficiency and self-responsibility aligned to the nurturing energies of the cosmos. She needed to parent herself, becoming an autonomous, self-supporting member of the extended family of humankind (North Node in Aquarius).

Mercury
Mercury in a parental house can indicate that in a previous incarnation the soul interacted with the present-life parent as friend or sibling, and the sign on the cusp will describe that old pattern. It may also be linked to communication karma with a parent, perhaps delineating a meeting or a clash of minds. In Aries, for example, Mercury can be self-opinionated, full of its own ideas which may clash with those of a parent. If Mercury is in one of the Air signs, it is liable to function more in accord with parental values and ideals. Mercury in a Capricorn-attuned soul, particularly with difficult aspects, may find itself repeating a conflict with fixed, old-fashioned parental ideas. Where Mercury is afflicted, communication with the parents may be, or may have been, difficult or distorted in some way - through hearing disorders, for example.

Venus
A soul incarnating with Venus in a parental house will, unless there are difficult aspects, expect to incarnate into a harmonious environment with people with whom it has experienced pleasant past incarnations. Such a soul chooses, on the whole, parents who enable it to learn through a good early relationship, although with Venus in Scorpio, Taurus or Cancer it may experience an echo, or re-run of old jealousy and possessiveness. This can surface in the child or parent who is jealous of the interconnections between other family members and this may lead, for example, to an intense rivalry between mother and daughter for the father's attention. Such a case may indicate that the souls were old lovers, and that this relationship is close to the surface in the present life. This was particularly noticeable in the chart of a child who had fourth house Venus in Scorpio. Right from the moment of his birth he would scream in rage whenever his father touched his mother, whether in his sight or

not. The parents' sexual relationship was being seriously disturbed by the child's evident jealousy. As the mother had her Neptune conjunct the child's Venus, it was suggested that she should 'talk' to the child whilst he was sleeping to assure him that he was much loved, but that their old interaction as lovers was no longer valid. After a few weeks the child settled down and accepted the relationship between his parents.

Mars

Mars in this placement, particularly if supported by other indications, may delineate a violent or aggressive interplay with a parent in the past - especially if reinforced by Saturn or Pluto aspects or a Scorpio emphasis - and the soul may have issues of self-assertion or courage to work out this time around.

There may also be unresolved will issues coming forward. A fourth or tenth house Mars making Saturn or Pluto interaspects to a parent's chart may be linked to a past-life pattern in which there was a master/slave type of interaction. Mars can also point to an issue with the masculine energy - possibly to the soul needing to integrate this into its experience - or to a reversal of roles, in that it has formerly been involved with the parent(s) as a male and now is dealing through the female gender or vice versa.

Jupiter

Jupiter in a parental house expands the incarnating soul in some way, although there may be karma due to previous overindulgence to overcome, particularly when Jupiter is in Taurus or a Fire sign.

Jupiter in the parental houses can also indicate a past connection with a former teacher or priest who is now a parent, especially if Jupiter falls in Sagittarius, Pisces or one of the Air signs. The parent may also be perceived either as a fount of all wisdom or a worker of magic who is either revered or feared depending on the past experience.

Chiron

With Chiron placed in the fourth house, the soul expects home to be traumatic, wounding and unsafe. This is the child who is 'not at home when at home'. There could have been painful wounding by parents in a past life - who may or may not be the present life parent(s). This wounding may continue in the present life in some way. Another possibility is that the child may incarnate into a family with a wounded parent - through illness, emotional dis-ease or another cause entirely.

One client of mine incarnated into a family where the mother had pursued the father for some seven years before they married. She was convinced that they were destined to be together and looked on his other affairs as mere distractions. However, when they married, it became apparent that he intended to continue his promiscuous lifestyle. When my client was born, with Chiron in Sagittarius in the fourth house, the parents were apparently in love and quite happy in their relationship, although by the time his sibling was born some three years later, the marriage had all but broken down.

The father was virtually living with another woman and 'had to be brought home for the birth'. He believed his wife had conceived the child as a result of a brief holiday affair - which was not the case. When he saw the child, however, he conceded it was his. The mother suffered from severe and protracted post natal depression and was hospitalised. For the next four years, my client was passed around the family and various friends and when he finally returned home to live, his father had developed cancer - although this was strongly denied by his parents 'who wanted to protect him'. An intelligent child, he knew that the prognosis was grim, and that his father was still continuing to have an affair outside the marriage. Although the home masqueraded as happy place, it was actually very painful for him to be there - yet it was exactly what his chart stated he expected, something confirmed by the regression therapy he undertook as part of his healing work.

Saturn

Saturn in the fourth or tenth house is indicative of former harsh disciplinarian-style parenting or of the lack of a father-figure. Either way, the soul experiences an emotional coldness and distance which restricts and inhibits its self-development and throws the soul in upon itself. It may experience being deserted by a parent through death or divorce. For example, a client (fourth house Sun in Leo conjunct Saturn opposing the Moon) experienced the death of both parents in a car crash when he was two. He was brought up in an orphanage - an experience he said he much enjoyed as it was a stable, extended family situation with disciplined but kindly house-parents. When Saturn is benignly aspected, it indicates an earlier experience of constructive discipline leading to self control and self-confidence.

Saturn can be the authoritarian or an authoritative parent, the difference indicated by the aspects and sign energies: Capricorn is an example of the former, and Leo is usually the latter. It can also be indicative of a past experience of, or the present-life need to take up, some kind of family responsibility related to position, inheritance or profession, for example. Such a duty may have been onerous before and entailed giving up what one wanted for oneself.

Uranus

With Uranus in a parental house the soul incarnates with the knowledge that life is likely to be chaotic and full of change, or with the expectation that the parent will probably be unreliable, unstable or unpredictable. This is how it has been in the past and, as always, what is expected is manifested. Mutable signs can cope more easily with this and Cardinal signs are pushed into an early independence, but Fixed signs, which require more stability, may find it problematic and adopt strategies designed to either control life and make it safe, or to stabilise the parent as far as possible. This is one of the placements with which the soul as a child either feels it necessary to always be at home, in order to ward off change, or to be aware of it in time to cope (Uranus in Taurus, Cancer or Virgo, for example), or seeks its freedom elsewhere at any opportunity (Uranus in Gemini or Sagittarius, for instance).

Neptune

Neptune on the parental axis can indicate a long-standing over-idealisation of the mother figure and the feminine or of the father and the masculine. The child may experience the parent as an elusive figure who, whilst appearing close and loving, cannot be pinned down and never quite meets emotional needs and expectations. This illusion also applies to the child who is brought up by a surrogate parent, often in the form of a nanny, or who experiences the mother or father as a rather unreal victim, martyr or saviour figure. Such a parent may appear to need to be saved, pitied or escaped from. It can also apply to the parent who escapes from reality into illness, drink or drugs, or to the image of such a parent brought back from the past which now prevents the child from fully trusting that it will receive the support and validation it requires for its development.

On the other hand, the Neptunian child may incarnate into a family in which the arts, music, poetry and the imagination are valued and encouraged as a means of self-expression, or in which its spiritual nature is concretised through an innate acceptance of other dimensions of reality.

Pluto

Pluto in this placement delineates a long-standing power struggle with a parent, frequently the mother, who may be dominant and manipulative. She may also be instinctual and deeply frustrated, trying to live out her unfulfilled desires through her family. The father may be strongly authoritarian, particularly when Sun or Saturn aspects are involved. The child can perceive the parent as all-powerful, even when this is not his or her innate nature.

For example, a woman who was typically Sagittarian looked on her children as friends and thought she had encouraged them to grow and expand as much as possible. She did not appear, from outside the family, to be in the least dominant. However, all three of her children had Pluto in the fourth and experienced her as the significant parent. Her daughter commented that her mother was 'so good at feminine pursuits' that she found it hard to take them up herself, in case she could not live up to such a high standard. Her mother's response to this was that she 'just did it', it entailed no effort on her part, and she certainly had not realised that her daughter felt intimidated and inadequate. On further exploring the family dynamic it emerged that the mother had been the dominant and significant parent because she had had to be - her husband, an army doctor, was away for long periods and they had in any case been divorced when the children were still teenagers. For many incarnating souls who have Pluto in the fourth house, however, this dominance can be experienced as soul-destroying, leaving a deep sense of inadequacy and resentment which is then carried over into the experience of being a parent or partner.

LOVE AFFAIRS: THE FIFTH HOUSE

The fifth house describes the soul's experience with love affairs in the past – and its attitude to them in the present life. This is a much lighter kind of relationship than that shown in the seventh house. It is affairs that give pleasure, or pain, without responsibility or the necessity of long term commitment. So, someone with Saturn in this house may have karma from love affairs in the past - and could meet the previous life partner in an effort to reconcile that past.

The soul with Neptune placed here may, on the other hand, have had fantasy relationships in the past or still has the illusion of a perfect love waiting. In the meantime, Neptune is not averse to several illusory soul mate relationships. Jupiter is prone to flings, which usually come about through the expansive, open heart of the soul with this placement who has learned to enjoy such things in the past. In some cases, especially where Jupiter is in one of the more repressive signs like Capricorn, the soul can be struggling to regain some of that joy.

The Parental Fifth House

Karma between parent and child can sometimes be ascertained from an examination of the fifth house in the parental chart, which indicates the expectation parents have incarnated with regarding their children. For example, a father with fifth house Saturn may either look on the child as a burden or as a creation to be valued and cherished. The mother with a fifth house Saturn may try for a child for several years before she conceives, or may feel inadequate and fear the responsibility. Much will depend on the aspects, the sign in which Saturn is placed, the type of parenting received by the parent and earlier incarnations. Saturn in Capricorn in aspect to the Sun, for example, may indicate a responsible attitude, but the fear of inadequacy may lead to authoritarian parenting. With Saturn in Cancer the soul may long for a child but experience considerable difficulty in becoming a parent, or lose a child, in order to change an old smothering pattern of mothering.

A woman with Mars in Pisces in the fifth house incarnated with an expectation of conflict with a child, and illusions, instability and restriction around mothering (tenth house Neptune opposing Moon-Uranus in Capricorn). Her daughter (twelfth house Moon conjunct Saturn-Sun-Uranus and a fourth house Pluto) anticipated rejection and separation from the mother as they had past-life karma to resolve. They quarrelled violently (mother's Pluto conjunct daughter's Mars). The mother's Aries Saturn conjoined the daughter's North Node and her Neptune opposition to Moon-Uranus squared the daughter's nodal axis.

Her daughter did not meet the mother's self-centred expectations of how her child should act, and she was totally unforgiving as a result. The daughter had to learn to nurture herself and provide her own emotional sustenance. Their past-life contact had also included a violent confrontation and this had been carried forward into the present interaction. Although the daughter was anxious to resolve the karma between them, all she could do was to practise the spiritual discipline of forgiveness and absolve herself from adding further to the cycle of cause and effect. She could not force her mother to accept or reciprocate the forgiveness, but she could offer her unconditional love and remain open to the possibility of one day healing the wounds between them.

RELATIONSHIP KARMA: THE SEVENTH AND EIGHTH HOUSES

The seventh and eighth houses in the chart - together with signs, planets and rulers - show how the incarnating soul will give and share itself within a relationship and the karma that relationship holds.

Planets in Seventh House

The seventh house delineates the incarnating soul's karma concerning one to one relationships of all kinds. This house shows the soul's expectations, and the type of partner who brings these issues to the fore. Both the planets in this house and the aspects to them illustrate the working of the karma.

Sun

The soul incarnating with the Sun in the seventh house has the need to develop itself through a relationship. The karma may, for example, be one of too much detachment or attachment (Aquarius, Cancer or the Fixed signs), of selfishness or unselfishness (Aries, Libra, Pisces or the Cardinal signs), sensual gratification (Taurus), neurotic perfectionism (Virgo), jealousy (Scorpio) or infidelity (the Mutable or dual signs). With this placement, the soul can learn about the intimacy which Robert A. Johnson says 'derives from authentic contact with another human being who possesses both strengths and limitations'. Its lesson can be to share itself in a relationship, whilst maintaining its own integrity and honouring its own needs, and those of another. The Self is affirmed in its identity by and through its interconnection with another:

> 'Almost paradoxically, a sense of their own power, purpose and individuality is found through partnership and relationship ... Through the ups and downs and entanglements encountered in the

attempt to form vital, honest and life-supporting alliances, the
identity is shaped and strengthened.' [1]

The Sun in the seventh house may also indicate that the male partner
was the soul's father in a previous life, or that the soul has in the
past been married to the present-life father. Either way, the
incarnating soul may have to deal with incestuous feelings arising
either in childhood, if the father was formerly the husband, or in
adulthood, when the husband was formerly the father. These feelings
may never become conscious but may pervade the underlying
structure of the relationship, causing subtle disharmony and
emotional difficulties. Conversely, one of the partners within a
seventh house Sun relationship may take on a fatherly role through
living out the powerful solar principle on behalf of his or her mate.
This is frequently true of both marriage and partnerships entered
into for business reasons. In such cases, one partner will act out the
dynamic Sun energy and the other will passively allow this. The
passive partner may have to learn to confront and own his or her
own power within the relationship.

The working of this type of karma can be subtle and complex.
For example, a woman who has a natal seventh house Sun-Pluto
contact will most probably have the karmic pattern of an
authoritarian father and project all her power on to men. She may
have been aware of her father's incestuous feelings, if not actual
behaviour, in childhood and may subsequently marry a man who
imposes his authority on her. Initially, she may be content to play
the little wife at home, but in reality is frequently the power behind
the throne living out all her aspirations through her husband. The
situation could be further complicated if she has Mars-Saturn-Pluto
aspects in her chart for instance, by her helplessness or an addiction
to violence. (Pain has become linked to love and her will has been
suppressed). When this woman, under the pressure of transits and
resulting inner changes, eventually begins to develop her own sense
of authority and takes back the projection of power (thereby dealing
with the karma attached to her Sun-Pluto aspect), conflict may well
develop within the relationship. But she may still interpret this as
'love' and be unable to release from the situation. She may also face
hostility from a husband who has been used to having a compliant
wife. Exercising that inner authority in her life may result in the
decision to leave the relationship, or to state clearly that she is going
to be autonomous within it. Either way, she will go through a period

of isolation and adjustment until a new way of relating which allows her to manifest her own considerable power is developed.

In a different scenario she may enter into an inferior role in a profession traditionally dominated by men. Spurred on perhaps by a need to be equal to a man she may aspire to succeed in that masculine world, being driven by ambition and a need to prove herself. She may also be trying to live out her father's ambitions for her or to emulate him, perhaps compensating for the son he never had. Under the pressure of transits and the need to reclaim her power, her promotion into a traditional male power base may be opposed and she may have to examine her values and ambitions. The resulting struggle helps her to reclaim her own power and consequently either her career will take off or she will find another way to express herself.

Moon

The Moon in the seventh house signifies that the incarnating soul is meeting past emotional or mothering karma through its relationships. For many souls with this placement, the past pattern has been to see themselves through the eyes of another, reflected back, rather than recognising themselves as they really are. Conversely they may see themselves as someone else wants them to be, or see someone else as they want them to be - all of which would be coloured by past precedents.

Souls for whom this is a deeply ingrained pattern feel naked, uneasy and incomplete when alone. Lacking a sense of Self from which to interact with the inner or outer worlds, they are vulnerable to anyone who appears to offer them a mirror in which to see themselves or who stirs up emotional needs from the past. Consequently they are an ideal hook for the projections of other people and for the false identity to which they are thereby exposed. The seventh house Moon may also reflect patterns within the incarnating soul through the interaction with another. A man (figure 10, inner ring) with seventh house Chiron and Moon in Scorpio conjunct the South Node opposing the Sun and Ascendant and widely T-square fourth house Pluto-Saturn-Mars conjunction in Leo, was 'idyllically happy' with his wife (outer ring) until she decided to have a child which he did not feel ready for. She had a Grand Trine of seventh house Uranus to Mars in Scorpio (conjunct his Moon-South Node, so this was an old conflict with him around mothering) and her Jupiter-Moon conjunction in fourth house Pisces, together

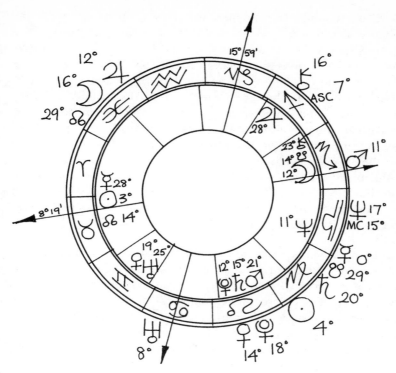

Figure 10 - Mothering Issues

with a Moon opposition to Saturn-South Node across the parental houses and an eighth house Pluto-Venus inconjunct to the Moon, indicated that they had both incarnated with expectations of emotional difficulty and constriction around mothering and jealousy of others. The adult interplay most probably repeated a pattern from childhood with their own mothers. From the moment of conception the relationship deteriorated rapidly. Her husband was extremely jealous of the child and particularly opposed breast-feeding (Cancer was his fourth house cusp sign). He had a Venus-Uranus conjunction which activated her seventh house and had had difficulty committing himself to the relationship initially, although his Neptune semi-sextile the Moon and her Neptune quincunx to the Moon reflected the idolisation in the relationship. His T-square and her Grand Trine and Moon inconjunct to Pluto-Venus had inherent difficulties and conflicts about mothering.

The birth brought these issues to the surface for them both.

He ceased to idolise her and manifested all the thwarted small child jealousy of which his Scorpionic Moon was capable. There was a Saturn-Pluto-Mars conjunction from his chart to her Venus-Pluto, and his Venus-Uranus squared her Saturn. They had been extremely symbiotic and dependent on each other. She described them as having been 'each other's best friend, totally inseparable until the birth'. Following on from their separation, he had a nervous breakdown and came to her for support which she interpreted as a mothering need, and which with her Moon in Pisces inconjunct Neptune she was happy to provide as she still felt that he was her soulmate. She believed that in a past life she had been his mother and that he had been extremely jealous of his siblings despite the fact that he was her favourite child. This situation was reactivated and reflected back to her by the birth of their daughter.

The karma of the seventh house Moon may also be one of excessive emotionality within a relationship, the soul having no control over how it reacts to a stimulus and over what past emotional patterns are triggered. In the previous example the Scorpio Moon husband felt deeply rejected and abandoned when his wife brought an 'interloper's into the family. Jealous and unable to accept the child, he reflected the rejection back on to his wife. She did not perceive it as his difficulty but as a reflection on herself as a bad mother and failure as a wife (fourth house Moon in Pisces opposing Saturn-South Node).

The lesson for the soul with a seventh house Moon is to learn to respond rather than react blindly, and to recognise how a past life trigger can intrude into the present, and the feelings it produces. The soul must become conscious of, rather than identified with, the emotional forces within itself and step beyond them so that it chooses how to act. The pathway of a fully conscious and aware relationship is a difficult one and can entail moving away from long-held beliefs and expectations.

> 'Human love is so obscured by the inflations and commotions of romance that we almost never look for love in its own right... But... we can begin to see love within us - revealed in our feelings in the spontaneous flow of warmth that surges toward another person, in the small, unnoticed acts of relatedness that make up the secret fabric of our daily lives.

We can learn that human relationship is inseparable from friendship and commitment. We can learn that the essence of love is not to use the other to make us happy, but to serve and affirm the one we love. And we can discover, to our surprise, that what we have needed more than anything was not so much to be loved, as to love.'[2]

The soul incarnating with the Moon in the seventh may also have karma with the mother in the present life arising out of a former life when they were married, or the soul may have been the mother of the partner to whom it is now married. This tends to result in emotionally incestuous or possessive behaviour, a mode of action frequently reflected by a mother who is unable to let go of her son. The unconscious need for a wife to act as mother can be carried over into adult relationships as in the previous example. This is reflected in the number of elderly men who seem unable to refer to their wives other than as 'mother' despite the fact that the children have long since left home. The lesson that these souls must learn is to release from the past interaction and to enter into a relationship unfettered by the apron strings of the past.

Mercury

The soul incarnating with Mercury in the seventh house has karma around how the mind or language have been used to communicate within a relationship in the past. This can range from the chronic nagger or scold (frequently linked to heavy aspects to Mercury when it is in an Air or Earth sign), to criticism (particularly linked to Virgo or Saturn), over-intellectualisation of the feelings (Air signs or Virgo), verbal barbs (Gemini or Scorpio) or intellectual domination by a partner (Pluto aspects). The need in the present life is for honest and caring communication between the partners.

The past-life pattern may also have been that the present-life partner was once a friend or sibling. A client had her seventh house Mercury in Gemini conjoined by her husband's Sun. The marriage had not been consummated because they both felt more like brother and sister, with a deep friendship between them. She said that ever since they had first met she had been convinced that this was a much loved brother from a past life. Although they were devoted to each other, eventually her husband wished to have a sexual relationship and moved out. They remained close friends, however, without engendering any jealousy in the husband's new wife, who recognised and accepted the special platonic link between them.

Venus

On the whole the soul with seventh house Venus incarnates expecting relationships and partners to be a source of contentment, growth and harmony - allowing for the aspects made with any outer planets! However, Venus does have its dark side particularly when situated in Taurus, Scorpio or Cancer, and there may be past issues of possessiveness, jealousy and revenge to overcome.

Much will depend on the aspects to Venus as to the incarnating soul's expectations and past experience, and to the aspects between the charts of the partners. If the charts are compatible with easy aspects, then this placement may indicate a contact coming forward from the past in order that both partners can overcome old difficulties and offer each other the opportunity to grow through a new type of relationship. On the other hand, easy aspects may indicate two loving souls who have chosen to be together to build upon and further develop their union. Problems can arise if the incarnating soul seeks to grow *through* another instead of by its own efforts, and it will then tend to blame the partner if things go awry, rather than look within. The lesson to be learnt from Venus, therefore, is to be both autonomous and harmonious within a relationship, seeking to share love and bring beauty into the life of another whilst retaining fundamental independence and identity.

Mars

With seventh house Mars, much depends upon the sign and aspects as to how the karma arose and will manifest. The negative, passive signs may have karma around repressed aggression or difficulties in assertion within a relationship; the soul may need to learn to express its own will rather than being dominated by that of another. The positive, outgoing signs are more likely to have karma linked with violence and aggression within a past relationship and the soul may need to compromise between its own ego or assertion needs and those of a partner.

If Mars has difficult aspects the soul may seek out an aggressive, dominant partner with whom to work on, or on whom to project, its own will and assertion issues. Such a partner may be a direct link back to the past, or may have been chosen simply because he or she epitomises the type of aggressive energies needed by the soul to manifest the positive side of the energies within itself.

A client (seventh house Mars in Scorpio in Grand Trine to

Uranus and Jupiter) who had just split up from her husband responded to the reading I had given her:

'I am very familiar with my Will! It can over-ride most obstacles in life. It was, of course, one of the things that first attracted my husband to me but in the end he saw it as a monster. It always carries that danger. I am very assertive but not very aggressive [the Grand Trine is in Water], although people often cannot tell the difference, I find. At least I don't hate easily as I think my Will would be very damaging under such circumstances... I was not approved of as a child, too strong a Will, too clever by half [Saturn conjunct Mercury-South Node in Virgo]. One of the reasons I fell in love with my husband was that he appeared to approve of my cleverness and my success. I found myself opening emotionally when I had sat on my emotions too long from hurt [Saturn square Chiron-Moon in eighth house]. Ironically, this opened up the healer [twelfth house Jupiter] in me and my computer career [Uranus in aspect to Mars] became unimportant... Equally ironically and very painfully, it became clear that my husband did not approve of this change and he used to talk of my 'crackpot and loony' friends and activities. I do feel now that I have the freedom to be who I am [Sun in Leo, Aries Ascendant].

I was fascinated by your psychic reading concerning a death in war consumed by fire or an explosion of some kind - by the way, it is almost certainly the First World War as I gave up history at school rather than study it. I have a definite past-death memory prior to that in the Middle Ages with a similar end. I was trying to do some kind of alchemical experiment and caused an explosion in which I was burned to death. I have always known this and got an awful shock when I realised that most people didn't believe in reincarnation. I have always put my fear of fire and my terror of letting go down to that experience. The letting go bit is a real nuisance. The experiment went wrong because I wasn't paying sufficient attention and now I am very scared of being out of control [Saturn square Chiron-Moon in Sagittarius, Pluto conjunct Venus-North Node]. That means I cannot relax enough to achieve orgasm, which is silly... I only hope I work through that sometime.'

The seventh house Mars may also indicate the lesson of expressing anger within a relationship in a clean, non-judgemental or non-blaming manner. It may be a soul who has always suppressed anger in the past, perhaps for fear of being disliked or rejected, or it may have experienced the guilt induced by being told: 'You make me angry'. Such a soul may have suffered the misplaced anger of another soul who was unable to express it to the source of its anger, or been subjected to the constant rages of an angry partner - it may also have been the angry partner itself. As a result, it may need to recover the energy and vitality of the suppressed emotion rather than suffer the consequences of old rage, such as constant tiredness, petty irritations or other health and relationship problems.

Jupiter

As with all Jupiter placements there is a possibility that over indulgence and aggrandisement are part of the soul's karma around relationships, or that partners will be a source of great expansion and growth. Jupiter in this house can mitigate other difficult aspects within the chart and the incarnating soul with this placement can begin to positively affirm itself through its contact with another soul. The partner chosen may be benignly expansive, or prone to sensual self-indulgence, and there may be a direct link with a previous life in which the karma arose, or a spiritual link to support the soul in its quest to overcome the past. The sign on the cusp and the interaspects between the charts delineate the type of karma involved.

Jupiter has the gift of faith and the power of creative visualisation and this placement can bring growth-enhancing experiences of mutual trust through a deep, spiritual relationship. The sensual joy of Jupiter can be extremely helpful in overcoming past sexual frustrations or frigidity; as can the simple act of learning to trust and open up to another soul - a lifetime's lesson in itself if there are difficult Saturn or Pluto aspects to contend with. However, the expansiveness of Jupiter can accelerate the soul's learning process and attune to the joyous energy immanent throughout the cosmos. Partners may act as mentors to aid the soul's evolution.

Saturn

Saturn is the Lord of Karma and the soul incarnating with seventh house Saturn has usually encountered difficult and repressive or burdensome relationships on its journey. One of the challenges for this placement can be to lower the defensive walls it has built around itself and its emotions. Old fears may need to be overcome and trust regained. However, the strength of Saturn manifests in the face of adversity and hardship overcome, and the soul with this placement has the possibility of entering into a stable, enduring partnership based on mutual love and respect for each other.

The soul with seventh house Saturn usually encounters a partner with whom it has direct karma from a previous life, old debts and obligations to work on or a promise to be honoured. Although at times the partnership, whatever form it takes, may appear laborious and limiting, through this interaction the soul becomes more aware of its own strengths, its inner resilience, discipline and integrity. If it has in the past tended to opt out of relationships when difficulties arose (Air and Fire signs on the cusp or Uranus aspects to the Moon or Venus), then this may be a valuable opportunity to see a relationship through. On the other hand, if the soul has tended to be stuck in a rut (the Earth signs) or to immerse itself in some form of sacrifice (the Water signs or Neptune in aspect to the Moon or Venus), it may be time for to decide when it is appropriate to stay in the relationship and when it is better to release from the interaction and let go of the past. The soul may have to recognise that there is no value in endlessly repeating an interaction that is on the road to nowhere. The urge of the Self is towards growth, not stagnation.

Chiron

Chiron in the seventh house is indicative of a deep wound around relationships and the soul with this placement often meets difficult karma in order to be released from suffering in this area - but also attracts healing relationships once the pain has been exorcised.

A client with Chiron in Taurus in the seventh also had Mars-Saturn-Venus and the North Node conjunct at the point of a Finger of Fate with tenth house Neptune and eighth house Pluto. She had always found relationships extremely painful and questioned whether she would ever find a man she felt safe with as well as being attracted to. She strongly believed she had been physically tortured in a past life and her main concern was with a friend about whom she asked: 'Why did this friend who tortures me come into my life, and how can I recover from these wounds?' In the synastry between the charts the 'friend' had Chiron conjunct the North Node in Leo opposing the client's Mars-Saturn-Venus-North Node - a reversed nodal connection. In addition the friend's Sun, Mercury, Uranus, and Saturn all activated the client's seventh house. The connection to her friend appeared to be an old one with a reactivation of the karmic pattern of torture. Through the relationship she was offered the opportunity to break away from the suffering stemming from her tortuous relationships, leaving behind the emotional games and insecurities of the Leo South Node conjunction and the Finger of Fate. This could result in her healing the wounds of the past.

Uranus

In traditional astrology Uranus in the seventh house, or Aquarius on the cusp, signifies divorce or separation. In karmic astrology Uranus may indicate that in the past the soul has not been committed in its relationships or has had problems with intimacy, or that the time has now come to be more free in the way it interacts with another. Uranus in this placement is committed to transformation, and if it cannot improve its relationship at the same time as it transforms itself, then it may have to change partners to do so. However, it may also be that a different, perhaps more unconventional, way of relating is needed: one which offers the soul the space it craves to be an individual without excluding the experience of interacting with another which it needs in order to grow. The soul with Uranus is the planet of universal love that teaches the soul to recognise and love humanity in its interconnected multifacetedness. With seventh house Uranus the soul needs to relate to the organic whole and its individual segments. If the problem in the past has been with intimacy, the soul is challenged to develop trust and closeness in relationships without sacrificing individuality. To open itself fully to another human being is an enormous evolutionary step for this placement.

The partner represented by the seventh house Uranus may bring the soul a lesson from the past around freedom or commitment; it may be someone to whom the incarnating soul failed to commit itself, or someone from whom it needs to separate to become an individual. The sign on the cusp and the aspects to Uranus from the partner's planets will elucidate the underlying karmic lesson.

Neptune

In Neptune the soul may encounter its previous delusions and projections, or it may meet a spiritual companion from the past for its present stage of the journey. It may also lead to present life illusions and denials. Neptune finds it difficult to face everyday reality, especially when this is unpalatable. Not all partners attracted by Neptune in the seventh are trustworthy, even though they may feel like a soulmate. Even when the souls are old and close partners, the spiritual lesson may centre around boundaries - or the lack of them.

Boundaries and separation are something Neptune finds hard to face. A client with Neptune in Scorpio in the seventh inconjunct the Sun in the twelfth and Venus conjunct Chiron-Mercury in the eleventh had an old soulmate relationship with her husband. He died when she was still young and she refused to accept the reality of his death, insisting on the continuity of the relationship. She became obsessed with the Spiritualist Church, seeking out mediums to contact him, and said that he was still with her constantly and that they would work spiritually together. She wanted to work off all her karma so that they could 'be together for eternity'. She refused to entertain the possibility that she was holding back his spiritual evolution, and her own.

Queen Victoria was another woman who was never reconciled to the reality of her beloved husband's death - despite the fact that she had a picture of his dead face pasted onto his side of the bed. His shaving water was brought to her bedroom each morning just as it had been when he was alive. She entered into perpetual mourning for forty years. Marriage to Prince Albert had given her an outlet for her extremely passionate nature (Venus in Aries) and despite her reputation for prudery, their personal life was highly erotic. She gifted him with titillating statues and salacious nude paintings to maintain his interest in things sexual - mirroring her libidinous Venus semi-sextile to Pluto. She had Neptune in Sagittarius in the seventh house, conjunct Uranus and trine Venus. Whilst her Neptune idealised her dead husband, her seventh house Uranus is reflected in her highly unconventional relationship with her servant John Brown. It is not known whether the two were actually lovers, but they were exceedingly close and it was even rumoured at the time that they had secretly married.

Neptune, perhaps more than any other planet, is capable of extremes and can indicate the potential for both the highest or the lowest to emerge through a relationship. The karma may be that the soul has been deceived or seduced in the past and now meets its deceiver or its illusions again; or it may be that it has idealised a union and not seen its partner clearly. It may have had unrealised or unrealistic expectations of love which held it back from unconditionally loving another and, therefore, it may have to learn to clearly perceive not only *what* love is but also *who* the partner is:

'Love is a force that acts from within, that enables my ego to look outside itself, to see my fellow humans as something to be valued

131

and cherished, rather than used. Therefore, when I say that 'I love', it is not I who loves, but, in reality, Love who acts through me. Love is not so much something I do as something I am. Love is not a doing but a state of being - relatedness, a connectedness to another mortal, an identification with her or him that simply flows within me, independent of my intentions or my efforts.

Love is the power within us that affirms and values another human being as he or she is... rather than the ideal we would like him or her to be or the projection that flows from our minds... Love causes us to value that person as a total, individual self, and this means that we accept the negative side as well as the positive, the imperfections as well as the admirable qualities. When one truly loves the human being rather than the projection, one loves the shadow just as one loves the rest. One accepts the other person's totality.' [3]

This is the lesson of unconditional love, to love what *is*, not what might be, and it is the karmic purpose of seventh house Neptune.

Pluto

As with all Pluto contacts the karma behind the seventh house Pluto is deep and devious. It almost always embodies a power struggle, both in the past and in the present interaction, unless the incarnating soul has reached a high level of spiritual evolution and awareness. Pluto has the potential for a creative relationship which heals old wounds and releases ancient resentments. However, for many souls incarnating with such a placement it is those wounds and resentments which await attention, together with the obsessions and compulsions relating to relationships which those wounds engender.

Seventh house Pluto offers the opportunity to fully and finally release from the compulsive karma of the past. This may involve a meeting with a past partner with whom there are power and emotional difficulties to resolve, or it may bring the soul into contact with a powerful force for transformation in the shape of an old soulmate or a new teacher. Pluto offers the soul a companion for its inward journey and can lead to a deep understanding of the interplay between men and women as it is expressed through relationships, with a consequent unlocking of the creative energies of partnership. In the Plutonian union of two individual souls coming together in aware relationship, the energy released is much more than the sum of its parts. It is true transformation and regeneration.

Planets in the Eighth House

The eighth house has links with the cycle of conception, birth, death and rebirth, and with the different levels of consciousness. It describes how the incarnating soul will share itself with others, what the subtle colouring of that interaction is, and how the soul will be connected to the cosmos.

Personal planets in the eighth house bring the soul face to face with the need to give of itself in a direct experience of the vibration represented by that planet, the planetary energy being a resource to draw on and develop through relationships. Outer planets placed here may incorporate subtle lessons in the encounter with others, widening out the concept of relationship still further, particularly into manifestation of the oneness of life.

Jupiter

With Jupiter in the eighth house the incarnating soul has a resource of creative energy and links to higher levels of consciousness. Attuned to Jupiter, it can share the vision of what may be and transform it through creative visualisation and affirmation into what is. The soul attuned to the energy of Jupiter is thereby able, through relationship in the fullest sense of the word, to draw out of another soul its potential to 'be'.

Saturn

Saturn in the eighth house may represent restriction and limitation on how the soul shares its resources and gives of itself to another. In the past it may have repressed its sexual energies, possibly as a result of a vow of chastity, and it may therefore encounter difficulty in the present incarnation with this area of life. This placement is symbolic of a defensive wall erected between the soul and others in the past, or of a lack of confidence in its ability to give of itself, based on poor self-esteem. The soul may blame other people, however, for its failure to relate rather than recognise that its own inner isolation and restriction are the cause of the problem. The karmic lesson is to transcend the limitations of its inner sense of worthlessness and to find within itself a core of value through which it can relate.

Chiron

With Chiron in the eighth house the soul will have had a traumatic experience in giving itself to another person. At a deep level, this placement expects pain in how it shares itself and is trying to heal this old pattern. The lesson can come about through what seems to be unbearable pain in the present life. I had a client with Chiron in Scorpio in the eighth house who had had a 'perfect relationship' with his wife whom he had known since childhood. They were soulmates in every way and had lived for each other, which is why her death from cancer at the age of 35 was devastating for him. When he came to me, he re-experienced several past lives where they had also had idyllic lives together. He went into the between-life state and was reunited with his wife as she was in the present. It was an extremely moving reunion and the room was filled with a presence of overwhelming love. Eventually, she told him that she had been watching over him but that it was time for her to move on. Her spiritual progress required it. He asked her why she had left him. She explained to him that, despite the great love between them, they had agreed before incarnating that they would learn how to separate and follow their own pathways. The only way this could be achieved was through her death. She wanted him to start his new life without any guilt or regret, saying that he had to experience a new facet of love.

After they had said goodbye, and he had returned to normal consciousness, he confessed that he had just begun a new relationship but had been feeling extremely guilty. Now, with his wife's blessing, he felt free to explore its possibilities.

The eighth house Chiron often experiences a significant life change after a death. This may be connected to having suffered a particularly difficult or formative transition to the spiritual realms in a past life. Chiron can also act as the transformer. Loss is not always a negative experience. A woman, whose husband had disappeared was liberated by the declaration of her husband's death seven years later. Having previous lived an extremely sheltered and protected life she was now freed to be herself.

Uranus

Uranus in the eighth house often points to an ambivalence and ambiguity concerning sexual orientation, and an unconventional approach to relationships. It may be that the incarnating soul found it difficult to make relationships in a past life, being too aware of its separateness and too attached to its freedom. On the other hand, the present ambivalence may be based on past experiences in which the soul was overwhelmed by its own sexuality, withdrawing perhaps into celibacy as an escape from instinctual pressures, or in which its sexual outlet was unusual or was considered perverted or different in some way. This particular placement shows up consistently in the charts of souls with a homosexual or bisexual orientation rather than a heterosexual one. It may indicate that the soul must learn to integrate the masculine and feminine within itself, moving back towards the asexuality of the eternal Self. On the other hand, it may simply be that Uranus insists on being 'different', in which case the soul is setting up new karma for itself in the future as it experiments with the extremes of dispassionate, deviant uranian 'relationship'.

One client had a Saturn-Mars-Uranus conjunction in Gemini in the eighth house, forming a Grand Trine with Neptune and the Sun, and the Moon in Capricorn. He suffered from shyness and found it difficult to form personal relationships; he was unwilling to become committed to one relationship, preferring a variety but not able to achieve that either. His difficulties matched both the repressed emotional energy of the Capricorn Moon and the eighth house Saturn, while his dual Gemini-placed Uranus was seeking the widest possible range of experiences. It seemed that he might one day surprise himself with his own inventiveness and the number of opportunities to be explored once Uranus had overcome the restrictions of Saturn and he had shed his inhibitions. The eighth house conjunction would never give him tranquillity in the emotional sense, but he could begin to make changes willingly and more smoothly instead of letting them come up with great force. Stephen Arroyo says that the eighth house represents a longing for emotional peace and release from compulsion, and he points out that this cannot come through suppression and repression but will only be attained if the longing is brought out into the clear light of consciousness and if the past is then outgrown.

In the past-life part of the reading, the above client was told that he had been a handsome boy, a slave to a wealthy Roman who pampered him and showed him off to his friends. But he had also used and abused his body in a private sadistic homosexual relationship, giving him much pleasure. Later he was converted to Christianity and welcomed martyrdom, as his sense of having lived contrary to the Will of God was so overwhelming. (This is a scenario that is archetypal and I have heard of several regressions to similar situations in Roman times). The life my client described tied in with an earlier incarnation in Babylon in which he was described as 'a pretty painted boy who played the whore' living a sybaritic existence, and to a later life as a religious recluse.

In a follow-up session the client stated that he had felt sexually guilty all his life, but could never pinpoint the reason and he described having had curious fantasies and an attraction towards other men. This had interfered with his forming the kind of relationship with a woman which he desperately wanted. Once he recognised his old pattern and that the fantasies were memories of those times, he was able to transform his relationships and express what he regarded a normal sexuality. But this particular client was also fearful of what else might be lurking in his past. He was once told by a clairvoyant that he had been a Jack-the-Ripper figure who used and abused women and then killed them. Although the feeling of that life fitted the symbolic pattern of his eighth house planets it did not ring true to either of us. He was much relieved to be assured that although the potential for that kind of behaviour could be seen in the chart, it did not appear to have manifested. The experience does, however, illustrate the damage which can be inflicted by an unthinking reading of a past life with no further counselling or interpretation available.

Uranus has the potential for truly aware and creative relationships, based on an acknowledgement of, and respect for, individual difference and recognition of mutual essence. It offers the soul an opportunity to move away from the stultifying patterns of the past into a new and original mode of relating.

Neptune

With Neptune in the eighth house the lesson is to learn to share the unconditional love and vision that it channels down from the higher levels of consciousness through the soul merging itself into another. Or it may be that the soul has to be more realistic about how much it gives of itself as there may have been a previous tendency to sacrifice all; to immolate and lose itself in a relationship, thereby forsaking its separateness and integration. The sign on the cusp can be helpful here, and so can the aspects to Neptune. Virgo on the cusp or Saturn aspects are more likely to indicate restriction in the past and point to a need to open up to another soul in the present incarnation. The Neptune in Libra soul may well have sacrificed too much of itself in a past relationship and now needs to learn to channel the energy constructively into a mutual sharing rather than self-immolation, in order to discover the true meaning of union and relationship.

Neptune in this house represents the soul's potential to offer to another soul a sharing and merging into a higher level of Being through the sexual pathway of mutual bliss. It is the pathway of Tantric yoga and Taoist practices, and the soul with this placement can benefit from the study and practical application of these principles.

Pluto

The lesson for Pluto in the eighth house is for the soul to re-attune to its old awareness of the cycle of birth, death and rebirth, the creative energy underlying the universe. It then has a powerful energy to draw on for healing and transformation, which can be shared with other souls on the same journey.

Pluto in this placement may indicate that the soul is trapped in a pattern of power and exploitation, or that it may be too egotistical and manipulative in how it shares itself. As Debbie Shapiro has pointed out:

'Power can easily be misused... People will be impressed, but not empowered. Dishonesty, a breaking of agreements, subtle bullying, the need to be right at all times, a quick temper, and a misuse of principles are some of the indications of ego involvement.'[4]

A client with Pluto in the eighth (square to Venus in Aries and trine to Mars in Scorpio) was engaged to a man for many years and eventually married him despite his powerful mother having opposed the union (his Moon in Scorpio was conjunct her Mars). The marriage had sado-masochistic overtones as her husband insisted on dominating her (his Mars trined her Saturn and was conjunct her Pluto, and his Pluto squared her Venus). She tried many times to leave the relationship but never succeeded as he had considerable power over her through the contact to her Pluto and its reflection of her own inner energies. In many ways it seemed she was addicted to him and to the violence and conflict of the relationship which was based on an old pattern of manipulation and dominance.

When Pluto moves beyond this level into the area of transpersonal power, it is intimately connected with the energy of the cosmos, the eternal creative source, and it can become a channel for healing the earth and all those upon it through its relationship to the whole.

THE ELEVENTH HOUSE: GROUP KARMA

Planets in the eleventh house show the soul's previous interplay with groups of people and also with friends. If Pluto is placed here, there will have been power struggles in the past, catalytic Uranus has striven to bring in change, conservative Saturn to maintain the status quo and Chiron may have been the group scapegoat. A soul will take these expectations into its wider relationships and may expect a current friend to act in the way that a friend acted in the past. Neptune conjunct Chiron, for instance, could have been betrayed and will unconsciously expect that betrayal again - or to meet that old experience once more within a group.

TWELFTH HOUSE: THE HOUSE OF KARMA

When you stand on the Ascendant and look out around the chart, the twelfth is unseen behind you - hence its traditional association with hidden enemies. But the twelfth house is also the house of karma. Planets of particular relevance to karmic relationships are:

The Sun and Moon

If the soul is born with the Sun in the twelfth house, then there is karma with the present life father. If the Moon is placed here the karma is with the mother and there will be strong personal connections. The sign on the cusp, and the aspects to the Moon, describe past conditions and how the karma emerged. Scorpio, for instance, has traumatic memories of being mothered and may need to heal old traumas with the mother. Libra or Gemini, on the other hand, may indicate that in the past the mother was a friend and that she has now chosen to undertake a greater closeness and responsibility These roles will most probably have been played out many times.

The nature of the interaction is indicated by the sign on the cusp of the house and aspects to the Sun or Moon. If the sign is an authoritarian one like Capricorn, the issue is autonomy, while an independent sign such as Aries is seeking to individualise. A man with Aries on the cusp and Sun aspecting Pluto, for instance, was subordinate to his authoritarian father who ran the family business. In regression, he found that the positions had been reversed. In the previous life, he had been the father who held his son down. His son ultimately rebelled and gained the power - which he had maintained in the present life as the father.

The twelfth house Moon can also indicate karma around the emotions. The soul may be dealing with the consequences of excessive sensitivity and emotionality from the past (Water signs), with a tendency to rationalise the emotions (Air signs), suppress them (Earth signs), or to create emotional conflagrations that consume both parties (Fire signs).

Venus

Venus in the twelfth house indicates strong karmic issues around relationships which need to be balanced out. The soul tends to be drawn to partners who embody the old way of relating. If the ingrained patterns are understood and a new type of partner sought, relationships can improve dramatically. The sign on the cusp indicates the source of the problem. Leo, for instance, demanded attention and had to be bowed down to as head of the household. Capricorn too wanted authority, but also had problems expressing feelings. Taurus found it hard to let go and was consumed with jealousy, as was Scorpio whose old passions and intrigues will come home to roost. Possessive Cancer held on, clinging to the past whereas with Aquarius the karma stems from being too detached. Aries was too selfish, Libra too giving. Virgo imposed high standards of perfection. The dual signs, Gemini, Sagittarius and Pisces, had a problem with commitment and faithfulness

This placement can also indicate that the soul has had strong incarnations as a woman or has close past-life links with the women with whom it is now in relationship. In the latter case, relationship difficulties can be experienced. The contact will feel totally right on one level but adjustments have to be made for the present life personas - which may not be as compatible and may cause friction. On the other hand, if the past life pattern was one of discord, the new personas may be more harmonious. The possibility is there for the past to be healed through a more loving relationship.

For a full explanation of planets in the twelfth house, see ‘*Patterns of the Past*’.

5

THE KARMA OF INTERASPECTS

If any association is allowed to work upon the faults, upon the
vanities, upon the material expressions, it is harmful. If it is used to
strengthen the spiritual import of the life, it is turned to helpfulness.
Edgar Cayce

A soul frequently attracts a partner with whom there has been
previous contact. Lessons are on-going, promises have to be kept,
purpose has to be fulfilled, reparation may be needed, breaking away
can be called for. The connection, and reasons for coming back are
laid out in the interaction between two charts.

The type of karma embodied within a relationship, and the
lessons to be learnt from it, can be ascertained from the connections,
known as synastry, between two natal charts and, in particular, from
the contacts of the outer planets in one chart to the personal planets
in the other chart and vice versa. I often feel that synastry should be
more appropriately written as sinastry. Sin is separation from
wholeness and the synastry between charts often shows where the
separations come, and also where the similarities are. So much of
synastry is a reflecting pattern, and so many partnerships repeat and
mirror issues from other relationships.

Examining the natal chart and its interplay with others can
therefore throw light on the underlying processes and evolutionary
forces at work both within the individual and those with whom
contact is made. Overcoming karmic obligations and outgrown
karmic patterns can, for some souls, lead to fulfilment of the purpose
of incarnation, opening the way to reintegration with the divine
and a return to the source of Being. For other souls the way will be
opened for further emotional learning and evolution through fresh
relationships.

The aspects across two charts are called interaspects. Some of
the outer planets do, of course, move rather slowly and so, with Pluto
and Neptune aspects in particular, other factors such as natal aspects

or an appropriate house being triggered are required to support the karma of the interaspect. As many people born in the same era share interaspects, it may indicate that the issue of the outer planet (Neptune, unconditional love; Pluto, power, for instance) is being worked on a collective or universal level, so that anyone who deals with the underlying karma or who develops positive qualities is helping the whole to evolve. The wide orbs that I recommend do tend to throw up more interaspects than conventional synastry, but I have found through long experience that this catches the underlying theme of a relationship which might otherwise be lost. Obviously the tighter the orb, the more significant an interaspect will be, particularly if it repeats both ways or gets tighter by progression.

Interaspects between the personal planets alone indicate the degree of superficial sexual attraction that will affect the partners. These inner planet interaspects are relevant to the present life and are not karmic. They are comparatively easy to resist and may not always be acted upon. Outer planet and nodal contacts to the personal planets, however, delineate older and deeper karmic interaction and soul purpose that is much more difficult to avoid. It irresistibly pulls two souls into relationship - or tries to. However there is a choice, even when it does not seem so. As with all karmic aspects, the key is to recognise the pattern and its triggers, and to develop a new way of responding rather than reacting in the same old way. Outer planet energies often manifest negatively within karmic involvement, but this does not have to be the case. A couple may express the transcendent, higher octave energies of the outer planet within their relationship. In addition to the old karma embodied in a relationship, interaspects also signify how the karmic purpose of a relationship can be developed by harnessing the positive, constructive side of the outer planet energy to mutual growth.

If the karma signified by an interaspect is personal to the two people concerned, the outer planet contacts from one chart to the personal planets in the other will be repeated. So, if each Uranus aspects each Venus across a set of charts, no matter what the aspect or width of orbs, a 'freedom-commitment' issue is personal to these partners and will have been worked on, or created, through several lives. This repeating interaspect has been called a 'double whammy' - a title which graphically conveys its effect. It almost always indicates previous life contact between the parties.

One way interaspects - an outer planet in one chart aspecting a personal planet in the other chart - show a karmic issue that is common to the couple but was not generated between them. In other words, it arose through and with another person, usually but not inevitably in another life. One-way aspects may also have to do with projections that go on within the relationship. For instance, whereas two-way Mars-Pluto contacts could *potentially* indicate that one of the partners murdered the other in a past life, a one-way contact could manifest in such a way that when one partner recounted to the other an experience of being murdered previously, the other partner would feel that he or she was being accused, no matter how unconsciously, of being the murderer. This could hook into that partner's own issues, especially around guilt and potential violence. These could then be carried into the relationship *as though they were a part of it*. Unless the couple were particularly aware of what was going on, these underground feelings would in time erode the relationship.

One-way interaspects may reflect a collective learning opportunity. This is the 'hundredth monkey syndrome'. When enough people have learned a lesson for themselves, it transfers into the collective consciousness and spreads so that other people instinctively know how to do this thing. At a personal level, however, distance from the cause of an issue can enable a couple to find a new way of dealing with it and transfer what they have learned into a relationship where the karma was created between the two people concerned. The Uranus-Venus contact, for example, may indicate that the people concerned are seeking the opportunity to have an intimate relationship but would find it too difficult to develop this with a partner with whom there had been a long history of commitment issues. If the partners learn to give each other the space this aspect needs, and at the same time become closer and more open with each other, then the skills learned can later be transferred into a relationship where the previous interplay between the parties needs to be transformed.

A one-way aspect may also indicate the potential for fresh karma to be set in motion, showing new lessons to be worked on this time around, or qualities to be developed. It can also indicate possibilities to be manifested, especially where it echoes a natal aspect between the same planets in one or more charts. The partner may provide an opportunity for a quality or skill to be incorporated into the relationship and from there into the soul's attributes. This is not always immediately apparent and can arise in what appears to be the most negative of circumstances. If, for instance, there is a natal Venus-Neptune aspect and a one-way synastric aspect between the same planets, the partner with the natal aspect has the opportunity to further develop unconditional love. He or she may find themselves in an alcoholic relationship. In practising true unconditional love, standing back rather than trying to enable change, that partner could aid the alcoholic to find the space that facilitates moving out of a pattern of dependence.

With outer planet to inner planet contacts, one persona usually plays out the role of one planet and the partner the other planet. It is not necessarily the person who has the heavy-planet element of the interaspect who acts out the role of that planet. Saturnine contacts, for example, may manifest either through Saturn playing the heavy or through the personal planet taking on the colour of Saturn and acting out its role of control or limitation. The roles often switch around during the course of a relationship especially as changes are activated by passing transits or progressions coming into closer orb.

Orbs

When assessing the karma inherent in a relationship, it is appropriate to use much wider contacts than the 2° orbs which are usual in synastry. For conjunctions, trines, squares, oppositions and inconjuncts (quincunxes), I use 8° orbs with 6° for a sextile and 2° for minor aspects. But I may expand even these orbs if the natal charts map the issues strongly and if, by doing so, an 'almost-interaspect' becomes a double whammy. So, for example, an interaspect square of 10° would be considered valid if it accompanied a 4° conjunction, especially if there was a natal aspect between the planets involved.

How to Find Interaspects

Finding interaspects is like finding aspects on a natal chart, except that there are two charts to consider:

- Look at the degree in which the Sun falls on one chart.

- Then look at the degrees in which outer planets (Jupiter/ Chiron/Saturn/ Uranus/Neptune/Pluto) fall on the other chart.

- If any of these outer planets fall within eight degrees either side of the Sun-degree, write them down.

- Do the same for the Moon and Venus, Mercury and Mars.

- Then take the Sun, Moon and Venus degrees on the other chart. Look at the degrees in which the outer planets fall on the first chart. If any of these planets fall within eight degrees either side of the Sun, Moon or Venus degree, write them down.

- Now go down the lists and put a cross where the Sun, Moon or Venus in one chart aspects an outer planet in the other chart, and the Sun, Moon or Venus in the other chart aspects the same planet in the first chart. This is a 'double whammy interaspect'.

- Finally, note whether any planets aspect the Nodes across the charts.

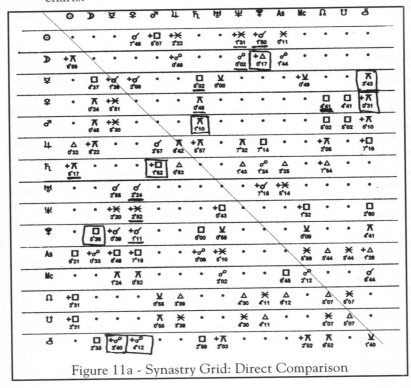

Figure 11a - Synastry Grid: Direct Comparison

```
☉  ☌  ♀  7.8        ♂  ⊼  ☽  0.7        ♆  ✶  ☿  2.3
☉  □  ♂  5.1        ♂  ✶  ☿  5.5        ♆  ✶  ♀  2.9
☉  ✶  ♃  2.4       [♂  ⊼  ♄  1.2]       ♆  □  ♅  0.7
☉  ✶  ♆  1.5      ● ♂  □  ☊  5.0        ♆  □  Mc 1.5
☉  ☌  ♇  1.8        ♂  □  ☋  5.0        ♆  □  ☋  3.0
☉  ✶  As 0.2        ♂  ⊼  ☋  0.2

                                        [♇  □  ☽  5.6]
☽  ⊼  ☉  7.0        ♃  △  ☉  0.5        ♇  ☌  ☿  0.7
☽  ☍  ♃  0.8        ♃  ⊼  ☽  6.4        ♇  ☌  ♀  1.2
☽  ☍  ♆  0.0        ♃  ☌  ♂  3.9        ♇  ⋎  ♄  6.0
[☽  △  ♇  0.3]      ♃  ⊼  ♃  6.7        ♇  ⋎  ♅  1.0
☽  ☍  As 1.7        ♃  ⊼  ♄  5.9        ♇  ⋎  Mc 0.2
                    ♃  ⊼  ♆  7.5        ♇  ⊼  ☋  4.7
                    ♃  □  ♇  7.2
☿  □  ☽  4.6        ♃  ⊼  ☊  2.1
☿  ☌  ☽  1.6        ♃  □  ☋  7.3        As □  ☉  6.3
☿  ☌  ♀  2.2                            As ☍  ☽  0.5
☿  □  ♄  5.0        ♄  △  ♆  1.7        As □  ♀  6.8
☿  ⋎  ♅  0.0        ♄  ☍  ♇  1.4        As □  ♀  7.3
☿  ⋎  Mc 0.8        ♄  △  As 3.4        As ☍  ♄  0.1
[☿  ⊼  ☋  3.7       ♄  △  ☊  7.9        As ✶  ♅  5.2
 ☿  ☍  ☿]                               As ✶  Mc 6.0
♀  ⊼  ☽  0.4                            As △  ☊  3.7
♀  ⊼  ☿  5.9        ♅  ☌  ☿  2.9        As ✶  ☋  3.7
♀  ⊼  ♄  0.8        ♅  ☌  ♀  2.4        As △  ☋  1.5
● ♀ □  ☊  4.7       ♅  ☌  ♇  7.2
♀  □  ☋  4.7        ♅  ✶  As 5.2
[♀  ⊼  ☋  0.5
 ♇  ☍  ♀]
```

Figure 11b - Synastry Table: Direct Comparison

Most computer programmes will quickly calculate interaspects for you either as a grid or as a list. The easiest way to work with these is to underline in red one-way interaspects and put a red box around each-way interaspects, see Figures 11a and b.

Synastry: Main issues

Jupiter: Expansion, mentorship and learning, profligacy, over-indulgence, going out of control and over the top.

Saturn: Debts, duties, burdens, separation, support, self-sufficiency, transcending limitations, finding wisdom.

Chiron: Scapegoating, wounds, healing, integration.

Uranus: Freedom, commitment, magnetism and sexual attraction intimacy, space, individuality, catalyst, transformation.

Neptune: Subtle debts, mystical unity, delusion, illusion, deception, hypnotic fascination, unconditional love.

Pluto: Symbiosis, absorption, manipulation, domination, intensity power and control, rebirth, healing, transmutation.

JUPITER INTERASPECTS

Jupiter interaspects are usually expansive and growth-inducing - although with Jupiter there is always the possibility of going over the top. Where Jupiter contacts a personal planet, Ascendant, Midheaven or the seventh or twelfth house, the Jupiter soul will help attunement to the highest potential and growth possibilities. This contact is particularly helpful in the mentor and mentored or employer and employee relationship as it can assure success in the chosen field. The Jupiter contact is often indicative of former teacher and pupil, or priest and priestess, and the partners are naturally drawn back into a spiritual interaction and a kind of mentorship where one oversees the progress of the other. Between parent and child, this can bring out the best in both parties. It frequently occurs in synastry where a child is disabled or disadvantaged in some way and the parents lovingly support the child to become what he or she is meant to be, rather than trying to force them to be something for which they are not fitted and which may go against the karmic purpose of the incarnation (see chapter 6). When Jupiter is adversely aspected however, or located in Taurus, for example, the karma may be one of intemperance, unrestrained sexuality, or profligacy.

Jupiter-Saturn

In addition to Jupiter to the personal planet interaspects, a Jupiter contact with Saturn can be significant, indicating an old expansion-contraction scenario of spendthrift-miser and similar karma. A typical example was two business partners with a Jupiter-Saturn square between their charts, and a trine from the tenth house Sun in one chart to the seventh house Jupiter in the other. The partner whose Saturn squared the other's Jupiter stated that he considered his role to be to teach his partner the value of money as this was something he had never learnt - in any of his lives. Unfortunately his partner did not see the need for prudence, or budgets, and bankrupted the company twice. Eventually, however, the persistence and faith of the Saturnine partner paid off and they established a successful joint business in which each took equal responsibility, thereby fulfilling the potential of the Jupiter-Sun trine, resolving the dilemma of the Saturn-Jupiter square, and encouraging mutual growth.

SATURN INTERASPECTS

Saturn is the Lord of Karma so it is not surprising that Saturn interaspects feature strongly in karmic relationships that have to do with duty and purpose. One of the most common karmic interaspects within a parent-child, marriage or other love relationship is a Saturn to a personal planet interaspect. Saturn is the glue that holds a relationship together, or the ball and chain that pulls the partners back into old interconnection, depending on the karmic history underlying the contact. People with Saturn interaspects usually feel that they want to be together, but the feeling may be stronger than that. The partners feel they *have* to be together. They owe each other something - at a soul level there is an indissoluble bond.

Saturn can indicate a soul who has in the past had authority over its partner, or to whom there is a sense of debt or responsibility, or a feeling of having to repay something from the past. The old interaction may have involved one partner saving the life of the other, or having metaphorically done so through an act of kindness or allegiance, or of having made a promise in the between-life state to work on something together. The souls want to make the relationship work - even though it may appear to be heavy going at times. Particularly with the double whammy contact, the souls have a desire to see things through, to do all that is necessary. Promises such as 'I'll always look after you/be there for you' may have been carried forward. These may be appropriate in the present life, in which case they may still need reframing somewhat - or they may have been carried over unwittingly and need rescinding completely (see Chapter 9). Saturn can find it difficult to let go of the need to learn a lesson or to fulfil the promise.

On the positive side, relationships tend not to last without Saturn. Some people may find them heavy going, but they see it through to completion, however long that may take.

At the commencement of the Saturnine relationship there is usually a sense of security, of being comfortable and a feeling of each person having known the other 'for ever'. After that first meeting, however, there may be an initial stepping back from the person, a pause for breath, as though the soul knows instinctively that here is someone with whom a relationship will be serious and growth-inducing, and that it may be hard work as well. Saturn contacts are rarely entered into lightly, without some forewarning of what is to come.

Once the commitment is made, however, then the negative aspects of the interconnection usually start to appear. Things get difficult and the so-well-known person suddenly shows traits that are far from comfortable, or reveals hidden baggage. Illness or poverty may intervene. In this situation one of the partners can have a strong sense of duty towards the other: 'I cannot leave him, I must see it through', being a usual comment about the relationship. Unlike the Pisces or Neptune self-sacrificing attitude, which fears or deludes itself that the other person cannot live without them, the Saturnine attitude is practical and pragmatic. With this placement the soul feels committed to the relationship and knows that there is a reason for any problems or stumbling blocks and tries to resolve them or to support the partner moving through them.

The lesson to be learnt by the soul who is undertaking a Saturn role within a partnership, whatever the interaspect, is to let go of fear and authority and to accept and encourage the growth of self-sufficiency and the ability to stand alone in each person concerned. A co-dependent or overly controlling partner, for example, has to learn to stand aside placidly and allow the other soul to control his or her own life, regardless of the mess that may be made of it. A Saturn-attuned person can, even with the best of intentions, be heavy-handed and be perceived by a partner as critical or nagging, even when trying to be constructive and helpful. A child or partner who is sensitised to such things by previous experience may, for instance, perceive him or herself as constantly criticised or called upon to shoulder all the burdens in the family. Lightness of touch has to be developed and humour used to overcome a tendency to moralise. Once some degree of progress has been made, the Saturn soul can experience fear around loss of control of the other person or of the situation. The soul therefore has to transcend its own limitations to ensure a complementary, balanced growth within the relationship.

It is partners with many Saturn interaspects, and especially Saturn-Moon, who are most likely to stay in an unproductive dead relationship long after it would have been more sensible or more appropriate to move on. The partners in such a relationship stay more out of duty or 'because it is the right thing to do', or because they hold strong moralistic beliefs against divorce, than out of love. One partner may demand eternal repayment from the other for sins of the past. The purpose behind the relationship may, however, have been of finding a mutually supportive way to end the relationship and the Saturnine debt.

In its positive aspect, Saturn can bring stability and responsibility to a partnership which allows for repayment of karmic debts in a constructive and soul-enhancing way, or for a steady evolution and integration of positive qualities into the relationship.

Saturn-Sun

With this combination, in addition to the general Saturn issues, the two souls may have made a previous commitment, even when the interaspect only goes one way. They agreed in the between-life state to be together. If the contact goes both ways, the old issue may still be present - especially the belief that 'we have to do this' or 'I owe it to him/her'. One soul often feels that his or her support is vital to other person. With Saturn there is always the underlying sense of duty or debt but it is particularly strong with Sun-Saturn interaspects. One person feels responsible for the other - a role that can interchange as incarnation develops. This interaspect is often seen between parents and children, or in relationships where one person becomes sick or incapacitated. Some heavy karma may be involved, but it is equally likely that this is a case of loving someone enough to help them learn some hard lessons. It is usually impossible to assess the whys and wherefores of this while still in incarnation although it may be accessible to far memory or regression to the between-life state.

A client with an Aquarian Sun conjunction to his wife's Saturn regressed back to a lifetime during which he had been a gaoler for a group of religious prisoners. He had allowed them to escape as he had not felt they had committed a crime and could not see them die. He had later been executed for this but after the regression he commented that at least he had died with a clear conscience. In passing he noted that his present-life wife was amongst the group, although in that lifetime they had had no other contact. Clearly, however, he had saved her life at that point. Their present relationship was a difficult one, but both partners were completely committed to working it out as they felt it was their destiny to be together.

In situations where the interaction is particularly difficult, an old vow or promise has usually carried over inappropriately. Ties need to be cut and the promise reframed in an appropriate way (see Chapter 9). The soul could well be learning that caring about someone is not same as caring for them. Some burdens need to be put aside.

A Saturn-Sun double whammy interaspect may indicate that the souls have been in a parent and child relationship in the past - and may still be working on some of the issues from that time despite the role change. Whilst the parent-child relationship may be supportive for the child, reversing an old pattern, there can also be a replay of the tendency for the child to be valued mainly for what it achieves and consequently feels a pressure to live out the parent's desires. (This usually relates to the father but not always so). The same situation can cross into adult partnerships as the 'child' continues to seek approval and validation from a partner onto whom this need is projected. If a partner also has Sun-Saturn natally, then the partner may be a perfect hook for this projection and may act out the stern parent role. The child - or the adult - may struggle to break free and express his or her own potential with varying degrees of success depending on other aspects involved, both in synastry and natally. When the parent becomes elderly, the situation reverses and the 'child' may have to look closely at whether there was an agreement to care for the parent or whether this is an imposed or implied duty that may, or may not, be appropriate.

The double whammy may indicate a past situation where one soul has been in authority over the other and consequently the souls have decided to balance this out by reversing roles in the present incarnation. On the other hand, old roles may be played out until something intervenes to change them. This is not necessarily a negative or retrogressive step: A Sun in Pisces client volunteered to return to her ex-husband to support him in dealing with cancer. They had remained friendly after the divorce and she wanted to be with him 'to repay a debt'. Her Saturn was conjunct his Sun and opposed by his Moon, her Pluto was trined by his Sun, sextiled by his Moon, squared by his Venus and conjuncted by his North Node, and her Sun trined his Saturn. She felt she needed to understand both his and her own behaviour in the past, and knew that his present approach to his condition could not bring about a recovery. She hoped that by being with him at such a difficult time, she could overcome any past karma left in the relationship and perhaps help him change his attitude and therefore the prognosis of the disease. She did not however make the mistake of thinking she could do it all for him - a common Pisces misconception.

Saturn-Moon

Whilst all the Saturnine karmic issues apply, with the Saturn-Moon interaspect the emotional contact between two souls either in the present life or in the past may be experienced as depressive and heavy, or supportive and caring. It all depends on previous experience. There may be mothering issues coming forward from another life which are lived out again and again until resolved. Unresolved or unfulfilled emotional needs and 'oughts and shoulds' frequently carry forward and are projected into the present interaction. A mother and child or an adult couple who have this interaspect, regardless of whether it repeats both ways, may find that their relationship replays emotional repression, deprivation, and mothering issues together with those of seeking validation, that stem either from childhood in the present life, or from another life entirely. It is as though the soul with this ingrained pattern - usually indicated by a natal Saturn aspect to the Sun or Moon - simply has to go on working through these issues with any available substitute parent. Such a substitute parent will often be strongly Saturnine in character and is therefore frequently unable to fill the deprived soul's needs or facilitate finding the qualities within their own self that would bring about healing for the past. Such a 'parent' may be considerably older or emotionally unavailable or blocked. If the 'needy' soul can learn to parent his or herself, find inner worth and value, and develop autonomy, then the relationship can shift into a more mature partnership in which the partner who is playing out Saturn can loosen and warm up.

If one soul feels it is the other's duty to care for it due to a promise or a karmic treadmill situation, or perhaps because there is recompense or retributive karma, the interplay can be problematic - especially if the other partner has no intuitive awareness of the underlying karma. If both souls feel that they want to love and support each other, however, then this interaspect is constructive and growth enhancing.

For souls with a one-way interaspect, it may be the first

opportunity in many lives for change. If one partner changes too quickly, however, the fear response of Saturn may be triggered in the other partner - who could, of course, be working on the same issue. But two people rarely develop at the same pace. In such a case, the Saturn partner may need to be offered reassurance and encouragement to proceed at his or her own pace. (Some signs find it easier to change than others, so a knowledge of basic astrology is useful here).

All the Saturn issues of duty and dependency come up with this combination but souls handle them differently according to their karma and past experience, and how many emotional expectations from the natal chart are activated by the synastry. How much planning was done in the between-life state is also relevant. If souls discussed things, planned carefully and gave assurances to each other, then although some difficult tasks may be taken on, the souls will feel they want to be together and help each other. If the planning was sloppy, or missed out completely as so often happens with a deeply ingrained treadmill, one soul can feel trapped by the other and will want to escape from the situation. When the other partner senses this, the inherent reaction is to hold on tight and to become more Saturnian in his or her demands. A good sense of humour, especially the ability to laugh at oneself, helps to deal with this interaspect as with all Saturnine contacts.

Saturn-Venus
This is another heavily karmic combination but one which can lead to long and stable partnership because these souls are deeply committed to each other, despite the fact that they have all the usual Saturn issues to work on. Alternatively issues around love and duty may lead to souls staying in a relationship simply because they feel they have to. A promise to love, honour and obey throughout eternity, for instance, may have to be rethought. Retributive or recompense karma too has to end sometime, especially if the partners have become entrenched in a payback rather than a supporting scenario.

With a contact between Saturn and Venus, the relationship may involve one partner - frequently the male, and not necessarily the Saturn partner - becoming a financial burden on the other, or developing a chronic illness or other dependency that may require an unusual degree of support. This interaspect is common in the charts of alcoholics or addicts and their partners and may be offering the partner an opportunity to repay something from the past by standing by, and offering support, whilst the addict goes through a karmic lesson.

Souls with this interaspect can also be working on intimacy and commitment issues - especially when combined with Uranus-Venus. There may be a need to compensate for past coldness. The two people concerned may be stuck in a pattern of lack of love with an emphasis on duty or security or an inability to express feelings. A couple could be bringing forward issues from a loveless marriage to rework and learn the value of devotion for instance. When the souls do find deeply committed love, the relationship then gives great satisfaction to both parties.

With Saturn it can be helpful to look beyond the Sun, Moon and Venus. Mercury and Mars interaspects also indicate specific relationship karma:

Saturn-Mercury

With this interaspect, one person's mind could have been overwhelmed by Saturn in the past, whenever that was, leading to situations where one soul is constantly criticised, mentally bullied or overpowered by the other and forced to follow a set of standards and behaviour patterns that do not innately belong to that soul. The two people concerned may have been parent and child, teacher and pupil, guru and disciple, or employer and employee. On occasions they may have been married before - usually indicated by the double whammy interaspect. The challenge is for both souls to develop independent minds, accepting each other's need to grow and learn in individual ways, putting aside criticism and beliefs regarding 'the ways things ought to be'.

This particular interaspect is often seen when both people are living by what one person's inner critic finds acceptable, or are following one partner's inner voice rather than each developing their own inner voice. If the mental control can be loosened sufficiently for each to listen to their own soul, they may find that they individually have very different beliefs. In this case, great tolerance is needed. Such a situation throws up an enormous challenge if the aspect is between parent and child or if a parent and child interplay has been projected onto a partner. People who have always been told how to behave or what to believe often find it difficult to think for themselves initially, and may need guidance from outside the relationship if they are to become autonomous.

Saturn-Mars or Pluto-Mars

Specific issues around will and power arise with these interaspects as well as the more general karmic issues. Both of these contacts can indicate that there has been abuse or violence in other lives and it is common for past relationships to have been of the 'master and slave' variety. There may also have been psychological pressure or covert violence rather than outright hostility. One person is used to having power over the other, controlling their life. Now the challenge is to let go, to allow that person to develop their life according to their soul's need.

Saturn or Pluto in interaspect to Mars can bring in the possibility of old violence resurfacing, lessons around the use of the will being reworked, and conflict emerging within the relationship. This can result in both a marriage-type of partnership, in which the essence of the interaction is fear and control, or it can surface within a business partnership in which the underlying conflict can make decision-taking a dangerous pathway. No matter what the present life relationship, with such a contact one soul may feel that the other has all the power and the authority, and that self-assertion is something to be feared as it may cause the underlying violence of these planetary combinations to explode. However, the issue of assertion and of the right use of the will within the partnership is basic to the interconnection and has to be tackled at some stage. For this reason, it is often easier to work through one-way aspects before moving out into a relationship invoking each-way contacts where the personal input from other lives would trigger a much deeper fear and the possibility of a repeat of earlier violent interaction. Even if there has been no past life contact, violence may be part of the karma-in-the-making between the parties.

This interaspect shows up in the synastry between the Tsar of Russia and Lenin (there is some doubt as to Lenin's correct date of birth but the Mars aspect stands for either date). The Tsar's Mars is trine Lenin's Saturn, and his Pluto is conjunct Lenin's Mercury, indicating the possibility of an old violence and mental manipulation or psychological pressure underlying the current interplay - although this would not necessarily be personal between them. The Tsar had a Neptune-Moon conjunction in the Aries eighth house, indicating the potential for a sacrifice of himself and a confusion in perceiving the extent of change and its effect on his life. He may have believed himself to be infallible and immortal with a divine right to rule. Lenin had Uranus conjunct the North Node in Cancer in the eighth, symbolising the potential for revolution and the sharing of new ideas of equality and freedom. When these two came together, there was an inevitable clash as each fought for control - just as there would be in a present-life relationship with these interaspects.

CHIRON INTERASPECTS

Chiron indicates a karmic wound and an opportunity to integrate the energy or qualities of a planet it aspects. These interaspects can be the key to a whole new way of relating. The challenge for any interaspect between Chiron and an inner planet is to heal pain from the past in the area indicated by the personal planet. The Sun and the Moon usually indicate karma carried forward from when the couple were in a parent-child or emotional relationship; Venus may indicate an old emotional hurt, Mercury a mental hurt, and Mars painful issues around will or assertion. When the interaspects operate each way, the wound was inflicted or created between the two people concerned who have decided in the between-life state, that the time has come to heal the cause. Present life scenarios may rerun the wounding before they are ready to resolve it. One person is offered an opportunity of making up for past hurts, the other of forgiving and letting them go.

Chiron has strong links to the scapegoat, and the karma between a couple with repeating interaspects may be where one partner was scapegoated by the other, or where one partner took something on for the other - a more positive form of this interaction. With this scenario, recompense or reward karma may feature in the relationship. In the present life, the partners or the parents need to avoid bringing scapegoating into the relationship. A mother who makes her children the focus of her world and in the process holds the child culpable for the sacrifices made - or the wife who does the same to her husband - create a situation of karmic enmeshment that requires healing. Blame or shame is just as wounding as emotional rejection or abuse and these may feature in present or previous lives.

If the Chiron interaspects are one-way, one person could be learning how to heal on a personal level before going into a relationship with individual or mutual wounding attached. Such healing can take place either by confronting the issues or, more gently, by simply experiencing what it is like to be in a loving, accepting relationship - something the soul might not have enjoyed for many lifetimes. If the interaspect relates to the present life, then deep wounding could take place and karma be set in motion. In a more positive manifestation, one partner could support the other through a major illness or other life-changing situation. The partners can also be the trigger for shadow aspects of the self to be integrated, or for potentials to be developed within the context of the relationship. At its highest level, this contact can be initiatory: the old wounded self dies and falls away to make way for the new, reborn Self.

URANUS INTERASPECTS

Uranus interaspects to the Sun, Moon and Venus have to do with freedom/commitment and intimacy dilemmas. One or both of the partners, depending on the natal chart, will usually have difficulty settling down or committing to a relationship and may have issues about opening up to a partner. It is common for one person to be highly committed and the other to be aloof, and then for the roles to suddenly switch around. Where the partners do get it together, one partner may insist on considerable freedom within the relationship as closeness feels more like suffocation. If the other partner then tries to insist on more commitment, the first one has a strong desire to take off.

Uranus interaspects often accompany Neptune or Pluto interaspects, bringing to a head the need to break free from a suffocating or illusory situation. On the other hand, Neptune or Pluto may represent the fact that the souls are trying to find a way to resolve the commitment issues and be together. If this is the case, then it can be difficult to assess from the charts themselves which will be the stronger need - natal charts throw some light on the matter but therapy or counselling may be needed to fully explore the complex interaction. Couples handle such contacts differently, and much will depend on how far the relationship has progressed in the current life. If it is simply going around the same old treadmill, the Uranian need to break away will become more urgent.

The past interconnection shown between Uranus-Venus or Moon contacts in particular relates to intense, passionate but sporadic sexual encounters. The scenario could well be a mistress situation, a husband or lover who goes away to war or who travels frequently, or a couple who cannot live together but cannot live apart, and a married man and his unattainable 'love'. Uranus interaspects can also relate to a couple who have had difficulty in sustaining a close, intimate relationship in the past and who have never learned to be emotionally open and trusting with each other. The relationship is characterised by aloofness or unpredictability. At one moment the partner may appear to be loving, and then will shut him or herself away. For such a couple, freedom may mean the opportunity to pursue sexual relationships outside the partnership, a so-called open marriage, or that one or both parties is not free to commit fully. The past life scenario could also be one of coldness and separation within an arranged marriage, or extreme independence or dependence of one party on the other. There may also have been a considerable difference in social status, making it impossible for lovers to marry. In some instances, Uranus interaspects, especially with Mercury, could relate to two friends from another life who did not venture into a love relationship then and who are cautious about doing so in the present regardless of how attracted and comfortable they feel together now.

Uranus interaspects with Venus in particular frequently indicate that one or both of the souls, depending on whether the interaspect repeats, never really became committed to the relationship as a long term event. There would be occasional, intensely exciting contact, particularly on the sexual level, alternating with long periods of separation due to war or other manifestations of Uranian chaos. Uranus interaspects to the Sun, Moon, Venus or Mars can all indicate a tremendously strong sexual attraction, which is irresistible, and yet even with this magnetic pull there can be a powerful 'can't live with you, can't live without you' theme. This may have run through many lives as the souls are attracted and repelled time and again.

In the present life, the couple with these interaspects face the challenge of being two individuals who come together in a committed, close and loving relationship but who allow each other the space to be themselves, and to do their own thing as and when necessary. Two clients of mine both had dispassionate, uncommitted Aquarius on the seventh house cusp in their natal charts, along with Uranus-Venus and Mercury aspects. In their synastry, there were repeating each-way Uranus-Venus interaspects. When they met, on holiday, there was an instant sexual attraction and they discovered many shared interests - some quite unusual as befits Uranus. Indeed, it was the astrology book she was reading that brought them together! She treated it as a holiday romance, but to her surprise he called her as soon as she returned home.

Living several hundred miles apart, they met for occasional weekends during which they frantically tried to make up the missing time. It was intense and frenetic and could not be sustained. They broke up. He moved much nearer to her and they got back together again. As he had a job where he lived in and had to be on call, they still spent relatively little time together. When they did spend longer periods, they travelled and so received the constant stimulation that this interaspect so enjoys. He then moved to another location - and found another relationship. When that broke apart, they tried living together again. For much of the time he was in the accommodation that went with his job and the relationship worked reasonably well, but she was worried he was not as committed as she was. A friend eventually pointed out to her that he was actually more committed than she was - it was her who talked of breaking up as she felt she could not sustain the uncertainty. Both had huge issues around intimacy and neither found it easy to talk to the other on emotional matters, but gradually they became more committed to each other. By this time they were great friends as well as lovers.

A turning point was reached when they bought a house together, which to her was a potent symbol of commitment and after many emotional upheavals, they finally learnt to talk about feelings. After seventeen years together, they are now in a stable partnership that encompasses many unconventional interests. Each gives the other space to pursue separate interests, and yet they are able to be immersed for long periods together in their mutual pursuits. Their past life contacts involved at least two lives where they were of a different status to each other, and some of strong intellectual companionship, but, so far, they have not discovered a past life marriage. In their present life, they still have to take this momentous step.

In the present life Uranian contacts may be lived very intensely, but the frantic pace cannot continue or the relationship will burn itself out too quickly. The other major enemy of the Uranian relationship is boredom. This is not an interaspect for twenty-four hours a day togetherness. Uranus interaspects need more stimulation than most partnerships offer, and part of the lesson is to recognise that, just because a Uranian partner goes off to do his or her own thing, this does not mean that infidelity will inevitably happen. Despite its commitment dilemma, unfaithfulness is rarely the issue. Compromise is needed in order to build into the relationship the freedom to explore other areas of life whilst retaining the secure base of a committed relationship. The two people mentioned previously solved some of their problem by travelling extensively alone, often in connection with their work, as well as together. The karmic lesson is to build a unit consisting of two individuals coming together to form the relationship, to which both are committed, or to break free from the past attraction once and for all.

The soul intention for Uranus interaspects may have been to let go of the other person, finally separating and moving on. If this is the case, Uranus rarely looks back longingly - so lovers who hope a partner will return may have a long wait. But then again, this being unpredictable Uranus, they could well return out of the blue. A soul who commits out of duty is trapped, but a soul who commits from a place of freedom can grow through that new way of relating.

If the interaspect arises between parent and child, the parent has to learn to let go of the child and allow the child to live his or her own life. A child may be compelled to forcibly break free particularly if there are also symbiotic Pluto interaspects across the charts. When the Uranian interaspects are between members of a family, this often indicates an interaction from another life or is reworked in childhood and then carried over into adult life and outside relationships. At its extreme, it may indicate a soul who has decided it is time to look for its soul-family rather than stay with biological ties.

A client's Sun-Pluto conjunction in Cancer conjoined her daughter's Uranus. This was only one facet of an extremely complex chart interplay and a network of past relationships, but it was found that the mother had been an all-powerful Mother Superior and the daughter one of her novices. The relationship had been an immensely old one, stretching back to Egypt and beyond when it involved a close love bond between two sisters. In the present life the daughter had a conflict between seeking a close contact with her mother (a natal Pluto-Venus aspect giving her a desperate craving for more and more love) and needing to free herself from her mother's authority (her Uranus conjuncting her mother's Sun-Pluto in Cancer).

This dilemma was reflected in her relationship with her lover, who was anxious to settle down and have a family, and in the Uranus interaspects with his chart. Once she had resolved her feelings about her mother and gained personal freedom by cutting the psychic umbilical cord between them, she was able to commit herself to marriage. It was suggested that she should negotiate a 'marriage contract' which would set out and honour both her need for her own space within the relationship and the somewhat unconventional type of interaction she required in order to function freely.

Uranus-Sun

Whilst all the Uranian issues are closely bound up with Uranus-Sun interaspects, with this combination the past life interconnection could indicate close yet platonic companions, especially those who share revolutionary ideas. It can also indicate people who are strongly attracted but come from different walks of life. An attachment to freedom is often featured, either as an ideal or as a way of life and love. Uranian contacts have a tendency to be different to the norm, sometimes to the extent of defying convention altogether. Often these people have been unable to marry or to be together in a stable partnership. The souls may not have been particularly reliable where each other were concerned, or one person may have consistently let the other down or failed to meet obligations. When a love bond is a feature of the past, it is rarely an on-going day to day affair. It is much more likely to be transitory and yet intense. It may also be impersonal, as when one is the mistress of the other or the wife to whom a man has had to commit but to whom he is unattached emotionally.

Uranus-Moon

In addition to other Uranian dilemmas experienced in relationship, in other lives emotional intimacy has been particularly difficult for this interaspect and the souls carry forward an inability to surrender to each other. Individuality will have been more important than partnership. There may have been an absolute dependence or a steely independence in the past interplay, neither of which condition allowed for any real emotional sharing. One partner could have been emotionally detached from the other and was experienced as aloof and unreachable or even alienated from the family.

As this interaspect insists on freedom, one partner may have taken on an unconventional lifestyle which put the relationship outside society. One or both souls has usually built up a strong shell to protect inner feelings and, as with the natal aspect, may give off a message: 'I don't need love'. As intimacy is problematic, the souls are often attracted to each other when one or both is unavailable. If both are available, then commitment becomes an on-going issue with both taking turns to be the uncommitted one, or else the unavailability is projected onto the other person.

Uranus-Venus

Although all the facets of Uranian relationship will have made themselves felt in the past, and will continue to feature in the present, this combination is the most likely to have had powerful, intense, passionate relationships which were not translated into marriage or other committed forms of relationship. There will have been a distinct tendency for one soul to refuse to take responsibility for the other in previous lives - which may also carry over into the present life. This is particularly so if the contact is between parent and child. The child may find him or herself shunted between parents following a marriage breakdown, or may find him or herself the recipient of unstable, unpredictable mothering - in which case the soul may decide that leaving home as soon as feasible is necessary for the child's own sanity.

If there is a double whammy, souls with this interaspect often rush into marriage after meeting up again, only to find that the old issues come up to the surface equally quickly. Also likely is magnetic attraction which goes nowhere because one partner is a commitment phobic who simply cannot enter into long term relationship. As a result, the couple find themselves in a dilemma of needing to separate and yet wanting to remain together. There is a powerful attraction-repulsion mechanism at work here as well as deeply ingrained freedom/commitment issues. Such relationships often feature several separations and returns. Marriage, divorce and remarriage are common (see Chapter 8).

A couple with this interaspect face the challenge of being in a committed, close and loving relationship but also of allowing each other the space to do their own thing as and when necessary. Expressed positively, Uranus brings about radical transformation in former patterns of relating.

NEPTUNE INTERASPECTS

As Neptune moves comparatively slowly, many souls share Neptune interaspects. A single one-way Neptune interaspect is, therefore, not necessarily significant, except on a collective level, unless it is backed up by natal aspects and other factors that reflect Neptunian issues. It may well be that whole generations are working on such issues and it makes little difference who they are experienced with, the learning process will go on. When the aspects repeat each-way, however, the souls will probably be part of the same soul group.

Neptune interaspects are idealistic and perfectionist and usually have the sense, if not the actuality, of a soulmate contact. They are characterized by longings and a desire to merge back into the beloved, to become one again. Such relationships can be deeply spiritual, indicating a soul-bond with a connection that has crossed time at a deep soul level. Neptune debts are those of love, they go beyond duty or reparation.

However, Neptune contacts may also be illusory - or confused. The relationship may be perceived by one partner as blissful, when it is far from that. It may not actually exist at all - it can be all in the mind! Neptune interaspects are the most likely to point to an 'if only' life.

Experienced in regression, such lives have a certain quality of wistfulness rather than a deeply felt emotional charge. They are fantasies that existed in the head of one of the people concerned at the time. The soul so wanted it to be that way that it was remembered as though it actually happened. So, for instance, if a spinster had romantic dreams of her future husband, they could later be remembered as though they actually happened. This can be seen also in the accounts of women looking back to a 'fiance lost in the war'. The relationship may actually have been a casual friendship, but the lack of suitable men after the war could have given this a gravity that it did not have at the time. If someone is in a difficult marriage, they look back to other suitors and fantasize how it would have been to marry him or her, and again it becomes 'fact' with the passage of time.

Neptune interaspects are problematic because, when the souls are extremely close or when there is a powerful fantasy at work, boundaries are diffuse and ill-defined. One or both souls involved may feel part of the same whole - as though they have come from the same soul or soul group. But this is not always the case, although it may be. Telepathy is common between people with Neptune contacts, particularly with Neptune-Mercury interaspects that repeat both ways. One soul knows what goes on in the other's head. This is fine when both partners want to be in that kind of relationship but it can cause enormous difficulties, as we shall see. The lesson in the present life for souls with Neptune interaspects may be to live separately - a painful prospect for Neptune.

Neptune represents an extremely subtle karmic interconnection in which there is at first sight a recognition of soulmate contact by one of the people concerned. Unfortunately this does not always turn out to be the case in the present incarnation, although it may relate back to another life. Nor does it mean that a couple are destined to be soulmates in the present incarnation. Neptune contacts to the Sun, Moon, Venus and Mercury can bring an almost mystical unity or hypnotic quality to the relationship, and telepathic contact can continue even when the partners are physically separated. Indeed, this can be one of the most difficult aspects of the relationship - or lack of relationship. For instance, a client's Neptune was conjunct an ex-lover's Moon which in turn sextiled her Pluto-Saturn conjunction. Her Moon was square her ex-lover's Neptune. She described the relationship:

'It is nearly six years since I met this man and three years since we broke up. For six years I have not known a single day without him being 'around' in some way. I don't seem to be able to get rid of him. This was the best and worst relationship I have had - it still hurts. I saw very little of him.'

In the past there may have been strong spiritual and psychic bonds forged through early temple training, (it was a characteristic of many ancient religions that couples would make a mystic marriage). If this is the case, then tie cutting at a spiritual level may be needed before separation can be achieved on the earth plane. Couples may also have been in a contemplative order together, or experienced many loving incarnations in which there were no boundaries or separation. The psychic contact and communication on the spiritual level continues in the present incarnation despite physical distance and, in many cases, the active opposition of one partner to the whole idea. I have seen cases where one soul is not in incarnation at all, but the contact continues. (In such cases it is often helpful to look at the synastry with the death chart if known).

Neptune interaspects are prone to seeing things as they were rather than as they are now. So, a soul that has been close to someone in another incarnation does not see the new personality that has been put on, and expects that the soulmate will behave as before. Past lives may not feature at all if a desperate need for love fastens onto someone with whom there is a one-way Neptune interaspect.

For these reasons, Neptune interaspects can indicate a high degree of illusion or delusion, or incorporate deep deception, particularly when the soul taking the role of Neptune is deluding or deceiving itself and projects this into the relationship. With Neptune contacts the soul may squirm for a while and try to avoid the truth, but it will be brought up repeatedly until it penetrates the soul's consciousness, and the partner is seen clearly for what he or she *is now*.

A client whose Venus was conjunct her ex-husband's Neptune said that on first meeting she had been wary of him, but soon 'fell under his spell' and believed that 'this was the most wonderful relationship I could ever have. It seemed so perfect ... I felt as though I had known him for ever, we were meant for each other.' He had a hypnotic effect on her, (she was undergoing a Neptune transit to her Moon at the time and was particularly open to emotional delusion), and when, six months after the marriage, she suddenly realised the extent of her illusions about him she 'felt just as though someone had snapped their fingers and brought her out of a hypnotic trance.'

The relationship had consisted of lies and deception on his part, and by the time she found out the truth he had conned her out of a considerable amount of money in the form of loans to get him back on his feet again. She had agreed to lend him the money because she felt a subtle sense of debt to him and wanted to help - the all-pervasive influence of the Neptunian contact.

'Wanting to help' is typical of Neptune contacts as is the feeling that one person would die for the other. The debt is different to that felt by Saturn. Whereas a Saturn contact feels that it has an obligation out of duty, the Neptune contact volunteers out of love.

Partners, or parent and child, with Neptune interaspects are prone to projections (see Chapter 9). 'Good' qualities may be projected because this is what the soul wants to find in a partner or parent - with consequent disillusionment if they do not actually embody the qualities. This may relate to qualities the partner or parent had in a previous-life relationship, or to what the soul considers desirable. The soul may be so eager to find these qualities that no analysis is given as to whether they actually exist. The soul simply assumes that this so-beloved soul must be that way. Neptune does tend to look at relationships through rose-tinted glasses, so the partner is 'perfect' and 'all I've ever dreamed of' - until reality intervenes. Or the parent is 'wonderful' and 'marvellous' - but can rarely be pinned down. The soul may also project his or her own positive qualities into the relationship - or quasi-relationship - if these have not been owned and integrated as *mine*. The challenge here is to recognise who has exactly what qualities and to look at how each soul can develop missing qualities for itself.

It is equally common, however, for undesirable qualities to be recognised where they do not exist in the partner because this is what the Neptunian soul expects to find in a relationship. So a soul who expects infidelity may accuse or suspect a faithful partner of unfaithfulness because the soul has experienced this in the past and projects the resultant fears and suspicions in any relationship. On the other hand, Neptunian people are highly intuitive and may pick up on fleeting thoughts and feelings which the partner had no intention of putting into practice. The Neptune-attuned soul may read those feelings as actual, concrete experience, and thus provoke unwarranted guilt in the partner.

Guilt is a common feature of Neptune interaspects. It may stem from projections, illusions or deceptions - whether from the present or past lives. It can also arise from not meeting the impossibly high dreams of perfection to which Neptune is prone. If a partner has a romantic illusion of what love should be, and a relationship fails to live up to this, both parties may feel guilt at the apparent failure. They may not perceive the solid achievements that they have put in place because these play no part in Neptunian dreams.

Neptune wants to merge, to be one, and there may be little or no room for individuality or separation in the Neptune vision of perfection. Here again, a sense of failure may quickly create guilt because the parties have not totally merged. This is especially difficult for blunt, straightforward sun-signs such as Taurus or Sagittarius, who do not subscribe to the Neptunian picture of wedded bliss. However, if Neptune interaspects are a feature of the charts, there may be an unconscious yearning for this blissful state - which would suffocate the independent sun-sign partner should it actually manifest. Such a conflict between what Neptune seeks and how the Sun or Venus placements wish to meet relationships is powerful. How, and indeed if, it is resolved will depend on how the couple have handled their relationship(s) in the past.

The deceptive nature of Neptune can be apparent in different types of interaction, particularly those which do not appear to have an underlying love bond. A typical example was a client whose boss at a new company had promised her the world: a new car, a good salary, travel and excellent promotion prospects. When these failed to materialise, she looked at the aspects between their charts: his Neptune squared her mutable Sun-Mercury, her Neptune was inconjunct his mutable Sun which in turn was conjunct her Uranus. She recognised the situation both as an old pattern reasserting itself and karma-in-the-making, often a feature of mutable placements, and changed her job rapidly. Anyone working for someone with whom there are Neptune interaspects would be well advised to have everything clearly set out on paper first. You then have something to back up what will be widely differing versions of 'what we agreed'! Repeating Neptune interaspects to Venus or the Sun or the Moon often indicate an unrealistic idealisation of one of the partners, people or parents involved. This is based on the soul's past interaction with that person and the expectation that they will remain the same, leaving no room for change, human frailty or fallibility. This idealisation leaves the soul open to disappointment and disillusionment. A Scorpio client with a fifth house Venus-Neptune conjunct an old friend's Neptune had a past life extrapolation into the present which was unsatisfactory to say the least:

> 'He's been in and out of my life like a shadow, going away for long periods of time and never making any attempt to get close to me. Recently he contacted me again. After having been a drunken drifter for too long, he's changed his life around - seemingly overnight - and now has a house in the country and a talent for the stock market. He is an extremely complex, secretive, clever individual (reflecting her own Scorpionic qualities) and I feel a very deep bond with him. For years I cried lonely tears, only wishing for some receptivity on his part. Am I meant to suffer unrequited love or are we in the fullness of time meant to be together?'

His Aquarian Venus conjoined her South Node and she was being pulled back to the past with a yearning for, and illusion of, perfection reflected through a Neptune-Moon interaspect. The reality, however, was more likely to be that his detached Aquarian Venus would never give her the close and fulfilling union she was seeking. It seemed like a classic case of unrequited love, and for her own growth she would need to let go of the past, grieve for what could not be, and then move on.

Neptune contacts can also indicate a degree of collusion between the partners, whether conscious or not. Reality takes on a different colour, usually rose tinted, when imbued with Neptune. A woman will ignore and pretend not to know that her husband is seeing another woman, for instance, because it would break her picture of the perfect relationship. The partners, or parents, of addicts often collude with the addict (see Chapter 6).

Notwithstanding, a couple with Neptune interaspects have the potential to make a bond which not only develops unconditional love and compassion, but which also takes the souls to a new depth of interconnectedness, beginning the task of union with the divine whole.

Neptune-Sun

In addition to the general Neptune issues, Neptune-Sun has some specific issues to meet. This combination usually feels like soulmate connection, even with one-way interaspects. The person is so well known from the first glance, it can feel 'like we've been together for ever'. This may be so, they may have been part of the same soul group and lived through many lifetimes together, but unfortunately this is not always the case.

Double-whammy souls have almost certainly been together life after life in close relationship. Each soul knows intuitively how the other thinks and feels - and may expect that, because the other soul has always been a certain way, it will continue. In the present life, the soul has put on a new personality, however, so these in-built expectations may not always be realised. Checking that intuitive perceptions are valid helps to separate past from present.

With each-way interaspects, a deep soul-bond may have become suffocating and needs to be severed. This can be difficult because the Neptunian bond frequently carries on when two people physically separate. It operates at a mental, emotional and spiritual level and has to be cut on all those levels if the souls are to exist independently.

This contact can also indicate souls who have come back for

a spiritual purpose, or so that one soul can support or facilitate the other during spiritual evolution. It brings up issues of how much help is appropriate, and when it would be more apposite to step back and allow the other soul to learn a lesson no matter how hard. The Neptune-Sun combination, as with such so much Neptune, is a challenge to practice unconditional love.

In either men or women, Neptune-Sun contacts can also be working through an idealised picture of male energy and of the fathering archetype. As with the natal aspect, Neptune-Sun interaspects may bring into the relationship an elusive father figure for whom the partner becomes a surrogate, and with whom a soul is seeking to merge. Many issues that more properly belong with the biological father or with a father from another life are then subsumed into the interplay. It can be a difficult task to sift out what is projection and what is real. All illusions and delusions have to be revealed, especially in partnership, and a more realistic expectation developed. This is not an easy task when nebulous Neptune is involved, and the soul with natal issues to reinforce the interaspect may find itself experiencing several relationships which work through different facets of the internalised, ideal, picture. They may meet one facet with one person and then the opposite with the next for instance. The soul also has to withdraw any projections put upon the relationship.

Neptune-Moon

As the Moon represents the past, there can be considerable emotional karma between a couple with this aspect, in addition to the more generalised Neptune issues. They are likely to be dealing with deeply ingrained emotional expectations and needs, many of which will be to do with being let down in the past - a feeling diametrically opposed to all the wonderful Neptunian fantasies of perfect togetherness that also come into the relationship. Each soul wants to know whether it can trust its emotions around this person, who feels so familiar and yet slippery. Will it be the wonderful blissful union that the soul hopes or will illusion and delusion mar the picture once more? How much can the soul trust its intuitions and how much probing is needed to find truth? So often in the past the Neptune-Moon contact has been deceived into feeling that everything is wonderful when it was not, especially if this is a double whammy case. Even if it is not, one or both souls still carry the archetype of deception, and recognise, at some deep level, the possibility of lies and deceits intervening as in previous relationships with other Neptunian souls.

This interaspect contains an idealised picture of feminine energy. Men with the natal aspect carry high expectations of purity and perfection which they project out onto women in their life through the interaspect. Even without the natal aspect, men can project their mothering issues onto the partner, especially if the reality in childhood was disappointing or too well fulfilled - as in the chosen child syndrome. Women who are expected to play out the ideal mother role find that it seriously interferes with their role as wife. Confusing relationships result as libido and lust have little place in the romantic Neptunian ideal relationship. With Neptune, the relationship may appear to be close and loving, and yet have blocks around sexual contact. It may be difficult to see partner a clearly as Neptunian obscurities and fantasies intrude into the reality of the relationship. There are few boundaries between the partners and feelings can be passed without speaking. As the Moon is so much a part of the past, the lesson for souls with this interaspect may be to separate, however painful that may be.

Neptune-Venus

As with all Neptune interaspects, the challenge here is to love the partner unconditionally and yet maintain the space and sense of self that allows no violation of boundaries. The difference with Venus is that a relationship rarely ends, or flourishes constructively, until the ability to love unconditionally has been tried and tested. Whether with a one-way or repeating interaspect, the souls carry forward the tendency from other lives to allow anything and everything to happen: to be walked all over because that was what passed for unconditional love in the past. 'If you loved me, you would allow this' is a deeply imprinted message. Problems are encountered if the partner has in the meantime developed the ability to say 'No' and to establish boundaries. The soul who is acting out the Neptunian role will push for the kind of collusive, delusive, co-dependent relationship that passed for love in the past, and the partner will have to resist. If these abilities have not been internalised, the soul may give in to the pressure, taking the couple back either into personal karma or into familiar territory.

This interaspect also has the ability to see the pearl in the heart of the other person, to tune into what might be rather than what is. As a result, pressure may be put on one partner to change. What would be more appropriate, as it would leave space for the partner to change and yet avoid manipulation, is to leave space for new possibilities to unfold through accepting the partner as he or she is. This can be incredibly healing and, if practised from the heart, may in itself bring about profound change in both partners. The challenge, as always, is to true unconditional love.

The past pattern for Neptune Venus interaspects may have been one of collusion and deception, but this is not always so. Idolisation and idealisation are equally common. The tendency as with natal Venus-Pluto is to place the beloved onto a pedestal and not see them for the fallible, mortal human being they really are. Notwithstanding, there can be enormous soul love between the parties, especially with a double whammy contact. If supported by Saturn interaspects to ground in reality, the relationship has every chance of success. If it has not, it may remain a beautiful dream or an unattainable fantasy in which one longs for the other but the feeling is not reciprocated.

Couples with Neptune-Venus interaspects often forget to do the between-life planning clearly and carefully. They just assume that their great love will pull them back together, or that next time that elusive lover will be theirs. They may want to be together but somehow find that they are married to someone else, or that they are mother and son, and so on. If this is the case, regression back to the between-life state to see exactly what each intended can be helpful as can reframing any promises to be together for eternity and the like.

With a one way interaspect, one person may yearn for the other and be met with coldness and disinterest. This can also occur with the double whammy if the planning was careless. Looking into past lives frequently reveals that a lover was unattainable in the past, and one soul made a vow to be together next time, without consulting the other. This can be enough to pull them back into incarnation together, but not enough to make the soul who did not make the vow believe that they should be life partners. On the other hand, the two may have been life partners through many incarnations but have decided that this time, for their individual growth, they need to be separate. Things are rarely straightforward when elusive Neptune is involved.

Neptune contacts with Venus can, however, be extremely

healing through the unconditional love and acceptance of frailty which allows the 'weaker' partner to be loved for what he or she is in a non-judgemental way. This can pave the way to self-acceptance and self-love by the other, who thereby gains inner strength. As John and Kris Amodeo explain:

> 'By accepting and loving others as they presently are, instead of holding back until they meet our idealised images or romantic expectations, they may feel a sense of safety that finally enables them to release the pain of past hurts. These accumulated bodily held hurts and frustrations, which often originate from previous rejection or unreciprocated love, have an opportunity to heal within the context of relationship characterised by a growing sense of trust. Such a relationship may then become a therapeutic one in that we are resolving conflicts and growing towards a healthier, happier dimension of being.'[1]

Neptune-Mercury

Neptune interaspects to Mercury frequently have deep intuitive insight into the partner's motivation and desires, whilst maintaining secrecy about the soul's own. There may be a history of lies and deceptions, and the couple share the need to learn the value of open and honest communication. On the other hand, this interaspect can indicate strongly telepathic qualities and a meeting of minds on the level of spiritual ideals and values. This aspect is frequently seen between couples, not necessarily in sexual relationship, who work together as healers, counsellors and teachers - roles for which, if the double whammy is present, they have had considerable training in other lives.

A Neptune-attuned partner may also have an understanding of its partner which can be helpful when working on the inner levels, particularly with spiritual intentions or psychological patterns. It frequently arises in love relationships when there is a mental affinity that goes beyond words. Such an aspect always features when a client says: 'He feels that I have a line into his head, that I understand him in a way no one else can, not even himself.' The partner may not always be too comfortable with this, feeling invaded and lacking in privacy but, if there is an openness to working on him or herself, then this can be an extremely helpful aspect. A meeting between Neptune and Mercury may be the catalyst required to set someone on to the inner transformational or spiritual pathway.

PLUTO INTERASPECTS

This combination can be one of the most entrenched and difficult to break out from. The karma is extremely powerful, often of the treadmill variety. The souls involved have been here many times before, although not necessarily together. Pluto is a generational planet and a soul may be working on universal issues through interaspects with people born within the same decade or so, especially if wide orbs are used. There could be a Plutonian undercurrent which pervades any relationship in which a Pluto interaspect occurs, regardless of whether the souls have met before or are working on Plutonian karma themselves. Power issues and how to empower people are a universal theme, as is the abuse and misuse of power, and cosmic evolution requires that these themes be addressed. The interaspect is particularly significant when it is a double whammy with close orbs, and where it is supported by similar natal issues in the charts of one or both partners.

Pluto is the planet of extremes and is intent on getting to the underlying core so that it can be transmuted. Therefore, Plutonian relationships tend to be both extreme and intense, often having an edge of compulsion and obsession to them. Such relationships often entail a trip down into the unconscious or to taboo places where other souls fear to tread so that outworn patterns can be brought to the surface for transformation. The Greek god Pluto and his consort Persephone, whom he abducted into the underworld, almost certainly had double whammy Pluto-Venus aspects between them. There is an almost alchemical process at work here. At times the interplay can seem to be destructive, and then transformation takes place and the relationship becomes exceedingly positive. Persephone transmogrified from an innocent young girl to a mature woman who held the keys to Hades. Having regained her own power, she was a guide for the souls of the living who wished to venture into Pluto's taboo realm to pluck its treasure. All the great heroes of Greek myth consulted Persephone before setting out on their initiation trials.

As with all manifestations of Pluto, it can be extremely difficult to see exactly what is going on - Pluto seldom removes his helmet of invisibility when he makes himself felt in a relationship. He is recognisable, eventually, by the effect the relationship has on the soul's progress. Even when the relationship is, apparently, negative, Pluto can reveal treasure. As Stephen Arroyo puts it:

'What I am experiencing... may be of great value to me. He may be pulling me down into the depths, but perhaps I need a journey into the depths of life and of my own mind and emotions in order to purge myself of useless psychic waste, old fears, outmoded attitudes, or compulsions. ... I may come back to the surface with a great wealth of inner understanding and with more courage than ever before.[2]

Pluto interaspects to the personal planets, whether each way or not, indicate amongst other things, old dependency versus independence issues centred around power, absorption, manipulation and separation. Especially with, but not necessarily limited to, the double whammy connection, in the past one of the souls has been engulfed by the other. This is often in a parent-child relationship in which the psychic umbilical cord was never cut (Moon), or where a parent or partner had strong power over the child or spouse (Sun). Pluto to the Moon can also indicate a particularly symbiotic or devouring mothering interaction. The interplay in the present life may include subtle domination of the child or spouse, or by the spouse, often through illness or apparent weakness, and with considerable emotional blackmail involved.

If the domination began in the present life childhood, it will extend far into adulthood and pervades all attempts by the 'child' to have a relationship. This may either cause the incarnating soul to experience such difficulty in separating from the parent that it never enters into an adult relationship, or leads it to try to recreate with its adult partner the patterns of its childhood. The man with Moon-Pluto aspects can, for example, coerce his wife into a mothering role, or the woman with Sun-Pluto aspects can unconsciously manoeuvre her husband into an authoritarian father role. This is particularly so when natal aspects provide perfect hooks for the projection. This interaspect can indicate that one or both partners bring into the relationship huge fears around, or expectations of, abandonment or rejection. It will perhaps colour the interconnection to such an extent that one soul will try to elicit exactly this to relieve the tension of waiting for it to happen.

The previous interaction shown by Pluto interaspects to the personal planets is usually symbiotic or parasitic, as in the type of relationship in which one partner feeds off or lives through the other. The relationship may have been so vampirish and debilitating that one soul had to leave the relationship in order to survive; the partner who was left behind feeling abandoned as a result. At times, the leaving may have sbeen through terminal illness or other death experience. Pluto is also ruthless and, as one of its extremes, this interaspect may show a past life experience of degradation - something which is always a potential for the present life too. If the Plutonian partner is spiritually unaware, then he or she can drag their partner into some very murky places. Plutonian facilitation or enabling scenarios often include drug or emotional dependency.

The interaspect symbolises a needy partnership with two souls entwined. At its extreme it can have been obsessive or absorbing, one partner being incapable of autonomous functioning within the relationship because it was so wrapped up in the other. One partner may also have been abusive or dominant, having total control and power over the other. The relationship in the past could have been as lovers, business partners, arranged marriage partners, master and slave, emasculating mother and son or authoritarian father and daughter. Venus contacts in particular signify an old symbiotic love interaction, although this is possible with any personal planet interaspect to Pluto. Pluto-Mars contacts can include former violence - physical, verbal or emotional - or a festering resentment which may manifest again as an underlying feel to the present relationship, or which may erupt into open aggression between the partners depending on the natal charts.

Souls with these interaspects are frequently caught up in power and symbiosis. Now the challenge is to develop intimacy without smothering; relationship without possession. Each person has to own their own soul. Interdependence is possible with Pluto but it takes work to move out of dependency or co-dependency. With this interaspect, both souls need to acknowledge each other's right to grow as an independent individual following his or her own pathway, in charge of their soul's destiny. When Pluto works positively, enormous transformation can take place through a relationship.

In the initial meeting in the present life of souls with a Pluto contact there can be a strong magnetic pull from the Pluto partner, and the other partner may be all too willing to fall back into the old pattern. That pattern almost certainly includes being manipulated or dominated and may generate an overt or covert power struggle. With a Pluto contact one of the partners usually feels that he or she can transform the other into something better. The task is to set the other free to be an individual, to put manipulation aside and allow the partner to grow spontaneously according to his or her own life plan. This may involve one partner totally removing himself or herself from the relationship in order to live freely, or it may require a re-negotiation of the terms of the partnership so that both partners may function autonomously. Tie cutting can help Plutonian relationships release from the karmic expectations and patterns of the past.

The Plutonian emotional connections pervading past relationships need not be of love. Resentment and hatred shows up regularly as does ancient rage and jealousy (often reinforced by Pluto-Moon or Mars interaspects occurring as well). Many of these themes will be projected onto or experienced through a present life partner, heightening the power struggle. Plutonian relationships continually replay these emotional themes, and the domination which accompanies them. These, especially when they are projected onto another, are particularly challenging in a work-related context or between husband and wife. It is helpful for the souls concerned to understand that either there is nothing personal about this (one way interaspects), or that old patterns are being played out which can be changed (two way interaspects).

Pluto represents power, and empowerment. Souls who have been through the Plutonian process and who have been stripped of their psychic dross are open to new ways to experience relationship. Once each partner has voluntarily relinquished control over the other, sex becomes a tantric activity, further enhancing mutual power. In their constructive manifestation, Pluto contacts can bring in immensely creative energies of rebirth and regeneration to heal and transform relationships.

Pluto-Sun

In addition to all the other Plutonian issues, Pluto to the Sun interaspects carry a strong projection of power and issues of abuse and misuse. With one-way interaspects, one partner projects power onto the other in a reflection of a previous pattern with some other soul. With the double whammy, particularly when supported by natal aspects such as Saturn to Pluto or Mars, one person has given away power to the other in the past which they now need to reclaim. In two-way aspects, one partner may have held all the power for lifetimes or the souls have switched roles from time to time, but the mutual projections have been around a long time and underlying issues of abuse will have to be addressed. These projections of power need retrieving from wherever the soul has placed them - usually a powerful male figure, but women too can be excellent hooks for power issues. The overpowered soul has to reclaim power. The person holding the power puts pressure on to the person who is powerless to remain that way. Ultimately that soul has to own its power, which may necessitate breaking out of the relationship altogether. This can in itself create an intense power struggle in which the previously dominated partner seeks to establish autonomy and the formerly domineering partner tries to retain control. The task is to take back that power and become empowered in an equal partnership.

Pluto-Moon

The Pluto-Moon combination has to deal with particularly symbiotic and toxic emotional issues that arise in the past as well as the ubiquitous power and manipulation factors. This combination also signifies cumulative mothering karma. Pluto-Moon contacts carry a powerful mothering bond, and issues around mothering and being mothered. There is a strong possibility of projection of these issues onto a partner *even if the partner was not involved in their creation*. If the partner is a good hook for the projection, that is to say they have a natal Moon-Pluto aspect or a Moon in Scorpio, then the relationship may replay devouring-mother scenarios in order to work through the issues – or to remain on the karma treadmill.

With one-way interaspects one partner can act as a mother to the other, or a partner will project issues that more properly belong to that partner's relationship with their mother into the love relationship with an adult partner. However, two-way Pluto-Moon interaspects between mother and son can indicate an extremely incestuous emotional scenario with its roots in past-life sexual contacts which have carried over inappropriately. Although these are not usually acted out, the mother still regards the son as 'mine' and is viciously jealous of any woman he comes into contact with. She will treat her son as a surrogate or substitute husband and the tie can continue right up to her death and beyond.

I had a Scorpio client who had a powerful repeating Moon-Pluto interaspect with his mother across the charts. Both of them had close natal Moon-Pluto aspects, with his Moon falling in the seventh house. His father died when he was fifteen and his mother told him: 'You have to take your father's place now'. He did exactly that, replicating his father's alcoholism - in which his mother took an enabling and facilitating role. She preferred her son to be weak and dependent to his becoming well again. He was extremely alienated and had few relationships as an adult. Eventually, in his mid-thirties he found a supportive relationship and weaned himself off alcohol. But the mother did not approve of his partner and wrote letters to her that would have been more appropriate to a wronged wife. She demanded that her son be returned to her. 'You have stolen him away from me and he depends on me', and similar sentiments were repeated over and over again. The man's partner commented that the relationship was always a threesome with Mother standing firmly in the middle. When she died fifteen years later, the couple were finally able to be fully together, although the memory of Mother still lingered.

On looking at the past life scenarios between this mother and son, they had been married in several incarnations and the emotional ties had never been broken, nor had the psychic umbilical cord in the present life. No matter how much tie cutting the son tried, it was not until his mother died - and, as he believed, was reunited with his father - that anything could sever the suffocating bond.

With two-way interaspects there may be a mother-child relationship coming forward with all that entails - especially as the repeating Pluto-Moon interaspect can indicate souls who have karma around abandonment, domination and rejection in the past.

Within adult relationships, childhood expectations may be projected onto the partner so that the issues are rehashed or reworked in an effort to release from them. As with all Pluto interaspects, the relationship may be experienced as suffocating or devouring. Old issues around jealousy, rejection, resentment and similarly toxic emotions pervade many adult relationships in which Pluto-Moon features, and while some of these may belong to the couple's mutual past they are just as likely to be projections from individual experience. The challenge is to make the contact emotionally nurturing without stepping into a mother or child role, and to move beyond the toxic emotions into a different way of relating.

Between partners, this interaspect signifies that a new way of interacting has to be found. With issues of abandonment coming forward, one partner might be afraid of stating personal and intimate needs for fear of rejection. Underlying power struggles and possible symbiosis must be addressed, together with the fears that the possibility of separation brings up.

When between mother and child, karmic mothering issues need to be reworked so that the child cuts the psychic umbilical cord, and the mother has to let go. Often the mother, or the soul taking the mother role, tries to live out her, or his, own unlived potential through the child - or to force the child into the mould the mother was pressed into by her own parents. A girl child might find her mother refuses to allow her the education she is capable of 'because you will be getting married', even though this is no longer a relevant concept in today's world. If she is expected to live out the mother's unlived life, pressure could be put on the daughter to become a doctor or teacher, which would fulfil the mother's own thwarted aspirations. She might also be herded into a marriage that the mother deems suitable to a man the mother herself would wish to marry.

The Pluto-Moon mother recognises no boundary between herself and her child and, therefore, assumes that what would have made her happy will be sufficient for her child. (Cynics have commented that such a mother actually wants her child to be as miserable and unfulfilled as she is, and this may have some truth to it if the interaction is an old one and is backed up by the mother's natal aspects).

Even with one-way Pluto-Moon interaspects, the issues can run so deep that it is difficult to disentangle the purely personal side of the issues and their roots in a past life from a general projection into a relationship of Plutonian issues. A Pluto conjunction and a Mars quincunx to the fifth house (love affairs), a Moon in Leo and several Neptune interaspects, all featured in the contacts between the charts of two men involved in a violent sexual relationship. The Pluto partner responded to an initial reading of his chart by requesting a follow-up reading on this specific relationship saying:

> 'The medieval woman experience you described [which I saw for him through far memory and which was extremely traumatic] is very close to me still and it is agonising and affects any close relationship I enter into - and by close I don't mean obviously sexual. It's more of fear - fear I will lose them and that they will betray me - and this fear makes me cling at times which is unhealthy for all concerned... the only time I ever loved anyone it ended up with all three of my medieval experiences repeating themselves: rape, betrayal and horrific violence... I know this sounds strange but although he [the

most recent partner] was brutal in many ways I felt he was my child, although he was four years senior in age. When he betrayed me I felt as though an innocent child had been destroyed in front of me.'

In the synastry between the charts there was a Sun conjunction to the Midheaven, and Stephen Arroyo suggests that this correlates with past familial ties wherein one person was the child of another. The Pluto-Moon mothering contact in the present life was therefore reinforced by a past life experience of being parented. The Neptune contacts were strongly idealistic and at first they had both tried to see the relationship as a spiritual one. However, in addition to the Pluto-Mars interaspect, a conjunction of Saturn to Mars, a Pluto trine to the Sun and a Pluto-Sun quincunx, indicated that the old power struggles featured in the charts erupted into rape - another karmic pattern between them. This was followed by six years of domination by the Moon partner of the Pluto partner in a reversal of the previous mother/child relationship. Eventually the weaker partner was able to break free and begin to work on his own inner energies. He recognised that the contact had served its purpose, having acted as a catalyst, and it was time for him to move on.

Pluto-Venus

With the Pluto-Venus interaspect, as with the natal aspect, there is a deep, desperate need for love, and huge issues around manipulation, dependence and abuse. A partner may appear to be the needy and demanding one in the relationship, with strong dependence on the other. However, almost inevitably, both partners actually share the fear that there will never be enough love, both existing in the Pluto-Venus black hole that sucks in all the love and affection it is given, and yet never feels is enough. Plutonian relationships are compulsive and obsessive. One partner will play out the needy, dependent, role and the other the power-over role, but these may switch during the course of a life or lives almost as though the two people cannot help themselves.

When the interaspect goes both ways, or when Pluto-Venus features strongly in the natal chart, there is an enormous challenge to love without possessing, manipulating or demanding. Emotional abuse is common, as is a parasitic feeding off the other person's energy. With relentless symbiosis frequently present in past life interplay (whether personal or not), letting go may be a major task for the present life that the souls face together or apart.

With the double whammy partners could have been in a relationship where one had total control over the other. Typical past life scenarios include domineering parent and abused child, master and slave, a masterful husband and a submissive wife who was owned body and soul by her husband, lovers who were totally wrapped up in each other so that no one else existed, or a love where one person was obsessed with the other - a feeling which may or may not have been reciprocated. The love may have been abusive, collusive, dependent or all-consuming, but rarely allowed for any independence on the part of the submissive or abused partner.

Even when the love was mutually all-consuming, one partner would eventually have felt suffocated by the relationship and needed to come up for air. If this was not achieved, all the separation and space issues carry over to the present interaction. Whilst it can, initially, feel remarkably safe being enfolded in such an intense love, it soon begins to weigh heavily - particularly as Plutonian issues such as jealousy and power struggles inevitably raise their head. Such jealousy may be part of the old interconnection - a lover who believes he or she owns his or her beloved body and soul may be consumed by jealousy at their slightest glance at someone else.

Old patterns of manipulation may need to be overcome when this interaspect is present. In the present life, as in the past, there can be an unspoken underlying threat: 'You'd better do what I want or else...' If the souls have been together in the past, the partner on the receiving end of the threat knows just how vindictive and vicious a thwarted Pluto partner can be. Even if they were not together, few people want to challenge what they instinctively know could be a nasty enemy.

Stephen Arroyo says of the natal Pluto-Venus aspect that the soul attracts partners who exemplify Plutonian characteristics.

> 'Hence the person often comes to feel lonely, unloved, used, neglected, dominated or utterly emotionally exhausted and consumed. But it is in just these times of despair that such a person can begin to tune in on the depths or his or her inner resources in order to really understand the need for a deep, fulfilling love.'[3]

This is typical of a negative Pluto-Venus interaspect encounter. Eventually the soul recognises the pattern and wants to change it. With Pluto-Venus interaspects, it is vital to get some space and independence into the relationship. The challenge is to develop trust and interdependence so that when this is achieved the love becomes alchemical or tantric in its ability to transform the old outworn pattern into new energy for the relationship. Such a contact is incredibly powerful and can transmute karma and open up the possibility of a totally satisfying relationship on all levels.

Pluto-Mercury

This contact can indicate old mental games, manipulation and coercion. There may have been enforced adherence to a strict set of beliefs, and pressure to behave or think in a certain way. Pluto is capable of seeing right through to the heart of someone, knowing exactly what motivates them at the deepest level of their being. This enables one person to pull another's strings, especially to achieve a desired response. This creates a subtle, usually covert, psychological pressure which creeps with relentless force into the present contact. One of the partners often feels in danger of losing his or her mind, or totally at the mercy of the other.

A client with this interaspect found that her husband waged a ceaseless underground war of nerves against her in an attempt to force her out of their joint business and push her towards a breakdown, so that he could avoid paying her off. When this did not work, he resorted to a slow poisoning of her body and it was only when she had her food analysed that she was able to put a stop to it. But of course, with Pluto involved, she was not able to prove that it was his doing. In the end, she was so manipulated and terrorised by him that she allowed him to divorce her without the settlement to which she was entitled.

This, although extreme, is typical of the lengths to which Pluto-Mercury contacts can go. In this case it arose in the present life, but it could equally well have been a past life scenario between them - had the aspect repeated both ways it probably would have been. When this contact works well, the person who has the ability to see into the heart of the other facilitates gentle change by helping that person look within. It is an extremely useful aspect to have in counselling, for example, but can also be helpful in family interaction as long as the temptation to use it for manipulation is avoided. Pluto-Mercury contacts can focus powerful mental energy - indeed, the souls may have learned to do this in the past through esoteric or occult pursuits.

Pluto-Mars

This contact almost inevitably occurs between partners who are, or have been, involved in the misuse and abuse of power. If the double whammy is present and backed up by natal aspects, it is likely that the two will have been in abusive situations in the past. On rare occasions it indicates that they were both involved in a situation where someone else abused power, with the two of them as victims. They could also have perpetrated atrocities together. It can show old aggression and issues around assertion which, unless sensitively handled in the present life, can pull them back into the old pattern.

A client (seventh house Mars in Libra) was married to a man with a Mars-Pluto conjunction in Leo which squared her nodal axis; her Mars squared his nodal axis, his Saturn was trine her Mars and his Mercury squared her Pluto. The marriage was full of conflict and her husband, who was an immensely wealthy man, had all the power in the relationship. When she eventually told him she wanted to separate, his response was to cut off all finance. Their old karmic interplay, in which money had been used as a weapon, had been one of business partners and the pattern was being repeated. In the present incarnation, he was more concerned with the convenience of having a wife than with having a loving relationship and he said she could stay on as housekeeper 'with sexual duties'. He also stipulated, however, that she would have to agree to do exactly as he wished in bringing up the children and running the home, including giving up her job. Her response was to withdraw a considerable sum of money from a joint account he had forgotten about, secretly buy a house in a different part of the country where she had found a job, and move out. It appeared that she was both dealing with old karmic patterns within the relationship (through her seventh house Mars and his Mars-Pluto conjunction) and being offered the opportunity to totally change the way in which she used her will. However, the underhanded, devious Plutonian fashion in which she intended to deal with the situation indicated that she was moving into the power games associated with both Pluto and the Leo North Node, setting up more karma between them, rather than owning her own power through negotiating for change.

The challenge here is for both partners to be assertive in their own right, channelling the strong Pluto-Mars energy into joint projects rather than into the love between them - which could well become sadomasochistic if Pluto was left to run amok.

6

NODAL CONNECTIONS

> Despite the infinite variety of circumstances and aspecting possibilities, there is probably no more favourable indicator for relationships than a North Node conjunct another person's planets.[1]
>
> Tracy Marks

The Nodes are notional points in the sky rather than actual bodies, nevertheless they have a powerful effect on relationships. In the natal chart the Nodes have to do with moving out of the past and into the karmic purpose for the present life and aspects to the Nodes indicate forces that will help, or hinder, that process. In synastry, planets in one chart aspecting the Nodes in the other person's chart can propel that person into a new way of being, or pull them back into the past. The connection can also indicate the karma between two people: Pluto refers to power issues, Neptune to delusions or spiritual soulmates, whilst Uranus acts as a catalyst for change and so on.

If a couple have the Sun and/or the North Node in the same sign, they are growing in the same direction. If they have the Moon and/or South Node in the same sign, they are coming from the same place and will instinctively feel comfortable with each other. When the North Node or Sun conjuncts the South Node or Moon in the other person's chart, that person is what the first person is trying to become. The relationship usually works well for a time, but then the people concerned may need to move on as they grow. This can occur in all types of relationship. If a teacher, for instance, will not let the pupil develop further because of control issues or ego, there is a need to break free. If two lovers have got all they can out of a relationship, they may need to move on to another learning experience.

ASPECTS TO THE NODES

In the natal chart, planets which conjunct the South Node pull the soul back into old patterns. If Venus is conjunct the South Node then the soul continually falls into an old way of relating. The Moon on the South Node retreats into deeply ingrained emotions, applying the feelings of the past to the present and extrapolating a scenario which has nothing to do with the immediate situation. The past emotional ambience of relationships is indicated by the sign in which the South Node and the planet are placed. Cancer for example has an inherent possessiveness, Libra a need for relationship no matter what the cost and so on. The challenge for the soul is to move into a more constructive expression of the qualities of the sign in which Venus or the Moon is placed, and work it into both new and existing relationships.

Mars conjunct the South Node may represent an old anger which is disowned and projected out onto the world or the partner. A woman with a first house Libra South Node-Mars conjunction was jilted by her fiance with whom she shared the conjunction of her South Node to his Mars. During counselling she denied being angry and said she understood the cultural and religious pressures which had led to his decision (the Libra South Node bending over backwards to be fair and adaptable). As she said this, an extremely large angry wasp buzzed in through the window and circled around her head. It then got stuck and its angry buzzing punctuated her further denials of anger. When she went back to her room, it had been invaded by a swarm of wild bees which were clearly demonstrating both her anger and her feeling of trapped helplessness within the situation.

Aspects to the South Node in the natal chart may be the source of powerful sub-personalities or dissociated complexes operating from deep within the sub-conscious. It is as though a facet of a previous life personality has been transported whole and unchanged from that incarnation and located deep within the instinctual functioning of the present personality. From its firmly entrenched position it makes forays into consciousness, disrupting and sabotaging attempts by the developing Self to express itself more constructively through the North Node. Saturn, for example, can indicate a fearful, dependent and depressive sub-personality, constantly inhibiting growth through its needs for safety, defensiveness and limits. There may also be a powerful inner critic or saboteur figure who wrecks any possibility of growth through its undermining internal comments and doubts. This figure often makes itself known in relationships as 'standards' from another life that are unconsciously used to assess a prospective present life partner or are extrapolated onto the relationship in general. The 'oughts' and 'shoulds' of the past are applied to present behaviour, which prevents growth and binds the soul to its emotional blockages.

In synastry, conjunctions to the South Node can pull the partners back into an old way of relating which breaks through into the present relationship without warning. It manifests as behaviour in one or both partners which appears to be out of character and which usually conveys the most destructive aspect of the conjoining planetary energy. South Node conjunctions in natal charts or in synastry need to be reworked so that the trapped energies can be released into consciousness and used constructively. A Saturn-South Node conjunction, for instance, has reserves of inner strength, discipline and resilience - once the fear is released - and Mars has the courage to assert itself in difficult situations.

Conjunctions to the North Node in the natal chart propel the incarnating soul forward into new patterns of behaviour, emphasis being placed on the planetary energies. If Venus conjuncts the North Node, then relationships are an important part of the soul's purpose for the present life. The soul wants to find a new way to relate, freeing up restrictions from the past. Whilst relationships may be difficult, depending on other factors, they will be where a soul grows most.

Planets squaring the nodal axis indicate the potential for synthesis of the past and future, but the soul may experience pressure from both ends of the axis and may find this destructive. Uranus, for example, may offer a creative resolution of the nodal dilemma, or it may be disturbed and antisocial, acting out all the archaic energies inherent within the opposing forces. Trines and sextiles to the Nodes may help with the integration of the energies, but the soul will vacillate back to the old ways.

A transit may be the trigger required to bring in a more harmonious functioning of planets and Nodes, particularly where the aspect is a close one, as the transiting energy can mediate in the natal conflict. At times, such triggers may, however, act as a brutal catalyst to resolve the seemingly unresolvable, literally propelling the soul into a new way of being through the inner dynamics of the irreconcilable opposites.

THE NODES IN RELATIONSHIPS

In the synastry between charts, contacts from the Nodes or planets can indicate an old soulmate relationship, with lessons and possibilities for growth through the new interaction. Unfortunately this does not always indicate, as so many people feel a soulmate should, loving harmony in the relationship. Most people regard their soulmate as their other half (see Chapter 10) but this is a fallacy. A soulmate does not necessarily equate to 'happily ever after' either. Although on a deeper spiritual level there is the feeling that here is a soul who truly loves and who offers an opportunity to grow beyond the confines of an old way of being, the circumstances in which that growth can take place may be extremely difficult. The lessons learnt from such a contact are often impossible to understand from the perspective of the earth plane. They can occur in the context of different types of relationship, which may or may not include sexual interplay.

Planetary contacts from the partner's chart to the South Node pull the soul back into an antiquated way of relating, which may initially feel comfortable and familiar. However, if progress is to be made into the new North Node constructive expression of the planetary energies, sooner or later conflict emerges - either internal or between the partners. This is particularly so if the other party is not expressing the energies of the Node or planet positively. Ultimately, unless the expression of energy shifts into a different mode, it may be necessary to move out of the association in order to express that energy constructively. The difficulties and frustrations of trying to deal with a South Node conjunction may finally push some souls into breaking through to their North Node or to a positive functioning of the aspecting planet.

A client's Scorpio South Node was conjunct her husband's Venus-Saturn. She described him as a wounded animal. 'He lives alone, but with us, sleeps alone, thinks alone.' His Saturn-Venus conjunction showed that he perceived himself as inherently unlovable, and that he had difficulty in relating. His behaviour pulled his wife back into the emotional pain and trauma of her Scorpio South Node. When she had had enough of that pain, she realised that she could not help him and decided to 'move on to expressing my own purpose and becoming a better human being'.

For other souls, however, this lesson may take a long time to learn and it may therefore be repeated through many incarnations. Some nodal contacts repeat ancient patterns. I was asked to look at the synastry for a client and a mysterious 'Mr X' with whom she revealed afterwards there was a feeling of an old illegal relationship.

They shared, in this life, memories of lovemaking in the past which coincided exactly. Mr X's Libra North Node was conjunct her Neptune, his South Node her Jupiter. His Venus and Mars were trine her Aquarian North Node and Mercury and Jupiter were sextile to it. Her Moon was inconjunct his North Node, sextile Mars.

In the past-life part of the reading I saw her as a lady of high rank. He was a slave. There was a passionate relationship between them, but one which had ended violently when he was discovered in her bed and killed. Later relationships had continued the theme of dangerous liaisons and secrecy (not always as lovers). In the present life he was married and they were unable to be open about the deep love they had rediscovered for each other. They were still playing furtive South Node-Neptune games. His North Node indicated that he needed a relationship which met both his own needs and those of another. Her Neptune conjunction to his North Node helped him to identify those needs and taught him about unconditional love. It also gave them a telepathic contact and accounted for the shared memories which arose spontaneously between them. However, the Neptunian tendency to not have things out in the open was being continued and her Jupiter conjunction to his Aries South Node pulled him back into an old pattern of selfishly indulging sensual needs, with which she enthusiastically concurred. Her Jupiter in Aries was extremely headstrong and she kept the relationship going for years when he felt it might be more appropriate to end it.

There was a danger of repeating a pattern of disaster and violence indicated in the Mars sextiles to the North Nodes. As a way of moving out of the difficult situation and away from the emotional games of the Leo South Node, she accepted a challenging job abroad which allowed her to explore her Aquarian North Node. The relationship had inspired her to explore her own spirituality and ability to love unconditionally; it had also reconnected her to earlier knowledge and skills which included metaphysical abilities and awareness of the spiritual forces inherent in the universe. She was able to harness the positive energies of Jupiter and Neptune and incorporate them into her way of life.

Present life relationships can replay destructive patterns as the souls are stuck on the karmic treadmill. The souls have an opportunity to change but do not always take this. In a case where the partners had been married for almost forty years, the wife was convinced that one of them had murdered the other in a past life, but she was not sure who did what to whom. There was no astrological indicator for this, but the feeling was symbolic of their involvement which killed individuality. She described their marriage as 'a continual battle for domination'. Her Venus was conjunct his North Node in Leo. Instead of working on owning and expressing their own individual power, each was trying to have power over the other.

An alcoholic husband's North Node in Libra conjoined his wife's Moon. The couple had been separated for years but the wife still stayed with her husband two or three nights a week on a platonic basis and 'a decree absolute seems to be an emotional trauma'. She felt 'responsible for his security and happiness, feeling as a mother'. She was continually moving back into her old Libra Moon pattern, which reflected to him the qualities he was trying to develop. However, for the dilemma to resolve she would need to move into her Sun in Taurus and Capricorn North Node which would mean finding security within herself rather than through her husband's apparent need for her.

Planets which square the nodal axis in synastry can, as with natal squares, pull two ways, resulting in disintegration, or they can assist in the resolution of the nodal conflict. A client had a Grand Cross in her chart. Her Pluto-Mars-Uranus opposition to Saturn squared her South Node-Moon opposition to Venus-Jupiter-North Node. Her ex-boyfriend locked into this Grand Cross: his Pluto-Uranus-Mars conjoined hers, and his Sun was conjunct her Saturn, squaring the nodal axis (Figure 12). He wanted them to get back together again, but she explained:

> 'There seems to be a lack of communication on some level. I feel like he is not 'seeing me'. There is an uncomfortable feeling, sometimes of sadness or seriousness and I can't put it down to anything that is happening now and here ... [She also had a] strong feeling of not wanting to interact with the world much and I retreat into meditation (Neptune conjunct her Midheaven and opposed her Sun). Everything seems so complicated. At the same time I feel there is something I have to accomplish this time. On a deep level I feel very secure and strong but when it comes to interacting with the world I sometimes feel lost and lonely.'

Those feelings reflected the inherent conflicts of the isolation and discomfort of Saturn in Pisces squaring the Moon-South Node

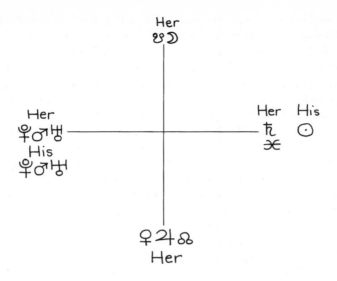

Figure 12 Grand Cross

opposition to the Venus-Jupiter-North Node (indicative of a potential for a different way of being). Her boyfriend's Sun in Pisces could have shown her a way to integrate her Saturn energies as a channel for Neptunian inspiration. However, he was being typically Piscean and 'not seeing her', his energy was manifesting on the unconscious level and he was not aware of her separateness. The relationship could have offered her the opportunity to move beyond the fear and loneliness of her Saturn energies into her strength and the potential for self-expansion through good relationships which the Jupiter-Venus-North Node offered her. She would then have had to deal with the potentially violent and explosive karma between them contained in the Pluto-Mars-Uranus square to her nodal axis and the planets that were conjunct to it. The relationship was a fated one, which required a high degree of spiritual evolution and awareness on the part of both partners before it could be resolved.

When there is a North Node to North Node conjunction there can be a deep soul bond and a unity of purpose. The two souls come from the same kind of past experience, and so instinctively understand each other, and are trying to develop along similar pathways. So long as the relationship is one of mutual support, the two can aid each other in harnessing the best qualities of the past to each one's individual growth and to the development of the relationship as a whole.

When the synastry between charts forms a Grand Cross which includes the Nodes, it produces what one of my clients calls a 'Shit or bust' confrontation. The souls face very directly both their own karma and the issues of the relationship. These are continually in their face, each moment of interaction triggers an issue mapped out in the Grand Cross. If the souls are not ready to do the work, then the relationship falters but if they can keep the impetuous going and find a way to resolve the issues, it brings about profound soul growth. The Grand Cross formed from interaspects which include both nodal axes is extremely significant as it shows facets that the souls are virtually compelled to work on together - what might be called fate - even though the souls are evolving in different directions. With the cross formed from the axes, the fundamental intention and direction is 'at cross purposes' as one axis forms a right angle to the other. However, this does not have to have a negative effect on the relationship. A Node squaring the other nodal axis may provide the impetus for that soul to make the transition between South and North Node purpose. It acts like a planet squaring the Nodes would do, propelling the soul(s) into a resolution of the opposing ends of the axis. It offers an opportunity for profound spiritual growth and may be why the souls have been drawn together in relationship. Although it is unlikely to be an easy passage, it will be life changing for one or both parties depending on whether it is a mutual shift. Planets which conjunct points on the Cross will aid or hinder the process depending on whether they pull the soul back to the past or propel it to the future. How constructively the transforming nature of any outer planet involved can be utilised in the relationship will be crucial to its success or failure.

So, for instance, a couple with a cardinal Grand Cross between the Nodes, his across the Cancer-Capricorn axis and hers Aries-Libra, spent the first half of their marriage with her working to support him whilst he qualified as a doctor and completed his postgraduate and consultant training. Just at the time when they felt she could begin a family and he could take over as breadwinner, she was diagnosed with a serious illness. Her South Node was in Aries. She had been extremely comfortable with taking the independent, active role in the relationship but had not yet found an equal partnership in which she made a creative compromise between her needs and the needs of her partner. The illness seemed to be forcing her to be dependent and yet the challenge was for her to explore interdependence. As her partner had his Moon in Libra, he already knew how to do this and could facilitate her learning process. Her husband's challenge was to move from the emotionally cool and self-sufficient Capricorn South Node into the much more caring and nurturing Cancer North Node. His patients would undoubtedly benefit from the experience too. In being with his wife during this traumatic time, he developed a compassion which spilled over into his work. As his Saturn was conjunct her South Node and her Saturn formed a septile (51°) to his North Node, this was clearly a karmic situation for them both. Between two partners, the septile shows that the relationship is moving into a new evolutionary cycle. The husband's Saturnine internal locus of control (the inner voice which contains all the oughts and shoulds imposed by authoritarian figures from the past) and his conventional medical training were challenged by his wife's desire to seek complementary healing. Each learned from the other, strengthening their relationship with their mutual support.

Reversed Nodal Connections

The reversed nodal placement occurs in the natal chart when the sign of the Node falls in the opposite house to its natural zodiacal placement. So, if the North Node in Aries was in the seventh house with the South Node in Libra in the first house, that would be a reversed nodal placement. In synastry, the reversed nodal connection occurs when the North Node on one chart falls in the sign of the South Node of the other chart. The Nodes are always in exact opposition, which means that the South Node of the first chart falls with the North Node of the second chart in the opposite sign.

Reversed nodal connections show themselves particularly in relationships where there is a strong spiritual bond, and the souls have intended to come together for mutual growth, or where there are lessons to be learned from or through each other. The fundamental dynamic of two oppositions moving in diametrically opposed directions means that, whilst the souls can learn from each other, they are evolving differently. One is moving to where the other has been, and vice versa. The faster they learn, the quicker they grow away from each other. So, a relationship which feels totally right when it starts may quickly develop into something which feels wrong at an energetic level. Unless the souls concerned realise what is happening, the relationship can easily fragment. If the association is one of pupil and mentor, that may be as it should be. Once the pupil has learned, it may be time to move on, unless the relationship can adapt. But the mentor may also need to acknowledge that he or she learned from the experience too.

A reversed nodal connection can be of enormous help in soul evolution, as we shall see, but if it occurs in a partnership it can also bring its difficulties. As each soul is growing away from the South Node whilst moving into the North, it feels as though they are leaving each other behind when the other person makes the shift into the North Node. However this need not be the case, as the constructive qualities of the South Node have to be integrated with the new qualities being developed through the North Node so each partner will manifest a fusion of North and South Nodal energies.

In discussing the reverse nodal connection between charts, Tracy Marks, who exhaustively researched this connection, feels that it is of 'noteworthy karmic and evolutionary significance' as the other person is naturally what we are trying to be. This connection usually indicates a soulmate connection, but as she points out:

> 'Such a "soul" connection may take the form of friend/friend, teacher/ student, parent/child, employer/employee or virtually any other kind of bond. It does not necessarily indicate the potential for marriage or partnership.'[2]

Miracles Do Happen

David Lawson and Justin Carson (see Chapter 10) had an 8° orb reversed nodal connection across the Cancer/Capricorn axis - one of the major evolutionary jumps that a soul makes. In esoteric astrology, Cancer is the Gate of Incarnation into Matter and Capricorn the Gate of Initiation into Spirit. With a Cancer North Node, a soul is on a personal evolutionary cycle and with a Capricorn North Node a soul has moved into a more collective spiritual cycle. This nodal axis is concerned with nurturing, gaining inner authority, and integrating the male and female cosmic energies. As I said in Patterns of the Past[3]:

> 'The disciplinary skills which the Capricorn South Node has developed in the past can be harnessed in a constructive way to the soul developing the ability to take a caring responsibility for itself and its family... [and] the Cancer North Node has the potential... to

move into nurturing both itself and a family in the widest sense of the world, supplying food and nourishment for the soul as well as the body...

Cancer ... [is] concerned with the inner world of dependency and vulnerable emotions, Capricorn ... with the outer world of achievement and self-sufficiency. The Capricorn North Node seeks success through a career. From a secure material foundation an inner spiritual strength develops...

The Earth Mother, boundless in her giving, has to unite with the stern Father-God to soften his heart with love so that together they will find an outlet for the universal love energy: just enough control and just enough free will to provide optimum conditions for growth. To reach this goal may involve exploration of the inner world of the psyche, of the archetypal energies invoked by the words 'Father' 'Mother' 'God' and 'Goddess' and of the anima-animus principles. These energies need to be recovered into consciousness and reintegrated into the Self in order to achieve wholeness.'

David and Justin were a perfect embodiment of universal love in action. Their *Healing Workshops* took personal development and healing to a new level and transformed the lives of many people in the process. They also built an extraordinarily caring and close-knit extended family that transcended blood connections and which spanned continents. When I asked David and Justin to contribute a piece on soulmates to *Hands Across Time* in 1996[4] I did not look at their astrology. But having studied it at length in between times and again for this present book, I realised how well things they said in that book illustrated the reversed nodal connection:

Justin: 'I hadn't clearly defined what my 'perfect partner' would precisely look like... interestingly enough, and this is only coming into my realisation now, as I think about this, [David's] professional abilities and confidence and indeed breadth of experience is currently beginning to resemble to a fairly accurate extent the type of 'match' I had been looking for ten years ago. So in a sense the fulfilment of my original creative daydream is just beginning to catch up on itself after a substantial period of time. Perhaps this demonstrates that the person I found was indeed not only the person I wanted but also the seed of who he would become and what we will become together, and had it all arrived packed and wrapped and 'ready to go' we might have missed out on a substantial part of our 'growing together'...And the past nine years have most certainly been a growing. We have lived together, worked together and relied on each other.'

David: 'Justin and I are very different to each other and yet our spiritual similarities seem to shine out for other people to see. I suspect that it is our similarity of spiritual purpose combined with our obvious intimacy that has prompted many people to ask if we are brothers...When we began to teach together, pioneering the study course programme in the UK based upon the work of Louise L. Hay... we would often find ourselves speaking with one voice. One of us would start a thought, beginning a sentence, and the other one would complete it. Ideas that appeared to land from the ether would arrive in their entirety or in parts to both of us at exactly the same time. Course participants probably saw us as a creature with two heads, one head (Justin) was most likely to keep them entertained and inspired with hilarious anecdotes while the other head (me) was an endless source of practical healing wisdom and intuition. Our own reality was that both of us could cover the ground that was usually attributed to the other and that when we worked together we would tap into something far greater than our individual talents and gifts... [Both are dual sun-signs, Gemini and Pisces, which find it easy to blend together and yet it is the reversed nodal connection that is also at work here].

We were engaged in a full time, live-in, loving, working partnership twenty-four hours a day. Friends were both delighted and horrified for us. How could any two people spend quite so much time together without driving each other crazy?...All I can say is that it worked very well for us. Sure, we had our disagreements about our different approaches to life, but we never fell out about anything.'

David recently described himself as a space cadet who moved between the worlds but needed to become more grounded, and Justin as a grounded guy who was opening up to spiritual possibilities - things they could teach each other from their South Nodes. In *Hands Across Time* David went on to say that he realised after a few years that for the relationship to grow, they would have to take time out for their own individual creative pursuits:

'But I did not then know what catalyst would be required to set us on a wider path. When that catalyst arrived, it did not shatter my happiness, but it was shocking and it challenged me to test and re-test everything that I believed in. For both Justin and myself, it stretched our capacity to love and trust each other and it continues to do so...'

In April 1992 Justin was diagnosed with an aids-related cancer. At the time there was an exact Uranus-Neptune conjunction in transit to Justin's North Node in Capricorn - close to David's South Node, pulling David into the more independent, Capricornian, way of being that he had already learned. Uranus is sudden and unexpected, its effect is instantaneous. Their life was transformed in a flash. In June that year there was a solar eclipse exactly on David's North Node in Cancer - close to Justin's South Node pulling Justin back into the emotional depths of the cancer. An eclipse is a time when the light of consciousness is blotted out and karmic forces arise so that soul intention can proceed. The initial effect of an eclipse is felt in the months leading up to the event, but it takes about six months afterwards to work itself through and for the full effect to be felt. David has since commented that during the years of his illness, Justin became more Cancerian and less identified with his Gemini Sun. In addition to the South Node in Cancer, Justin had Jupiter, Mercury, Uranus and Venus in Cancer. Interestingly, when David programmed for a relationship (see page xx), he visualised himself in a loving relationship with a Cancerian man. Describing the impact of the illness David said:

> 'Dealing with the practicalities of continuing to run our business, with the weekly regime of Justin's chemotherapy and our own limiting judgements about healers not supposed to be anything but gloriously healthy all the time, pushed us both into making new decisions about our lives and relationship. Something had to give and give it did. Hoping and trusting that this would not be the end of our teaching career, we postponed some courses and I chose to lead others on my own. The workshops that I led without Justin were my own respite from nursing him full time, and although I had been a teacher before we met, they also reminded me of the individual qualities that we both bring to the material we teach and that we could still be creative together without always being in the same room at the same time [The soul with Capricorn South Node has undoubtedly been a spiritual teacher in a past life. David remembers lives as a priest of Anubis and also a sacred scribe in ancient Egypt, a native American shaman, and a holy brother in various religious orders.] It felt essential for me to engage in something that expressed and enhanced our fundamental health and sanity.'

The transformational effect of that Uranus-Neptune transit was visible:

> 'During this time, Justin emerged from his cancer, like a butterfly from a cocoon. Perhaps he was a butterfly with slightly dented wings, but his spiritual awareness had grown enormously, adding greater

emotional depth to the charm and humour he had always possessed [the effect of his trip back into his South Node].'

Justin was one of the generation who had the early Uranus Opposition: the traditional and often spectacular astrological mid-life crisis. His natal North Node is conjunct Mercury and Uranus so the potential was there for enormous insights as Uranus conjuncted the South Node and opposed itself. This is a time when life gets shaken up, and when the unlived life pushes for expression. It is a time when the soul's intention comes to the fore. Justin wrote with typical eloquence about the effect of the experience:

'Part of my process of growth has been a serious illness, and we are weathering that together. In my better moments I can see the illness itself as part of my education process, although I would, frankly, have preferred to have learned my lessons in a different way. However, that has been the way I have learned, and am still learning. It hasn't always been a lot of fun and it has moved our relationship in a way that I wouldn't have expected, and one in which I frankly wasn't prepared for at the beginning, but for which I am truly grateful for the process...'

David ended by saying:

'Justin [has] changed from being pretty, charming and attractive to being truly beautiful and wise. He is powerfully charismatic and connected to inner resources that make me marvel with respect and admiration. Our purpose in being together is much bigger than any words that I could use to define it. We have provided each other with a foundation for our creative and spiritual growth. We have loved and laughed and enjoyed companionship. Our shared journey is growing sweeter, the present more exciting, and the future less important. When you are in love, each present moment is the best time of all. This love story is still work in progress.'

In living with aids for seven years, Justin 'walked his talk' and put their healing philosophy into action with great effect. But faced with a particularly unpleasant manifestation of the virus, he chose not to have toxic treatment. As transiting Saturn passed over the cusp of his eighth house, he set off on his next 'awfully big adventure'. The Cancer-Capricorn axis is about nurturing and David has the North Node in Cancer in the eighth house. When Justin came home to die, David was his primary carer. Transiting Uranus was on David's Moon at the time, separating him from the past and acting as a catalyst for his emotional growth. With enormous love and tenderness, he set about making Justin's death a positive experience for everyone concerned.

Some years before Justin's death, a psychic friend had suggested that they had been exceptionally clever in making a karmic choice to share their experience of Justin's illness. As David explained:

'In choosing to go through this process together, we were both undergoing the alchemical transformation of karma through dis-ease, and the spiritual evolution that can come with the role of carer. We were each simultaneously experiencing and learning from the two roles.'

Through their powerful soulmate connection and emotional empathy, they shared the impact of what each one individually experienced (a manifestation of the reversed nodal connection in action). So David, sensitive Pisces that he is, felt the subtle energetic impact of Justin's illness within his own body. 'Sometimes I could even feel the energy of his medication coursing through my veins.' After Justin's death, David realised the wisdom of their friend's insight:

'Karmically, Justin and I were able to accomplish an enormous amount in a short space of time. I now wonder whether I will need to manifest a major illness in my body this lifetime. I feel like I have been through the process already and emerged with a new sense of wholeness, even in my loss. Almost by osmosis, the finest qualities of Justin have been absorbed into my psyche and have enhanced similar aspects of myself. The most obvious example is a growing confidence in my wicked sense of humour - this has been particularly noticeable during a year's academic study of religion, death and dying!' [Eighth house North Node.] A typically Piscean way of David owning aspects of his own personality that had previously been embodied by Justin, thereby fulfilling the promise of the reversed nodal connection.'

The reversed nodal connection works particularly well in a mentor-pupil relationship. Christine Hartley was my spiritual teacher for over ten years, particularly in the art of far seeing. We had a reverse nodal connection between our charts and were spiritual soulmates. I wrote in *Patterns of the Past* about our reunion in the temple at Philae - years after her physical death. On a magical Egyptian evening, as I watched the sunset turn the temple a deep rose pink, I was suddenly aware of Christine beside me.

I had followed the time-honoured ritual of paying the backsheesh man for the privilege of being allowed to land after hours, and was able to wander without the usual hordes of tourists around.

Once again I was able to walk the halls with Christine whilst she instructed me in the inner teachings of the Osiris-Isis Mysteries, as she had done many centuries before. It made no difference that the temple had been moved, the energy impregnated in the stones was enough to take us back to that deep spiritual contact.

Christine Hartley was more than twice my age when we met and in addition to the reversed nodal connection our charts have Jupiter conjunct Jupiter, and Sun in opposition to the Sun. Her South Node-Mars conjunction conjoined my Pluto-North Node conjunction, and her Chiron was conjunct my Moon. Her Neptune-Pluto conjunction enclosed my Mars. She was the spiritual midwife for my far-memory abilities, and the healer of several of my emotional wounds. We shared many experiences and our lives had a similar pattern with significant events happening at the same age - something which occurs with nodal or reverse nodal connections. Despite the age gap we were close friends as well as teacher and pupil. I first met her, in this life, at the height of summer at Portsmouth Harbour station, just as the London train and the Isle of Wight ferry disgorged their passengers. Among the crowds, we found each other immediately and 'knew' each other. Christine and I had been together many times before and would chat about the old days as though it were yesterday.

Our contact in this life was preordained: Christine was instrumental in aligning me to my pathway, and for reawakening in me the spiritual knowledge required for my work. She spent many years urging me to take her place in reincarnation work, but it took me a while to be ready for this step. However, I felt unable to venture into her occult work. It would have been easy to fall back into the conjunction of her Leo South Node-Mars to my Pluto, and it would certainly have helped me to own my power as my North Node was urging. Our Gemini Mars conjunction to Pluto talked for hours on the subject, but I found it difficult to commit myself to the occult pathway and this was handed onto another of her pupils - with whom I also have a reverse nodal connection. When I completed my first public reincarnation seminar, some ten years after we first met and she had approved the proofs of his first book, Christine died the following night in her sleep as she had wished, 'just slipping away into the next world'. It was an appropriate time for her to leave and each of us had to take our legacy from her and move forward with it.

MURDER, MAYHEM AND NODAL CONFLICT

Other nodal patterns are also significant. In esoteric astrology, a natal mystic rectangle, consisting of two oppositions, two trines and two sextiles, signifies spiritual wisdom and soul intention. In synastry, its import can be far from spiritual, indicating symbiosis, and yet there is always the possibility that the relationship will transcend its everyday limitations and facilitate something amazing – or incredibly destructive and creative at one and the same time.

Playwright Joe Orton was murdered by his lover, Kenneth Halliwell, who then committed suicide. It was the culmination of a fifteen-year relationship which 'transformed Orton from a provincial nobody to one of the most talented, comic playwrights since Oscar Wilde'[5] and which totally destroyed Halliwell. Their Nodes formed a mystic rectangle in Cancer-Capricorn and Virgo-Pisces (see Figure 13). Their Suns opposed each other in Cancer and Capricorn. Throughout the troubled month leading up to the brutal killing, Orton had transiting Pluto conjunct his natal Mars. On the day he died, transiting Mars was exactly sextile his South Node-Neptune conjunction. Although birth times are not available for Orton or

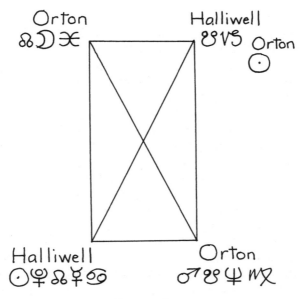

Figure 13

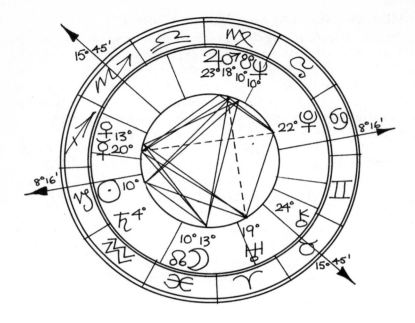

Figure 14 Joe Orton

Halliwell and the charts shown are for sunrise as these give a symbolic picture of the incarnation, the effect of the Nodes is clearly visible. The relationship between the two men illustrates the complex interweaving and shifting power balance of the nodal axis in the individual charts and in the synastry between the two.

Orton (Figure 14) had the North Node conjunct the Moon in Pisces (a placement which holds good whatever the actual birthtime, but the aspect widens as the day goes on), opposing a Neptune-South Node-Mars-Jupiter conjunction in Virgo, squared by Venus-Mercury. His capacity for self-destruction, especially in matters of love, was boundless, as was his ability to bring things into manifestation. He was operating on some old, and very dark, unconscious patterns from the past. The conjunction of Mars and Neptune to the South Node indicates both an old will dilemma, and the potential for Orton having had past-life experiences in which he retreated into drink or drugs as an escape from a reality which he found unbearable. In the present life Orton used this aspect more constructively in his writing, but nevertheless drugs and sex played a major part in his life. He was ambivalent over the relationship with Halliwell. Orton's biographer,

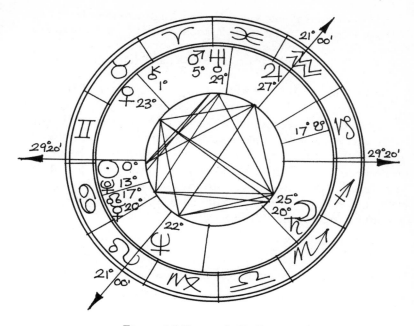

Figure 15 Kenneth Halliwell

John Lahr, repeatedly points out both Orton's loyalty to Halliwell (Figure 15) and his promiscuity (nodal axis square Venus in Sagittarius).

Orton's Neptune-South Node-Mars conjunction is constantly illustrated in his diaries, quoted by Lahr, who comments:

'The combination of sex, hashish and sun [in Morocco] fulfilled the Dionysian intention behind his comedies. They celebrate instinct and gratification and aspire to corrupt his audience into pleasure ... like the votaries of Dionysius, Orton was hounded by his passion. In his plays, Orton faced his rage and exorcised it with his lethal wit [Mercury in Sagittarius inconjunct Pluto] ... Morocco slaked the tension that was always erupting in Orton's life between his emotional needs [Moon conjunct North Node in Pisces] and society's social and sexual taboos [Virgo South Node and a virtually unaspected Saturn in Aquarius] ... the battle against society was difficult [Mars conjunct South Node] ... in England the strain could create a painful confusing rage ... When Orton discovered the theatre, he found focus for his energy and an answer to his needs [an outlet for the nodal axis] ... Theatre consolidated Orton's fascinations - literature, music

201

and make believe [Venus square Neptune] and made them legitimate labour [Virgo] … 'You can't be a rationalist [Virgo] in an irrational world [Pisces]. It isn't rational' … Orton wrote: 'I'm a great believer in the absolute logic of Alice in Wonderland' [Pisces incorporates Virgo].[6]

Orton met Halliwell at RADA. Lahr's biography and the Orton diaries chronicle their obsessive, claustrophobic, destructive relationship and its seemingly inevitable resolution through violence. In synastry each Mars trines the other Saturn, Saturn opposes Mars in the composite chart, and there are Pluto-Mercury-Venus interaspects and a Chiron-Venus contact. Halliwell, a literate man with a facility for language, was in the ascendancy when they met. He had money and owned a small bedsit into which Orton moved. According to Lawrence Griffin:

'he, Orton, would do anything Kenneth (Halliwell) wanted him to'. 'Halliwell was like a Svengali to John [Orton]. He took John over.'[7]

Halliwell's nodal axis dominated the interchange at that time.

'Halliwell asserted almost complete control [Capricorn South Node] over the relationship. Halliwell cooked and provided the food [Cancer North Node].'[8]

Halliwell initially nurtured Orton's talent (Cancer), but in the end his possessiveness and emotional instability alienated Orton who escaped whenever possible (Pisces):

'Once, hallucinating on hashish, Orton saw himself as a little boy being beaten by a teacher. The teacher was Halliwell [symbolised in Halliwell's Capricorn South Node].'[9]

There are strong Mercury contacts between the charts:

'It was Orton's mind, the gorgeous wicked fun it poked at the world which made him irresistible and obsessed Halliwell.'[10]

Halliwell's Mercury conjuncts Orton's Pluto which is inconjunct Mercury. Mercury-Pluto aspects appear frequently in the charts of 'black' comedy writers - practically the entire Monty Python team, for example. In synastry Mercury forms an exact inconjunct (quincunx) to Mercury. Orton and Halliwell were jailed for what Lahr describes as:

'mischievous literary vandalism. Books … were appearing on the [library] shelves with photographs and book jackets humorously altered … most perturbing to the court was not the abuse of private property but the care and intelligence with which Orton and Halliwell tampered with the books.'[11]

The synastry between the charts also includes a trine from Orton's North Node-Moon conjunction to Halliwell's Pluto, which opposes Orton's Sun; Halliwell's North Node sextiles Orton's Mars and Halliwell's Venus sextiles Orton's Pluto. Orton's Chiron conjuncts Halliwell's Venus and indicates an old wound in the relationship between them. Jealousy, anger, envy, resentment and revenge were the Plutonian undercurrents which pervaded the seemingly harmonious relationship, and which broke through the claustrophobic relationship with tragic consequences.

Halliwell's chart has Mercury and Pluto conjunct the North Node in Cancer, with a Scorpio Saturn-Moon trine to the Node. It is a depressive, emotionally unstable chart (Sun in Cancer square Uranus-Mars in Pisces, Grand Cross of Moon conjunct Saturn in Scorpio opposing Venus squaring Neptune opposing Jupiter, and Chiron inconjunct the Moon - an aspect which becomes tighter as the day progresses). The Capricorn South Node, the Chiron-Moon inconjunct and the Saturn-Moon conjunction indicate an old, painful constriction around emotion which is evident in a RADA assessment of Halliwell as 'stiff and rigid'.

'Seems to be unconvinced that acting is the expression of emotion. The result is that his approach is all mental [Mercury conjunct North Node in Cancer]'.[12]

In Lahr's words:

'Halliwell's instinct was always to retreat, rejecting the source of the pain before it could reject him [Pluto conjunct North Node] ... Halliwell was no stranger to horrific death. When he was 11 his doting mother had been stung in the mouth by a wasp and within minutes had choked to death before his eyes. Twelve years later, Halliwell came downstairs to breakfast to discover his father with his head in the oven, dead from asphyxiation ... The pain of failure, the waste of talent and the sense of betrayal the orphan feels towards those who have left him bred in Halliwell a festering and terrifying hostility towards the world. Halliwell had no reason to trust life [Pluto-North Node-Mercury conjunction in Cancer].'[13]

Orton found fame and notoriety as a playwright. Halliwell, who had literary aspirations of his own, found only failure. He progressed backwards from placing his name above Orton's on their early, joint, manuscripts, to being Orton's 'literary editor', and finally to signing himself 'Secretary to Joe Orton'. Orton was moving towards the integration of his nodal axis through his work: 'The liberties Orton took with language and plot were built on a disciplined vision [Virgo-Pisces].'[14] At the same time, however, Halliwell moved into crisis and disintegration:

> 'Orton's almost magical resilience inevitably sank Halliwell into deeper depression (Saturn-Moon). Unable to compete, Halliwell instinctively tried to punish and control Orton [Capricorn South Node]. In his sickness Halliwell, who needed love and said so [Cancer North Node demanding to be heard], became increasingly unlovable. His panic to make people draw closer only pushed them away and he broadcast his pleas for attention in his complaints about Orton's 'trolling', his demands on Orton's allegiance and his psychosomatic illness. [Orton was here offered the opportunity to fully comprehend this peculiarly Virgoan condition, but he declined. No doubt his South Node had already explored this previously]. Orton's sensual rapacity was a threatening reminder of Halliwell's emotional dependence.'[15]

Halliwell left a suicide note: 'If you read his diary all will be explained.' The diary chronicles a deteriorating relationship as the balance of power inexorably shifted from Halliwell to Orton:

> 'The diaries offer a rare, if unwitting glimpse of the punishing dynamics of a celebrity's self-aggrandisement ... The diaries are not just a chronicle of the drama between them, but a prop in it ... Halliwell could - and did - read their punishing contents. Everything about the diaries was provocative, a symbol of Orton's retreat into himself and away from Halliwell ... Orton was the centre of Halliwell's life; but, as he could read, Halliwell was an increasingly minor - and frequently irritating - extra in the drama of Orton's eventful life.'[16]

The relationship with Halliwell epitomised Orton's own nodal conflicts:

> 'The struggle between licence [Pisces] and control [Virgo], between identity and invisibility, between consciousness and "self-consciousness" [was] the mirror image of Orton's own struggles with Halliwell's neurotic problems.'[17]

Actor Kenneth Williams insisted that Orton had 'heart':

> 'If we're talking about compassion and sympathy, I'd say Joe had it. He showed tremendous loyalty to Halliwell. He showed it to me ... He was the most marvellous counsellor.'[18]

However, when faced with the challenge of his Pisces North Node for empathy in the shape of the demanding and suicidally depressed Halliwell, Orton could only retreat into his Virgoan Neptune-South Node conjunction, denying what was happening. Actor Simon Ward was 'puzzled by Orton's indifference to Halliwell's pain … no one could be as insensitive as that if you really cared about the person'.[19] Within days Orton and Halliwell were dead. 'Halliwell's final fillip was nine hammer blows to Orton's head.'[20] Their ashes were intermingled and scattered. The Cancer and Capricorn axis had finally been integrated and the Piscean Moon-Node desire to merge was satisfied. 'Through murder Halliwell achieved the public association with Joe Orton's career he had been denied in life.'[21] In his plays Joe Orton articulated many of the dilemmas inherent within his own and Halliwell's charts. As John Lahr put is: 'The joke at the heart of Orton's farce mayhem is that people state their needs, but the other characters, in their spectacular self-absorption, don't listen.'[22]

EARLY RELATIONSHIPS

The events of childhood do not pass but repeat themselves like seasons of the year.

Eleanor Farjeon

The incarnating soul's earliest relationship is with its biological family of origin and, as regression experiences have shown, includes the soul's interconnection with its parents whilst still in the womb. Biochemistry confirms that babies are extremely sensitive to the moods and feelings of their mother. The baby inhabits a chemical soup that carries impressions of the mother's emotions, her highs and lows. Many people under regression report being extremely sensitive to what their mother was going through, clearly picking up on her thoughts and emotions. And some found that, even at that early stage, they felt responsible for what their mother was feeling. After birth, they remained closely attuned to the mother's feelings and tried to keep her happy at all costs. They also assimilated what was going on between husband and wife. Some would side with one parent, others with another. These experiences were so empathetic that it felt as though the foetus was undergoing the experience itself. Indeed, several people found that they had been imprinted with emotional expectations that did not really belong to them, they were absorbed from the mother - something that can also occur as the child matures. Other people reported being deeply affected by their parents' sexual relationship. People conceived out of love had a totally different approach to incarnation to those from lust or indifference. If the parents had passion and zest plus a deep love for each other at the time of conception, the soul would eagerly anticipate birth and would seek a similar adult relationship. If the intercourse had been cold and passionless, a 'duty', the soul was less eager to incarnate and would later, unconsciously seek the same in a partner. If conception arose from an abusive, selfish act, then this is what the soul would see as 'normal'. In most cases this hooked into what the soul itself had experienced in other lives.

The poet William Wordsworth called birth 'a sleep and a forgetting', but Stanislav Grof's work[1] has shown that, during the birth process, past life recall is stimulated in the passage down the birth canal as each contraction cuts off the blood supply for a moment and the baby 'dies'. With each death comes a remembering, and so the feelings and expectations of other lives are also imprinted, even though the child apparently forgets these again after birth. Notwithstanding, some children remember their past lives well into childhood, especially if the last passing out of incarnation was traumatic. The soul, of course, carries the memories throughout each life, although this is usually at an unconscious level. Nevertheless, in those birth moments the baby is aware of any past life connections within the family. He or she may look forward to the meeting, or may be apprehensive as to whether necessary changes and learning can occur. How the child is welcomed into the world at birth will either reiterate old patterns, or offer the possibility of a new beginning. In addition to indicating the patterns of behaviour and expectation carried forward from the past, the natal chart also shows the environment into which these will be projected. (See *Patterns of the Past*.) It describes how the mother, father and siblings will be perceived, and how the family will interact.

There may be a direct karmic link between the souls within the family unit (which will be clear from the synastry), or karma related to the type of family interaction. Some groups of souls appear to incarnate together as families time and again. Others are more loosely connected, varying the experiences explored through karmic contacts and including friendship or enmity as well as love relationships. Parents are selected prior to incarnation on the basis of the experiences required by the incarnating soul, and the genetic and attitudinal inheritance that the family offers.

As Stephen Arroyo has pointed out: 'The child lives and breathes in the atmosphere that the parents create through their relationship to each other.'[2] No matter what the soul's own pattern might be, the baby initially learns about relationships through observing the parents relating to each other. If the child sees something he or she is expecting, the innate expectation is reinforced and the soul is set on its treadmill again. If the child sees something different, then he or she learns that things do not necessarily have to be the way things were before. This allows the soul to grow. Parents may be chosen for the new possibilities they open up just as much as for other gifts they may be able to offer the child. However, souls may be imprinted with the parents' unfinished business or unfulfilled longings - which may or may not have been carried down the family line. In such cases, when the soul matures work may be needed to heal and release from the imprinted material.

Old patterns such as lack of self-worth or conflict with authority figures are carried over by the incarnating soul from the past, and the appropriate family interplay intensifies inherent difficulties. Families, or one or other parent, are often chosen because they can provide exactly the right environment for expectations to flower. Even when the family situation is not that difficult, the soul may perceive it as such because of an ingrained belief that it must be so. One or other parent, or another significant adult, will play out the roles that the soul has come to expect.

For example, a woman came onto one of my workshops whose mother was in a coma and not expected to live. The woman felt that it was very important to attend the workshop as she would learn something which would help her, and her mother, to move on from an exceedingly troubled relationship. She did not share her situation with the group until the following day when she told us this story:

'Yesterday you spoke about how natal Moon-Saturn aspects expect bad mothering, and about the devouring mother syndrome of Moon-Pluto. You also said that part of the lesson was to learn to nurture ourselves rather than looking outside for parenting. Well, I have these placements, with Sun-Saturn-Pluto across the parental houses and the Moon in Scorpio in the eighth house, and I certainly had my expectation fulfilled in every way. But you also spoke of our choosing parents who fulfil our expectations and offer us lessons, and said that they might be part of our soul group in disguise. When we did the tie cutting, I found it very difficult to cut the ties with my mother and especially hard to let love and forgiveness flow between us, but I managed it and I felt much stronger as a result.

So, last night I went to the hospital to see my mother who was in a coma but who was hanging onto life. My relationship with her had been traumatic to say the least and I had not wanted to visit her previously. But I sat down and held her hand and said to her: 'Well, mother, if you were here to teach me about abandonment, and rejection, and lack of love, and abuse, and many other destructive things, you certainly succeeded. But I now realise that I chose you for this purpose and that by being like that, you also taught me self-reliance and turned me inward to look for my own nurturing. I am the person I am today because of the way you treated me, and that was exactly what I expected when I incarnated. So I forgive you and thank you for what you did for me.'

With that, my mother opened her eyes and looked at me: 'That's alright dear' she said. And she died. I came back today to tell you about this, and also to try to confirm that she was indeed part of my soul group.'

In the regressions that followed, this lady did indeed confirm that she and her mother had known each other before and were part of the same soul group. She understood that her mother had agreed to give her this experience of very difficult mothering so that she could overcome what had, through several lifetimes, become a deeply ingrained expectation, that she now wanted to transform into a positive learning experience.

It is these unconscious patterns which form the basis of learned behaviour: they include many defence and avoidance strategies fabricated to prevent taboo feelings and emotions from surfacing. These form part of the shadow side of the personality and are therefore rarely consciously acknowledged or recognised. The pressure of behaviour based on childhood circumstances and of experience carried over into adulthood, however, ultimately forces attention on to the issues involved, and offers the possibility of resolution of long-standing personal and parental karma and assimilation of the shadow.

The network of karmic ties and obligations pervading the family can be identified through the synastry between the natal charts. Karmic patterns and dilemmas such as control and abuse, dependency/self-determination, possessiveness/separation and freedom/commitment show up clearly in the interaspects across the charts between the inner and outer planets. Unfinished business, debts to be paid or pledges to be fulfilled, can be identified. Relationships may have repeated destructive patterns for many lifetimes, or may have swung between two extremes, but the karmic interaction can be investigated through the charts, and a way of resolution found. The knowledge that the chart and the parents have nearly always been chosen by the incarnating soul to support its progress in life empowers people to look differently at their childhood and parental relationship.

NATURE VERSUS NURTURE

Scientists and educators have long debated the question of nature versus nurture: how much of the personality is attributable to heredity and genetic factors, and how much to family and environmental influences. Studies of twins separated at birth show a remarkable congruency of experience, and yet twins brought up together often have markedly different personalities. One twin seems to exemplify the positive, outgoing qualities of the chart and the other twin the quieter, more passive side. This difference is rarely accounted for by the birth interval altering factors such as Ascendant or the M.C.

The concept of reincarnation throws new light on this dilemma. Without reincarnation the baby is a blank slate at the mercy of its genes and environment. With reincarnation it is seen as having an innate disposition carried forward from the past which affects how it interacts with both nature and nurturing. This concept can also explain why twins who incarnate with virtually the same chart may nevertheless express the energies very differently. The incarnating soul's past experience colours its perceptions, subtly influencing its expectations which will be reflected in its inherent response to new experiences.

The innate disposition is reinforced from the moment of birth. A happy, contented baby is automatically responded to with love and kindness. A crying, discontented one almost always engenders exasperation and, if it continues crying for long periods, may well provoke anger. The mother may feel inadequate and unable to cope, particularly when the baby is her first child. Thus, the level of nurturing available to that child is poor when compared to that of the contented child. However, an incarnating soul pre-programmed to expect poor nurturing will home in on the occasions when that expectation is met, and may totally ignore the nine out of ten times when it received perfectly adequate mothering. On the other hand, the child whose expectation is that its needs will be fulfilled will more easily tolerate the occasional frustration of unmet desires.

PARENTAL IMAGES: THE SUN AND MOON

In the child's natal chart, the Sun and Moon give an indication of the type of karma the child has to face with its parents and show how the incarnating soul will experience the parents relationship. A Sun-Moon opposition, quincunx or square, for example, delineates parents, or parental archetypes, fundamentally at odds with each other, whereas the conjunction, trine or sextile indicates parents who are basically in harmony.

The Sun and the Moon describe the parental archetype, what the soul has come to expect, and what the soul would like to meet if the archetype is expressed positively. Such archetypes are frequently lived out by the actual parents. If they are not, they lurk in the depths of the subconscious mind as a paranoid suspicion that 'this is what parents are really like' and may emerge at any time to be acted out by parents, employers and so on. The Moon also indicates the 'lunar food' that the soul has come to depend on for nourishment and nurturing. If this 'food' is supplied, the soul will feel loved and satisfied, it is not there will be a sense of deprivation no matter how good the mothering may be in other ways. The Moon also signifies the ancestral inheritance that passes down through the family, and the soul may have chosen that family specifically for this inheritance.

Aries
The Sun - Fathering Archetype: The Knight in Shining Armour
With the Sun in Aries the soul has had experiences in the past of a father who is courageous and brave, taking on the world at full tilt in true Aries style. However, the soul may also have had many battles with the father as egoism runs strongly through this naturally assertive sun-sign and Aries always believes it knows best. The challenge for the child in the present life is to become centred in the Self, and to learn to temper the impulsive action and hot temper which could trigger the wrath of the father.

The Moon - Mothering Archetype: The Amazon
What the soul with this placement seeks is a mother who is ego-boosting and who gives confident nurturing - a mother who aids in expressing this soul's fierce independence. What the soul expects is the selfish mother who has no time for her offspring and who puts her own needs first. The archetypal mother symbolised by Aries is fiery, passionate and outgoing, but she may be domineering, egotistical and selfish. She can put all her energy into child rearing, creating a chosen child who carries all her hopes. At its extreme, this mother consumes all in her path with her enthusiasm and emotional demands and can produce a competitive, self-centred child who must win at all costs. Less extreme, this is the mother who encourages her child to be independent and self-reliant.

The lunar food for this moon-sign is admiration and validation. This soul has a strong ego and finds it difficult to merge into the background. It needs to be recognised for the special fiery Arian qualities of courage and assertiveness. In the past, this soul has been looked up to and acclaimed. Attention, flattery and respect are inextricably linked to love. This demand will be apparent in adult relationships.

Ancestral Inheritance: A strong constitution, powerfully-held opinions and the ability to fight for causes are the inheritance of an Aries Moon. Initiating action, and then moving on before completion, will be a pattern in the family. Little is repressed with the Aries Moon, the temper is instant, flare-ups common, but forgetting is equally fast. Emotions and delicate nuances of feeling, however, tend to be trampled underfoot in an insensitive household.

Taurus
The Sun - Fathering Archetype: The Dependable Father
With the Sun in Taurus the soul is looking for a dependable father who can be relied upon to give the stability and security that this soul needs. What the soul might encounter is the stubborn and rigid father who assumes he knows how his child should develop. The routine so beloved of Taurus may profoundly constrict the child's growth unless the father is flexible enough to tolerate unrestricted growth in his child.

The Moon - Mothering Archetype: The Earth Mother
The soul with the Moon in Taurus seeks a mother who is dependable, orderly and nurturing. An earth mother who fulfils all the soul's needs. What the Taurus Moon most fears, and so often meets, is an overpowering, possessive no-sayer, who seeks to control both body and soul.

What feeds this soul is keeping the body safe and receiving affection. A Taurus Moon can put up with a lot so long as the surroundings are comfortable and the food is good and in steady supply. If body and soul are not nurtured appropriately then this soul may turn to comfort eating or addictions to 'stuff down' emotional needs - a pattern which is extremely obvious in adulthood.

Ancestral Inheritance: This Moon symbolises a home where there is an enormous emphasis on security, routine, wealth and status -

although the home itself may be deprived. The soul may look to wealth to satisfy a craving for more that is carried over from other lives. If the family is not rich in material goods, the soul may be learning that money is not everything.

Gemini
The Sun - Fathering Archetype: The Talkative Friend
A soul with the Sun in Gemini has had experiences of a father who is more like a friend. A pal with whom to enjoy childhood exploration and discuss the issues of the day. Unfortunately, what the soul might also have encountered is the father who is too busy exploring his own world to make room for his child, and who will promise anything just to get away. As a result, the father can be unreliable and untrustworthy. The challenge for the child is to recognise what is truth and what is not.

The Moon - Mothering Archetype: The Blue Stocking
The mother that this soul seeks is articulate and imaginative. She can enter into the soul's inner world and communicate articulately. The archetypal expectation is a playful, intellectual mother who encourages exploration and independence for her child. What the soul fears, is the manipulative mother who knows just how to play on feelings and emotions to gain control.

The lunar food the soul with Moon is Gemini needs is attention and mental stimulation. This soul wants to be listened to above anything else. There is a deep need to be heard. Talking can become a substitute for emotional satisfaction and demands may be made on adult partners to verbalise rather than feel the feelings.

Ancestral Inheritance: This family encourages communication and sociability, although there can be something of the social climber about the family. The inheritance is cerebral rather than emotional. What the soul is not encouraged to do is to participate in and share feelings honestly. True feelings may be covered up within the family and superficial feelings may not accord with those within. Any display of emotion may be frowned upon, or certain emotions will be taboo. There is something about the Gemini Moon that is difficult to pin down, and this is reflected in the family ambience. It may be secrets, gossip or matters that need great discretion, but something in the family background remains hidden.

Cancer
The Sun - Fathering Archetype: The Dedicated Father
The soul with the Sun in Cancer may find him or herself locked into an image of father as possessive and clinging, wanting to share everything with his child. He may suffer from self-pity and look to his child for emotional support. This father clings to the past, to family values and how things were. On the other hand, the soul may have experienced the excellent nurturing that Cancer is capable of and so looks to a father for supportive care.

The Moon - Mothering Archetype: The Smother Mother
What the soul with this Moon placement seeks from mother is comfort, nurturing and emotional closeness. It desires support for powerful needs. This soul desperately wants to experience overwhelming mother love and often confuses possessiveness with love. The desire is for abundant nurturing. What the soul fears is the highly protective, 'smother-mother' who holds her child close and allows no separation.

       The lunar food craved by the soul with the Moon in Cancer is emotional sustenance and validation for deeply instinctual, emotional feelings. Without a strong home base, this soul is lost.

Ancestral Inheritance: This placement may indicate a matriarchal family where the mother is all-powerful. With its strong bonds to the past and to the mother, the Cancer Moon often inherits factors through the feminine DNA. Old issues about being female also pass down through the genes.

Leo
The Sun - Fathering Archetype: Head of the Family
The soul with the Sun in Leo is used to a proud father who is the dominant member of the family. An autocrat or a benign dictator, all is well as long as the family follows his lead. If they do not, the displeasure is all too obvious, and yet this father can be a wonderful playmate for his child. Leo is all about warmth and loving and the father can express this in a most positive way to his offspring.

The Moon - Mothering Archetype: The Queen Bee
What the soul with this placement seeks is a warm, affectionate mother who can be looked up to as a positive role model - and who

can act as playmate and entertainer. What the soul dreads is the 'queen bee' around whom the world has to revolve and who demands constant attention from her child, or the drama queen whose histrionics turn each day into an emotional opera.

With this placement, admiration is essential sustenance. This soul desperately wants to be special. To be looked up to and adored is vital. If this homage is not received, the soul sulks and becomes a drama queen itself. But power also feeds this soul. In adult relationships, the soul expects the partner to provide the admiration.

Ancestral Inheritance: The ancestral inheritance from Leo is power and pride. The family is all-powerful and proud of its place in the world - which may have attracted hubris and a fall from grace in the past. Even when poor, the family has dignity - and may be too stiff-necked to ask for, or accept, the help it needs. Warm-heartedness and generosity feature strongly in the ancestral line, even in poverty.

Virgo
The Sun - Fathering Archetype: The Faithful Servant
With the Sun in Virgo the soul will have previously encountered fathers who were the faithful servant to someone else. Much will depend on how they dealt with this as to exactly what the soul expects in the present life. Virgo-fathers have an ideal of perfection to live up to, and may be highly critical if their child does not match their own high standards, and yet Virgo fathers are capable of great self-sacrifice on behalf of their children.

The Moon - Mothering Archetype: The Perfect Mother
The soul with this placement seeks a mother who is perfect and who provides an organised and yet creative environment. The fear, however, is that the mother will be cold and critical, setting impossibly high standards of behaviour and creating an emotionally sterile environment in which the child cannot thrive.

The soul with the Moon in Virgo is fed by reward and recognition for all the small services rendered, but is too modest to seek this out. In adulthood, this lunar food will be sought from a partner who recognises that such services are a way of showing love.

Ancestral Inheritance: The inner critic is associated with the cold and critical part of Virgo. Such a figure can be passed through the family line imposing impossibly high ideals of behaviour and service. The child soon learns to self-criticise and this criticism is applied to others if they do not meet the same high standards. Emotional coldness can be a feature of family life, although there are times when earthy common sense prevails. Virgo also has a connection with the psychosomatic effect of the mind on the body: the overly protective mother creates an offspring who has asthma, for example.

Libra
The Sun - Fathering Archetype: The Diplomat
The soul with this placement may have had considerable experience with a father who sought peace at all costs, to the extent that the child made him or herself virtually invisible. This father could have demanded that the child put his or her needs on hold, making sacrifices on behalf of the family. It is also likely that the child learned to repress any feelings of anger. The child comes to believe that being good is preferable to being him or her self – a misconception that is carried over into adult relationships with a resulting lack of congruence between the outward behaviour and the inner person.

The Moon - Mothering Archtype: The People Pleaser
What the soul with this Moon craves is a nice mother who will create beautiful surroundings in which the child can be admired and indulged. What the soul expects is the mother who is pleasant on the surface but who is inherently selfish and, in private, attuned only to her own needs.

Libra is nourished by peace and beauty. This soul craves companionship and admiration in harmonious surroundings. Poverty does not unduly worry this soul, so long as comfort is not sacrificed, but adult partners must be ready to create and maintain an harmonious environment.

Ancestral Inheritance: The ancestral ambience may be one of ease and plenty. Sensual stimulation and indulgence usually abound in Libran households, but even in poverty, this is the family who values beauty. The child learns how to make surroundings congenial no matter what. The family also values niceness. Harmony is maintained at all costs. Anger and conflict are forbidden. The child learns that anything is preferable to showing temper.

Scorpio
The Sun - Fathering Archetype: The Power Broker

Scorpio is a powerful sign and the soul with this Sun placement will expect the father to be equally powerful, an ideal hook for the projection of power until the child comes into his or her own. There is an element of self-destruction to Scorpio which may show itself in the father, but there is also a unique perspicacity with regard to his offspring.

The Moon - Mothering Archetypes: The Great No-Sayer and the Devouring Mother are both associated with this Moon

Power plays are a feature of childhood for the soul with this Moon. The expectation is that Mother will be all powerful, dominant and, quite possibly, abusive. The soul seeks an emotionally intense mother who provides the right ambience for the child to release and heal deep, dark emotional pain from the past. What the soul fears is the wrathful, devouring, frustrated mother who seeks to live out her own unlived life through her child. The mother may look to her child to fulfil her unmet emotional needs and has no hesitation in using subtle blackmail to ensure he/she complies.

Intensity and all-consuming passion provide fuel for the soul with this Moon. When emotionally nourished and fulfilled, the soul is empowered. Emotionally deprived, the soul retreats into abusive power plays. This soul's task is to find emotional nourishment from inner reserves rather than demanding emotional sustenance from others, and partners will play an important role in this. The soul will expect them to intuitively understand just how deep emotions run.

Ancestral Inheritance: The ancestral inheritance passed down this dark line is matriarchal, powerful and dominant. Lurking family secrets may include addictions, infidelity or illegitimacy. Death and destruction abound, as do secrecy and manipulation. It is not uncommon for a family member to simply disappear. Birth has a close relationship with death, although such things are rarely talked about. The emotional intensity heaves beneath the surface, but the family strives to keep a lid on it at all costs.

Sagittarius
The Sun - Fathering Archetype: The Adventurer

As Sagittarius is on a permanent quest, the father of the soul with this Sun placement may be unavailable when required. However, the soul will have an expectation that father is knowledgeable, exciting and adventurous. Freedom means a lot to this father - and to the child.

The Moon - Mothering Archetype: The Free Spirit

This soul seeks a companionable mother, one who is playmate and co-explorer of the world. The archetypal Sagittarian Moon mother is spontaneous and freedom-loving. She enjoys her children but may lack discipline herself and therefore be unable to provide the guidelines a child needs. What the soul fears, is that mother may be so busy exploring her own world, she will have little time for her child.

The soul with the Sagittarian Moon seeks companionship and attention - and emotional freedom. This Moon can live off discussing feelings - preferably other people's - so a partner had better be prepared for this. Learning to be truly intimate with a partner could provide soul food, as long as the partner recognises the need for emotional space.

Ancestral Inheritance: Lack of commitment and an inability to be intimate pass down through this lunar line. The family may trust to luck to get by, and may be none too honest in the process so the child learns - or relearns - that being economical with the truth is acceptable. Exaggeration is also a facet of Sagittarius that runs down the family line, somehow things are not all that they are cracked up to be. There can be conflicts between a desire to tell the truth and a reluctance to reveal all. As a result, emotional honesty is either brutally frank or non-existent. Tact and diplomacy have little place in this home.

Capricorn
The Sun - Fathering Archetype: The Stern Father

Capricorn is an authoritarian sign and the soul with this placement expects a stern, controlling father who sets strict boundaries. His offspring is required to conform to the conventions of the day. The father will no doubt be highly ambitious for his child, as Capricorn values material success. If the child fails to fulfil this, he or she may be disregarded as of little worth - an experience that will have occurred in previous lives.

The Moon - Mothering Archetype: The Voice of Authority

What the soul with this placement seeks is consistent, dependable, disciplined mothering. The soul needs boundaries and the opportunity to develop personal autonomy. What the soul fears, is a cold, controlling, authoritarian mother who demands that the child conform to her standards. If those standards are not met, then love is withdrawn. The absent parent is a feature of this Moon.

What feeds and nurtures the soul with a Capricorn Moon are success, approval and a sense of things being right. As a partner will learn, this soul wants to remain in emotional control and yet would be nourished by a genuine display of feelings.

Ancestral Inheritance: The family into which this soul is born may be materially successful but emotionally deprived. Childhood is often emotionally stultifying. The ambience passed down through the generations is cold and authoritative, no argument possible. The family is strongly patriarchal. Success in the outer world is valued, and the child is urged into a good career rather than being encouraged to develop innate talents and abilities. This soul may find itself in a family where depression or chronic illness is common. In this case, the soul has the advantage of having learnt emotional self-sufficiency.

Aquarius

The Sun - Fathering Archetype: The Eccentric

With this Sun placement the soul does not know quite what to expect of a father. There will have been lives where the father was unstable and unpredictable, as if coming from another planet. But then again, the father may have been the scapegoat for society's ills. On the other hand, the father may have been stuck in a rut of strict adherence to an unconventional view. And, there is always the possibility that the father was entirely absent. Now the soul is faced with the challenge of creating a new image of father.

The Moon - Mothering Archetype: The Unpredictable Parent

What the soul with this placement seeks is a freedom-loving, somewhat unconventional mother who nevertheless recognises the need for boundaries and guidelines. What the soul expects is an eccentric, unstable mother who can be something of an embarrassment and who finds it impossible to give consistent discipline.

This soul finds emotional sustenance in social interaction and working for society. However, a close, intimate relationship with someone who is able to appreciate a need for space would provide nourishment at a more personal level if a prospective partner can breach the Aquarian emotional defences.

Ancestral Inheritance: There is always something a little different about far-sighted Aquarius and the family will reflect this. The ancestral pattern may be one of fighting for freedom and the rights of the individual. Taken to extremes this could be the anarchist and revolutionary. Taken personally, it could be the loner who defiantly follows his or her own path, the independent thinker, or the humanitarian. However, Aquarius can also be cold and unresponsive; or unstable and unpredictable. The soul with this Moon is never quite sure what to expect and home is rarely a safe haven.

Pisces
The Sun - *Fathering Archetype: A Beautiful Illusion*
A Piscean-Sun soul expects a wonderful father, but is often disappointed. This is the father who is impossible to pin down. He appears to be all that the soul could wish for, until help or support is called for and then, inexplicably, he is not there. He often experiences great difficulty in actually seeing his child, somehow he imagines the child as an extension of himself. In other lives, the soul may have had experiences with an addictive father who took refuge in the bottle; or a man who was more involved in his visions and fantasies than his child. If he could share those visions, however, he could live up to all his child hoped for.

The Moon - *Mothering Archetype: the Fantasy Mother*
What the soul with this Moon seeks is a sympathetic, sensitive mother who enjoys entering into a fantasy world with her child. What the soul expects is to be engulfed by a mother who recognises no boundaries and sees her child as an extension of herself. Such a mother leaves no room for individuality or mutual growth.

This symbiotic Moon feeds off other people and wants to merge back into an emotionally melded relationship, which is seen as blissful union.

Ancestral Inheritance: The family will reflect certain underlying themes: dedication to an ideal, religious beliefs, escapism and addiction. The soul may be expected to sacrifice itself for others, or the parents believe that it is right to sacrifice themselves for their child. Personal space and individual boundaries are rare. The ambience is symbiotic and undifferentiated, with little room for individuality. Any attempt to break free from the family is met with disbelief. An attitude of martyrdom pervades the parenting. Two keynotes are: 'After all we've done for you...' and 'what have we done to deserve this?'

THE SUN AND MOON IN ASPECT

Outer planet aspects to the Sun and Moon show the kind of parenting the soul has received in the past and indicate whether the soul expects the present-life parents to be supportive. Some souls will have had good experiences with parenting, others not. Such experiences affect the soul's self-image and confidence, and will carry forward into adult interactions. Where there are several aspects to the Sun, the soul will be trying to resolve conflicting previous life experiences and find a fresh archetype.

Fathering karma

Aspects to the Sun by the outer planets modify the image of Father that the soul carries from life to life. They subtly affect the archetypal sun-sign picture of what the soul expects. As the soul is pre-programmed, experiences that reinforce the picture tend to be noticed and those that are different are often disregarded. Part of the challenge is for the soul to find a more positive assumption.

Jupiter-Sun

This soul has received strong and supportive fathering in the past and the expectation is, unless there are other aspects that mitigate against this, that the father will be a source of growth in the present life.

Chiron-Sun

The soul has been deeply wounded by a father in the past. The father may have left, willingly or unwillingly, or may have been abusive and harsh. Now the soul has to heal the wound of that old parenting.

Saturn-Sun

In other lives, the soul will have had experiences with a stern authoritarian father and will have come to expect emotional distance, or actual separation, from the father. There may be an absent parent in the present life - physically or emotionally - or a lack of affection. The father may also be much older, belonging to quite a different generation. The experience of father is often one of disapproval unless the child conforms to rigid behaviour patterns. The challenge for this soul is to father itself.

Neptune-Sun
This soul has usually idealised and idolised the father in the past, but rarely sees him clearly. The father himself may have been elusive and difficult to tie down. The child too may have been idolised in a past life, having experienced being a chosen child and seen as perfect by the parents. The karma here is one of over-idealisation. The child expects father to be wonderful - and indeed the father often appears to be so, until the child needs support when the father melts away. The present life father may be weak, unreliable and dependent - to the extent that the child ends up fathering the father. The challenge is to see through the idealisation to reach the real father rather than the one who is fantasized. The soul's task is to develop a realistic expectation of father.

Uranus-Sun
The soul has a picture of unpredictable, unstable fathering. A father who comes - and goes. The father may be a free spirit, or a man who has great difficulty in taking responsibility for his child and committing to relationship with that child. The father may remain physically present, but wish to be elsewhere. The child is challenged to find a new image of father.

Pluto-Sun
The karma here is around power and symbiosis. The authoritarian father has the power of life and death over the child. These expectations are carried into adulthood, the father remaining a powerful figure in the inner psyche unless that projection of power is taken back. The image of father is an extremely powerful one. The child in the past most probably felt that this was the most powerful figure in the universe, and this is projected into present life relationships. One of the fundamental tasks is to regain personal power from the archetypal father figure.

Mothering Karma

The Moon-sign is the archetypal picture of what the soul expects with regard to nurturing. Aspects to the Moon by the outer planets subtly alter the image of Mother that the soul carries from life to life. As the soul is pre-programmed, experiences that reinforce the inner picture tend to be noticed, and those that are different are often disregarded. Part of the challenge is for the soul to find a more positive view of the maternal energy.

Jupiter-Moon

The fortunate soul with Jupiter-Moon contacts has experienced some excellent mothering. It has been supported and urged to grow in past lives and now incarnates expecting the kind of parenting that will allow it to live life in the best way possible for its evolution.

Chiron-Moon

The soul with this combination carries a deep wound around mothering and being mothered. The mother may have been torn away in a past life, or the child may have had to be abandoned. The challenge in the present life is not only to mother oneself but also to heal the expectations of wounding by creating a healthy relationship with the soul's own mother and with offspring. This child frequently finds him or herself in the role of family scapegoat or the identified patient: the one who acts out all the family dis-ease and who takes on the burden of blame. The child may also have been made a scapegoat for the mother's unlived life, even though the mother may have chosen not to take up opportunities (see Chapter 3). If the mother felt she had no choice, then the child with this aspect is even more likely to have the blame shunted on him or her, although this will usually occur at an unconscious level in the mother. It may result in a mother who acts the martyr or victim role. The challenge is for the soul to nurture itself, healing its mothering karma.

Moon-Saturn

With Moon-Saturn aspects the soul has received poor mothering in the past. There may have been coldness and indifference, illness or poverty, death and separation early in life. Being the eldest or middle child in a large family could mean that the soul misses out on being mothered, for example, and often, if female, has to care for itself and younger siblings. The challenge for the soul is to mother itself.

Uranus-Moon

The soul with this combination has experienced unstable or unpredictable mothering in the past. The mother could not be relied upon, throwing the child inward onto his or her own resources. This can make for an extremely independent soul, but it can also lead to difficulties in making relationships. The challenge for the soul is to trust the maternal energy once more, whilst learning to nurture itself.

Neptune-Moon

This combination indicates an idealised or idealistic picture of mother, an illusion that may prove false and lead to great disillusionment. It can also indicate the kind of closeness between mother and child that operates on a non-physical level. This may be beneficial to the child, but it can also make for an overly dependent child contingent on the soul's previous experience. The soul must develop a realistic mothering expectation.

Moon-Pluto

As we have already seen, the Moon in aspect to Pluto indicates powerful karma around mothering and being mothered. This is smother or devouring love. There is a peculiar intensity about Pluto that doesn't let you off lightly. In other lives the soul will have experienced abandonment, rejection, persecution and the archetypal figure known as 'the devouring mother' - in other words heavy mother issues. The expectation now is that being mothered is likely to involve symbiosis, power struggles and a desire on the part of the mother to live out her unlived life through her child.

One noticeable facet of natal Pluto-Moon aspects is that the child incarnates with a strong soul connection to one or more grandmothers. It is as though the grandmother is the stable rock upon which the child can depend, and who can support the child, even through the most difficult of times with the rest of the family.

The aspect is often linked to the 'Jewish Mother' but, as Howard Sasportas once remarked, 'You don't have to be Jewish to be a Jewish Mother, although it certainly helps!' Jewish Mothers want the best for their children, especially their sons. They are fiercely protective, strongly possessive and highly ambitious for them. They will manipulate and control in an effort to get the child to do what is 'best for him'. Cutting the apron strings is rarely an option with this mother and the child remains tied well into adulthood. Such an experience will clearly affect adult relationships (see Chapter 8). The task for the soul with Pluto-Moon aspects is to let go of the past, to forgive both itself and all mothers who have contributed to the karma, and then to become creative and nurturing in its own right.

'HE WAS MINE FIRST'

A seventh house Sun or Moon indicates that a father or mother and child were likely to have been husband and wife in a former life. Aspects to the Sun and Moon, and the sign on the seventh house cusp, clarify the type of karma involved in the relationship and the ease, or otherwise, with which it will be resolved. This past-life sexual interaction between parent and child can cause difficulties such as physically incestuous or abusive behaviour. A father, for example, could feel it is his right to use the child sexually and to control it with violence. It may also result in emotional incest between a son and a possessive mother who deeply resents any other woman in his life, particularly on the sexual level.

A gay man with the Sun in the seventh house opposing Neptune, was extremely close to his mother and told her, as a child, not that he would marry her when he grew up - which is the fantasy of many little boys - but that he had been her husband in the past. He could not bear the thought of loving any other woman and his mother was extremely jealous of the few girls he dated in his teens. However, they were both happy when he started a sexual relationship with another man.

The mother used a workshop to explore past life links with her son, and found she had been married to him in several lives - which confirmed their feelings. To her surprise she also found that she had been married to her present life father with whom she had also been close. Her present life mother had been jealous of her and had made her childhood miserable, as she could not stand this closeness between father and daughter. 'Now I understand', the woman said triumphantly to me: 'He was mine first and she simply could not stand it.'

THE UNWANTED CHILD

The Moon carries with it the opportunity to learn the twin lessons of mothering and emotional equilibrium. A young man incarnated with Capricorn on the Ascendant (conjunct twelfth house Chiron).

The Moon in Aquarius in the first house opposed Venus in Leo in the seventh, forming a T-square to Saturn in Scorpio in the ninth. He was an unwanted, unplanned pregnancy and the third child in four years born to a middle-aged mother. His father had left home some days before his birth. Shortly after the birth his mother experienced severe post-natal depression (Saturn square the Moon) and entered hospital, returning there periodically over the next four years so that his early nurturing was intermittent and on the whole poor (the expectation of the Capricorn Ascendant).

His Aquarian Moon indicated detached, unpredictable and unstable mothering and yet paradoxically he was deeply attached to his mother, living with her until his thirties. He was unable to break away from what had become a suffocating bond, formed through fear, isolation and idealisation (Mercury-Venus square Neptune-Saturn opposing the Moon). He was initially disliked by his elder brother and sister, who blamed him (a Capricorn scapegoat) for the loss of their mother, teasing and tormenting him throughout his childhood.

The children were brought together by the early death of the father but they remained fixed in a pattern of childish interplay. He had incarnated with an inner sense of worthlessness and lack of confidence (Saturn-Moon) which was reinforced by his uterine and childhood experiences, and the development of a repressed personality. The emotional impact of these experiences was internalised - at one point in his childhood he was hospitalised for chronic constipation, a psychosomatic manifestation of his inner constriction. At the age of eleven he became a Buddhist, finding his nourishment and sustenance in his contact with the cosmos (Sun conjunct Jupiter trine Neptune), and rejecting worldly matters (wide Saturn-Neptune conjunction, ninth and eighth houses). In his mid-thirties he underwent the progressive transits of Saturn-Uranus-Neptune to his Sun, Jupiter and Mars, which enabled him to overcome the past conditioning and to leave home.

'I DON'T DESERVE TO BE LOVED'

Birth often brings child and mother face to face with innate expectations. Pluto on the Ascendant of the mother and an exact Pluto-Uranus-Virgo Ascendant conjunction of the child to the mother's Chiron, featured in a birth by vacuum extraction where the mother's contractions had almost ceased and the baby's heart was slowing. Both were near to death (Pluto). The mother expected birth to be a life threatening experience - she had died in childbirth in her last life. The baby had been conceived during a civil war (Uranus) and the mother had been coping with the breakdown of her marriage.

The child had incarnated with the expectation that birth would be life-threatening and traumatic and that the world was, in any case, an unsafe, unpredictable place to be (Pluto-Uranus). This was reinforced both by the toxic state (Pluto) of her mother's body (Virgo) and the way in which she herself was suddenly sucked out into the world (Uranus). She also had an eighth house Saturn opposing the Moon, showing an in-built expectation of rejection and isolation. Owing to the trauma of the child's birth she had to be cot-nursed for forty-eight hours and was denied the comfort of physical contact with her mother. The family moved house constantly during her childhood and she experienced continual disruption in her environment. Her father died when she was young and her grandfather, who acted as a surrogate father when she was very young, left her grandmother - although this was never acknowledged within the family. Her grandfather fell into a pattern of promising to visit her. She would be overwhelmed with excitement, waiting all weekend for him, only to be devastated when he did not arrive. Her experience of men, therefore, was that they let you down.

She married young and followed the family pattern by experiencing great difficulty in pregnancy. Her first baby died at birth and this was followed by two difficult births. She then left her husband and began an affair with a man whose birthday was the same as her grandfather's. He was older than her, and 'coincidentally' happened to be the age her grandfather had been when she was close to him. He even looked a great deal like her grandfather. The affair was an on-and-off one, and each time it was ended by him he would within a matter of weeks 'somehow call round and we'd end up in bed'. This went on for several years but she still felt that there was no one like him, he understood her in a way no one else did. His rejection had become entangled in her eyes with love - because he was repeating exactly what she had experienced from her so-loved grandfather. Eventually she became pregnant and he immediately broke off all contact, saying the child could not possibly be his. Then he returned. Then he left again, precipitating premature labour. After the child was born, he returned and they began to live together but he constantly threatened to leave. To her this was normal; after all, deep down inside she believed she did not deserve love and he merely confirmed her belief. She was unable to see that she was repeating a family pattern nor could she accept that she deserved something better and could change the pattern. Her in-built sense of being unlovable was too great.

ABUSE AND COLLUSION

Figure 16 is the chart of a woman, Ingrid, who was born to a violent abusive father whom she hated (fourth house Mars opposing Saturn-Uranus-Sun T-square) and a compliant, collusive mother, whom she nevertheless idolised. Her mother never gave her any affection and escaped through an early death (Sun inconjunct Neptune, Venus-Jupiter Grand Trine with Neptune and Saturn). Ingrid had a Scorpio South Node and manifested an overwhelming capacity for rage and revenge, stating that when her father, by then eighty years old, became senile and helpless she was going to: 'Get him and make him suffer.'

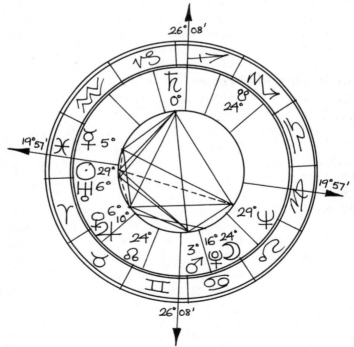

Figure 16 - Collusion

Ingrid carried her compulsive patterns of lack of self-worth (Sun square Saturn), acceptance of abuse (Saturn-Mars), and demand for love (Venus-Pluto) into her adult relationships. Her first child died at the age of seven months (wide Pluto-Moon conjunction in Cancer in the fifth). She eventually left her 'too nice' husband and five children and went to live with another 'not so nice' man. She had an abortion despite the fact that he wanted the child. She unconsciously used her children as a weapon against her men. She said that she felt responsible for her children's pain (Moon in Cancer, Sun in Pisces) and was acutely aware of their rejection of her, and yet could not connect the cause with the effect. She felt herself to be a victim: a typical manifestation of Pisces colluding with itself to subtly alter and avoid reality.

Ingrid requested a reading because she was 'unable to let go of her painful childhood and the hurt around her children, whom she could not release to the past' (a Cancerian Moon trait). She wondered what the lesson was that she had not learnt, but did not believe the answer she was given. As Susan Forward explains: 'Masochists look on their submission to mistreatment as love, whereas in fact it is a necessity in their never-ceasing search for revenge and is basically motivated by hatred.'[3]

PARENT-CHILD SYNASTRY

Synastry between the parental chart and the child's chart highlights karmic issues, old interconnection and plans for the present life. Any aspect, no matter how minor will manifest the karma inherent in the contact. In assessing these inter-aspects it is important to bear in mind that either person can act out the role of the outer planet, and that roles may change or reverse as the child matures. Interaspects are dealt with at length in Chapter 5 but in addition the following issues arise specifically between parent and child:

Jupiter Interaspects

Jupiter aspects to the personal planets or the angles across charts indicate a basic trust between the souls which comes from a long association and which can mitigate the effect of other, difficult aspects. Even if the contact or relationship is onerous, there is still a sense of rightness about it coming from the deeper levels. The interplay helps the incarnating souls to open up and grow in some way. It may be that the parent incarnates with the intention of assisting the growth of the child, or that the child will expand the parent. Jupiter is linked to faith, not religious belief, and knows that it is in exactly the right place at the right time. It accepts that it is learning the lessons it most needs for its soul growth. This sense of basic rightness can explain why, having experienced a deprived childhood, some souls might not be as severely impaired in emotional functioning as others who have experienced less hardship.

This contact has been particularly noted in the synastry between the charts of differently-abled children and their parents in cases where the latter seek understanding of the child's need to incarnate under difficulties, and value the child despite the handicap. They do not grieve for the child who might have been, as often happens with Saturn aspects, but rather seek to make the most of what *is*. The Sun or Ascendant of the child in these cases almost always falls on the Jupiter of a parent, and the child's Jupiter may fall on a personal planet in the parent's chart. When exploring the karmic interaction of these souls, it should be remembered that there is always a close spiritual tie and a deep desire to assist in *mutual growth*.

Saturn Interaspects

Saturn aspects to the personal planets between the charts indicate an old debt or sense of duty which is being repaid, either by the parent or the child. The difficulty is that the debt may surface as a deep sense of responsibility which is restrictive and repressive, particularly when an angle of a chart is involved. Issues of control versus self-determination may have to be dealt with. The parent may wish to control the child in order that past mistakes made by either of them may not be repeated, but the parent is often unable to accept apparent failure or see that mistakes can be a basis for growth. On the other hand, the parent can guide the child on to a pathway of self-development and self-control by applying sufficient discipline and giving the right balance of freedom to choose. The child who feels that it has a debt to repay may take on the burden of an elderly or chronically sick parent, or accept financial responsibility for the family by way of repayment.

A child may experience apparent rejection from the Saturnine parent, and be pushed into a separation which the child may need but not feel ready to accept. A woman with fourth house Saturn conjunct her mother's Sun was an unwanted late child - a fact she was always acutely aware of. At the age of fourteen she was sent away from home to work in a hotel. She only saw her parents once a month but sent her wages home each week because she felt she had to. Much later, as she was caring for her infirm mother to whom she had grown extremely close, she came to recognise that, far from rejecting her, her mother had been offering her what she saw as a good future, a way out of the poverty trap which had dogged her family all her life.

Chiron Interaspects

When Chiron interaspects occur between parent and child, the relationship is either offering the child an opportunity to heal old wounds - or for the parent to do so - or to replay old wounding situations so that the soul once more has an opportunity to heal the past. The family interaction may also include scapegoating, or for the child to take on the wounded-healer role that heals the family line. Chiron interaspects often pervade a whole family, in which case they are re-working an old dynamic where many issues will come together in an opportunity to heal ancestral karma.

Uranus Interaspects

Uranus contacts to the personal planets indicate a freedom/ commitment or control dilemma. It may be that the old contact was one of too much control and that the soul now needs to recognise and acknowledge the other's unique individuality and need for freedom. On the other hand, the parent may in the past have failed to take on responsibility for the child and now has to make a commitment. This was apparent in the contact between a father and the child he had abandoned in a past life. In the present life he felt very strongly, when divorcing the child's mother, that the child should live with him.

Neptune Interaspects

As we have seen (Chapter 5), Neptune contacts to the personal planets between the charts indicate an old closeness and a subtle sense of wanting to care for the other soul to the extent of giving up one's life for it. However, this is not always carried through. Many promises are made in the guise of Neptune but the parent, or the child, slips away having promised the world - so these contacts also contain illusions and delusions around what is or is not 'real'.

When between parent and child, Neptune contacts to the personal planets across the charts indicate an extremely telepathic link, although this is rarely conscious. It means that the child may subconsciously pick up on what a parent is thinking or feeling. If this intuitive knowing is not validated for the child by the parent confirming that it is correct, or worse still by the parent actively denying the insight, confusion and deception can mar the relationship. It can also create a pattern for future relationships in which deception arises. The child may either stay totally with intuitive feelings and reject logic and parental untruth, or may go along with the deception. If the child does not trust his or her intuitive feelings, these may be disregarded and suppressed long after the actual parental contact has been left behind. The soul will then have to re-learn to trust these inner perceptions again through a liaison with a Neptunian partner. However, the Neptunian interaspect can be utilised to talk telepathically to the child on a mental level, a technique which can be extremely helpful in conveying a sense of reassurance and safety or in ironing out difficulties.

Problems can arise in families with Neptune interaspects when individual boundaries are not recognised. For example, where the parent expects the child - or the child the parent - to react as he or she does or has always done in the past, or when the child is assumed, without consultation, to be in agreement. As with adult relationships where Neptune interaspects are strong, each person needs to continually check out: 'Am I hearing or understanding correctly?', 'Is my own expectation or ideal getting in the way?', 'Am I falling back into an old pattern which is no longer valid?'. Within these safeguards, there can be a loving communication on a soulmate level between parent and child.

The Chosen Child
Neptune interaspects may point to the 'chosen child' - the child whom a parent dotes on, who is extra special and with whom there may be emotional incest as well as a strong internal bond. This is the child who is, unconsciously, chosen by a parent to be 'a primary source of emotional support'.[4] The parent confides in the child, and make may him or her an ally against the other parent. Such a child has a great deal of idealisation to carry and may find it impossible to live up to parental expectations. The relationship with the parent

with whom the Neptune tie is strong will be invasive and enmeshed. As Dr Patricia Love explains, the chosen child so needs to be connected to a parent, usually because of low self esteem, that the parent has total control of the child. The parent frequently tries to live his or her own unlived life out through the child, and the child is afraid to do anything independently in case love is withdrawn.

Viewed from outside, the interconnection between parent and child may appear to be wonderful, blissful even. The two are so close, but the closeness is excessive. The syndrome has repercussions within the parental marriage as the parent looks to the child rather than the partner for emotional fulfilment and companionship. The other parent often feels resentful and yet cannot criticise a spouse for loving a child and so has no outlet for the resultant anger. This further widens the emotional gap in the parental unit, which leaves the child unparented by father or mother as the case may be. As a result, chosen child and parent cling closer together. In effect, the child becomes a surrogate spouse - and emotional incest has the potential to turn into sexual abuse as the child matures. With Neptune interaspects, there is usually a romantic, flirtatious undertone, but with Pluto the undercurrents in a chosen child situation are more abusive.

Given Neptune's links to escapism of all kinds, this interaspect is common where a child gets drawn into an alcoholic parent's own confusions. The child will be used for emotional support one minute, and as a focal point for the release of anger the next. But addictive behaviour is not the only scenario where this occurs. The result of a child being 'chosen' will be powerlessness, fluctuating self-esteem, lack of privacy or individuality, and difficulty in maintaining a relationship with his or her peers. In adult life, sexual dysfunction may be present and there will be problems with maintaining relationships.

In the chosen child syndrome, the parent uses the child to satisfy needs that would have been fulfilled more appropriately by another adult. As a result, the parent will usually have an inadequate adult support system to fall back on, and so turns to the child even more. In so doing, the parent will ignore most of the child's own needs. After all, if there are no boundaries between them the parent can rationalise that the child does not have separate needs - a typical Neptunian convolution. Within a family, there is a noticeable effect on siblings, with considerable sibling rivalry. Guilt often pervades the whole family: the chosen child feels guilty if he or she does not do enough for the parent, the non-bonded parent feels guilty at not fulfilling the parental role, and the non-chosen child feels unworthy, believing they must have done something to deserve this.

In adult relationships the effect is profound. First of all there is an enormous struggle for a chosen child to develop individuality and to separate from the parent. They can be held in the child relationship, way past physical maturity. Chosen children frequently have commitment problems, because, in their eyes and their parent's eyes, committing to someone else would be betraying the parent. Equally, they may choose an unavailable partner because, unconsciously, they know this will not be a rival to the parent. As no-one could possibly live up to the, apparently, wonderful bond between child and parent, a prospective partner will always be judged wanting - especially by the parent who will find fault and believe that so-and-so is not good enough for their child. If the child does marry, the close-bonded parent is a shadowy, but powerful, third party within the marriage. In such circumstances, intimacy is impossible. In addition, there is a lack of commitment to what should be the primary love partner because that role is still, at least in part, taken by the parent.

The way to heal the chosen child syndrome is to realign the parent-child relationship, bringing it into balance so that there is no excessive emotional enmeshment or disturbance. The love then becomes unconditional, freeing the way for the child to evolve emotionally and separate at an appropriate time.

The Colluding Parent

Neptune can also be linked to an old pattern of collusion - entering into another person's distortion of reality - and delusion, as in the case of a mother who felt an extremely old connection with her sensitive son, whom she always protected from his father. He was a classic case of the chosen child, which created considerable resentment in his sister and his father. The mother had Venus in Pisces opposing Neptune, squared by the son's Sun. Her Chiron opposed his Moon in Scorpio.

The son had Mars conjunct Neptune in Libra in the first house T-square the fourth and tenth houses (Capricorn-Cancer), and Chiron-North Node opposite Uranus-South Node. His mother's twelfth house Moon conjoined his Neptune-Mars and her Uranus opposed it, her Mercury was conjunct his Chiron-North Node and her Pluto in Cancer his Uranus-South Node. Her karmic Grand Cross contained powerful mothering issues and his interaspect T-square contained both pain (Chiron), escapism (Neptune-Mars) and the possibility for transformation (Uranus). Neptune acted powerfully upon both mother and son.

Having discovered that her son, then aged thirty, was taking drugs it took the mother a long time to assimilate the knowledge. Once she had adjusted to the fact that he was smoking heroin she deluded herself for many months that he would not inject - 'he had always fainted at the sight of needles'. Eventually she had to believe the evidence on his arm. She then colluded with him in his drug-taking, supplying the money and controlling the supply by giving a little less each day in an attempt to wean him off. Again it took her a long time to recognise that he was supplementing her controlled dose by buying more and taking sleeping pills. She arranged for him to go to an out-patient clinic and again tried to control his use of methadone by doling it out each day. This time he resorted to a chronic cough and codeine linctus to supplement the dose.

At one point the mother attended a 'Cutting the Ties' seminar. Half-way through cutting the ties with her son, she fell asleep but told no one. A few days later she arrived on my doorstep. Her navel was raw and bleeding - she had been in the middle of removing an umbilical cord the thickness of a tree trunk which joined him to her when she had lost awareness. She commented that she had not felt right about what she was doing as she believed she was cutting off the love he needed rather than the old emotional conditioning between them which is the object of tie cutting. It took over two hours of one-to-one work to finish that cutting, and she then slept for fifteen hours.

Shortly afterwards her son entered a clinic as an in-patient but refused to stay as he 'did not need all that head-stuff'. He did give up heroin, but turned to alcohol. When I last saw the mother, five years later, neither of them had yet recognised that he was an addict - now to alcohol - and that she could not 'do it for him'. She was unable to use the tough love of Chiron which may just have precipitated him into the crisis he needed to find the motivation to deal with his escape from reality - a deep-seated pattern in his chart.

The Neptune-attuned soul is capable of great personal sacrifice for another, including vicarious suffering. Nevertheless, this soul can play the martyr and delude itself into thinking that others need the sacrifice when it would really be more constructive for them to deal with their own karma. The mother who gives up her life outside the home to care for her child is a good illustration of this: her child may have in fact grown more through a mother fulfilled by her own career or while, perhaps, struggling with isolation and loneliness - if this was on the child's karmic script. In giving up everything the mother is adding a karmic burden to the child who then feels a guilty obligation to the paragon - an attitude which colours subsequent interaction in adult relationships. Then a similar sacrifice on the part of the partner might be expected, or it may prove impossible to find anyone who lives up to the impossibly high and totally unrealistic standard set by mother.

Pluto Interaspects

As we have seen, Pluto aspects to the personal planets in the other chart indicate dependency versus independence issues centred around power, manipulation and separation. Pluto aspects to the Moon indicate a particularly symbiotic or devouring mothering interplay, and Pluto-Mars an aggressive one. In the past one of the souls has either been absorbed by the other, often as a parent-child relationship in which the umbilical cord was never cut (Moon), or the parent had strong power over the child (Sun), or the child has experienced abandonment and rejection previously and now unconsciously expects this to occur in the present life.

The challenge may be for the parent to make reparation for earlier rejection, or to give the child yet another experience of abandonment so that this can be overcome. Death of a parent is often perceived as abandonment, even in adulthood. A client of mine, with natal Moon-Pluto, regressed to a life in which as a small child he had been left in the snow to die. His mother had been too tired to carry him further. In his present life, his mother died of cancer when he was young (they had repeating Moon-Pluto interaspects and he identified her as the mother in the earlier life). All his life he had felt abandoned. However, his own death healed this in that, when he was in a hospice, all his friends rallied round to sit with him. The experience of such devoted loving overcame the past.

The interaction in the present life can include a subtle and covert or overt domination of the child, a domination which extends far into adulthood and pervades all attempts to have a relationship.

Such a domination may come about through the chosen child syndrome, emotional blackmail, or through rejection or abuse of the child. All these things bind the child to the parent. There is considerable karmic and emotional enmeshment in a family pervaded with Plutonian ties.

Pluto has powerful links to abuse, and to emotional incest where a child experiences from a parent the kind of emotional involvement which would be more appropriate between spouses. One young woman, for example, had close double whammy Pluto interaspects with her father, whom she idolised. When she was a child, she and her father formed a powerful alliance against her mother, a deeply frustrated and angry woman. The father fell into the habit of confiding all his emotional angst to his daughter and using his closeness to her to compensate for the lack of companionship with his wife. When she was thirteen her father began an affair with a seventeen-year-old whom she knew quite well. At night, her father would sit on his daughter's bed in tears: 'If it wasn't for you', he would say, 'I could leave your mother and go and live with her. If you didn't exist, I could be happy.' Not surprisingly, the woman manifested an illness which nearly killed her. It was not until after many years, when she entered therapy, that she recognised just how abusive and inappropriate her relationship with her father had been.

At its extreme, the Pluto interaspect child can become a surrogate spouse with all the emotional projection that entails. But the child may also end up a punch-bag for the rejected spouse's resentment. Displaced rage from the mother's anger at the father in the above case would regularly land on the teenager in the form of blows for the slightest infraction of the mother's rules. It is common for the Pluto interaspect child to be made the scapegoat. They often experience a bewildering switch between being treated kindly as an emotional prop and then used for a release of tension or anger. This can occur either with the parent with whom there are Pluto interaspects, or the other parent.

Plutonion enmeshment may cause the incarnating soul to experience such difficulty in separating from the parent that he or she never enters into an adult relationship, or can lead to trying to recreate with an adult partner the patterns of childhood. The man with Moon-Pluto aspects can, for example, coerce his wife into a mothering role, or the woman with Sun-Pluto aspects may unconsciously manoeuvre her husband into an authoritarian father role. With this interaspect, both souls need to acknowledge each other's right to grow as an independent individual following his or her own pathway, in charge of their own power and destiny.

REFRAMING THE PAST

The promise to mother a specific soul, to provide them with a physical body in which to incarnate can be extremely powerful. Such promises are, usually, made in the between-life state and are, of course, forgotten when the mother incarnates. The other soul, however, waits for an opportune moment to incarnate. This can lead to complications if the first soul takes a different life path to the one envisaged.

I had a client who was Chinese and who had lived in China for the first forty years of her life. Through a series of apparent accidents she had become a highly successful business woman. As a teenager, she had been very much in love and had married against her family's wishes. Her husband died soon afterwards, under rather mysterious circumstances. She was four months pregnant and she was left destitute. Her family took her back, on condition that she aborted the baby. Although she would have liked to have had that child, in her situation she could see no other choice. She then went to work in the family business. She had several affairs, each of which ended in pregnancy and abortion by her choice. (China is a country that uses abortion as contraception and this is not unusual). She began to travel abroad with her work and started using western contraception, but it failed time after time.

By the time she came to see me, having moved permanently to England, she had lost count of the abortions she had had. When we talked about it, she said that the only child she had wanted was the first one, and yet each time she aborted another potential child, she felt tremendous grief. 'It is as though I am supposed to have that child, no matter what', she said, 'and yet I know I do not want to bring up a child on my own and I have not found a man I would want to be my child's father. And, in any case, I'm getting too old for pregnancy'.

I took her back to scan her former lives to see if there was a reason for the situation but she could not see anything. I guided her into the between-life state to seek the reason there. She quickly found a soul who was waiting to incarnate through her. She had promised this soul that she would be her mother and the soul was still there, waiting. I suggested she should ask the soul why the promise had been made. The soul said that the woman had been her mother once before, but had died in childbirth. The mother had stayed close to her child to 'watch over her'. When they met up in the between-life immediately after the soul's death, they had had an emotional reunion and the promise had been made there and then. Before incarnating, many years later in earth time, the promise had not been discussed again.

The woman told the soul how her circumstances had changed and how she did not feel able to be a mother. The soul told her that she should stick to her promise. A long dialogue then ensued. The woman kept begging the soul to release her, the soul was angry and felt rejected. I had to step in and suggest to the soul that she should talk to her guides. (I felt that as she had been hanging around the earth plane trying to incarnate again, she had made little progress since her last life and was stuck in a rut.) Reluctantly she did so, and came back to say that she would go with them. But, she was adamant that she and the woman had unfinished business that would have to be dealt with at some future time. At that stage she was not able to offer any forgiveness.

Had she been able to, the women would have renegotiated that promise during the therapy session, but it was not to be. I suggested to her that she should spend five or ten minutes each evening, sending love and forgiveness to the soul and holding compassion for her in her heart. In this way, the situation between them would have been subtly altered by the time she left incarnation. As it was, after a few months the soul appeared to her in a dream and told her that she was ready to let the promise go. Had she not done so, the karmic enmeshment would have continued into the next life.

SOUL SERVICE

The bond between parent and child offers many examples of soul service. A parent may have promised in the between-life to help the child work on its karma or to give support whilst an issue was dealt with. But soul service can come about through events of life which may not necessarily have been planned for. Such service may be incidental, or seemingly accidental. For example, a mother contacted me because of a health problem of her own, but mentioned as an aside that she was experiencing great difficulty with her son who was extremely aggressive towards her and said that he wanted 'to be a general with power over other people'. This ambition was perhaps not surprising in that his natal chart had an exact Moon-Mercury conjunction on an Aries Ascendant quincunx Pluto in Libra and Saturn in Scorpio.

Notwithstanding, I felt that he was experiencing 'undue influence' from a person from a previous life, when they had been soldiers together. (His Neptune conjunction to the South Node and Capricorn M.C, squaring his Sun-Mercury conjunction signified that this was quite feasible, particularly at a mental level). This third party was not in incarnation at the present time, the influence passing from the etheric realm, but he was living his life vicariously through the young man and exerting a powerful influence over him due to their mutual unhealed stuff from the previous life. I checked this scenario out with a therapist who specialises in spirit release work and she came up with exactly the same story. We therefore worked together to release the young man from this past-life influence.

When I looked at the synastry between his chart and his mother's, it was clear that they had been together before. There were repeating, each-way interaspects between Saturn and the Moon and Venus. This particular combination can often indicate a debt or promise of some kind being carried forward, either from a previous life or from the between-life state. The son's Saturn-Pluto conjunction fell in the mother's sixth house, his natal Moon was in Virgo in the sixth house, and her natal Moon was also in the sixth house, so there was an emphasis in the charts on the house and sign of service. With the mother's Moon conjunct her son's North Node, she was involved in his karmic purpose in some way. I came to the conclusion that she was offering him positive service through her request to me for a karmic reading. Although she had not specifically requested that her son be treated, in contacting me she facilitated this happening and rendered him an invaluable service.

I rarely use composite charts for karmic work as the synastry usually tells the story. I may sometimes look at a relationship chart if I want to probe deeper as this gives an indication of how and why the relationship functions. However, when I looked at the relationship chart for these two (Figure 17) there was a strong emphasis on Virgo with the Sun, Jupiter, Pluto and Uranus placed there. The chart had an outer-planet Finger of Fate involving Saturn,

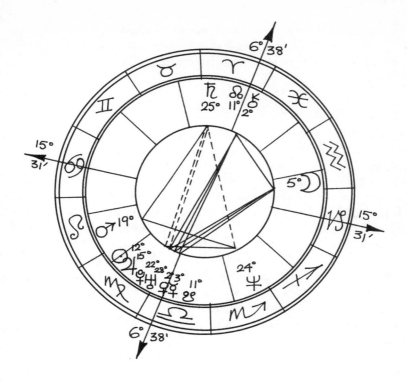

Figure 17 - Relationship Chart

the Lord of Karma, Pluto-Uranus and Neptune. Fingers of Fate involve energies that simply have to be integrated but as these are transpersonal energies it is extremely difficult to bring them into conscious awareness.

With both Saturn and the North Node in Aries, each person involved in this relationship had to become centred within their own Self. Knowing that Self however, was a difficult task. The Sun signifies the Self and the Sun-Jupiter conjunction was dissociated from the rest of the chart, signifying the potential for a past life persona or personas to break through and take over - and creating the possibility of release. Wherever dissociated or singleton planets occur there is a strong possibility of past life interference arising or of a soul energy split which could leave a person (or a relationship) open to interference from the past. Whilst it is unusual for this to occur through a third party, it does happen. However, the opposition of Chiron to Venus and Mercury indicated a strong possibility of reintegrating the boy's past life persona and healing the split, thus releasing the third party and the mother who had received the projection of aggression from a past life in which she was not involved.

KARMIC RESTITUTION?

Saturn-Moon is an aspect that anticipates that mothering will be a painful, difficult process. A client with a Saturn-Moon-South Node conjunction in Cancer in the fourth house conceived a child out of wedlock during the Second World War, following the death of her first husband, at a time when she was destitute and homeless. The child, a girl, had to be adopted although the mother later married the father and brought up his teenage children. The client had incarnated with the expectation that mothering would be a source of sorrow and difficulty to her (Saturn-Moon-South Node), and she had needed to learn to let go of her child, overcoming past possessiveness and a tendency to smother (fourth house Cancer Moon). She had also incarnated with six planets in the twelfth house, including Chiron, and was working on her karmic issues in an intense way.

When the client's daughter was thirty her adoptive parents died and she traced her mother. The daughter had Moon in Virgo semi-sextile eighth house Saturn, tenth house Neptune square Venus, and Chiron inconjunct the Sun. She also had four planets in the seventh house, indicating that she had considerable relationship karma. Her tenth house Neptune expected elusive mothering and her eighth house Saturn had karma regarding how she shared herself with others. The daughter already had a young child herself and shortly after meeting her mother again she gave birth to a son. She went into severe post-natal depression and rejected him, and he was subsequently fostered, made a ward of court and eventually adopted, thus perpetuating the family pattern. The daughter 'remained in torment, unable to love or make meaningful relationships'. The mother 'tried to help, but was filled with guilt and could find no solution'. At a later stage the daughter refused to see her mother.

Her mother asked whether this was karmic restitution. The interaction between the charts was not heavily karmic, and showed surprisingly few contacts. There were personal planets to Uranus interaspects, indicating a freedom/commitment dilemma, and reflecting the daughter's own Sun-Uranus conjunction opposing

Jupiter - an aspect which indicated that she may have grown and expanded rather more through her adoptive parents than her biological ones. A Neptune square to the mother's Moon indicated illusions, guilt, and perhaps idealisation of mothering. Saturn opposes Uranus, a change/maintenance dilemma. It appeared as though the daughter had needed to learn a karmic lesson about relationships and had chosen a mother who expected to lose her child, but not a mother with whom she had intense personal karma to work out.

It could, of course, have been that they were part of a soul group who had incarnated to help each other with some difficult lessons, although I saw no indication of this in the charts. The usual indications would be repeating Neptune-Moon or Venus aspects and nodal contacts but these were not present. With the Sun inconjunct to Chiron it also appeared that she may have had direct karma with the father, although this was not explored as he was dead and the mother was more concerned with the immediate effect of the interaction and the prospects for the future.

She found it difficult to accept that, having once given up her child, the child should return to her and then reject her. This, however, was the expectation and lesson expressed in her Saturn-Moon-South Node, which needed to move beyond the confines of the biological family and into a wider understanding of the meaning of relationship. It was also possible that, through the unconditional love offered by the Neptune-Moon interaspect and the empathy from her own experience, she could in time help to heal her daughter's wounds.

ANCESTRAL KARMA

The soul may choose to incarnate into a particular family because it has ancestral karma, a pattern carried down through the generations. This may be at a physical or emotional level of dis-ease, or it may be a repeating pattern such as the death or disappearance of a father, son or husband. If the soul needs these particular experiences itself, then there is a good chance that the family inheritance will provide fertile learning ground. Such interactions are characterised by a repeating pattern of a particular natal aspect, and interaspect, between charts.

In one family, in which six generations of women could be traced to have Moon-Pluto aspects, the husbands would die, or disappear in one case, just when the woman was involved in caring not only for her own family but also her elderly mother. As a result, it was a powerfully matriarchal family with ingrained issues about abandonment and rejection, and power. In the synastry, not surprisingly, there were many Moon-Pluto interaspects weaving down through the generations.

A pattern also emerged in which a woman would marry, have a child and then quickly have a fight with her mother, which would result in them not seeing each other for months. The grandchild would feel abandoned by the grandmother, the daughter rejected by her mother even when she herself had instigated the split. There were also Chiron interaspects involved and it was usually the illness of the grandchild that would eventually bring them all back together, although the underlying issues were never addressed. It was as if the only way the daughter could break free from the powerful mother-figure in her psyche was by removing herself completely. The client who consulted me on this was herself a grandmother who had become embroiled in the pattern. She was aware of being involved in something more than a personal pattern. 'It feels very collective', she said, 'I'm not even sure it merely belongs to our family'. This is typical of Pluto - it works at the collective level.

Ancestral karma may be inherited through the genes or through the emotional or intellectual ambience of the family. A parent may have an unfulfilled longing, for instance, that inculcates it into a child who then lives it out. The attitude or issue may be part of the child's karmic past, or it may be something he or she takes on by osmosis as it were through contact with the family. If the attitude is internalised merely to please the parent it can create problems in that soul's relationships with people outside the family, but if the issue also belongs to the incarnating soul, then he or she may have incarnated to be the lineage breaker who finally changes the pattern. This can mean facing the issue in a most intense way.

For instance, I had a client with the Sun inconjunct twelfth house Saturn and Chiron trine the Sun. From past life regressions, it was clear that he had struggled against society's norms for several incarnations, trying to bring in change. In his present life he had been born to a man who had control issues. The father was autocratic and heavily controlling, assuming he knew what was best for his son and telling him what to believe. He sapped his son's confidence and created a nervous child who was intimidated by any authority figure. In the synastry between the charts, the father's Uranus-Mercury adjoined the son's Chiron, and the father's Chiron sextiled the son's Mercury square Uranus. Not only were communication issues triggered by the father, but so was the deep wound which words can inflict. The son was terrified by the father's violent verbal outbursts over the slightest thing. These two had old, personal karma between them and, as the son grew older, he inflicted as much verbal pain as his father. This issue was only resolved between them after the father's death.

In the karmic chart, the Sun symbolises the archetypal father. In the son's chart there was an aspect with Saturn, the Lord of Karma, symbolising discipline and resilience and lessons taught through restriction, limitation, deprivation and strict control. The sheer discomfort makes change in the old pattern essential. This situation is often there so that inner strength can be developed by fighting against adversity - or against the father. In the process, a frightened child lacking in confidence emerges with an internalised sense of worthlessness - exactly what the father secretly carries but tries so hard to overcome.

As with most Saturn-Sun aspects, the child was only approved of if he did what pleased his father. The love he was offered was conditional on him being a 'good boy'. The father instilled in the child attitudes that profoundly affected him in adult life. Telling him things like: 'You are never finished until you sit down and tell yourself you are finished' ensured that, as a young man, the boy went through physical agony in an effort not to give in. The father tried to live his life through his boy, pushing him into a career where he could be the power behind his son's success. The father had himself wanted to be a doctor but the abandonment of the family by his own father meant that he had to go out to work immediately. He never had the opportunity to 'make something of himself' and forced it on his son instead. The father had the Sun and Moon in Capricorn inconjunct Pluto and disconnected from the rest of the chart, so there was a fundamental split which allowed something to rise up from a previous incarnation - and which passed on to his son.

The father ranted and rebelled against 'the system', seeing it as corrupt. He hated incompetence and bureaucratic stupidity. One of his favourite sayings was: 'Rules and regulations are for the guidance of the intelligent and the blind obedience of the idiot', something which shaped his son's ideas on life. When the career into which he pushed his son was foreshortened because of ill-health, the son became a journalist. He took up environmental campaigning and brought many of the issues his father has railed against for so long out into the public eye. It was only when the son met fierce opposition and had to fight to justify his beliefs that he was able to disentangle what he really believed from what he had inherited from his father. Following his father's death, he became much more extreme in his views, rejecting his father's somewhat conservative stance in favour of radical reform. It brought him into several head-on collisions with authority figures, and nearly wrecked his marriage in the process. But he said it was essential for him to stand up and fight for his values - something his father and his father's father had never been fully able to do.

THE LINEAGE BREAKER

Repetition of an issue is often part of the inherited ancestral karma a soul carries and there are times when a soul incarnates into a family not only to work on its own karma but also to deal specifically with the ancestral patterns embodied in that family. Such a person is known as a 'lineage breaker'. It is their task to heal the family back through the generations so that future generations will not carry that same karma. An eighth house Moon, South Node, Chiron, Saturn or Pluto placement may well indicate someone who has incarnated to transmute the family inheritance in this way.

Claire, a client whose karma with her father has already been discussed under Saturn-Sun contacts, has the Moon, South Node and Pluto in Leo in the eighth house inconjunct Chiron in Capricorn in the first house. Her mother told her that her great grandmother had met and married her great grandfather, an Irishman, in Jamaica. His younger sister, Elizabeth, was in love with an English soldier but had been forbidden to see him because he was of an inferior status. In the grief of their enforced separation, she died of pneumonia at the age of 25. In effect, it was passive suicide. Elizabeth had gone out riding in foul weather and died as a result.

Claire's sister, who had been told the story as a young child, always felt a great affinity with her as she too had fallen in love with a working class man and had run away to be with him. Claire herself fell in love with a working class man and lived rough with him, forming a rock band. But it was a tempestuous, difficult relationship and eventually he left, after which Claire attempted suicide.

Claire was aware that March, the date of her great-grandmother's death, had always been a significant time for her. Relationships would end then and, when she turned her life around after the suicide bid, appointments with doctors and healers and other important events would occur on the anniversary date. This is extremely common where the past is intervening on the present. Claire realised this when she read the line 'the sins of our fathers shall be inherited by the third and fourth generation' in a book, and she consequently had the soul of her ancestor put to rest on All Souls Day. Her grandmother died on the anniversary day. Claire said: 'It was as if a knot tied impossibly tight within my family has been unravelled, leaving us freer to be open and loving with one another, freer to give each other space and freer to take conscious responsibility for our own lives'.

I believe that Elizabeth may well have been a former incarnation of Claire, but that the tormented soul energy had remained split off when Claire reincarnated. Another view might be that Elizabeth' soul profoundly influenced Claire as she repeated the major events of Elizabeth's life.

Comparing the death chart for Elizabeth to the natal chart of Claire (the death chart is the birthchart into the between life state from where they interacted) several patterns and aspects repeat. Both had Jupiter-Mars, Saturn-Sun and Moon, Neptune-Venus-Mercury, Saturn-Pluto. In the synastry, Claire's Sun is conjunct Elizabeth's Neptune and her Neptune is on Elizabeth's North Node, making telepathic contact possible, her Venus is conjunct Elizabeth's South Node, a soul group or soulmate indication. Claire first became aware of her as 'spirit haunting me in my teens', which again is a common experience where there has been a soul-split.

In working on herself in great depth, and by having the soul of Elizabeth 'put to rest', it could well be that Claire actually reintegrated this lost soul energy into herself. It certainly worked as a lineage breaker for the family. Claire's sister's relationship flourished and was accepted by the family, and Claire herself emigrated to America and found happiness in marriage.

8

ADULT RELATIONSHIPS

No marriage is a start on a clean slate. It is an episode in a serial story begun long before.[1]

Gina Cerminara

The events of childhood do not end with puberty. They endlessly recreate themselves in adult relationships like the seasons of the year. Such events do not need to have also been a part of a former life, but if they have been then it strengthens the childhood carryover into adult life.

Loss of a loved one in childhood can profoundly influence adult behaviour within a relationship, for instance. A child who experiences the death of a parent, sibling or grandparent, may find themselves excessively possessive with an adult lover because the fear is that the loss will repeat again - especially if it is part of a karmic pattern that the soul instinctively recognises. Much patience may be needed on the part of the partner to reassure and overcome the deep-seated despair that underlies such excessive reactions. But childhood loss is not the only factor to make itself known. Situations arise that meet ingrained expectations, attitudes are confirmed, experiences cycle round and around. Roles replay themselves, sometimes with an understudy it is true, but the major characters are often drawn from past life contacts.

Joshua incarnated into a Jewish family. His chart has a T-square intimately connected with mothering and relationships: first house Venus in Scorpio opposed the Moon in Taurus, squared by a Pluto-Saturn conjunction in Leo, in the truth house. When we first met, he was on a path of self-development and avidly attending workshops which allowed him to explore both his own psyche and his family pattern. He was also interested in regression to the events which had led up to his present situation. Joshua carried the archetype of the matriarchal devouring Jewish mother (tenth house Pluto) and he desperately wanted to be loved and accepted by her. According to Joshua's past life exploration, his mother had been his wife (seventh house Moon) and in the present life she rejected his choice of wife, cutting her off ostensibly because she was non-Jewish and could not continue the matriarchal line of Judaism through her children. He incarnated with an expectation of emotional trauma, and rejection was bound up within that T-square. In previous lives Joshua had experienced the death of three women directly as a result of their having loved him (Pluto square Venus). He said: 'If people got too close, they would get hurt, I would cause them to suffer. I felt guilty.' In his regression work he also experienced considerable jealousy, trauma and rejection in relationships.

As transiting Pluto neared his Venus an astrologer told him to anticipate what he had been searching for all his life: a meeting with an old soulmate. This would be a karmic relationship, instant recognition: 'One where you walk in the room and she's there, you can't escape it.'

He could. The terror generated by Pluto and Saturn was too great. He spent the transit sharing a house platonically with a female friend who was undergoing a very karmic relationship herself. Once again he felt isolated, rejected and abandoned, and exuded resentment. And, just to complete the picture, his mother arrived to stay for three months whilst her own home was being renovated (Pluto-Saturn).

Joshua was like that line from a Winnie-the-Pooh song: 'I'm just a little black rain cloud, hovering over the honey tree.' He so wanted a relationship and yet the aura of gloom that he emanated was an effective shield against it happening. Just like poor old Pooh, whenever he reached for the honey, he got stung.

When I first met Joshua I felt he was isolated in the ivory tower of his twelfth house Neptune, cut off from the suffering of others and totally centred in his own misery. However, no one can stay static for ever and when the Pluto transit of the T-square was well underway he found a relationship based on an old friendship: 'One which is not in the least gut-wrenching, just comfortable.' He was able to move out of his total isolation and self-centred preoccupation and manifest some of the positive qualities in his chart through teaching and counselling work (utilising the Gemini North Node). This brought him into contact with many people and opened up a new direction to his life. Eventually he married the 'old friend' and settled into a stable relationship.

Joshua's story is typical of how a mothering pattern can profoundly affect adult life. The karmic patterns reinforced in childhood are carried over into relationships in adult life. They operate from a deep unconscious level and frequently precipitate totally inappropriate reactions when a trigger is inadvertently activated. Associations continue to be coloured by the past until a conscious decision is taken to examine the roots of the present response to, and interconnection with others. Such an exploration may involve entering into therapy or analysis, or undertaking regression in order to identify, and release from, the patterns of the past.

True Love?

It is possible that a bond of true love will unite a couple in marriage down through the ages, but this is not always so. Hatred can be the cause of powerful attachments. Some people will not let go of the person they 'love', and will reincarnate with that person again and again until they can do so. The lesson can be painful, especially when the recipient does not recognise the 'love' and rejects the supposed soulmate. Some couples find themselves living the consequence of ancient infidelities. Retribution can be part of relationship karma, as can recompense, reparation and enmeshment.

Physical attraction can be particularly strong where couples have known each other in the past, but it is not always appropriate to continue the relationship. It may be that the lessons the souls have come back to work on would be better learned alone. It could be that the intensity of karma makes it inadvisable for the couple to confront it until they have worked on the issues separately. It is possible that the couple do not yet have the spiritual strengths required to resolve the karma or that their purpose in incarnating is incompatible. In such cases, it could be advisable for the couples to pursue other relationships no matter how strong the pull of physical attraction.

In his readings, Edgar Cayce always emphasized that karma was not a matter of debt between couples - although I have found many cases where the souls concerned did feel that they had a karmic debt, subtle or otherwise, which they wanted to repay. According to Cayce, the issue was one of personal soul development:

'It is merely Self being met … a karmic debt of Self that may be worked out between the associations that exist in the present'[2]

In other words, the people around us are reflections of our self and the karma we must face. We create our reality, and the players on its stage, according to our psychology and our karma. This is what Carl Jung meant when he said: 'We meet ourselves time and again in a thousand disguises on the paths of life', and Krishnamurti when he stated: 'Relationship is surely the mirror in which you discover yourself'.[3]

When Nietzsche warned 'Be careful who you choose for your enemy because that is who you become most like', he was speaking a profound karmic and psychological truth. We take on the qualities of those we love and hate in equal measure because, deep down, we already have all those characteristics awaiting development or fully formed from another life. An enemy will trigger the unloving side of ourselves and we may have to face some unpleasant truths. But friends and lovers may equally bring us face to face with our shadows, and what we perceive in someone else could be what we most need to pay attention to in ourselves.

Thus, if someone complains that their partner is unloving, it is not the partner who should change but rather that the person asking for a reading should take the opportunity to redress what Cayce called 'imperfect attitudes'. They themselves would be well advised to seek to become more loving as this would overcome a previous inability to love. Equally, if they find it impossible to love someone, then they should work on being more accepting and tolerant so that they can develop unconditional love.

This approach may work, but it is not always appropriate. There are times when souls need to step away, and there may be other reasons why a couple should not marry.

SEQUELS TO THE PAST

Edgar Cayce frequently stated that no major human relationship is the result of chance. An opinion with which all karmic counsellors would no doubt agree. From a close study of his many thousands of readings, Gina Cerminara concluded (as quoted at the beginning of this chapter), that 'no marriage is a start on a clean slate. It is an episode in a serial story begun long ago.' This does not mean, however, that the parties would necessarily have been together before, it was the issues involved that were the serial story. I see in my own work couples and members of families who are starting out together for the first time. It is as though working through the issues at one remove, they can be more objective than if they have been over the same old ground together time after time.

For Cerminara, based on the evidence Cayce gave, all relationships are 'sequels to the past' - although her view takes no account of karma in the making. Virtually all the people Cayce read for appear to have been connected within soul groups and some had been in close relationship with each other before. Many incarnated together to continue karmic tasks, to close unfinished business or deal with karma. For quite a number of the people Cayce read for, marriage was a repeat performance. He said that they had had the same partners before. However, there were a number of people whom Cayce warned not to repeat the karmic relationship, and he told others that there were karmic influences that made it unwise to enter into marriage. He affirmed the presence of free will and new choices rather than repeating an old pattern.

ACROSS A CROWDED ROOM

I wanted a positive case history for this chapter, partly to offset all the difficulties I was writing about, but also to show that it is possible to circumvent what might at first sight seem to be barriers to love. I heard about this love affair when I was manning a bookstall to promote the first volume of this book, so it seemed appropriate to include Peter's story. Also, he has considerable astrological knowledge and so it would be interesting to see what he felt was significant in the synastry. Some weeks later he wrote to me saying that although he had found writing about a twenty-year relationship a somewhat daunting task, he wanted to do this to tell readers that really happy relationships can exist:

'So often in astrological books and articles relationships are seen as a battleground and I wanted in some small measure to redress the balance.

When I printed the charts I was surprised to see that Ellen's nodal axis was 3° from my Sun opposition to my Moon, which I felt was a major factor in the relationship. Interestingly I now have another friend who is a yoga teacher who was born eighteen and a half years after Ellen so she also has her Nodes conjunct my Sun and Moon'.

With the North Node conjunct the Sun, Peter is growing in the same direction as these women so both the relationships are important to him. In addition, in his synastry with Ellen there are double whammy interaspects between the Sun and Pluto, Venus and Saturn, and Chiron and Venus so this was a strongly karmic relationship. One-way aspects included Uranus square the Sun and sextile the Moon, which might explain the unconventional nature of their living arrangements, with Neptune inconjunct Venus showing the great love they shared. In their natal charts both have Neptune-Venus and Pluto-Venus aspects and the Moon in Gemini. This is their story:

'We met in the autumn of 1975 when we were doing our training to be yoga teachers. It was a case of seeing a stranger across a crowded room, although there wasn't a defining moment. I do remember at some point something inside me saying: 'That woman will be important in your life'. At that time I was 41 and Ellen 56. Her husband, whom she married at 21, had been her first love and I had only had one love affair before - to a woman 23 years older. Looking back I seem to have been drawn to more mature wise women since my teens.

In the autumn of 1975 transiting Jupiter was conjunct Uranus in my seventh house, transiting Neptune was conjunct my Sun, and transiting Jupiter was trine the Moon. In Ellen's chart, transiting Jupiter was conjunct Mars.

I offered to navigate for Ellen on a long drive to the Yoga Congress and found we had many interests in common, both of us having had mystical experiences at a time when such things were seldom spoken about. The weekend of 2-4 April 1976 seems one of the most memorable in my life. I was ecstatically happy without really knowing why. My transiting Saturn conjunct the M.C. and opposite Venus seemed hardly the start of a love affair but more like - I believe in retrospect - a meeting up again in this lifetime. Ellen had been happily married for twenty-six years and also had a father-in-law and mother-in-law to care for. While I, who had always lived at home, had an ailing mother to look after.

During the next few years Ellen and I went to many yoga and New Age events but only met at weekends due to our commitments. My mother died in 1979 then, quite unexpectedly, in 1980 Ellen's husband left her for a younger woman, which devastated Ellen but, in time, allowed us to deepen our relationship.

The next fifteen years were not without incident. On the down side I lost my home and business to developers followed by a two-year legal battle. I don't know how I would have survived without Ellen's support. And she had several medical problems. On the plus side, our lives opened up immensely. We travelled, and ran workshops in the far North West of Scotland for five years - many wonderful memories.

People remarked on how our partnership seemed to shine out from us, which was very flattering, and one friend suggested that one of the reasons was because I [Peter] had the mother he always wanted and Ellen had the child she had never had. There was some truth in that. [Peter has Pluto semi-square the Moon and could well project his mothering needs onto another woman, but as they had no interaspects, nor did Ellen have a natal aspect, these did not reflect the black face of the devouring Moon but rather the healing and transforming aspect.]

On a visit to Findhorn we were shown why we were brought together and what our job was in this lifetime. We were told that we had to be lightworkers and that we would achieve far more as a partnership than individually. We were to share our talents and knowledge with others but not under any particular flag (i.e. guru or 'ism') - advice that held true for the rest of our time together. We offered yoga and a wide knowledge of healing therapies.

In the winter of 1991 Ellen had a successful operation for colon cancer but in the autumn of 1995 (as transiting Pluto conjuncted her Ascendant) the cancer resurfaced and she was told she had only months to live. As there was nobody to look after her, I stopped work and moved in until she died on 26 June 1996 (as transiting Sun conjuncted Pluto). We parted very much in love.

Ellen didn't share my enthusiasm for cycling and astrology but was happy I did both. She was surprised by my number of older female friends ('Wise Women') while I had to adjust to her blood relations (Jewish Ancestry) with whom we had very little in common.

The story doesn't stop there as Ellen 'came through' to my clairaudient friend who she had never met, and interesting communication and advice has come through periodically ever since'.

'CAN'T LIVE WITH HIM, CAN'T LIVE WITHOUT HIM'

As we have seen, Edgar Cayce said that relationships were actually self meeting self and that through our relationships we had to work on ourselves and the issues that we have. It is fascinating how many charts reflect the same issues between the two people in a relationship. I have used the following example because just about every possible aspect to Venus is involved.

Margaret consulted me because she and her husband Nicos had been married, divorced, and remarried. Thirty years later, they still did not know why. In their natal charts both had Saturn-Venus, Uranus-Venus and Neptune-Venus aspects. In addition, Margaret had Chiron and Pluto aspecting Venus. As I had done work on her chart earlier, I reminded her that with Neptune-Venus she could recognise the pearl in the heart and see what the other person could be. But she could also go into rescuer, enabler or saviour mode, and make them into this wonderful, perfect person, which was not what it was all about. What it was all about was living with someone else as they were, allowing them to be themselves, giving love whatever happened, while still setting boundaries and not allowing herself to be knocked off-centre by the partner's behaviour.

This was important for Margaret because in the past she had been looking for perfect love. Her Venus in Virgo set impossibly high standards, and with the Neptune-Venus contact she expected idealised love at a deep level.

In addition to the Neptune-Venus-Virgo Madonna-Whore dichotomy, Margaret had Saturn opposite Neptune. This is religion versus everyday reality. The question is 'Do I live in the world, or do I go and meditate in my monastery or on my mountain top and think spiritual thoughts?' The challenge is to be a spiritual being in a physical body, and to use that body to pleasurably relate to somebody else. The underlying message Margaret had to grasp was that sex is not sinful! To further complicate matters, there was a Saturn opposition to Venus, which contains old messages from the past: 'I don't deserve love and therefore whatever happens, whatever I do, it doesn't matter, because I didn't deserve to be loved in the first place'. With this aspect, Margaret was challenged to accept herself and to allow herself to be loved, as well as to give love to other people. She then had Chiron, the wounded healer planet, squaring those planets and bringing in the expectation: 'Love hurts'.

There was great pain and trauma from the past, and that may have something to do with the inbuilt Uranian expectation: 'Well, I don't need love anyway. I'll be celibate, I'll be on my own, or I'll choose some different way of expressing love'. Her challenge here was to be able to say: 'Love heals'.

With Chiron, when you go back into the past lives, there are always things that need healing - especially painful relationships. I reminded Margaret that perhaps she had to learn how it felt to have this particular thing happen, or to be in that kind of relationship, for her soul's understanding. She was learning about love in all its facets through many lives, while she was moving eventually to the practice of unconditional love. But while here, in incarnation, she couldn't possibly expect to see the overall picture. With a Venus-Pluto aspect, her challenge was also about letting go and forgiving whatever was painful and hurt her in the past.

As Uranus sat exactly between the seventh and eighth houses, and Uranus is the planet that is different, anything you expect Uranus to do, it does not do - which makes counselling or prediction difficult. It is also traditionally known as the planet of divorce, but often this means that one person changes and the other does not, or there is a big commitment or intimacy issue. Margaret had a close Uranus-Pluto trine, so to a certain extent she would have resolved the 'I don't need love' and lack of commitment in her last life, coming in this time to test out whether she could actually put that into play. Of course, her husband was also part of the equation as he had the same issues, and it was absolutely classic to find herself in the situation of being with somebody and finding she could not be with him; then to get divorced, and get back together. Uranus sitting here is saying, 'Well, what else did you expect? This is one manifestation of my energy. There are others'. Uranus is a catalyst, a transformer.

These issues were reflected in the interplay between Margaret and her husband's chart. There are repeating each-way interaspects between the Moon and Neptune, Mercury and Uranus, and Uranus and Venus, emphasising the freedom-commitment dilemma. It was all summed up in Margaret's letter: 'Can't live with him, can't live without him. Here we are somehow at the end of a long turbulent period - we're still together, so what's going on?' This seems to be the relationship where she discovers if she has resolved her intimacy and commitment problems.

With Neptune-Moon, these two will have been together way back in the past and in a situation where they learnt to read each other's thoughts. I had a picture of them in some kind of religious order where they would be sitting supposedly praying, but in fact holding long conversations in their heads. My sense was that somebody came in who knew what was happening and separated them physically, yet the mental contact still continued.

But most significant was the emotional contact where they were totally subsumed in each other - what she felt, he felt, what he experienced, she experienced. There was no boundary and that was overwhelming and very difficult - you need some separation between the emotions. That particular life made one of them say: 'I've got to have some space. OK, at one level this is wonderful oneness, but at another level I need to get out of here so I can think for myself, feel for myself. I can't be overwhelmed by the pain'. There was certainly pain in there somewhere although it was not exactly clear what was going on. One of them was either ill or emotionally disturbed for some reason, and the other was not able to shut off from the pain even if they were separated. Through Uranus-Mercury there was also the need to be free at a mental level. In the past, two people go along a route which takes them away from the mainstream and they can understand each other and be different together, but the rest of the world does not understand what is going on. However, in the present, they can approach the world with widely different intellectual styles according to their Mercury placements.

There were also nodal contacts. Margaret's Uranus conjuncted her husband's North Node acting as a catalyst for change. It was an opportunity for him to move into his North Node, his spiritual purpose. But people who remind us of our spiritual purpose when we don't particularly want to know, can be uncomfortable to be around. With Nicos's North Node in Taurus, he was supposed to be finding a slow, steady evolution and yet he had her impatient Uranus behind him - not easy.

In addition, Margaret's Jupiter was conjunct his South Node so it was easy for her to pull Nicos back into the destructive Scorpionic mode (his South Node), which was deep and intense. This Node can sting itself to death, and Jupiter expands on anything that is there, so there were extremely dark emotions and experiences both physical and metaphysical. Through the relationship, Nicos was being called back into that turbulent part of himself when really he was trying to move forward.

With Margaret's Mercury contacting Nicos's Jupiter, she may think, consciously or unconsciously, that she is here to act as a catalyst for Nicos's growth, but he is also teaching her and is an activator for her growth. With a one-way Venus-Neptune link they have an opportunity to focus on the unconditional loving side of relationships, not demanding love but learning how to give it.

There were also one-way interaspects such as Sun-Pluto, a power and control issue - who pulls the strings? who holds the power? This was particularly difficult because as a native Greek (and with a Capricorn Sun) Nicos expected to be the head of the family and did not look kindly on Margaret's need for empowerment - she has Sun-Pluto in her chart. But Margaret would be challenging that strongly, especially as it was on her South Node-North Node axis. She was moving out of being the little wife at home who looks after the family and into taking her own authority and power. It would rattle Nicos's cage more than a little, but Margaret could find ways round it. The most important thing with Uranus-Venus is to give each other space.

It is somewhat similar with Neptune-Moon. They have to find a way to stand serene and untroubled by what goes on around them, to care about what the partner is feeling but not be engulfed by it. They could have a strong, committed, intimate relationship with Margaret not being intimidated by his passions or depressions; and vice versa. This I felt is why they are still together. That is the lesson.

When I explored their previous lives, I saw a girl in a simple tunic-type dress. She was demure, head down, looking from underneath the eyelids, shy and quiet but exuding sexuality. She had been captured, but the slaver recognised the value of his merchandise and treated her well. She had told him she was a virgin, and her brothers, who were with her, tried to keep her honour pure. When their ship docked, she thought: 'I'm not going to let anyone see how this is hurting and humiliating me'.

She was in a room, surrounded by men who clearly had money and taste, and were willing to pay for what they saw in front of them. It was not exactly an auction, they did not bid going up in price - they had to decide what their top price was and offer that, almost like sealed bids. Then a man came in who was older - Margaret's present-day husband. He was respectful but with an air of quiet authority said: 'Send her to me', and that was it. She was bundled up, a bit like a delivery package, and sent to him. Initially, for the first 48 hours, she thought she had done well. She was bathed, fed and looked after. But when he appeared the next evening, he proceeded to deflower her with relish. That was the only word I could use. There was little left in life that gave him pleasure; he had status, power and enough money to buy anything. He collected beautiful women, virgins that he could possess. He was not cruel and yet he wanted to possess her body and soul. When he was doing his deflowering, it was almost as if the innocence was taken into him. He was extremely seductive and wanted to imprint himself on her, yet there was no intimacy - partly because of a language barrier - but also there was no sharing of himself. He wanted to experience her.

He was not interested in her experiencing him. Nevertheless, because he took time, and wanted the sexual experience to be memorable, it was actually perfect sex in a way. The fact that it didn't have any love or real feeling, real intimacy, did not matter to her. As a physical experience it was perfect, and gave her something to measure everybody else against. When she was sold on, which brought huge feelings of rejection to the surface, she was aloof from other men. She went through the motions and let them take what they wanted, but did not give anything of herself. Part of her had shut off. This was where Margaret's notion of a perfect sexual act came from, but it was also the source of her feeling unclean. In her own culture she would have been married to a man who honoured and respected her.

There was a more recent life which had made less impression on Margaret. But I got flashes of someone who was beautifully dressed, and where a man came in and they embraced. A long period followed when they were not together, although on that occasion Margaret wanted commitment. He either was not in a position to marry, or did not want to marry, but it was clear that she would have been married to him heart and soul, absolutely his. In other relationships she had found commitment difficult because of a hankering for this perfect love. All Margaret could do in her present relationship was work on herself. She had to make the changes that transits at the time were urging, especially the owning of her own power. Sometime later, she reported that things between her and Nikos were good. Changes were happening, and given space Nicos was expanding and the relationship was the better for it.

SOLVING THE SPACE DILEMMA

It is not always necessary to separate to deal with karmic dilemmas. For many people, the present lifetime is one in which they intend to resolve old dilemmas or bring together opposite strands from previous relationships and it is possible to find a creative way to do this - although it may mean moving outside the conventional notion of relationship.

I counselled a client with repeating double-whammy Moon-Neptune and Mercury-Neptune interaspects, which indicate a strong spiritual bond; together with Pluto interaspects to all the personal planets, an emotional, symbiotic bond. She had undergone spiritual development with her partner in another life and as a result was able to communicate without being together. They shared telepathy and dream experiences when asleep. It didn't matter whether they were together or not, the experiences went on. Because of the Pluto interaspects, it was both powerful and suffocating and she had no space to herself, even inside her head. She felt the need to get out of the relationship to be able to breathe. As she said in her letter: 'He knows what's in my head and I know what's in his head. I can't hide anywhere'.

This is always difficult to handle within a relationship, but it was especially so as they also had Uranus interaspects needing freedom and space. The last thing Uranus needs is a sense of being joined to the other person by an umbilical cord that can't be cut: but at the same time she was desperate to escape she also felt that this was her soulmate.

She resolved the dilemma by organising a time-share. Part of the week she worked and lived on her own. They agreed between them that there would be no telepathy or shared dreams - and I taught her psychic protection techniques to cut the psychic link (see *The Way of Psychic Protection*). She then spent long weekends with her partner doing all the things they enjoyed sharing. He was fearful of this arrangement at first, his great terror was that she would find someone else and leave him. But as the months progressed, he learned to trust her and began to enjoy his own space. The relationship was much healthier for this unorthodox arrangement and still continues today.

ETERNAL TRIANGLES

> If two lives join, there is oft a scar
> They are one and one, with a shadowy third;
> One near one is too far
> > Robert Browning

There is a woman I know whose husband left her thirty three years ago, but she has never accepted it. She still sits at home, waiting for his return. He is living with another woman, waiting for one or other – or possibly both - to die to set him free from an intolerable situation. All three have Sun in Pisces, which perhaps explains why the situation has gone on so long. (In my experience, it is Pisces more than any other sign who does not end one relationship before beginning another, and who drifts from one partner to another and back again). It is an eternal triangle: all three are as tightly enmeshed as though they were living together. The wife will not let go, but then neither will the husband. Each refuses to instigate a divorce and yet he ceased loving her long ago. And the third woman is hanging on to him in the hope that one day she can marry the man she loves and whom she has regarded as her husband for over thirty years. Yet if she dies first, he has stated his intention of returning to the matrimonial home.

Robert Browning knew all about eternal triangles. His wife Elizabeth conceived a powerful attraction to another woman (see Chapter 3) who virtually consumed her before she broke off the relationship. Despite a passionate exchange of letters, there is no evidence that this was a sexual relationship, although the love that Sophie Eckley expressed was obsessive and that of Elizabeth intense. They were friends because of a passionate mutual interest in Spiritualism, something Browning did not want to get involved in. Eventually, as is so often the case, Elizabeth had to extricate herself from the situation when Sophie proved to be deceiving her.

Sometimes the 'shadowy third' in a relationship is a living person, at other times someone who has passed on but whose influence still pervades a new relationship. It may be the memory of a previous partner, or parent, or an actual person who becomes actively involved as an extra member of a twosome. Memories of previous partners, especially when they have passed on, are particularly difficult to work around, as there is a tendency to idealise the old situation, and the new partners are overly aware of themselves being critical or harsh. And yet, as one client of mine said: 'There hasn't a day gone by when I haven't felt the presence of his dead wife in the relationship. We are never alone as a couple, she is always there'.

If three living people are concerned, the threesome may be re-enacting an old scenario with the same old roles, or the roles may have changed but the script remains the same. So often when we look at the astrology of an eternal triangle, there are many similarities in all three natal charts and the synastry between them, plus a surfeit of soulmate indications, so that any two of the three could be in close relationship.

As one woman said: 'How can I possibly love two men with all my heart and soul at the same time? But I do'. In her case, the lesson was to let go of the first soulmate as he would not leave his wife and family and the relationship had no future. When she had dropped all her illusions and dreams around him, she could then enter into a relationship with soulmate number two. When she did this, she found the happiness that had been eluding her all her life. There are times when an additional partner enters into an existing relationship to act as a catalyst and break it down, leaving pain and chaos in their wake but also an opportunity for new growth. At other times they drift into the relationship and out again, creating change as they go.

There are times when the third person who enters into a relationship helps the other two souls come more into harmony, but it is equally likely that fragmentation will occur.

In the early 90s I was consulted about many triangle relationships. It seemed to be a time for ancient ties to surface again. (It coincided with Saturn, Uranus and Neptune coming together in Capricorn, sextiling Pluto in Scorpio. Scorpio is the sign of the avatar, the spiritual initiate entering once more into earth and activating Capricorn, the sign of transformation from incarnation into matter to incorporation at the spiritual dimension).

In many cases, the original partnership either split totally, or the extra person was accommodated into the relationship, usually at a cost to one or other partner. At the time I searched for specific astrological indicators but could find nothing that stood out across all the examples. The only common theme was the number of repeating aspects and interaspects especially to Neptune across all three charts, and the nodal contacts that indicated possible soulmates.

When I was working for a New Age Guru, his wife and his 'spiritual partner', I looked at eternal triangles in great detail. When speaking of soulmates, Plato says that there are some souls left from the original split who can never find their mate and so try to break into soulmate combinations or attach themselves to other lone souls. For a time, it will feel as if there is a fit. If the souls are together for enough lives, it may feel like a genuine soulmate connection, but this will not hold. The illusion will ultimately become clear for what it is. However, I was shown a rather different picture when I meditated on the beginning of the eternal triangle:

> Triangles hung in the air. I was told that the event I was to see was the start of many eternal triangles. This event appeared to take place on a planet far from earth…The beings here were humanlike, but not so solid. They hung ethereally in the air or walked lightly on the ground. Reproduction was by means of binary fission. The being

simply split into two (like Plato's soulmates). On sacred occasions, two beings could come together to make a body for a very special soul to incarnate into...

There was a catastrophe ...Many died. It looked like the devastation after a nuclear explosion... From then on, instead of splitting into two, many beings split into three. This created a pair and an 'outsider' who was forever trying to find a place to belong. The pairs would draw together naturally, shutting out the 'outsider'. The outsiders would try to form relationships together, but would always seek to return to their original triangle as this was the only place that felt like home. In this way, the eternal triangle was created. I was told that many souls live this out on earth, with the three souls concerned taking on many different roles and genders in an effort to heal the split.[4]

At the time, I assumed that this was an allegory rather than an actual event but since then many other people have had a similar picture. Astrologer Pat Gillingham did a channelling which spoke of these eternal triangles as 'triads'. Her communicator said that many such threesomes had been created a long time ago and had been drawn back together at the present time because they had work to do. According to him, the souls were symbolised by the planets Neptune (love), Uranus (will) and Pluto (power). Each would be attuned to one particular planetary vibration and were playing out archetypal love/will/power struggles which had to be resolved.

Another channeller spoke of triangles in a way which perhaps pointed out a new direction for eternal triangles: 'One point of a triangle attracts positive energies, another negative, and the third point harmonizes the two together. It has a similar harmonizing role with spiritual and physical energies also'.[5]

A positive side of eternal triangles can be enacted when three parts of a soul group meet up again, especially if the relationship is not complicated by sexual contact. One of the most powerful expositions of this was a case I wrote about in *Hands Across Time*. It concerned three women and, fitting in with what Pat Gillingham had been told, one had a natal chart which emphasized Neptune, another Uranus and the third Pluto.

The women had been drawn together through a mutual interest in healing. All had been part of a sisterhood in the far past, which had been fragmented and scattered. All were powerful women in their own right. When they first came together, there were a few explosions as each tried to find her place in the group. Strong feelings and jealousies surfaced which had little to do with the present life, but they worked through these. They met each one head on, nothing was allowed to remain repressed. At the same time, they offered each other unconditional love and support, and a place simply to be.

Whilst all were intuitive, each brought her own strengths to the healing group. One epitomised love (Neptune). She was particularly good at psychically diagnosing a soul's dis-ease. One represented will (Uranus). Her skill was in healing blockages from childhood - she was an exceptional energy transmitter. The third was attuned to Pluto (power). She was an expert at working through the body to heal soul traumas. After the initial period of adjustment, they would either pair up as necessary or, at exceptional times, all work together, but it did not matter whether they were physically together or not. Each knew she could call on help at a spiritual level from the others as and when it was needed. Being in telepathic contact, they did not need to be physically present. In a previous life the healing group they belonged to had been smashed apart, with a traumatic aftermath for them all. Now in the present life the sisterhood had been repaired. They were told: 'the soul group is being pulled together, new members are coming in all the time. Each one takes her rightful place. Not all the original sisters will come together, but they are in contact on the etheric levels. The healing purpose is being fulfilled'.

WHY SOME PEOPLE NEVER FIND THEIR TRUE MATE

To make life bearable for them, to avoid loneliness, to enable them to feel complete, to give them children - these are all reasons given by my clients for wanting to meet their soulmate. Such reasons are inherently selfish, they seek to make the small-self happy, rather than the other person or the eternal Self, and that is not a good basis for relationship. Rarer, but more positive, are the people who ask how they can find someone with whom to grow and evolve. Occasionally, someone will say: 'I feel I have much to offer a partner'. The one thing all these people have in common is that they are searching for someone with whom to spend their life. Yet I have as many if not more letters from people who are married and trying to find a way out, as it has not lived up to their expectations.

In her book on the work of Edgar Cayce, Gina Cerminara comments:

'The French have a brilliant epigram on the subject of the married and the non-marital state: 'Marriage is like a besieged fortress: those who are outside want to get in; those who are inside want to get out'... Marriage has brought so much psychological misery to so many people that it seems almost surprising that other people should still consider the married state a desirable one, that they should still be able to disregard its many threats to peace of mind and see only its promises of felicity. And yet...the unmarried generally have a sense of having been cheated of something precious – a sense of frustration and failure'. [6]

That sense of frustration and failure is extremely real, judging from my post bag. Whilst the single state may well be a positive choice, with the soul learning lessons of self-sufficiency and other such qualities, it is rarely seen as that. From twenty-five years of looking at this issue, it appears that some people are simply not destined for marriage. They may have made the choice at a soul level but are having difficulty adjusting to it here in the physical world. Few people are actually happy with their single state - and those who are, rarely consult a karmic astrologer to find out why. Most souls for whom the single state is an issue either do not find a partner or, having found a partner, the marriage is not destined to last. I regularly get letters from people whose partners have died shortly after marriage, or who move out of the relationship swiftly, leaving them alone again.

In the past, such people often dedicated themselves to the church, or to family obligations. Men could go off to war or some solitary pursuit, but women were limited in their alternative outlets. Nowadays, of course, sex is more widely available; women as well as men devote themselves to their career, and women can conceive children without having a partner just as men can adopt. Nevertheless, I am regularly consulted by men and women who feel that, whilst perfectly happy with their lives, they suspect that they may be missing out on something.

In some charts there may be astrological indications of a 'blockage', such as an old vow or an unresolved issue around sexuality and gender or intimacy. But there are times when there is nothing obvious in the astrology. In such cases, it can be helpful to go back to pre-birth to look at their life-plan for the current incarnation or to look at the karmic reasons for not attracting a mate - something which requires a skilled guide or expert in far memory.

Edgar Cayce did many readings on this kind of question. He told one frustrated spinster, for example, that several lifetimes back she had been married with two children. Her husband 'fell into disgrace in his community' and she committed suicide in a fit of post-natal depression. According to Cayce, her failure to find a partner now was because she deprived her husband and children of the love they needed then. As she had not honoured her responsibility to her family, nor appreciated family bonds, in her present life she was to go without these things in order to appreciate their worth.

In another reading Cayce told a woman who had been alone since a love affair which was purely physical and with great psychological incompatibility, that she too had committed suicide and abandoned a child, and so was deprived of one in her present life. In that other life she had been proud, haughty, self-willed and arrogant and died rather than suffer humiliation. In her present life, she exhibited exactly those same qualities again, together with an independence and brusqueness of manner that put prospective partners off. She was prone to fits of black depression, during which she contemplated suicide. After the reading, she never again wished to commit suicide. Cayce also told her that she could expect to marry much later in life after she had made herself as helpful as possible to all with whom she came in contact. In that way, apparently, she would make herself 'worthy of marriage', which was the karmic purpose of her present incarnation. For her, it was not the suicide which led to her single state, but the carry-over of the traits that had caused the suicide in the first place.

What many people are looking for in a partner is someone to make them feel complete, to fill in the gaps as it were. The doctrine of karma, however, says that they should seek to develop the missing qualities within their own self. So, if they are looking for love, they should practice love at every opportunity - which does not mean becoming promiscuous but rather showing love whenever and where possible, even in the smallest of ways.

Lack of a partner is so often regarded as being a negative condition when it can be a positive one. Being single may have been part of the soul plan for the present incarnation. The soul may be learning the difference between being alone and being lonely. Being alone can bring strength and independence, an ability to be happy in one's own company. It can offer the opportunity for spiritual insights gained through meditation, and the possibility of knowing one's inner self more intimately. Being lonely often brings dependence and barriers. It shuts off from spiritual comfort or insight and is constantly looking out there for answers.

Souls usually encounter what they expect. So, if at a deep level the soul feels unlovable, unworthy, inadequate or inferior, *for whatever reason*, this is what will be attracted. One of the most powerful ways to find a true mate therefore can be to learn to love oneself - not in a selfish, self-centred way but in a way which appreciates who and what you are in the fullness of your whole being.

Setting unattainable standards can be one of the pitfalls in finding a mate. If the previous experience was of perfection, then anything else tends to disappoint. If it wasn't perfect then, the soul might have decided it has to be now. Many people go into relationship expecting - or demanding - that everything should be instantly right. If it was, there would be nothing to work on! On the other hand, if the soul has always settled for something less, and therefore been disappointed in love, then, once again, that expectation will probably manifest once more.

Previous decisions and vows can profoundly affect the ability to attract a mate. If a soul has taken a vow of celibacy in another life, there remains a certain untouchable air about that person unless the vow is rescinded. They may make subtle movements of distaste and rejection which are perceived subliminally by a potential partner, who backs off. Disappointment or hurt in love, the decision that: 'I'll never risk that again' can have much the same effect. It is as though the aura freezes as well as the emotions - and prospective partners intuitively read the signals the aura gives out and so stay well away. Consciously the person wants to receive love, but subconsciously a little voice is saying: 'Remember that decision you made, well it was good sense, you'll only get hurt again'. Once the soul recognises that voice and, where possible, finds out where it is coming from and shuts it down, then a new attitude is possible.

WHY IT MAY BE INAPPROPRIATE TO MARRY

Edgar Cayce did a great many relationship readings, some of which specifically referred to the karma embedded in a prospective relationship. In response to a question as to whether marriage would be best for a couple's mutual development, he replied that it might be so, but that there were other potential partners with whom their growth would be better served, especially as they had some karma which would be particularly hard to deal with as husband and wife. In that case Cayce clearly felt that the couple should not marry. When asked a similar question by another couple, he stated starkly:

'No' and gave no reason. In other readings he left the couple to make up their own mind - which is what an astrologer, no matter how intuitive and spiritually aware, is advised to do. You can set out the factors as you read them and then leave your client to make the decision. Anything else is risking karmic enmeshment with your client. In response to one couple's enquiry as to whether they should marry or were there other partners with whom they would be happier, Cayce retorted that he could name twenty-five or thirty - going on to say that marriage was what you made it. But he followed this up by saying that the couple did have an issue which would have to be worked on together sooner or later, and so the choice was up to them.

In commenting on this and the inadvisability of marriage in certain cases, Gina Cermina points out that the souls, despite having mutual karma, may have other lessons to learn which are more important than the one they would learn together. In my work, I have certainly found this to be the case. It may be that one soul actually needs an experience of being alone, for instance. Gina Cerminara goes on to say that some couples should not marry because one of the souls may be spiritually insolvent. In other words, he or she has not yet developed the inner strength needed to face and work through the karmic difficulty. There are also cases, she feels, where the marriage would be 'too extreme a penalty for the delinquency, or the punishment does not fit the crime'[7] That is to say, whilst there may be some karma between a couple who are attracted to each other, it would not be sufficient reason for them to become embroiled in what would, or could possibly, develop into a difficult passage due to other considerations.

Some souls are still dealing with the consequences of unwise choices in previous lives, setting themselves the task of learning discrimination in relationships (frequently found in Neptune-Venus aspects or Venus in Virgo or Pisces placements). If this is so, it would be wise to postpone marriage until the issues have been unpicked as it were, as otherwise the couple may find themselves tied together for a repeat lifetime in which they go round and round over the same old ground.

Sexuality and gender may be hidden agendas behind failure to find a marriage or life partner, or in a marriage breaking down. There are souls that are suffering from a resistance to a gender change that has taken place (often signified by Uranus-Venus aspects or Venus placed in a dual sign in the natal chart). Extremely masculine women, for example, or effeminate men, may be resisting moving into a new experience and therefore do not find a suitable partner because they are unconsciously looking in the wrong place. This is something which can affect all and any souls at one time or another and not just those who have changed gender. The soul may have intended to have a same-sex relationship in order to develop certain qualities only available through that interaction, but society's mores may be pushing them into a more conventional marriage. As many men, and women, with same-sex leanings have found to their cost, marriage does not cure the condition. Until such time as the soul adapts to the new gender in whatever way is appropriate; it might be more constructive to be alone.

Still other souls are working on the continuity principle or karmic treadmill. Many people 'know' they will recognise their perfect partner instantly, and dismiss anyone who does not match up to this idealised picture - usually without even recognising that the selection process has taken place, or that they are looking for a partner from the past rather than for the present life. If such a person does find a match, they well marry for that reason - deluding themselves that everything will be perfect, though it seldom is.

In other continuity cases, old messages around love could still be operating and affecting the possibility of attracting a partner. Until such messages have been changed, it may be better not to enter a relationship. On the other hand, a soul in a previous life may have made a decision, or taken a particular stance which carries over from life to life as attitudinal karma. So, for example, a woman may have decided in another life to resist love. Or a man may have formulated a heartfelt desire to remain single and unattached. Such decisions carry forward and may need reframing, (they may show in Saturn to Venus placements, or Venus in Capricorn). But it might be better for the soul to live out the consequences of that earlier decision until it has been fully experienced and the soul is ready to move on.

Notwithstanding, there are souls for whom an informed decision to remain single will be a positive act. I knew a man who had become a monk in his present life, at a young age, despite being determined not to. He thought he had no vocation, and yet found an aptitude for the work. Having been a teacher, he moved into counselling work. In his forties, he fell in love - totally, head over heels, blissfully. But he decided not to marry. Having carefully considered the matter, he felt that he could help far more people through his spiritual work than he could gain personal satisfaction from marriage. He lived within a small community of brothers who shared a spiritual life that sustained him. When he looked at his past lives, he had already experienced relationships and children. He then had an interim life where, although married, he felt a powerful pull to solitude and spiritual work. This was something which was only resolved at the very end of his life after the death of his wife. By the time his present incarnation came along, his soul felt ready to move onto a different way of giving and sharing of himself. For him, his single state was a positive affirmation of who he was.

Once people view their single state as complete in itself rather than as a lack, they can be much more positive about their relationship to the wider whole. This gives them an opportunity to find strengths and develop qualities within themselves which could not have been accessed had they married.

Reclaiming the Heart

Handing your heart over to another, suffering from a 'broken heart' or being 'hard hearted' can be linked to past heartache and to dysfunctional relationships. The effect of not having a fully functioning, open heart can be devastating. Chuck Spezzano, creator of the *Psychology of Vision*, feels that 'the heart is the cornerstone of emotional integrity'[8]. He has identified various states that signify that the heart has been lost or broken which closely accord with my client's experiences both in regression and in their present lives. Few souls will display all of these characteristics, although they could if several past life experiences are coming together for healing. But the presence of two or more of the following signs may signify that there is work to be done on healing the heart:

Signs That the Heart Has Been Lost or Broken

No passion to life	Defensive	Guilty	Naive
No fire and zest	Sacrificial	Scared	Cynical
Takes but does not give	Remote	Bitter	Fearful
Life has lost its colour	Burned-out	Alienated	Greedy
Defines oneself by roles	Dissociated	Separate	Judgmental
Unavailable for relationship	Selfish	Needy	Cruel

Many of these states are, of course, emotional in origin. Defensiveness, for instance, arises when a soul has been hurt and feels the need to protect the heart, but so too does cynicism. Burnout occurs when the soul has given and given but has not allowed itself to receive nurturing in return, or has been unable to find love. A broken heart may lie behind a soul's tendency to sacrifice itself for a beloved. Such a soul could define his or herself by the role of 'parent' or 'wife' or 'husband' rather than who the soul intrinsically is - such a soul rarely feels it has any worth or value in its own right. The net result of a wounded heart is that life loses its zest and passion. A desperate soul whose heart is pained may be both needy and greedy, but it could become judgmental or bitter.

These states relate to many of the astrological patterns found in the birth chart that we have already examined but, just because one has carried over heartbreak or meets it in the present life, does not mean that the soul is stuck with that state for the whole of a life. Repairing a broken or lost heart is vital if healthy relationships are to be created and may be the task that the soul has set itself for this lifetime especially where Leo features strongly in the chart.

One of the most insidious ways to 'lose heart' is to hand it over into someone else's keeping. The ancient Egyptians spoke of the 'Lord of my Heart', Shakespeare of '[bearing me to] her, where I my heart, safe-left, shall meet'. Pop song lyrics are full of references to giving away the heart. Lovers have always been regarded as the repository for one's heart, which can create an extremely complex situation as Anita found when she did some work to free herself from the control of a powerful man.

Initially, Anita had been strongly attracted to this man and believed herself to be in love, secretly harbouring visions of him as a lover or husband (the kind of romantic illusion to which her natal Neptune-Venus trine is prone). In past life work she discovered that the attraction did not belong to the present lifetime, but was a residue from a life where they had been lovers, after which he had rejected her. In that life, despite no longer wanting her as a lover, the man had been extremely jealous, beating her if she so much as looked at another man. In her present lifetime, from the moment she met him she had found it impossible to have a relationship with anyone else. She said that she felt he had, in the other life, drawn a veil over her emotions so that she could not see anyone else, and that this had carried forward into the present (signified by a Neptune-Moon interaspect). People who knew her at this time commented that they had assumed she was married because she was so unavailable.

After she cleared that other life, she hoped to move into a new relationship but found that she was still blocked. I suggested to her that she should take back her heart, as I was sure he still held it. A friend took her through the exercise:

> 'I saw the man, and could sense both aspects of him - past and present. He was carrying my heart in a box. I asked him why he wanted to keep it and he said 'power'. I asked for higher help, and he eventually handed the heart over, and began to shrink and disappear.' [9]

However, this was still not enough to free her. In another regression session, she again found herself talking to the man in question. Her therapist asked her 'What has he got that's yours?' She found a ring in his pocket which she took back, and returned another to him. Rings are powerful symbols of a joining of the heart and can in themselves act as a tie, which is why it is advisable to return a ring at the end of a relationship:

> I saw what had happened. We had exchanged rings to hold us together for ever. I saw the scene the day it happened, back in the eighteenth century. I was very young, and we were in the garden together, very flirty, but with a sinister undertone. I said: 'I give you my heart for ever'. He said: 'Ah, but I want your soul!' To my horror, I saw myself saying to him: 'I give you my soul' and we exchanged the rings. It me it was just playfulness and an expression of love, but to him it was deadly serious - he wanted total control of me…I reframed the scene to say: 'I give you my heart for as long as appropriate'… He then asked 'Will you give me your soul?' and I replied 'No! I will never give you my soul' and faced him with arms crossed. He nodded to me, acknowledging my power. It felt as if he had met his match.

When Anita first wrote her story for *Hands Across Time* she said that she wanted to share it because she was amazed at how many levels there could be that needed to be released.

The man concerned was typical of men who carry projections of power. I have frequently seen this scenario with powerful Leo men and women - it works both ways. He had the Sun conjunct Jupiter and Pluto in Leo, together with the North Node (a generational combination which suggests that there may be more than personal karma being played out in the emotional power games associated with souls born in this era). Leo is the sign traditionally associated with the heart, and a Leo Sun has the challenge of opening the heart and becoming empowered, but not indulging in emotional power games. This man was a powerful, charismatic figure, a typically showy Leo who demanded absolute control in keeping with his Sun-Pluto conjunction. He was on a protracted emotional power trip into which all around him were drawn. His North Node sat on Anita's expansive, power-orientated Jupiter-Pluto conjunction - something that would be true of all women of her generation and was, therefore, not necessarily a personal soul contact. He could have played out the scenario with any women her age, just as she could have played out the scenario with any man his age.

His South Node on her Moon, however, indicated an old contact that could pull her back into past emotional patterns (see Chapter 6, South Node contacts). The degree of power he held over her was demonstrated by his Pluto opposition to her Mars-Chiron conjunction (again, something that would happen with all women her age). The old personal emotional pain and rejection were shown in the repeating Chiron-Moon interaspects. His Pluto sextiled Anita's Mercury whilst his Mercury was conjunct her Pluto - demonstrating how easily the mental manipulation and coercion of this contact could be played out by either party.

How lightly Anita had handed over both her heart and soul deeply shocked her. If such actions are multiplied by the number of lives in which similar experiences have happened, there may be a strong need to reclaim those pieces of oneself handed into the keeping of others. As roles change over lifetimes, these 'keepers of the heart' may have become friends, enemies, children and so on. It may be essential for the health of present life relationships to reclaim the heart and anything else that has been left behind.

How strongly rings and other symbols can hold people - and the power of words and how literally the soul interprets them - is graphically illustrated by my aunt's experience. She fell in love when she was fifteen. Ten years later she married her soulmate and they were married for almost fifty years. Then my uncle died. She was devastated and saw little point to life without him. All she wanted was to be reunited with him - she was a strong believer in life after death and there was the added complication that my uncle hadn't exactly gone anywhere. He was a constant presence in her home.

She lived for another twelve years, then was rushed to hospital with an acute illness. When I went to see her, she was furious that she was still alive. She was a strong-willed Capricorn and decided to refuse food and treatment, and eventually, she lapsed into a coma. The ward sister wanted to cut the wedding ring off as her finger was swollen. As she had worn the ring for over sixty years, I was unsure about this. I felt, wrongly as it turned out, that she would wish to keep it on. Several days later, the ring was removed late in the evening, and she died peacefully a few hours later.

Recently, my aunt communicated to me that the ring was a powerful symbol. As part of her wedding vows, it held her 'till death us do part'. In her mind, she had not envisaged her husband dying first. Nor had she realised that, when she had one foot in the spirit world and had been reunited with him, the prospect of her physical death would become somehow subverted to be the time when death parted them. As long as she wore the ring, her fear was that her death would part them. With the ring removed, her spirit was free to leave and be fully with her soulmate in the other world.

Guided visualisation is a useful tool for reclaiming the heart[10], changing an old script and reframing 'for ever' declarations of love. It is a powerful tool for changing the sub-conscious patterns from the past that govern relationships. The following exercise uses this power. It can be recorded, leaving appropriate gaps, but it is better if you can find a friend to read it to you as they can follow your own timing. Whilst it does use visualisation, it is not necessary to 'see' the pictures - some people are non-visual and 'feel' the experience rather than seeing it. (Pictures can be helped to form by looking up, with your eyes closed, to the point above and between your eyebrows.) Intent is the strongest power there is for changing the future and you need to 'act as if' whilst doing this exercise. If you act as if you are seeing, it will happen. You will also find that crystals such as Rose Quartz, Rhodochrosite, Rhodonite or Charoite (Chiron's stone) can help with this work. You may like to hold one over your heart as you do the exercise.

For the exercise, you need a quiet room where you will be undisturbed for the duration of the work. You can deliberately decide to do the exercise around someone you know, or you can ask to be shown who has a piece of your heart. You do not necessarily need to know the past life story, but it could be helpful to ascertain whether you made any promises or vows and, if so, rescind those. (Note: Entering into a past life is best carried out with an experienced therapist who knows how to heal and reframe experiences. I cannot emphasize strongly enough how dangerous it is to do this by oneself, see *Principles of Past Life Therapy*.)

Reclaiming the Heart Exercise

Settle yourself comfortably and establish a gentle rhythm with your breathing. Do not force it. Focus on your breathing for a few moments. As you breathe in, breathe in a sense of peace. As you breathe out, let go of any tension you may be feeling. Each breath takes you deeper and deeper into relaxation. Soon your body is feeling pleasantly relaxed. A deliciously warm, peaceful feeling spreads from the top of your head down to your toes. Give a big sigh of peaceful contentment.

Now, focus your attention on your heart. Feel its beat, hear its sounds. As you listen to the rhythm of your heart and feel its pulsating beat, let yourself relax a little deeper. Slowly, let your heart transport you into another space.

You find yourself standing in the temple of your inner heart. Its colour and dimensions are unique to you. Explore this temple; notice if it is broken anywhere. Notice if you meet anyone else (if so, remember to work with them in a moment). Recognise if there are heart strings pulling you in a certain direction. If there are, use a pair of golden scissors to cut the connection and then heal and seal this place with golden light.

You may already have become aware of someone who holds your heart, if so picture that person standing before you. If you have not yet recognised who holds your heart, ask to be shown this right now. (If there is more than one person, work on one at a time).

You see that this person holds a portion of your heart. It may appear symbolically. If so, look at its colour, shape and form. You may find that it is freely offered back to you, or you may find that the person wants to hold onto it. If they do so, ask their reason. They may well feel that they have to look after you, or you may have made them a promise, or you may have given your heart into their keeping. If necessary thank them, release them, release yourself, whatever is appropriate. State firmly that it is now time to reclaim your heart.

Now take a deep breath and focus all your attention. Firmly and clearly, reach out and take this heart back. Say out loud: 'I take back all that is mine and I freely give you back all that is yours'. Welcome your heart back with love and place it once more within you. (You may like to place a piece of rose quartz over your heart to symbolise this return.) If you experience any problems, ask for a guide, a helper, your higher self or an angelic being to come to your aid.

Repeat this reclaiming until there is no one left who holds a part of your heart. Check that you yourself do not inadvertently hold a piece of someone else's heart. If you do, then surrender it willingly and allow it to return where it belongs. Then check the inner temple of your heart once again. You will probably find that it is looking much better. You may well find that the symbolic pieces of your heart decorate the walls. If it needs any further repair, use golden light or place a crystal over your heart.

Take a few moments to open your heart and offer forgiveness to the other person and, if appropriate, allow yourself to receive their forgiveness and place it in your heart. Open yourself to divine love and fill your heart from that source.

Now consciously step out of that inner temple, but know that it is within your own heart, which is now whole and healed. Become aware of your breathing once again, and the beat of your heart. Slowly bring your attention back into the room. Take your attention down to your feet and ground yourself firmly. Picture a bubble of light enclosing you, sealing your energies, so that you are safe and protected. When you are ready, open your eyes. After a few moments of reflection, get up and move around the room.[11]

PACTS AND PROMISES

The pacts and promises made in another life, or in the between-life state, can strongly affect the present. They may involve another person or be personal to yourself. If a soul promised to always be there for someone or to always look after you, or never to leave, it can create relationship karma. If the declaration was made that 'you are the only one for me' this holds true across lifetimes. The vow holds the two souls together beyond death.

A woman found her partner, for instance, at the age of thirty-eight. She knew from the moment she saw him that they were meant to be together, although their path to a committed relationship was not easy. Before that commitment, she had always been held back from relationship by caring for her alcoholic sister and acting as support to her large family. Now, the woman wanted to have a child but worried about her sister as she 'wanted to be there for her'. In regression, she went back to promising her sickly sister that she would indeed always be there for her. She hadn't envisaged the promise lasting several lifetimes. She reframed her vow 'for one life only' and asked that her sister be helped to make her own spiritual progress.

Almost immediately, her sister went into treatment, which proved successful, and the woman found she was pregnant.

The declarations made in marriage, especially as marriage is a sacred bonding in most religions, exert a powerful hold. 'Until death us do part' is one thing, but 'eternally' is quite another. Such a declaration binds both parties and may not be appropriate in a new incarnation - it may not even be appropriate for the whole of one incarnation. Couples do grow and change and may need to move on. If they do not, they become stultified. W.B. Yeats, who suffered from unrequited love for many years, said: 'Too long a sacrifice can make a stone of the heart'. Many couples stayed together in the past because there was no other option. Love, if it existed at all, died and the heart turned to stone. But a vow could still bring a couple back into incarnation if it was not rescinded.

A vow made by one person may also trap a couple, as can wishful thinking. A person may say: 'I could make him (or her) so happy if only…' or may declare 'I'll make him (or her) suffer'. If you have ever demanded that someone be there for you, you need to release them as that demand is sufficient to create a trapped scenario.

The power of these vows is extraordinarily strong - but they don't always work out quite as the soul thought they would. One of my favourite stories is the client who was in the middle of a regression. She had been unable to marry the man she loved, remaining on the side-lines throughout his life. She yearned for him. As she lay dying she said: 'Next time he'll marry me'. She started laughing. 'He did', she said: 'He was the vicar who performed the ceremony this time around!'

Declarations that: 'I'll never have another relationship etc.', 'There'll never be anyone else for me' or 'I will always love/hate you' can have a powerful effect through many lives. It can pull couples, or parents and children, into relationship time after time until a way is found to heal the interaction and change. Even decisions to 'always love you' can be karmically blocking. It may be more appropriate for spiritual growth to let go.

Guided visualisation is a useful tool for changing an old script and reframing vows, pacts and promises whether these are to a higher power such as the profession of celibacy, poverty and obedience made by a monk which can seriously interfere with sexual relationships, or those made to another person. Visualisation is a powerful tool for changing the sub-conscious patterns from the past that manifest within relationships. The following exercise uses this power.

Renegotiating A Vow: the Quick Method

Settle and calm yourself as in the previous exercise. Now say firmly and clearly, out loud, 'I hereby rescind all vows, promises, pacts and arrangements that I have made in this or any other life, or in the between-life state, that are no longer appropriate and no longer serve me. I set myself free. I also set free anyone from whom I have exhorted a vow.' Clap your hands together loudly to signify the end of those vows.

Bring your attention back into the room, stamp your feet firmly on the ground, stand up and go about your business.

The More Specific Method

Settle and calm yourself as above. Now picture yourself back at a point in time when you made a vow or a promise (if you are unsure of when this was, or with whom, ask to be shown). Rerun the scene as it happened but as an observer - you might like to see it as though on a video screen. Notice who is present and what you are saying. If it is someone you do not recognise, ask who that person is in your present life.

Now look carefully at that vow. Is it still appropriate? Is it something you want to continue? Does it need to be reworded, or rescinded? Is it something from a past life that has inadvertently been carried over into the present? Have you demanded a vow from someone else that is still holding them to you? If appropriate, ask for an advisor to come to discuss the matter with you. If it is a promise made to a soulmate, have them be with you outside the scene to join in the discussion. Check whether it needs to continue. Check also whether you made a promise to a soulmate between lives.

Then see yourself in that scene using new wording. Be firm and clear: 'It is for this life only'. Or state clearly: 'I cannot do that' if what you are being asked will fetter your soul unreasonably. If the promise has to carry over into the present life, or if it has been made for or in the present life, set out the conditions under which it can operate. Make it clear that if your soulmate, or the other person, does not stick to the agreement, or if circumstances change, then the promise will be released.

When you are sure that the scene has been reframed to your satisfaction, let it go. Bring your attention back to the present moment. Take a deep breath and be aware of your body once again. Picture yourself surrounded by a bubble of light to protect you [you can use this bubble during the visualisation if you feel you need protection or extra strength

*during the reframing]. Then, when you are ready, open your eyes and get
up and move around.*

You can follow up this exercise by using positive affirmations. Tack
up where you will see it frequently a note saying: 'I am free from the
past' and repeat this regularly. If the promise was made to a soulmate
or someone with whom you are in relationship, discussing it allows
change, and may bring hidden issues to the surface for exploration.

SPIRITUAL DIVORCE

Marriages are not always made in heaven. If karmic ties have pulled
a couple back together again without careful planning, or if the
relationship has become inappropriate or not conducive to growth,
if it has been abusive or coerced, then a spiritual divorce may be
called for. The relationship may have been taken on to make
reparation, either to the person or in response to a single mistake; or
it may have offered opportunities to develop qualities either in oneself
or the other person that failed to materialise. In such situations, the
karma of grace operates. As Pauline Stone puts it: 'It is by no means
necessary to do penance for a lifetime on account of one karmic
debt'[12]

The concept of grace states that if you have done all you can,
then you can leave with a karmically clean slate. It does not work if
you are merely running away from an uncomfortable situation. If
you have genuinely explored every possibility and the way is still
blocked, especially if the other person is not prepared to work on
whatever brought you together, then you are free to leave.

It may be that your soul did not intend to be with this person
for a lifetime in any case, or indeed in this lifetime at all. In this
event, the spiritual divorce needs to extend back into the past
connection. The spiritual divorce technique is also useful if you know,
or suspect, you have made a mystic marriage in the past or where
you want to release from an apparent, but perhaps inappropriate,
soulmate (see chapter 9).

The astrological indications for spiritual divorce can be
difficult to differentiate from apparent soulmate connections. The
South Node and Neptune or Uranus with the personal planets tend
to feature strongly in the synastry, and if these are one-way
interaspects only (see Chapter 4) then it may be time to part
company. However, repeating close Neptune or Pluto interaspects
may also show that separation is called for. This is especially so if

the relationship never really got off the ground and consisted of wishful thinking and illusions rather than genuine give and take.

Exercise: *The Spiritual Divorce*

Relax yourself as in the previous exercises. When you are fully relaxed, picture yourself entering a temple or a church, or some other appropriate place. (Allow the picture to come rather than thinking about which it should be. You may go back to a current life wedding setting). Notice how you are dressed, are you bride or widow? Either may be appropriate.

You are here to meet your soulmate or marriage partner. You have come before a priest or priestess to have the breaking of your former union blessed. If you are wearing a ring that relates to that union, take it off and return it to the priest. (If you are wearing an actual ring on your finger, take it off physically and, when appropriate, return it to whoever it came from).

Looking at the other person, rescind the vows that you have made. Take back all those promises. If necessary, let the tears flow as you do so. Where healing and forgiveness are required, let these pass between you.

Say quite clearly: 'I divorce you, I set you free. I become whole again'. The priest or priestess then blesses your dis-union, allowing the divine energies to flow over you both bringing more healing and forgiveness.

Then say goodbye to the other person. Wish them well in their future. Accept their blessing and good wishes for your own. If appropriate, forgive yourself for any mistakes you may feel you have made. Then turn and walk out of the church or temple. Accept the congratulations of those who await you. Be joyous in your separation. Reclaim your power as a separate being.

When you are ready to close, surround yourself with a protective bubble of light. Feel yourself whole and healed within that space. Then slowly return your awareness to the room and open your eyes.

KARMIC ENMESHMENT

Karmic Enmeshment is a situation where two souls are strongly intertwined due to karmic situations - they incarnate together again and again in an effort to clear the situation. If relationship karma is unfulfilled or unresolved in one life, if a dependent is not cared for (as in parent and child), if someone who seeks their freedom is held onto, if someone else is blamed for the soul's own limitations or inability to move forward, if old promises remain, or if intentions have not been fulfilled, then karmic enmeshment comes into play.

To hold others culpable for the limitations a soul puts on itself is to invite karmic enmeshment, and creates a situation where the souls are drawn back together as one struggles to become free from the other. The same is true in associations where one person feeds off the other. Symbiotic relationships and situations where one person owns the other body and soul - as in master/slave scenarios and some marriages - also create the same kind of enmeshment. The lesson is to let go, even of what is passing for love (unconditional love does not hold on). One soul may have to learn to stop blaming the other. If one soul has failed to take appropriate responsibility for another - as in a situation where a child is abandoned, for instance - then releasing the enmeshment may first involve giving appropriate parenting or care, possibly to the extent of caring for someone for an entire life if they are ill or disabled, and then setting the soul free to go on their own journey.

Letting go is an enormous karmic challenge. People do tend to hang on, to what passes for love, to the way they feel things should be; to hopes, dreams and illusions. Letting go sets everyone free to take their own path. If it really is true love, if things really are meant to be that way, then it will happen. But if it is not, then the soul is freed by letting go, stepping out of the karma, and moving on.

Cutting the Ties

Tie cutting is an exercise that helps anyone, not just those who may want to escape karmic enmeshment or parental expectations. It cuts away all the karmic conditioning, the expectations, 'oughts and shoulds' that have built up during the relationship. It allows the clear expression of the purpose behind a relationship and the manifestation of unconditional love. It is extremely powerful and should only be done when you are completely sure you are ready for the cutting.

Tie cutting can be used between parents and children, present or past partners, or anyone else to whom you feel a strong tie. The person concerned does not have to be alive. It is an excellent way to release those who have passed on so that they can continue their evolution elsewhere. Nor do you need to know with whom you have to cut the ties before you begin the exercise. One client of mine did a 'blank cutting', creating the circle and asking for whoever she needed to cut from to appear. She was surprised to see an old headmaster - but he was an abusive man who held much of her power. When she cut the ties, she reclaimed that power.

The unconditional love and forgiveness that form part of the exercise are potent healers. If you feel you are not ready for that stage, move onto the next part of the exercise but try it again at a later date to see if you can use forgiveness - it is extremely beneficial for your personal growth if you can.

It has been suggested that tie cutting may interfere with the other person's autonomy and freedom of choice. This is not so. What you are doing with this exercise is removing the other person and all the issues attached to them out of your personal psychic space. You are not invading them or invalidating any choices they have made. I have conducted tie cuttings with hundreds of people, and all have reported beneficial effects.

Before you do the following exercise, make sure that you are in a quiet space where you will not be disturbed. The human mind is fantastically inventive and can be most graphic in its representations of the ties. Nets, hooks and ropes are common symbols. The exercise begins by using two circles. Do not let these overlap - if they do it can tell you a great deal about the relationship! Peg them down if necessary or use a cylinder of light that completely surrounds you from the top of your head down to the ground. Part of the exercise includes burning the ties after the cutting. This transforms the energy that was held in the ties. If you have a tie that it feels inappropriate to burn, ask to be shown the right way to transform it.

It is most important that all the cutting, healing and sealing is done in one go. If you blank out or fall asleep, go back to the beginning and start again, telling yourself that this time you will remain alert and complete the cutting. If you find visualisation difficult, you can work with your hands, seeking out the places on your body where you intuitively feel there are ties and removing them with a cutting motion. Then place your hand over the spot to heal and seal it.

Tie Cutting

Settle yourself comfortably in a chair. Breathe slowly and easily. Raise and lower your eyelids ten times and then allow your eyes to remain closed. Look up to the space above and between your eyebrows as this will help the images to form. You can either see yourself projected onto a screen in your mind's eye or in front of you, or you can picture the images happening all around you. Picture yourself standing in a meadow or on a beach or other comfortable place. At arms length all around you on the ground mark out a circle (you can use paint, light or whatever comes to mind). In front of your circle, but not touching it, draw another circle. Standing in the centre of your circle, ask that the person with whom you wish to cut the ties will come and stand in the centre of the circle in front of you.

When the person appears, explain why you are doing this work. Tell them it will not cut off any unconditional love between you but it will free you from all the conditioning, the expectations, the oughts and shoulds, promises, etc, that have arisen in other lives or in the present one.

Ask to be shown how the ties between you manifest themselves. When you can see these clearly, ask to be given the appropriate tools to remove them. Remove them from yourself first, and then from the other person. (If you find this too difficult, ask for a helper to remove them from the other person). Pile the ties up outside the circles. As you work, heal and seal each place with light as the tie is removed. Make sure you get all the ties, especially those around the back or in hidden places. When you are sure you have removed all the ties (except those of pure, unconditional love), ask for healing light to surround you, and the other person, so that all the places can be healed.

Allow unconditional love and forgiveness to flow both ways between you. Give and accept forgiveness as appropriate. When this is complete, move the other person back out of your space to their own space, back to where they belong. (They will most probably move out of sight. If there is any problem with this, ask for a helper to escort them out of your space. If the person is a current partner, then it may be appropriate for them to remain within sight but out of your personal space).

Now turn your attention to the ties. Build a big, blazing bonfire and throw the ties onto this. As the ties burn, the energies ensnared in them will be transmuted and released. This is your creative energy, let it come back to you, helping the healing process. Move as close to the fire as you can, drawing in the transmuted energy. Fill yourself up with the energy. Let it empower you.

When you feel ready to complete the process, move back to the place you started from. Notice how much lighter and freer you feel without those ties weighing you down. Feel the edges of your aura - the energy field that surrounds you. Let these edges crystalise to keep you free from inappropriate ties.

Slowly become aware of your body sitting in the chair, and your feet on the floor. When you are ready, stand up and move around.

9

WHAT DO I SEE IN YOU?

Relationship is surely the mirror in which you discover yourself.
Krishnamurti

The simple answer to the question: 'What do I see in you?', over and above karmic considerations, is: 'Myself'. At a deep and fundamental level, like attracts like. The qualities we seek in others in order to make us feel complete are precisely those that our soul has set us the task of discovering in ourselves. The things we dislike in our partners are exactly those things we dislike in ourselves. As Steve and Shaaron Biddulph put it: 'We have trouble living with our partner because we have trouble living with ourselves.'[1] They, like Edgar Cayce, believe that we attract a partner who embodies what we most need to learn, or relearn, about ourselves. If we can turn our attention inwards, and withdraw our projections, then we can recognise within ourselves the qualities we have been seeking 'out there'.

This can take enormous pressure off a partner and allow them simply be themselves. After all, few people want to be idealised, or demonised, or pressured in any way, especially to change or to live out someone else's expectations. Nor do most people necessarily want to know what makes them tick. Many people who try to share karmic insights with a partner are met with indifference, or even hostility. In a letter written in 1951, Carl Jung said:

> 'In the end people don't want to know what secrets are slumbering in their souls. If you struggle too much to penetrate into another person, you find that you have thrust him into a defensive position.'[2]

All we can do is work on our own soul growth and recognise what our relationships are trying to tell us, rather than our partners. If we take responsibility for our own feelings, then we can make the changes our soul is calling for - and neutralise relationship karma.

THE KARMIC MIRROR

We can look at our relationships as mirroring our own inner psychic reality. We create the situations we need to play out our karmic scenarios, to meet our ingrained expectations. The actors in the drama have often been known to us in the past, but this is not always so. New characters can be drawn into our unfinished business. Indeed, we may choose to work through something with someone with whom there is no karmic charge from the past. In this way we may learn the lesson and then apply it to a relationship where there is a karmic link. So in what appears to be a repeating past life situation, the cast may change from incarnation to incarnation but the underlying theme will be the same.

Our surroundings and companions react to us consciously or unconsciously in response to our frequencies at any given moment in time. If either party fails to understand and adjust to these frequencies but react to them instead, a further chain of reaction is set up which carries over into another lifetime. However, by going back into the past we can sever that connection and change the interaction - and we can also alter it by tie-cutting in the present life.

A prime example comes from the regression experience of one of my clients. She found that she had said 'I hope you rot in hell' in response to some particularly nasty behaviour towards her in a past life. However, as she said, she was most surprised to find that she had to do another life with that person to watch and be part of his hell. She had thought the hell was nothing to do with her, but she was suffering by seeing this other person that she had once loved suffer. As she realised during the regression, she had actually set this in motion by her thoughts and words in that other life. Now, by forgiving that person in the other life and taking the words back, she was able to set them both free. Although the person who was suffering would continue to do so - he was working through his own karma on this - she did not need to stay in the situation which had been exacerbating things. She moved out and he became much less bitter. Both of their lives improved. Things are rarely what they seem at first glance.

PROJECTION

Many relationships, whether karmic or not, suffer from projection. This occurs when someone sees something which belongs 'in here' out in the world or in another person. It is as though one, but usually both, partners in a relationship are reading from scripts, but each script is for a different play that they have written from their unique viewpoint, based on past experience. Partners may believe that they are taking part in the same play, but in reality each is playing out a role assigned by the other person *in his or her head* in his or her play. It is not a shared reality. Projection is rarely spoken about and, even when it is, as we shall see, it is difficult for either person to recognise their particular projections.

Projection in relationships can manifest on many levels - including the physical, emotional, mental and spiritual planes. A soul may project back into the past, bringing forward 'what has always been' to mean this is how it is now, or it can introject 'what I want to happen' into the future. There are many varieties of projection:

- The soul sees what it expects to see – conditioning from the past produces a preconceived image, which may be far from true.

- The soul sees what it wants to see and disregards the rest.

- The soul projects an idealised or demonised picture onto someone else.

- The soul expects a partner to behave as they did in another life.

- Expectations that the soul has brought from another life are mirrored by a partner.

- Behaviour by a partner mirrors issues from the souls own unrecognised behaviour.

- Something unpalatable that the soul cannot own as *mine* is projected out onto another person.

- The soul sees its own unrecognised strengths in someone else.

- The soul projects past life behaviour and expectations by a partner into the present life.

- The soul recognises a spiritual connection and acts from the belief that it will be perfected in the present life.

Projections can change as a relationship progresses. What starts out as ideal, quickly becomes the exact opposite if the projection is not owned. In negative projection all the soul's worst fears *appear* to be confirmed in a relationship by the partner's behaviour. In the stages of relationship (see Chapter 2) souls may successfully negotiate the shadow projections and power struggles of the early stages - where many relationships flounder - only to face them again at a much deeper level during the leadership stage when chronic soul problems can be encountered and healed.

As we have seen throughout this book, many relationships embody at least some element of projection or mirroring, but the following case history was more graphic than most in its detail. In my introduction to a section entitled *The Mirror of Our Being* in *Hands Across Time*, I quoted W. B. Yeats: 'We are mirrors of stellar light and we cast this light outward as ...magnetic attraction, characterizations, desires' and I asked:

'If we lived alone, in isolation, would we ever come to know our self fully? This seems to be a task for our soulmate: bringing us face to face with all the issues that need our attention... all those unrecognised and unloved aspects of our self that we have been avoiding for so long; offering us the opportunity to love. And also bringing us the love we seek. This love may not always be apparent at an everyday level of being, it may have become warped and twisted, but it is there at the level of the soul, at the place where we make our deepest connection. If we seek love conditionally, if we limit it, put 'ought's and 'buts' onto it, try to hedge it around with cast-iron guarantees, then what we get back will be conditional love. If we approach love with the view: 'If you are right, then I must be wrong', or 'You're doing this to me', then we will never resolve the duality of an I and You position. If we always see what we are seeking 'out there' in someone other, we can never be whole.' [3]

I chose Christie and Tyrrell's story to illustrate my point because he came from a psychotherapy background and therefore understood the mechanism of projection all too well. Also, the synastry was classic -the two were mirrors for each other. There was a powerful sexual attraction, and a sense of knowing each other from before. However, they approached life and relations in totally different ways. For Tyrell, communication was all important. Shared feelings and thoughts were necessary for him to experience closeness. For the more tactile Christie, it was shared sexual and sensual experiences that led to emotional closeness. Each had the astrological indications of the problems the other was encountering: Tyrell's Uranus-Venus contact brought a huge problem with intimacy and the desire to run away. Christie's Venus-Saturn conjunction square Chiron brought the feeling of being unlovable and the expectation that love would be cold and distant. Both had the freedom-commitment issue, which Christie played out by going abroad to work for months at a time, much to Tyrrell's discomfort. As a result, he felt abandoned where he could have felt trapped, and she felt trapped where she needed to be free.

Christie's Leo Sun and Cancer Ascendant was on Tyrell's Descendant. Tyrell's Sun-Venus-Ascendant conjunction in Capricorn, was on Christie's Descendant. His Moon and Venus were in her seventh house. She was the powerful woman he sought, but feared. He represented what she was expecting in relationships and what she wanted to find, no matter whether he was actually like that, just as he projected on her.

The double whammy interaspects include Venus-Saturn and Venus-Uranus and Mercury-Saturn with her Neptune conjunct his South Node, and his Sun squaring her Nodes. It is no wonder they knew each other so well when they met; they must have felt like instant soulmates. One way interaspects include Mercury opposite Uranus and Sun square Neptune. A one-way Mars-Pluto aspect showed the potential for the violent abuse which Christie perceived as coming forward from another life. However, this is not personal between the two of them and it would appear that Tyrell simply formed the perfect hook for her expectations to hang on. Christie has a Pluto-Mars semi-square in her natal chart and this inconjunct aspect usually projects its issues outwards, and lives them through another person.

I am very aware that by writing about a relationship I fix it in time, as it were. So often the story goes on, expands and changes as it takes its life course, but my readers do not know this. What they read is, for them, as it is. In Hands Across Time Christie and Tyrell told the story of their relationship from very different perspectives[4] - so different in fact that readers wondered whether text had been missed out. No, it was not. These were the individual accounts of that joint relationship, even if they did seem to be living in totally different worlds. And, perhaps not surprisingly, by the time the book was published, Christie and Tyrell had separated. In fact, by the time I updated the story for *Deja Who?* things had moved on again, as they had for this current book.

Initially they had felt so right together although Christie in particular showed enormous resistance to commitment - and projected this onto Tyrell. They had chosen the date and time of the wedding astrologically so they could 'face as much of themselves as possible within the relationship'. They quickly became their own projections - Tyrell felt that everything Christie 'did to him' he had done in previous relationships and that now he was facing 'instant karma'. What mattered now was how he dealt with it.

Christie's point of view was that they both had very different needs, neither of which were being met. She also felt Tyrell treated her as a patient rather than the lover or wife she expected to be.

Examining their relationship so closely for *Hands Across Time* brought the inevitable split forward. I had suggested to Christie that perhaps Tyrell was not the handsome French stranger who had abused her trust in another life, but she was adamant. In her mind Tyrell was indissolubly connected to a man who had in that past caused her to live in the 'darkness of losing the love and acceptance of a community' (her tribe). She felt he was responsible for all her ills. She could not forgive him.

When they were divorcing, she took her revenge. Taking all that she felt was owed from that previous life, she drained him dry of energy and resources. He became extremely ill from psychic attack. As I saw it, all he could do to counteract the past was to continuously forgive her so that the relationship would not need to be taken into another life.

This is a peril of the past intervening in the present. Christie totally believed in a past life she saw and it prevented her from entering into the intimacy she sought, but which she fought against strenuously. By taking refuge in the excuse of past experiences she avoided taking responsibility for her actions in the present.

Tyrrell felt he knew Christie when he first met her, but his instinct was to keep away. He did not want a relationship - up to that point he knew where he was going with his life. When Christie came on the scene he was drawn into the romanticism of the meeting. She was an attractive woman with an extremely flamboyant character - totally different from the English women he was accustomed to.

She made it clear at that first meeting that she wanted to be in a relationship. So why did he go against that initial: 'Keep away!'?

> 'I used to take on challenges in relationships to bring out what I felt was hidden in the person. In Christie I felt there was a lot of bluff about the way she presented herself and I told her that she was 'busted'. Part of her did really want to be seen for who she really was - that was a strong part of the connection at first'.

Seven months later they were married. Each felt they had married someone totally different, but they struggled on because somewhere underneath each felt there was love and learning to be had. Tyrell, as a therapist, expressed the relationship as looking in a mirror. Christie did not see it this way at all. To her, what was in front of her was how it was.

Seeking guidance one day, Tyrell came across the myth of Perseus. Perseus was challenged by the king to go and cut off the head of Medusa, but any man who looked upon the face of Medusa - horrendous, framed by writhing snakes - became paralysed with shock. This was the face of the negative feminine, a dark shadow aspect of woman and man. Perseus looked in the reflection from a burnished shield to cut off Medusa's head. Out flew Pegasus, 'potent with the positive feminine qualities of creativity and spirituality'. Perseus then freed the chained Andromeda from being sacrificed - another metaphor for freeing the anima, the feminine. Tyrell saw this as a perfect summary of what was happening for him: Christie was forcing him to look down deep inside.

Tyrell and Christie separated, but after six months Tyrell was exhausted and ill and he was spiralling downwards towards the dark feminine he found so difficult to face.

In Tyrell's original text for *Hands Across Time*, he wrote 'presumably Medusa's death results from natural causes!' He felt vague when he wrote it and has discovered since is that it is not possible to remain in the cave of Medusa without a clear purpose. 'She does not die of natural causes, her *darkness* dies through her being clearly seen in the mirror (or in oneself), brought forward and then integrated.' He was reminded of this quotation:

> 'If you bring forth what is within you, what you bring forth will save you. If you do not bring forth what is within you, what you do not bring forth will destroy you.'
>
> The Gnostic Gospels of Thomas

Tyrell chose to embrace the dark feminine side of his nature and became involved in a project that allowed his creative energy to flow.

This continues to fit in with the myth of Perseus, as Pegasus (creativity and spirituality) is released. Tyrell realised that for him the dark feminine is merely the unrecognised and learnt how to welcome that part of himself - he started to see happiness through the integration of the healthy inner masculine and feminine rather than something outside of himself:

> 'Our primary responsibility has to be to ourselves - to take ourselves to the limit of our potential, and if another person offers to help us on that path, no matter how they do that, then that person deserves thanks. Thank you, Christie'.'

I asked Tyrell whether he thought the relationship was karmic. He looked confused for a moment and then said:

> 'I would have to say that everything is karmic but the trap is not to see it as such. Because as soon as you start seeing things as 'karmic' you never break the circle. Everything we talk about is flow and releasing and as soon as you bring in a concept of rigid karma, it creates a circle'.

Tyrell had felt that he could not do a tie-cutting with Christie until the divorce was over. To me, the divorce was merely the formal ending, but for him somehow the marriage would not be over until it happened. Christie prolonged the divorce way beyond what was reasonable - she was like a cat playing with a mouse. She was a Leo after all. When we discussed this, he realised that he could be free now, at that moment. He came to see me and we did a tie-cutting that operated at many levels. Initially both the circles kept moving and tried to overlap each other - always a sign that there is still an attachment there - which was why he had been open to psychic attack from her. There were several ties to remove - and some illusions. When these were cleared it revealed the deep soul love that remained, but cut away all the expectations and projections. By the time he left, he looked clearer. He was finally freed from the past connection with Christie, whenever that past might be.

I found that their composite chart was very revealing. The natal Venus-Moon conjunction in Scorpio chart was almost exactly squared by Pluto in Leo opposite Jupiter in Aquarius, together with twelfth house Saturn sextile Venus. The basic fear in the relationship was that there would never be enough love and that greedy, needy dark hole was further inflated by Jupiter. Neptune semi-sextile Venus, however, still hoped to find perfect love, whilst the composite Libra Sun was looking to complete itself through a partner. The composite North Node's position in the seventh house indicated how essential they were to each other's growth. That they might separate could, however, be gleaned from its placement in independent Aries. First house Neptune was the lens through which the projections took place.

When I began working on this book I wanted to find out how Tyrell's projections were going. Had he managed to integrate his own dark feminine and deal with his fear of intimacy? I knew he had made a powerful connection with a woman in one of my workshops sometime after his marriage finally ended. Walking in late to the workshop his attention was drawn to the back of a woman's head - just the top few inches - but it was enough to cause a powerful tremor to run through him. Fear, excitement? Both possibly. What he saw was the transiting Neptune to his Venus picture of his ideal woman fleshed out, but, as with all Neptune transits, there was always the possibility that this was a delusion. Again he decided he wasn't ready for a relationship.

> 'The workshop began and soon I was in a position to see the woman who had triggered such a strong wave of feeling. Looking at her brought another wave, and this time there was no doubting the feelings - deep attraction and profound terror. I chose to listen to the terror knowing that we would be working in groups and couples, and asked you to ensure that I was not grouped with Anna at any time. You questioned my reason and I explained, which led to the inevitable 'But perhaps it's something you need to face...' [What he had actually said to me was: 'She's another Leo and I can't go there again!']

They did end up working together and Tyrell managed to explain to Anna that he wasn't ready for a relationship or able to take the pain that one may generate. He was already projecting forward at this stage and possibly picked up on the potential pain embedded in her Chiron conjunction to his Sun. They hugged at the end of the workshop and went their separate ways - with some obviously unfinished business between them.

Tyrell had confused dreams that night and woke in a similar state. Any decision was taken out of his hands when Anna called and asked to meet: "I say 'seemed to be taken out of my hands' because I, of course, always had free choice, but I preferred at the time to think the decision was made for me." Anna came down the following weekend and it was the beginning of a short, passionate relationship. Tyrell believed Anna showed quiet compassion and had great integrity. Her Sun in Leo opposed his Venus so she was another perfect projection of his anima qualities. They talked a great deal about what a relationship would involve:

> '*because* we talked about these things honestly, I believed that we were both prepared to work on them, even when some weeks later, it was becoming clear that she was wanting to run. This energy was so powerful that on two occasions when I was in her bed, I felt as if the bed were tipping up and I was sliding off the end - something a previous partner of hers had also experienced.'

The contact between them was strong and Tyrell picked up on the negative thoughts Anna was having about the relationship, which she confirmed. It was just becoming a matter of time before it would end. Anna had been raised to put her career needs behind those of her husband. When this failed in her first marriage she broke away. Her boys were sent to boarding school leaving her the space she felt she needed. Tyrell had found someone who had already demonstrated her need to be free:

> 'and perhaps more importantly, in my view, shown a lack of real heart connection with her own children [a projection of Tyrrell's own issues from his Pluto-Moon opposition and Saturn trine to the Moon, and a reflection of their different social backgrounds. For Anna, boarding school was the norm. For Tyrrell, it was not]. Yet I still continued to try to fool myself that it would work out, because my part in *her* play was to seek the intimacy she most feared.

Anna's periods of emotional withdrawal increased and eventually she wanted to end the relationship some three months after the original meeting. Tyrell was hurt by Anna's apparent unwillingness to work through the issues. After the initial romance wore off she started to project onto Tyrell her negative beliefs about love and men - and at that point she withdrew from the relationship. This caused him to switch into his negative beliefs about women: 'They're in it for what they can get. You can't trust them. They leave you'. (Natal Saturn aspect to Venus-Moon in Aquarius).

Tyrell wondered how much of the relationship was real. Probably very little (at the time it ended, transiting Neptune had retrograded back out of orb to his Venus), yet the feelings were very intense - simply because she was the perfect subject for his projections, both positive and negative, and the trigger for the most powerful feelings of attraction and rejection. Put most simply - love and hate. He confessed he was shocked by his own hate.

So, what was going on in this relationship? The first clue was that transiting Uranus was conjunct Tyrell's Moon at the time, and transiting Neptune was conjunct his Venus. Neptune is heavily involved with projections, idealisations, illusions and self-deception. With this transit it was exactly the right time to meet his soulmate or ideal woman, but with Uranus conjunct the Moon it was also time to confront his own fears around intimacy and commitment - which he saw in his account of the relationship as 'Anna's stuff'. He could not do both at the same time, so attracted an unavailable partner who played out the 'scared to commit' role whilst he could pretend that, this time, he was ready for full commitment. It could just as easily have gone the other way, as it did at that first meeting, when he appeared to back off and Anna to pursue him.

The interaspects between the charts throw more light on the dynamics. His Sun conjuncts her Moon and his Moon opposes her Leo Sun. She was instinctively what he was trying to become, but that Capricorn Moon can inhabit a very cold and lonely place - as can his Aquarian Moon. Neither had learned in the past how to be intimate yet a powerful attraction was operating. Tyrrell's Moon and Venus conjunct Anna's North Node in Aquarius meant that he was instinctively what she was trying to grow into and could teach her the emotional detachment that is part of her karmic purpose - providing of course that he was truly dispassionate rather than just out of touch with his deeper feelings. She, on the other hand, could help him to open his heart.

The double-whammy Saturn-Sun interaspect indicates they were here to help each other learn a difficult lesson. But this was the only repeating interaspect and proved to be insufficient 'glue' to hold the relationship together through the difficult initial phase in which one-way Neptune interaspects to the Sun, Moon and Venus highlighted projections and illusions. Venus-Pluto also brought out the fear of being swallowed up and consumed by a relationship. But despite this there was the possibility that, with the nodal contacts, they had both confronted their fears and negotiated the 'Romance', 'Shadow' and 'Dead Zone' stages of relationship (see Chapter 2) in which projections and shadows are owned. With those powerful nodal contacts, the stages of relationship were speeded up and compressed into a very short period of time and they confronted their issues more intensely than most people would in a lifetime of relationship. This often happens when there is a 'soulmate' contact pushing the soul to resolve its old patterns and breakthrough to something new. When I went back to Tyrrell with this piece for his comments, he said:

> 'After reading your text, I feel I want to add a couple of notes. You refer to my perception of Anna's behaviour to her boys as my projection - in fact my projection was that I ignored it, and other significant signs of lack of loving, and continued headlong into the relationship. Yes, there is a part of me that fears intimacy, but that part was not predominant in the relationship with Anna. I opened up to raw, heart-opening and vulnerable depths, believing we had a future together.
>
> It was my hefty projection on her that enabled me to go into those deep places, and a possibility is that because at some level I knew it *was* a projection, maybe I also knew that I wouldn't have to stay there for long, as the relationship would finish.

So the relationship left Tyrell knowing that he is able to commit to a relationship, lose it and survive. Also that he needs to approach relationships with care, not opening up too deeply until he sees the real person behind his projection:

> 'I do feel that the strength of our projections is directly related to the lack of strength of our (real) selves. So that while relationships are critical testing grounds, the gaps between them are equally important for integrating what we learn from them, which is always about strengthening the Self.'

Many people go into a relationship not recognising how much they project from previous relationships, or from their hopes and wishes for the future. Sometime ago one of my clients, a Leo, wrote to me asking if I would take a look at his potential for relationships. His old patterns of disembodiment and negativity were dissolving so what came next? Before I could do the reading, I had another letter. He wanted me also to look at his life purpose because I had already told him that he needed to make a connection to his higher Self, which was progressing well. He could see that part of his search for a relationship was actually his need to deepen that connection. His drive for relationship was also a need to express the love that came from his Self.

A few days later, another letter arrived in which he shared more insights he had uncovered. Women were still on his mind but what was different was that he now felt he had something to offer and was looking salvation within himself rather than in a relationship. He said: 'I need a positive growthful relationship - not an idealised soulmate...' Having withdrawn the projections that he had previously put upon his ideal woman, he was now ready for a real relationship.

REPEATING PATTERNS

I did a series of synastry charts for one of my clients, Amanda (natal chart Figure 18), over several years as she moved through various relationships. One of her relationships contained a Grand Cross (see Chapter 10), but in working through several partnerships, it was fascinating to track how the issues came up and repeated themselves

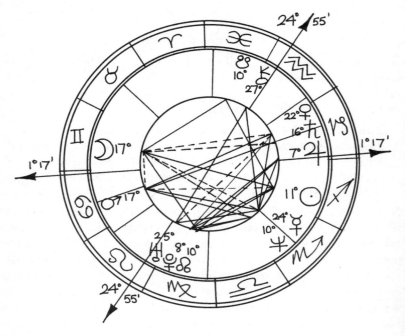

Figure 18 Amanda

within the different relationships, and to see how she drew to herself men whose charts reflected her issues.

Amanda has a Saturn-Venus conjunction, which brings in with it the message: 'I don't deserve to be loved', and although it is a wide connection, it is emphasised by Venus in Capricorn. Its opposition to Mars shows some conflict in male/female past life personas that also fed into that feeling of not deserving love. Her challenge is to learn to love herself, and to, as it were, warm up Venus, which, being in Capricorn conjunct Saturn, feels like it is in a rather cold and lonely place. There is a deep inhibition with both Capricorn and Saturn, suggesting that in the past Amanda has not been able to express her feelings. In her chart it is particularly significant as it bridges the seventh and eighth relationship houses.

More subtle, but still important, are the other two aspects to Venus: an inconjunct from Uranus and a quintile from Neptune. Quintiles are particularly karmic aspects, signifying her intention to sort out her love dilemmas this time around. Inconjuncts are also strongly karmic, implying something that she has simply got to work out in her present life. The inconjunct to Uranus gives the message that it is safer to stay free and uncommitted. Being intimate is a big challenge for her, and she could choose whether to work at developing this with men or opt for celibacy. Another choice would be to consider the way she copes with the problems that stem from having been male in another life, and work on feeling more at ease with the current life situation. This is potentially frustrating as of course women can't necessarily do the same things as men and they are not treated in the same way. It is always difficult to know which way the unpredictable Uranus will go, but as it was, she dealt with the 'previously male' issue through her work and the intimacy issues in her love-life - which often overlapped into 'work'.

With Neptune the challenge is, of course, to love unconditionally. To be able to see that the person Amanda loves is simply human. She could recognise their shining, spiritual self, accept that they have that potential, but has to learn that if they are not like that, that is okay. This was the challenge with all the relationships she consulted me about. She would enter into them with high ideals and hopes, encounter the difficulties, and then the man would come crashing down off his pedestal.

Charts often reflect a dilemma through several placements and aspects. If we look at the relationship house of Amanda's chart, the Descendant is in Capricorn, a sign which needs security, stability, and to conform to the norm and to what society expects. So people with Capricorn on the Descendant seek a stable, long-lasting relationship, which does not altogether accord with what Amanda's Moon and Sun are looking for - they want freedom and space to explore. She also has Venus conjunct Saturn in Capricorn, so there is a part of Amanda that is looking for stability but which may encounter sternness and control issues (a problem with one or two of her men). It will depend whether the Venus is resonating on the strong, authoritarian side of Capricorn, or whether she has found her own inner authority, in which case she would meet a more flexible side of Capricorn in the person with whom she had a relationship.

In the second relationship she had asked me to look at, we had a chart where the emphasis was on Capricorn. Hans had Sun, Moon and the South Node together in that sign so he was re-working his Capricorn, and developing more of its positive qualities. That was a good start, and his Sun conjuncted Amanda's Venus which is always a comfortable feeling no matter what else is going on in the charts. The difficulty for Amanda's Venus is that there are both inner and relationship boundaries to break through - particularly when she meets someone whose Capricorn planets slot so closely into her own. Fortunately, Jupiter, which is trying to open things up, sits close to Hans's Mercury. At least they could talk about the struggle to grow beyond the limits and the restrictions.

Her Jupiter, however, conjoined his South Node, as did her Saturn, and Saturn conjunct the South Node pulls one back into an old parenting pattern, or an authority interplay of some kind. Yet the Jupiter-South Node paradoxically pulled back into expansion and growth. Jupiter may sometimes be over the top, though not in Capricorn where it is usually rather restrained and symbolises growing in a way that can lead to stability. It could also pull back Hans into what he was trying to grow out of - the judgmental South Node. He wanted to move into his North Node in the much softer more caring and concerned energy of Cancer, where Amanda's Mars, which conjuncted his North Node, gave a kick-start to his purpose and his whole growth process.

As Amanda's Mars was widely triggering his Sun there was a sexual spark and, for him, familiarity about Amanda because he had the Descendant and almost the whole of his seventh house in Gemini - and she had the Moon in Gemini. This is a connection which was based on the past, and which felt comfortable and familiar because so much was being reflected back and forth between the charts and the people concerned - which was exactly how the relationship turned out. They remained friends even after they had split up as a couple.

Looking at the synastry, this clearly was a strongly karmic association from the past based on a need for freedom or commitment: Sun-Uranus and Neptune-Uranus, emphasized by the one-way Moon to his Uranus interconnection, particularly as it picked up the Venus-Uranus quincunx in Amanda's chart and the conflict of her commitment-orientated Venus in Capricorn versus the freedom loving Sun and Moon on the Gemini/Sagittarius axis. This is her ongoing conflict: 'Do I really try and make it work? Do I settle down? Do I commit to this? Or do I have to break free?'

With Pluto interaspects as well, the old interaction was in a close, symbiotic relationship, feeling the need to break free. They were not used to living together and giving each other the space and the freedom they needed. The challenge in the present life was to have a relationship which was not symbiotic nor making either feel complete through the other person, but one which allowed space and the freedom to be an individual.

When I looked at the past lives, there was a sense of there being an old vow, an old promise, which had kicked in - reflecting Amanda's Venus in Saturn in the eighth house. This kicking in of old vows was a feature of her relationships and so Amanda stuck with this one a lot longer than the Uranus contacts usually would, with Saturn saying: 'Work this through, find a new way to be, repay the debt'. They tried to find a way through. It was powerful stuff, but somehow easier to work with once they had a sense of it being planned to fulfil a promise.

The shared life that resonated most strongly with me when I tuned into Amanda's past lives was one connected with those old whaling ships that went out from somewhere like Nova Scotia. When they married Hans was then a mate, but because of an accident he became the acting captain. It was a harsh life and my sense was that Amanda had been quite horrified by it, especially as things like the blubber had to be melted down once the ship returned to shore, and the wives were expected to help. Amanda, as she was then and in her present life, thought this was horrible; the smell, the stench, and the actual killing of the whales. Hans, as he was then, accepted it, because he had never known anything else. He was born in that community, whereas Amanda had come in from outside - her father was the manager of the whaling factory.

She met this man who was the love of her life - a strong, instant feeling of 'that's the man I'm going to marry' and went headlong into it, although she had previously been cosseted and kept away from the realities of what the whaling factory did. Never knowing whether her husband's boat would come back or not became a worry when she married. When Hans came home it was very passionate, strongly sexual, and for the first couple of trips it was like a honeymoon.

Then a ship was lost and she suddenly realised that the sea is cruel, a ship is likely to sink. In the next picture she was pregnant, and I could see her talking to the unborn child saying: 'Your Daddy will be back soon, and before you're born he'll be back, he'll be here for the birth', and just hoping and praying that this was so. When he came home things were different, because there she was with this huge bump, about to give birth, and he saw her in a new light. She'd really been mistress more than wife to him, and it was a sobering thought that soon there would be a new life that he was also responsible for. When the child was born, he looked at the two of them and said: 'It will be all right, I will be there for you'. But it was almost as if he'd crossed his fingers behind his back, because he knew that he could not leave the sea.

For years it was fine, and there were more children, and when she was pregnant or had the children to look after she didn't have to go into the factory to work when the whales came back, which was a relief. The trips seemed interminably long. She would get pregnant before he went, and then when he came back she would be about to give birth, and by the time he left again, she would be pregnant again.

Then the awful day came when his ship went down and she knew it the moment it happened. She clutched her heart and said to a child: 'Your father's dead. The ship has sunk'. And this child, who was a teenager tried to say: 'Don't be silly, mother, you're just having a flight of fancy', but she knew. Eventually, word came that she was right, but she had been in deep mourning ever since that moment when she 'knew'. There was a memorial service in the church, although there was no body to bury, and she needed to see his body, to confirm that, yes, this is over. But it never really was over, because she was conscious of him in his spirit - she could sense him around and still had a strong contact. The telepathic link between them didn't stop; it simply carried over into the present life.

The issues from that past life reflected themselves in the present relationship. They had met, had an intense affair and parted, but she felt an inconsolable loss and they moved in together again. It was difficult to totally commit, for at some level Amanda felt that she was still grieving, and was afraid of losing him. By the time she moved on, much of that had been sorted, but her personal issues had not been resolved.

In her next relationship the same dilemmas were mirrored again. Anthony had a similar challenge around intimacy, commitment and unconditional love with a Sun-Venus connection in Taurus square to Uranus. There was also an opposition to Neptune, bringing up the idealisation and the Madonna/Whore dichotomy from Amanda's chart. But he had the potential for totally accepting Amanda as she was, if he could detach from his idealisations and dilemmas from the past.

What made the relationship different was that Anthony did not have a natal Saturn-Venus aspect. Saturn-Venus believes: 'If this person can love me, they can't be that special, otherwise they wouldn't love *me*'. It was a doubt that Amanda had expressed when asking for the reading, and until she worked past it and learned to love herself, the thought could still arise unbidden. Its other manifestation is: 'I'd better dump this person fast, before they leave and hurt me'. If both people have this natally, neither will have the confidence to make things work. As Anthony did not carry this burdensome belief he was able to have patience with Amanda and understand her insecurities - which left their relationship free to confront other issues.

This was not just someone Amanda had met out of the blue and was having a first relationship with, however. From the repeating interaspects, we were looking at an old relationship and it was the second time they had met up in the present incarnation. There were repeating Sun-Chiron aspects and, as with her other three relationships, a Sun-Chiron sextile, an easy aspect in theory, but making it so easy to slip back into an old pattern. As Chiron is about wounds and healing, this was another opportunity to heal and be healed of relationship difficulties from the past. But it can be a bit like lancing a boil - the pain has to come to the surface and drain out, before it can be healed. When the aspect is a sextile, it is initially easy until you wonder: 'Well, how did I get here? Why has this pain suddenly emerged?' If you can look on it as: 'Well, it's the old pain, it's where we're both hurting at a soul level, and we can help each other to heal', then the relationship can progress. But if you see it as something which is done to you by the other person, then of course the association tends to break down.

Amanda and Anthony also had a repeating Moon-Saturn connection. Saturn connections are needed to ground a relationship, and it can either be regarded as an anchor or a ball and chain. One person sometimes plays Saturn 'the heavy' while the other person plays the Moon, reflecting things back and behaving in a very instinctual, habitual way. But underlying everything the couple were kept together by a sense of: 'We wanted to do this. We decided before we came that we were going to be together'.

The interaspects also included Pluto-Venus: just the thing to make natal Venus-Uranus panic. This interaspect gave them the most difficulties because what comes forward from the past is symbiosis and dependence. Such partners need to give themselves space, lightness, and see themselves as two separate people rather than two halves of the same whole. They are learning to be individuals who have a close inter-dependent partnership, but not a dependent liaison.

The Saturn-Mars interaspects repeating both ways reflected Amanda's will issues. Sometimes this can bring in violence from the past. This may be conflict, or aggression, or being caught up in something such as a war situation with conflict all around. It can also be conflict between the two people: one may try to impose their will on the other, triggering the Saturn-Mars part of Amanda which feels powerless and helpless. Anthony also has an opposition aspect, and so the two of them are working with the same feeling of powerlessness and needing to reclaim the will. It is easy to project that on to each other, and see the other as holding you back, or as trying to force you to do something you do not want. But really it is an opportunity for both to reclaim will, power, and assertion, and use it together.

The other aspect which repeated was the Saturn-North Node contacts, and this again was reiterating that sense of: 'We've got to learn some difficult lessons, it may be traumatic, it may be heavy, but we can see each other through it'. It also repeated Amanda's own North Node trine to Saturn, which feels it has a task to do. On the other hand, Amanda's Uranus squared Anthony's Nodes, and there would be times when one or both of them would want to run like hell! Yet on another level Amanda could act as a catalyst for him, trying to help him move from his rather entrenched, safe, secure, materialistic Taurus sense of self, into his Scorpio North Node. This was a scary place for him concerned with exploring the dramas and traumas of life, but it also promised the inner sense of security that recognising oneself as an eternal being gives. Amanda has a North Node conjunction to Pluto with the courage to go into those scary places, so she could help Anthony develop that inner sense of security he needed, as part of her own learning process.

The one-way aspects that they were dealing with were the ubiquitous freedom versus commitment. The desire to be intimate was brought to the surface as again was the possibility of idolisation with Neptune-Moon. There were all the so-familiar issues of telepathic contact, knowing what was in his heart, and the challenge to unconditional love.

Amanda has Venus in Capricorn, he has Moon in Capricorn, and that helps them understand each other. She knew he could find it difficult to express his feelings openly and warmly, because she has those same experiences of suppression and repression, but she could also make it safe for each other to express their feelings. They would get a sense of security from that shared understanding. Nevertheless, it was hardly surprising Amanda had some doubts.

When you meet somebody with whom there is a karmic link you usually feel comfortable with them initially. Then you take a big, deep breath, and stand back and say: 'Hang on - this could be serious. I can see where this could go. Am I ready for this? Do I want this?' And then you get into it. You say, 'OK, I will go for it'. And then when you are deeply immersed in it, things like the symbiosis of Pluto and the heaviness of Saturn come up, and if you can think back to that original feeling of being comfortable and understand that the relationship is merely reflecting many of your own issues, you can have this sense of: 'Yes, this is meant to be'.

The first life I saw for them explained their close contact and the Saturn-Mars issues. They were Roman slaves who had been brought up as children together. The man who owned them seemed to be quite an enlightened man who educated his slaves, because he wanted scribes. He owned them body and soul but wanted to bind them to him through respect and love rather than through fear.

Going forward two or three years, when they would then be about fourteen or fifteen years old, they were waiting on the guests at a banquet. Their instructions were to pick up the gossip, things that would be said unthinkingly in front of a slave. Anthony was by now an attractive young man, sent to flatter the women, and was being trained to give the women sexual favours. This caused jealousy, because a lot of the men there would have liked to have had him for their pleasure. Amanda and Anthony, however, seemed to have reached an understanding that they were going to be lovers - *very* discreetly.

The owner's wife wanted Anthony for a body slave, with all that that implied. Anthony was concerned that he would be unfaithful to Amanda, but she was more pragmatic than he, saying: 'Well, if you refuse there's going to be trouble, you'd better just go along with it. And I know in your heart that you love me and that this is a job, and this is how you keep your position, and it's okay'.

It was the period when Christianity was becoming more accepted, quite late on in the Roman Empire. The wife had been converted to Christianity and wanted her staff, the slaves, converted too. Her husband agreed because it was fashionable, but he didn't really embrace it. What he did not realise was that he was bringing in a morality that had not existed before, with the result that Anthony, the slave, wanted to marry Amanda. He wanted to be, in the sight of God, her husband. He told his master that his conscience would no longer allow him to serve the wife. But the man refused and immediately sent Amanda to the country, so Anthony ran away too. This was of course the one thing that slaves must never do, and they were both put to death. At the end he was looking at her and saying: 'I will be with you' - as they both believed in the imminent resurrection of their bodies. Eventually they were drawn back into incarnation together, but in the present life, Anthony and Amanda did not take up the potential for a deeply committed relationship. However Amanda will continue to attract relationships that throw her into freedom-commitment dilemmas so that she finally resolves the conflict between the different parts of herself.

Amanda was sure that another of her relationships was with a soulmate, something she shared with so many people who consult me. But Soulmates need a chapter all to themselves.

10

SOULMATES

Two souls with but a single thought
Two hearts that beat as one
                    Friedrich Halm

Soulmates are both a powerful karmic fact, and one of the biggest illusions of all time. The origins of soulmate are in the Greek philosopher Plato's description of 'original beings' who had two heads, four arms and legs. These beings angered the gods with their overwhelming arrogance, and were split in half:

> It is from this distant epoch, then, that we may date the innate love which human beings feel for one another, the love which restores us to our ancient state by attempting to weld two beings into one and to heal the wounds which humanity suffered.[1]

Plato says that ever the two halves sought each other and that, should they find their other half, there was a danger that one would be subsumed by the other as they lost all interest in anything else. This is similar to the Plutonian symbiosis that can arise between couples who are dependent on each other for many lifetimes.

Another difficulty pointed out by Plato is that, of the original beings, one third were female, one third male and the remaining third were hermaphrodites. So, if Plato is to be believed, the 'other half' of a soulmate couple may well be of the same sex - and not everyone looks for their soulmate within their own sex. In any case it is clear that souls can change their gender in different lives. Nor are soulmates necessarily lovers: friends and parent-child contacts are just as likely to be soul partners. Nonetheless, people still cling to the idea of a one and only soulmate throughout eternity:

> We two shall build, a bridge for ever
> Between two beings, each to the other unknown,
> This eager wonder is at the heart of things
>   Tagore

305

Most people believe that they have only one soulmate, someone who makes them feel complete and totally at one. But, in my long experience in looking at karmic relationships, this is rare. Yes, there are couples who go through life after life together, but this may become an unproductive and sterile relationship in terms of karmic learning and, eventually they have to part. It may be better to refer to this type of relationship as a soul partner.

In my experience, there are far more people who have several soulmates, sometimes within one lifetime. These 'soulmates' are frequently part of a 'soul group' who have travelled together through aeons of time. They may not, on the surface, always appear to be the idyllic soulmate that so many people dream of. It can be quite a surprise for someone who appears to be their most hated enemy, abuser and the like, to actually be a member of their soul group who is helping them to learn a difficult lesson.[2] The soul contract is set out across charts and can be gleaned from repeating each-way interaspects and nodal contacts.

Illusions and delusions are rife within so-called soulmate contacts - and so is karma. A person you meet may feel like a soulmate, and yet want nothing to do with you. You may have met a soulmate and had a devastating time. My postbag is full of heartfelt pleas to tell the writer why their soulmate refuses any contact or why they do not recognise them. Other people want to find this elusive being, the special soulmate, and refuse all other types of relationship. Thus they put their emotional life on hold - sometimes permanently.

SOULMATE ASPECTS

Soulmate indications are shown in Neptune to inner planet interaspects such as Venus to Neptune, especially when these repeat both ways, and in Sun-Moon-Venus contacts to the Nodes across the charts. When looking for soulmate indications consider all aspects, even minor ones, and use 8° orbs. (Both indications need to be present for a true soulmate contact.)

Sun, Moon, Mercury, Venus or Neptune interaspects with the South or North Node, or Venus contacts to Neptune, either one or both ways, *feel* like soulmates. One or both people involved feel: 'This is the person I have been searching for all my life. I know him (her) so well. I can tell what he (she) is thinking, he or she is always in my head'. And conclude: 'We are meant to be together'. If the aspects to the North Node or Venus contacting Neptune operates both ways, this may well be case. If this is so, the karmic purpose for the present life, or the souls' challenge, is unconditional love. This contact usually indicates that the two people concerned have been soul partners for many lives, but not necessarily that they intend to stay together throughout the present life. It may be time for them to split and go their separate ways - in which case there will most probably be Uranus to personal planets interaspects.

When the contact is to the South Node, the previous connection is passing away. The souls are learning to let go and move on, although they may be in relationship for many years in the present life. This is a difficult and painful process, especially recognizing that the soulmate is not necessarily a once-and-for-all other half.

We have already looked at the reversed nodal placement between David Lawson and Justin Carson. It is worth noting here that Justin's Moon was exactly conjunct David's South Node (widely conjunct Justin's North Node-Mercury-Uranus), David's Jupiter squared Justin's nodal axis and Justin's Jupiter was conjunct David's North Node (soul growth and expansion), and David's Neptune quincunxed Justin's Sun. Justin's Neptune quincunxed David's Sun, with repeating Neptune-Mercury interaspects as well. A classic indication of soulmates from the past. These two had to meet, it felt right and comfortable, and there was a powerful attraction:

Justin:' Without knowing what was about to happen, the first thing I ever said to my prospective partner was: 'That'll be £2.00 please'. [He was taking the money at the door of a seminar]. From then on everything happened at tremendous speed. We met on the Sunday and by Thursday he had moved in, my normal sense of caution [Capricorn Moon] about these things having completely gone to the wind'.

David: 'At first glance, Justin was not the person I would have imagined that I would choose to spend my life with. Although he was charming and attractive, bright and talkative, with an enquiring mind and a flirtatious nature [a true Gemini], he appeared to be the epitome of the social butterfly [Gemini Sun] and the worldly city boy [Capricorn Moon]... Nevertheless I found him extraordinarily compelling. At the end of the seminar...I found myself unable to leave...When the charming, compelling man I had met a short time earlier offered to give me a lift back to north London I accepted, without a moment's thought. I seemed to resolve my immediate inexplicable dilemma, while very soon creating a whole new one...His brightness was seductive and by the time we neared my home, I knew that I did not want to get out of the car and lose sight of him...I moved in four days later'.

David was fascinated with the concept of a soulmate, as he said:

'A friend had told me that a true soulmate was someone who embodied the other half of our own soul, and that if we met this person we would feel so complete that we would lose all incentive to follow our own spiritual purpose and we would forget about our great spiritual potential. He said that most people who formed close spiritual relationships actually did so with a person who was similar to their soul twin. This connection would be described as being like two pieces of a jigsaw puzzle that were a good fit but did not fit together perfectly. The similarity was close enough to allow for a powerful attraction and create special spiritual opportunities but different enough to allow for the growth and positive transformation that comes with individual purpose. This theory made great sense to me at the time so I set about finding the man who would provide me with an 'almost perfect fit'.

Justin remained unconvinced about the existence of soulmates from past lives:

'And is David my soulmate? To be honest, I don't know! I do know that life would not be the same without him, indeed I suspect that I might not even be alive without him. One aspect of my healing has in part been the fact, I am sure, that I haven't been ready to leave, to be without him. I don't think that I believe in reincarnation in the classic sense. I suspect that it is unlikely that I was ever a slave in Cleopatra's court or an amoeba in some primeval slime, but I am sure that at the end of this life there will be some new adventure to explore - some new learning - and if some part of David was there too, hopefully on some sort of equal footing, then I would be truly blessed'.

Two years after Justin's death, David was sitting in his regular psychic development circle at which there was a new group member.

'Tom had never known Justin and was meeting me for the first time. He looked across the room, said there was a man standing next to me and described Justin pretty accurately. Tom then proceeded to give me a message from Justin saying that he has now changed a number of his beliefs. Justin wanted Tom to tell me that I was right about many aspects of the spirit world: evolution beyond life on earth, reincarnation and karma. He now fully understood that I had always had a foot in both worlds'.

We will look at their synastry in more detail later. If you have already read chapter 6 you will be aware that Justin died eleven and a half years after they first met. The relationship was amazing, perhaps too amazing to sustain for a whole lifetime. And perhaps, in view of the one-way Uranus-Sun and Moon-Uranus contacts across their charts, they had planned to part. In such a case the challenge is not to yearn for what might have been, but rather to recognise all that you had between you and then move on. To look out for the next soul partner, to take the risk of something new, with fresh potential to explore.

Tracy Marks, who studied this aspect extensively in practice, feels that a North Node contact to another person's personal planet is indicative of a soulmate connection[3] but points out that much will depend on how the energy of the planet is being manifested. It is clear from my own studies that whilst a soulmate or soul group connection does underlie the contact and it is a definite point of growth, the relationship may not necessarily be easy or one of conventional 'lovers'. As I have said in *Hands Across Time* our soulmate is here to help us learn some hard lessons and the relationship can appear far from one of love:

> 'In chart after chart I have seen a pattern in which the Sun, Venus, or one of the other personal planets, is conjunct the North Node in what outwardly seems to be an ideal relationship and yet may suddenly fall apart for no reason, or where the relationship never gets going at all as one party seems not to notice the other exists - or rejects the relationship after 'one perfect night'. I am conscious, however, of seeing a biased sample of charts, as it is at the point when a relationship has gone wrong that I am usually consulted. I do not often see charts illustrating a relationship which is still ideal. Up to the crisis point there has usually been a great deal of complacency in the relationship, accompanied by lack of mutual growth. The answer to why it has all gone wrong lies in the soul's need to grow.'

A woman whose Virgo North Node-Neptune conjunction conjoined her partner's Sun and North Node, described their relationship as 'the sort of fairy-tale romance you read about in romantic novels, as if made in heaven'. It suddenly became catastrophic after she lent him a considerable amount of money and he become evasive and unavailable. The negative Neptunian energies of delusion and deceit manifested and she later discovered that he was seeing another woman. She was, however, reluctant to take legal action to recover her money in case he wanted to come back to her. Her fantasy was that the perfection might be regained. Her South Node in Pisces pattern had been to be rescuer and victim and her North Node in Virgo was demanding that she move into a more discriminating mode of relating. However, the Virgo energy was obscured by the influence of a Neptune conjunction to the North Node which made her yearn for the unattainable and meant that she was able to overlook the deception and deceit in the search for her lost ideal love.

How sad and bad and mad it was - But then, how it was sweet!

We have already seen in Chapter 3 how both Robert Browning and his wife Elizabeth (natal chart Figures 4a and 4b) had strong Saturn-Venus aspects and how he plucked her away from her overbearing father, whisking her off to Italy where they lived for seventeen years in connubial bliss - or almost so. The interaspects in their charts show an old soul contact that looks very much like soulmates: repeating Venus-Nodes contacts, one-way Moon square the Nodes plus innumerable repeating double whammy interaspects which include: Sun-Chiron, Sun-Pluto, Moon-Saturn, Moon-Neptune, Mercury-Saturn, Venus-Jupiter, Venus-Uranus, Mars-Chiron. The relationship with Browning not only healed Elizabeth's physical illness and her addiction to morphine, it seems to have considerably aided her emotional health as well.

The relationship and composite charts for the two of them (Figures 19a and 19b) show erotic Venus in the seventh house. In the relationship chart, Venus is at 0^0 Gemini, showing the deep friendship embedded in their relationship. The interaction is cerebral. In the composite chart Venus is in earthy Taurus, the passion has become physical and is no longer all in the mind. Bearing in mind that the composite chart shows *how* a relationship functions, and the relationship chart *why* it is as it is, this is most appropriate.

Long before she met Browning, Elizabeth admired his 'passion'. A biographer, Margaret Forster, says that despite being a reclusive spinster, Elizabeth was no stranger to passion, which she channelled into her own poetry. This was not merely passion with a sexual connotation, it was a spiritual feeling that connected her to the creative life force. It was Elizabeth's dream that one day she would find a true poet whose *poetic* passion matched hers, and in Browning, she found her poetic soulmate. Their initial correspondence was to discuss their work, but Elizabeth articulated a need to know him 'by refracted lights as well as direct ones.' After their first meeting, he wrote an impassioned letter proposing marriage, which she rejected. As she did several more proposals. In keeping with her natal Saturn-Venus inconjunct, she told him she was not worthy of his love, but Robert responded in exactly the right way to overcome the pessimism of Saturn. He told her that she would be doing *him* a great honour. Margaret Forster says:

> 'He would not allow his love to be pushed away into a dark corner, to be hidden in case it vanished, but displayed it repeatedly so that she would become familiar with it and learn to trust it'. [4]

Eventually she acquiesced to his proposal, but she did not tell her authoritarian father who had thwarted her plans many times. She preferred to elope.

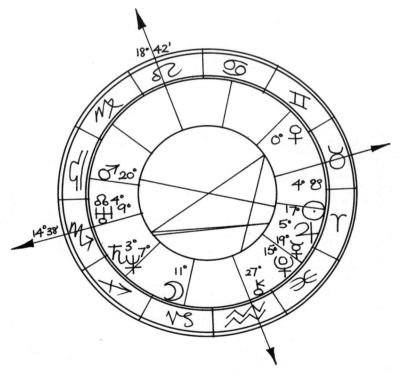

Figure 19a Relationship Chart
Elizabeth Barrett-Browning and Robert Browning

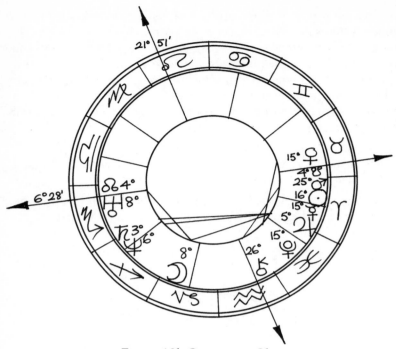

Figure 19b Composite Chart

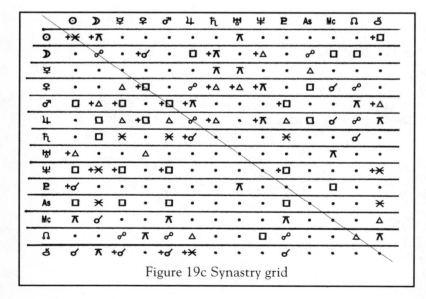

Figure 19c Synastry grid

In the relationship chart, Venus opposes Saturn-Neptune in Capricorn and squares Chiron in the fourth house, bringing the stability they both desired and showing the unconditional love which may have been promised in another life to be together again and heal old emotional wounds - although of course when Elizabeth died, Robert experienced considerable pain. Notwithstanding, with all the South Node conjuncts in the synastry, this separation was also most probably a part of their life plan.

That Elizabeth had been dependent on Robert to break her free from the depressive black hole in which she found herself is shown in the composite chart by a Pluto-Venus sextile, in the relationship chart by Saturn-Neptune opposing Venus, and in the synastry by a Saturn-Venus trine (see Figure 19c). There were times during their marriage when depression threatened to overwhelm her again, and this is what led her to Spiritualism and the obsessive friendship with another woman. But the relationship proved strong enough to overcome this. It may have been intended to heal lifetimes of emotional wounds for them both.

The relationship helped Elizabeth to recover the power she had projected onto her father and brought her to motherhood in her own right - natal Mercury, Mars and Pluto conjunct her Sun inconjunct the Moon. Elizabeth's own mothering had been blighted by her mother grieving for her brother's death and by the overwhelmingly dominant nature of her father. With Sun conjunct Pluto inconjunct the Moon, there would have been powerful undercurrents in the household and considerable karma with both parents. But only one parent can play the domineering role at any one time and in the Barrett house this was undoubtedly the father.

Nodal aspects between Elizabeth and Robert's charts include the double-whammy: his Venus-Jupiter conjunct her South Node and his Venus inconjunct her North Node - indicating a soulmate relationship. With his Saturn conjunct her North Node, her Mercury conjunct his South Node, her Mars-Pluto conjunct his South Node and her Neptune square his Nodes also figuring (see Figures 4a and 4b), there would appear to be a karmic intent to help each other evolve and grow.

The relationship picked up where it had left off in some other life. They knew each other intimately from the start, sharing thoughts and feelings without words. In particular they shared 'intuitions of the heart'. There were no barriers between them: '[I] am inside of him and hear him breathe' (Elizabeth) and '[we] know each other for time and, I trust, for eternity'. (Robert). A graphic description of how a double-whammy Moon-Neptune contact is experienced in a relationship, although the double Sun-Pluto might at times have become too symbiotic without the intervention of Venus-Uranus. The one-way interaspects in the chart include Robert's Neptune square Elizabeth's Sun, and square her Mercury and Mars, and her Neptune square his Venus. Hardly surprising they didn't need words to know what was in each other's head, or that this had been the case even before they met. As an old friend told them 'if two persons were to be chosen from the ends of the earth for perfect union and fitness, there could not be a greater congruity than between you two'. After Elizabeth's death, Robert wrote in her bible these lines from Dante's *La Vita Nuova*: 'Certain am I - from this life I shall pass into a better, there where that lady lives of whom enamoured was my soul'. Elizabeth virtually wrote her own epitaph in a poem *My Heart and I* which Robert published posthumously for her:

> Yet who complains: My heart and I?
> In this abundant earth no doubt
> Is little room for things worn out:
> Disdain them, break them, throw them by,
> And if before the days grow rough
> We once were loved, used – well enough,
> I think, we've fared, my heart and I

Effectively, what this poem says is that all that matters was that she was loved. Even if they had not made a mystic marriage in a past life (which is a strong possibility with Neptune-Moon and the Venus-Node connections), it certainly appears as though they had in their current life.

SOUL COMPANIONS

As part of on-going work regarding Amanda's relationship patterns, which we have already looked at (natal chart Figure 18), she asked me about a man she had recently met 'again'. They were convinced they were soulmates and that they had something to do together, beyond a sexual relationship. When I looked at their charts, and at their past lives together, I felt that they came into the category of soulmates who were together to help each other grow. (The lives in this case history are those I psychically saw for her rather than those

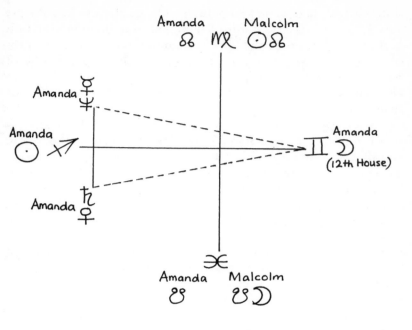

Figure 20

obtained through regression, although she had already had some regression experiences which supported my far seeing).

Both births were on the full moon. Amanda's chart has a Sun-Moon Sagittarius-Gemini opposition forming a Grand Cross with her Nodes, and her partner Malcolm has the Sun-Moon across Virgo-Pisces, forming a Grand Cross in synastry (see Figure 20). Full moon charts are always interesting as the Moon is the deeply ingrained instinctual, pattern that has developed over many lifetimes, and the Sun is what has to be built into the present life. When the two oppose each other, tension builds between the desire to evolve and the need to stay entrenched in the past. The past life energy is particularly strong at full moon and so for Amanda the communicative but emotionally elusive Gemini Moon energy is powerful. This is reinforced by its placement in the karmic twelfth house, indicating what has gone on in the past. The opposition to the Sun shows qualities Amanda is trying to develop in this lifetime.

With some pairs of signs the Sun-Moon opposition is a huge

315

shift - as with Malcolm's rationality versus intuition (Virgo-Pisces) axis. However, the Sagittarius-Gemini axis is a different vibration of the same thing, the emphasis being on the communicative aspect of the Gemini Moon shifting to the more philosophical side of Sagittarius. This is the eternal quest for knowledge while the challenge is to simply be, rather than always striving to become or to understand.

What made Amanda's opposition particularly interesting is that it forms a mutable Grand Cross with the Nodes of the Moon, and that also involves a shift from the past into karmic purpose. There is a strong service orientation with the North Node in Virgo. Where Amanda is coming from, with a South Node in Pisces, is reflected by Malcolm's Sun-North Node in Virgo and his Moon-South Node in Pisces. Not surprisingly with this Grand Cross, Amanda's relationships strongly mirror the issues in her chart. Pisces so much wants to be one with the universe and this becomes confused with merging into a partner. She is searching for unification, but on the way she frequently gets caught up in the victor/martyr/saviour syndrome, and all the soul dramas that spiral around it.

It is an enormous soul lesson for the Pisces-Virgo axis to develop discrimination, because Pisces either gives indiscriminately, or has the urge to save (or become) the victim, and Virgo demands boundaries and detachment.

Amanda's Node is quite close to Pluto, so it is pulling in strong transforming energy to aid her process. The old patterns have to be burnt away in order that the new energies can emerge and because the Grand Cross is mutable, it can go either way. Amanda can either develop a considerable part of its potential, or she can glide along and never quite get round to it - or go off on another tack and do all the things that the dual signs, Pisces, Sagittarius and Gemini are distracted by. If this happens then Virgo can be quite a hard taskmaster, saying: 'OK, you've done that, now come back to the lesson, come back to the service, come back to the discrimination, and come back to the fruitfulness'. So the ease of Amanda's Gemini-Sagittarius will be tempered by both partners need to 'put the nose to the grindstone' and get on with their lessons.

There is a wide Finger of Fate also powerfully interacting with the Grand Cross in Amanda's chart. The Sun-Moon opposition is the backbone, with Saturn-Venus on one side and Mercury and Neptune on the other. Fingers of Fate are exactly what they sound like and call for a big shift. Amanda is trying to integrate energies that in the past have been at odds with each other, but she is also trying to fulfil the potential of some latent power. The challenge is to balance these possibilities and express the energy through the Sun (which is the release point for the Finger of Fate rather than the twelfth house Moon at its point). So we come back to sixth house service-orientated matters.

If we break the Finger of Fate down into its composite parts, we notice that Amanda has Saturn-Venus in the eighth house. It is possible she has developed lack of self-love and low self-esteem because of religious, moral or cultural perspectives. As we have seen, this is an aspect which so easily prostitutes itself for security and safety and what passes for love - or what doesn't pass for love. This soul may be drawn into sexual servitude. With her past life history, however, Amanda can go way back and discover the time when prostitution was sacred and when she was the mediator for the goddess. However, the synastry with Malcolm brings up all the doubts about being lovable.

On the other side of the Finger of Fate are Mercury and Neptune. They do not form a conjunction, but are feeding their energies into the Moon and so must be considered as such. With this combination, Amanda can channel high sources of inspiration down through the Finger of Fate, as long as she doesn't become sidetracked by illusion, delusion and deception. This is a Neptunian tendency, and something which the South Node in Pisces will have done many times. This present life, however, is asking her to view people and love - or the things that pass for love - more realistically. When she is able to love herself and access her higher energies, she will be able to express them in service to others through the Virgo North Node. As her evolution involves Sagittarius, questing and exploring also come into this. It has many potential applications when she has integrated the planetary energies.

Amanda's Saturn-Mars powerlessness has been a big lesson in this present life and challenges will continue to be triggered by Malcolm's chart. When I did the reading, Amanda was moving to a point where she could really begin to express and assert herself - she would face the challenge of transiting Pluto coming up to her Sun. She needed to be aware of the danger of giving away her power or falling into the martyr/saviour trap and this was where her soulmate came in.

Meeting Malcolm happened at an important time for Amanda, and he activated various parts of her chart. She had asked me about her purpose so I reminded her that the Sun in the sixth has to do with the work that you *have* to do. Chiron on the Midheaven is concerned with serving people in a healing capacity. It is also what a partner whose Nodes formed a Grand Cross with hers could be expected to facilitate in some way.

If we look at how her relationship with Malcolm slots into this, we note that his Sun conjuncts Amanda's North Node, which is one of the indications of a soulmate purpose in coming together. They have been together before and so feel comfortable - the contact is emphasised by his Nodes being squared by her Sun, with his Nodes sitting on that Grand Cross. It has a sense of destiny and purpose behind it. Malcolm's Sun conjuncts her Pluto and her Sun squares his Pluto - a double whammy pointing to power issues. Much will depend on whether she had a previous opportunity to take her power back or to break symbiotic dependence, for they can either be empowered as a couple, or she can give her power away to him.

That is one part of the synastry. Another extremely important part has a repeating Moon-Saturn connection which can hold them together while they work through their purpose. The challenge is to use the positive discrimination of Virgo appropriately and have the strength to allow the other person to learn by their own mistakes. Together they can achieve anything they set their minds to.

We can also see the mirror of relationships at work here again. The one-way aspects, which will come up in the present life, concern Amanda's will. The fact that Malcolm's Saturn opposes her Mars means that, like so many of her men, he brings up her assertion/aggression/right-use-of-will issues. As they were born within three months of each other, they have similar Saturn and outer planet placements, so at a karmic level they are working on the same issues. This is reflected through a Sun-Pluto aspect in Malcolm's natal chart.

The charts and synastry mirror each other: Malcolm has a Pluto-Moon opposition and in the synastry there is a one-way Pluto-Moon opposition. This can be to do with metaphysics, transformation, healing the earth - working on the Earth Mother vibration - or it can show itself as Malcolm becoming Amanda's little boy, her child, and bringing his own 'mother stuff' into the relationship. In that case the issues that come up may not belong to their personal relationship together - although having his Moon conjunct her South Node she was quite likely to have been his mother before.

The Moon-Pluto issues are not necessarily personal to the two of them (the interaspect would need to repeat both ways for that), but Malcolm has mothering issues to work through and the relationship offers an opportunity for this. The devouring mother archetype lies behind Moon-Pluto and it would be easy for Amanda to play the mother to Malcolm. If they could keep this mirroring at the level of healing then it's fine, but if they fall into 'little boy and mother' it could be destructive. That came up strongly in the relationship until Malcolm recognised his mothering issues and separated them out.

The relationship also worked as 'cross-mirroring' to help Amanda resolve her fathering issues (Sun-Pluto). At times, Malcolm took on the father role so she could play out her father-power issues with him. But that was at the personal level. At the much bigger soul level there was great opportunity here for transforming some powerful blockages, and it was possible for Amanda and Malcolm to heal some ancient patterns in each of them. As the relationship panned out, they did work on many of these issues but the pressure eventually forced them to part as the intensity was too great, and the projections too complex, to sustain.

As I did the reading, I saw a series of pictures that led me to feel that this couple had been learning together for a long time. Although I don't believe in linear, chronological time stretching way back into the distance, it did seem nevertheless to go back 4,000 - 6,000 years. They were a couple who were promised to each other from birth. The astrologers cast charts and said: 'These two have come in to be together' and that was that. One of them, and I was not sure who was then male, nor did it seem to matter, was born of a high lineage of priestesses, and the other was born from a royal line. Although they were promised to each other, they weren't going to have a conventional married life. They would come together at specified times, in sexual relationship, but most of the time they would be apart doing other things. They underwent a sacred marriage and on occasion there was a strong physical connection because they acted as a conduit for the god and goddess. For the rest of the time, whichever one of them was taking the priestess role had strongly religious duties to perform, and the other had a governing role as an official whose title was 'Observer of the Royal Presence'. Somehow the fertility of the land which was vested in the king was acted out through the Observer of the Royal Presence who was almost a substitute for the king (it was never clear why).

The priestess was usually celibate otherwise, and totally involved in the spiritual work. But the 'observer' seemed to have carte blanche to do what he liked. He could take other wives and could have a family as long as he came to the temple five or six times a year and performed his obligations. This gave him great freedom, which initially wasn't a problem, but there was a sense of - *resentment* was perhaps too strong a word for it, yet I could not find another one - from the priestess. Here was this man who had enormous freedom of choice for partners and for expressing his sexual beingness, while she was restricted.

Also, I felt that there were certain days when there were duties and obligations on the priestess to be available for men, in the role of the goddess. She couldn't make a choice, she had to wait for the man to choose her. Because a lot of men were in awe of her, she frequently was not chosen, and that did not feel good. By this stage in the reading I felt Amanda had probably taken the priestess role in that life but I still was not entirely sure. It was almost like two facets of a soul, and may indeed have been a life where the souls were just beginning to individualise into two, having been up to that point one soul.

There came a point where the priestess was allowed a choice. She could either stay with the temple, or go back into the world and resume a life there. I saw a discussion where she was asking this man: 'What would happen if I came into the world - would I be with you or not?' And he was saying: 'I already have a family, I have all I need'. I could feel an enormous tension in her; she couldn't openly admit that she would have liked a different answer. There was a shutting down of emotions and feelings.

She decided to stay in the temple as it seemed a safer place, but she had already handed over her duties to her successor, so there was no longer the sexual contact with the man. The priestess withdrew more and more into her own self and her contact with the goddess and after a few years when she had to perform the sacred rites of being available for men, which was still part of her duties, she was all goddess. Word got out and whereas men were earlier in awe, now they were queuing up and she began to feel used - the energy was all going out but nothing was coming back.

At this point the man re-appeared, standing in line. She had never considered that that could happen, but he had heard about what a powerful conduit she was, and he had also been missing their own sacred connection. When he entered her chamber, her initial reaction was that everything between them was finished - but she couldn't refuse him as she was the representative of the goddess. Her feeling was divided. The exultant power surge of 'I've got him now' was countered with the thought 'If I do this, it'll bring everything up again and I've closed it all down'.

When the sexual part finished, she begged him not to come back, although part of her wanted him to. He was ambivalent too but it became an addiction, with him coming back at every opportunity and it became a very intense relationship. When he asked: 'Can't you now leave and be my wife?' she replied: 'No. The moment of choice is past. I have to stay here. I have to dedicate my life now and as I get older and older less men will want me and eventually I'll be sitting here and I'll be rejected by everybody, but that's part of my lesson'. He responded: 'No. I won't allow that. As long as I'm alive, as long as you're alive, I will come to the temple and we will be together'. It was that vow that linked them on a soul level because finally it became 'In another life, we'll be together'. And she agreed, without really believing it.

When they met again in another guise there was a subtle recognition, a feeling of needing to be together and yet not quite knowing what lay behind it. That was a master/slave relationship, and they were drawn back together to know what it means for one person to have mastery over the other, but it was sexual mastery as well - extremely erotic because of the past contact.

I then skipped to a much later life where they were both the same sex. They were walking in a monastery, a classic picture of two monks who are friends, but who are not allowed to become particular friends. There was a great sense of brotherhood being encouraged, but not individual friendship. They were just taking pleasure in being in each other's company, interested in the same things, and in discussing ideas. It was a gentle friendship, yet homo-erotic underneath because of the old contacts (which open the lower chakras), and although on the surface they did not seem to be aware of it, the abbot picked up on the underlying current, and separated them. He sent one off to work at a sort of outpost, and the other stayed at the monastery. Again, there was a promise, without really knowing what it entailed. They had a secret meeting where they swore undying eternal friendship, and in an unguarded moment one of them said: 'If it hadn't been this way, I would like us to have been husband and wife'. And the other responded: 'Well, maybe, who knows, we'll have to see'.

And so they incarnated together again in that role, quickly, because they had flipped back in. That relationship felt much more equal. It was comfortable, like a reprise life, where they did all the things that had not really happened before, such as having a family. But for both there was a hungry soul behind the outer happenings, and that soul wanted to grow, to be of service, and in that life this soul was a little bit censorious: 'There's pleasure here, there's comfort here, but what have we learnt?' The answer appeared to be to look after a family, to do all that they had not done before, but there was a discontent towards the end and a feeling that they could have done more. And so the present incarnation is about doing more. It is not a sense of duty or responsibility exactly, although that is there in the background, but the importance of directing the energy into the proper channels.

I ended the reading by reminding Amanda that service is doing willingly whatever you are called upon to do. It is not doing things for recognition and reward or appearing to be a good person, it is identifying a job that needs to be done and getting on with it. She reported back that this was indeed an important part of the relationship and it was what she missed when they finally parted. However, she also said they had come a long way towards resolving their issues so 'who knew what the future would bring?'.

CONTINUING THE MIRACLE

There are times when two people deliberately set out to the meet their life partner - whom they may or may not regard as a soulmate. We have already looked briefly at the relationship between David Lawson and Justin Carson, but the full story is even more extraordinary. David first met Justin in his sleep:

'My first conscious impression of Justin was the feeling that I woke up with on a summer's morning in 1987. The feeling was warmer and more golden than the August sunshine that was squeezing its way through the blind that covered my bedroom window. A new light was dawning from within me too and gently filtering into my conscious mind as I opened and then slightly shielded my eyes from the brightness of the day. I knew that I had met him. I had contacted the man that I had been planning to meet and, on some subtle level, we had discussed the possibility of sharing our future. I did not have any tangible idea of what this person was going to look like when we finally physically met, nor did I remember the specifics of what we had discussed but I knew without a shadow of a doubt that I had met him. The feelings were too strong to ignore'.

Quite apart from the fact that David is a sensitive, extremely psychic Pisces, the couple had repeating, each-way Neptune-Mercury and telepathic Sun-Neptune, Pluto-Mercury interaspects between their charts. They could see straight into each other's heart and know exactly what was going on, no matter what the distance was between them. These two did not need to meet physically to communicate, nor did Justin's death end the contact. The relationship continues on a spiritual plane, just as it did before they met:

'We had a number of similar meetings during that August and into early September. There were more mornings of waking up with that special feeling and with a sense that this man and I were forging some unique spiritual contract between us. If I had consciously known what was contained within the small print of that spiritual contract, I perhaps would have been both more fearful and more excited about the roller-coaster ride that was to come. My relationship with Justin has been the most positive, thrilling, growthful, challenging and terrifying relationship of my entire life!..

I did not plan to meet a soulmate as such, but I was actively planning to attract my ideal partner and create my ideal loving relationship for some months before Justin and I found each other. Indeed, in our own ways we were both consciously planning for a relationship and using positive thought techniques to make ourselves magnetic and available for the right person to come into our lives'.

Justin:' I have to say that the concept of looking for a soulmate is curious if not slightly spurious. I have heard it said that life is what happens while you are making other plans, and I suspect that the same thing applies when establishing a relationship. If you spend all your time looking for it, it will probably recede further and further into the distance. It is obviously appropriate to prepare yourself both spiritually and emotionally but you probably cannot plan for it or look for it.

In my case my preparation for finding my relationship consisted of doing affirmations related to what I wanted to create for myself in my life, and forgiveness, both of myself and past relationships, so that in a sense when the next one was imminent, I was ready for it'.

David's description of how he set up the meeting with his 'almost perfect fit' is helpful for anyone who wants to attract the best possible relationship:

> 'On a regular basis, I sat in meditation and imagined the kind of man that I would like to share my life with. I wanted someone who was as interested in his own personal and spiritual development as I was in mine. I wanted a man who would help me laugh at life, and who would support me in the powerful flow of positive thought that I had started to develop over the previous few years. I created a detailed profile that included a clear sense of the impact that I would like my ideal partner to have upon my life and emotions, as well as a list of the qualities that I would like my ideal partner to embody. I realised that preparing the ground for this special union required me to make positive changes within myself, so that my beliefs and behaviour allowed me to be available for it. Love can easily pass us on the street corner if we have not learned how to look for and recognise it, and in my experience recognition of love always comes with a willingness to love ourselves. I created a series of positive affirmations for daily use; I burned old love letters that kept me attached to the past, forgiving my past relationships and releasing myself from old, worn out expectations of how relationships are supposed to be'. [An appropriate course of action for someone with Venus in Taurus, which could otherwise hold onto comfortable notions of how things ought to be, and to resentments from the past - although David does have Uranus in Virgo and the Moon in Aquarius, a combination which likes to move on.]

Without realising it, Justin was using a similar technique, which he called creative daydreaming:

> 'For a period of time I ran a thought alone the lines of 'I now create a perfect spiritual, sensual and loving relationship with a beautiful man for ever'. One of the things I do for a living now is to teach positive thinking and I joke that in the process of developing that perfect relationship I had a series of what I can only describe as practice runs. I would meet someone and think: 'Oh, this is IT. I'm in love … oh… okay, so I'm not'.

But then Justin went to a seminar and was asked to stand at the door taking the money, and the rest is history. His spiritual, sensual and loving man walked into his life and never left.

So what can we learn about soulmates from their synastry? Well, apart from those Node and Neptune interaspects, the most significant repeating each-way aspect is Saturn-Venus. From the karmic perspective these two had been together before and had agreed to help each other with some extremely difficult lessons in life. David's support throughout Justin's illness was crucial to his repeated recoveries, just as Justin supported David in his individual creative endeavours. Even Justin's death fitted into David's lessons in life. With Venus trine to Uranus conjunct Pluto, David needed to let go when it was appropriate. As he says, during the darkest days of Justin's illness he would:

> 'do deals with God in the hope that Justin would return to me alive and well. I have moved through years of believing that, whatever happened, he would always make a miraculous recovery, to a year when I really did think that he was going to die, and began to prepare

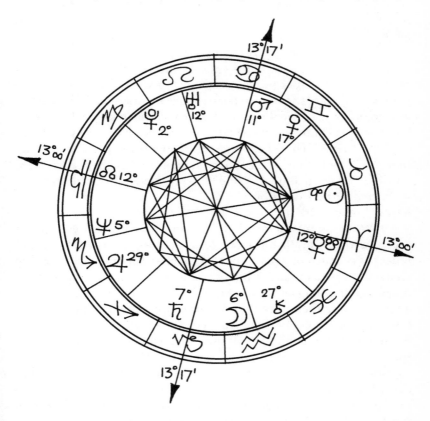

Figure 21 Justin Carson and David Lawson:
Relationship chart

myself for that eventuality, searching inside myself for the grace and willingness to let go if Justin most needed to leave. Just when I had found those inner resources and was ready to surrender, Justin's recovery was the most profound and the most miraculous of all'.

And, of course, eventually Justin did need to move on and David was there, supporting him every inch of the way. But even in his dying process, Justin also supported David in keeping with that Saturn-Venus connection. I was with them both for the two weeks before Justin died, just before Valentine's Day, and almost his last request to me was that I should buy David an enormous bunch of roses and present them to him on that day with his love - that, and a request to look after David at a joint television appearance we were scheduled to make a few days later. Justin was most insistent that David should go as it was important for his career (Capricorn Node).

The remainder of the aspects between them were one-way. The Sun and Moon to Pluto contact showed the potential for a symbiotic or interdependent relationship while their contact to Uranus pointed to the need to maintain personal space. Both contacts mirrored David's own Pluto-Uranus to Venus issues, which were brought to the fore when he had to face so intensely the possibility of Justin's death. That these aspects are in a trine, point to the fact that David had resolved them in a previous life and had found their positive side - which he was able to express when he unhesitatingly supported Justin's decision not to have any more toxic treatment, letting him go with love.

What fascinated me when I began work on this present book was how the relationship chart for David and Justin (Figure 21) reflected so much of what I knew of them as a couple. Relationship charts show *why* a relationship operates. The nodal axis squares the nodal axis in David and Justin's natal charts, forming a Grand Cross and propelling them into their separate and joint soul purposes. In the Relationship Chart there is a mystic rectangle of Mars, Neptune, Saturn and the Sun: part of their function is to integrate the spirituality of Neptune with the practicality of Saturn. Their healing, psychic development and Angel courses were strongly grounded in everyday reality and yet were inspirational and spiritual. They resolved the mystic-pragmatist dilemma and taught how to live with spiritual intent in the practical world – and, fittingly for Sun in Taurus and Jupiter in the second house, showed how to bring abundance into everyday life. The North Node, fittingly, falls in Libra, right on the Ascendant so that the purpose of the partnership is to go out and teach the world about positive, loving relationships!

A Grand Cross is formed with a Mars-Saturn opposition (which again falls on the natal nodal axes). Saturn is the Lord of Karma and this planet squaring a nodal axis signifies an important task, with Mars to give it impetus. There is a further Grand Cross involving Uranus opposite the Moon and the Sun opposite Neptune. This was a transforming relationship on all levels.

What stood out for me in the relationship chart was that Venus in Gemini, the sign of the twins, was virtually unaspected - other than a sextile to the communications planet Mercury and the Nodes. This placement suggests twin souls, and all the communication that was so typical of David and Justin's relationship is embodied in that contact. It is in the ninth house of publishing, which would fit in with the books, tapes and videos they published on prosperity and positive thought, and yet the challenge was to integrate Venus into the rest of the chart. Their relationship was not only about teaching and communicating love, it was about *living it in the moment*. It is worth repeating what David said some four years before Justin died:

> 'Our purpose together is so much bigger than any words that I could use to define it. We have provided each other with a foundation for our creative and spiritual growth. We have loved and laughed and enjoyed companionship. Our shared journey is growing sweeter, the present more exciting and the future less important. When you are in love, each present moment is the best time of all. This love story is still work in progress'.

David's North Node is in the eighth house. His experience of loving and living with Justin through and beyond death expanded David's awareness of the two worlds and of soulmate relationships. Typically for the eighth house, David puts his experience into his teaching and one-to-one sessions. Clients increasingly ask him to show them how to attract and manifest loving relationships. David feels that this is an on-going expression of his and Justin's joint purpose, which included a very visible and public modelling of a loving relationship. This purpose was set out in the composite relationship chart through the Libra Ascendant conjunct the North Node, and the ninth house Venus in Gemini.

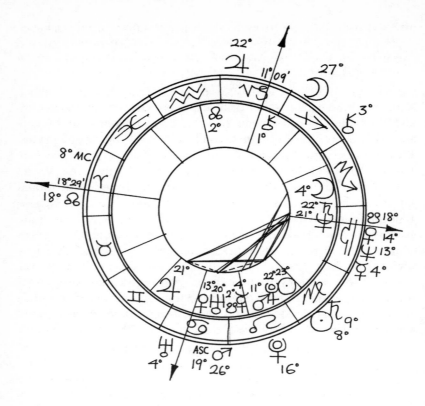

Figure 22

SERIAL SOULMATES

Soulmate meetings can be wonderful experiences, but their cost may be high and the lesson hard. Gwen, an American who had already had the experience of meeting one soulmate contacted me. She said that her soulmate had died but she had learnt many lessons from the experience (Pluto was sextile Venus in her natal chart and she needed to complete the change in her pattern of relating). She had subsequently been told by an astrologer that she would meet her second soulmate (an experience for which her Venus-Neptune conjunction yearned) and that they would have a long and happy life together. She was introduced to a man:

'It was magic, just like the time I met my first soulmate; we felt instantly attracted and each felt we had known one another before.

> We spoke about reincarnation on our first meeting... On his third
> visit he told me he had been diagnosed as having a terminal illness
> and he felt we needed to teach each other some lessons and that we
> don't have much time. We feel so close to each other he has asked
> me to be with him when he dies... How can fate be so cruel?'

What she didn't tell me then, but which soon became apparent, was
that Tom was gay and that he had Aids. I also learned some years
later that he was in fact soulmate number three, number one having
died from a drug overdose and number two from liver cancer (see
Hands Across Time for more details).

The nodal axes of the charts (Figure 22) form a wide Grand
Cross out of element, Gwen's Aries-Libra to Tom's Aquarius-Leo, so
that they may seem to be at cross purposes in their life direction; she
is working on herself at the personal level, he at the universal.
However, her North Node exactly conjuncted his Aries Ascendant
and his Sun trined her North Node; his Venus squared her Nodes,
and his Descendant-Neptune-Saturn conjuncted her South Node-
Neptune-Venus; her South Node conjuncted his Mars, and his Mars
trined her North Node. This does not appear to be the 'long and
happy life' and yet it had the potential to be fulfilling in terms of
soul growth and companionship. They had lessons to offer each other
through the contacts to the Nodes.

Her initial response to his news was to rush around frantically
trying everything for him (his Mars activating her Libra South Node).
I suggested that one of her lessons was to learn to 'let go and let
God', thereby allowing the quality of unconditional love to flow. A
past-life contact which surfaced was one in which Tom was a sickly
child and Gwen was his mother, who literally willed him to live.
She was aware, on first hearing of his cancer, of a strong motherly
energy and of wanting to force him to live. Once she had recognised
this as a past-life pattern, however, she was able to let go of these
emotions and concentrate on releasing him to take responsibility
for himself.

In his imaging and regression work Tom discovered an
ingrained sense of 'ought' and 'should' which was an external locus
of control (the tenth house North Node needed to develop an inner
source of direction). He was afraid to allow his own images to emerge
in case they weren't right, despite the fact that in imaging work there
is no right or wrong. Tom linked this to his father and to a feeling he
had as a child that here was a man who knew everything, but with

whom he found himself in increasing conflict as he grew older (Saturn and Jupiter sextile the Sun-Pluto conjunction, Saturn square Uranus, Chiron in Capricorn in the ninth house near the Midheaven). This in turn linked back to an old life in which his present-life father had been his teacher, passing on the law and mores of a society which were becoming obsolete and which were overturned shortly after his death. Tom worked on this block and was able to focus on his inner locus of control and self-healing power.

To stand a chance of recovering, Tom needed reclaim his power and make it clear to his soulmate and his family that he was quite capable of doing so. He was way beyond the stage when conventional therapies could cure him. His one chance was to use his power of self-healing to reverse the process of the cancer. Gwen was thus offered the opportunity of sharing the compassion and acceptance of the Libra South Node conjunction with him through unconditional love, instead of losing herself in the relationship. Her Neptune conjunct Venus and the South Node in Libra could be expressed in a higher relationship where the soulmate relationship would be that of companion and teacher. Such a relationship would also release her from the manipulative past pattern of the Pluto sextile to Venus and the overly adaptive and accommodating Libra South Node. She could also, if it was Tom's time to move on, support his soul in that process.

Part of Tom's karmic lesson and purpose, indicated in the tenth house Aquarian North Node, was to help in the evolution of both his own inner authority and of that of mankind, and part was to resolve his seventh house Neptune-Saturn dilemma. In *The Karmic Journey*, I wrote that it 'may prove necessary for him to act as a scapegoat by dying; to facilitate both a family (tenth house) and wider group (Aquarius North Node) understanding that death can be a growth-enhancing process and is not, in any case, The End'. Tom felt he could help his parents to deal with death more effectively than they had before by encouraging them to come to terms with his life-threatening illness and sharing in his death - he looked upon it as his gift to those with whom he shared his life. Conversely he may have needed to take his knowledge out to the world himself, particularly if he had succeeded in correcting his dis-ease, in order to teach that one must take responsibility for oneself and that death can be a creative activity. His soulmate companion offered him support in taking this step, the Mars-Node contacts were used courageously and did not invoke the aggressive, ego-conflict level of functioning.

In the event, Tom died some two years later, but Gwen said later that they had said all there was to say. There was nothing left to do. They had put all their karma to rest. Tom died peacefully at home, with his friends all around him, just as he wished.

When I was with Gwen in the States a few months later, I learned more about her serial soulmates and their effect on her spiritual development. Number one was a drug addict and eventually, no matter how much her Libra-Neptune-South Node wanted to stay in relationship, for her own sanity she had to leave. He died shortly afterwards, but she was unable to face the funeral and got on a plane instead. Number two was a Southern beau to match her Southern belle - an old connection which was renewed for some seven years. She was then told he was dying of liver cancer. She had a horror of hospitals that amounted to a phobia and, after the first visit, once again got on a plane. He died soon after and again she missed the funeral.

When she met Tom it was obvious she had some karma around hospitals, death and dying. She nursed Tom devotedly when it became necessary, both in hospital and at his home and did everything for him - even laying out his body. She had resolved that this time she would do all she felt called on to do and more 'so that when soulmate number four comes along, this will be a live one!'

As an aside to this story, there is an interesting tale around soulmate number two, although I do not have the astrology. Paul was the adopted son of elderly parents whose first son had died of liver failure. When I was in the States I stayed with his mother who confided to me that, as a strict Baptist, she could not believe in reincarnation. However, she said, she chose Paul (an older child than they had wanted) because he was the image of her first son, and when they brought him home, he seemed to know the place already. She felt that her prayers for God to bring her son back had been answered. Sadly he carried the same deadly seed as her first son and, although he lived much longer, ultimately it was the same organ that failed. I noticed there were lots of photographs of him, an extremely handsome man, and I learnt that he wanted to be a film star. A few nights later, unable to sleep, I was watching T.V. when suddenly on the screen was the face I had been seeing in all the photographs. But this was a former matinee idol who had been bitter at his failure to make it to the top, and had turned to drink and died young of cirrhosis of the liver. It is rare to find such a close physical resemblance passing through three incarnations, but in all three, his good looks were of supreme importance to him.

As for Gwen, when I last heard from her she was with soulmate number four. But this time it was different. No illness, no death in the foreseeable future. As she said: 'I intend to live with this one'.

SEEKING THE TWIN

Soulmates are often referred to as twin souls or twin flames. Different people have alternative definitions of these terms but they tend loosely to mean the same thing: someone's 'other half' or twin. One explanation for twin souls, which comes close to what Plato had to say, occurred to me sometime ago whilst listening to a programme on twins. The researcher said that as many as sixty percent of pregnancies are twin pregnancies in their early trimester. That is to say, the fertilised egg splits and two foetuses share the womb together for a few weeks. Then, one twin is absorbed by the other so they become one again. One foetus may also be lost by miscarriage or stillbirth. This can leave a lifelong sense of incompleteness and longing, an experience for which a client of mine, Tim, seemed to find confirmation during a shamanic experience in South America.

Tim is an extremely psychic and sensitive Pisces with the Sun and North Node conjunct Chiron in the seventh house and Venus-Saturn at the head of a Finger of Fate with Neptune on one side and Pluto-Jupiter-Uranus on the other. He undertook a classic shamanic journey. The drugs he was given shattered him, took him apart so that he had to put himself back together again. Then, late on in his journey, Tim was at the Temple of the Moon with a shaman called Augustine. He was given San Pedro cactus before going into a cave where he lay in the foetal position. He became conscious of being a twin and experienced the pain of the twin being miscarried:

> 'It was really heart wrenching. It was like losing someone, a relationship breaking up.... I also felt the pain of losing the other half, of how I have carried that pain all my life, in everyday life it has always been there. It affects how I do things. I also felt how I did not want to be born because of that loss. I wanted to stay in the womb because it was a safe space, and nearer to where I had come from.

Tim then went into a powerful healing memory of a past life during his birth in a teepee as a native American. The child was welcomed by the whole community who were closely involved in the birth. Drumming was used to stimulate the baby into birth:

> 'The drumming became more erotic, began to move around more, like a swaying and sensual dance...It was wonderful to be born with that feeling instead of being induced with drugs as happened in my present life...[5]

When Tim left the cave it was dusk, exactly the time he had been born for the first time in this present incarnation. But now he had been reborn. He is convinced that the miscarriage his mother suffered, apparently just before his conception, was actually of his twin and that he himself stayed in the womb and was born ten months later. Until the shamanic healing he had felt incomplete, but was now whole. For the first time in his life he was able to enter into a committed, long-term relationship which is still strong six years later.

THE MYSTIC MARRIAGE

An extremely powerful soul bond that lasts across time was once made through the 'mystic marriage'. It was created by a joining of two souls on the physical, mental, emotional and spiritual levels and was intended to last for ever. A mystic marriage often lies behind an apparent soulmate connection.

Initiates were carefully prepared for this ritual, with the training extending over many years. An Egyptian papyrus still exists with most of the steps set out, although the last few are missing. The couple developed telepathy, out of body experiences, and other metaphysical abilities. They had to proceed together, for if one lagged behind, the other could not continue until they caught up. The mystic marriage was made in order that spiritual work, which did not end with death, could be carried out.

As the bond does not cease with time or distance, at least one of the partners involved in a mystic marriage will usually know exactly what is happening to the other, even if they are not in physical proximity. Clients will say to me: 'We met in our dreams before we met physically' (see David Lawson and Justin Carson's story) or 'There hasn't been a moment since we met that I did not know exactly what he was thinking and feeling, even though I was on the other side of the world'. Some clients feel that they are controlled by the other person, others that they have been psychically invaded. It is possible to have made more than one mystic marriage over the centuries, or such a union may have failed at the last minute but still binds the souls because of all the intermediate stages that have already been passed through. Wise priests annulled the union if an initiation failed, but this was not always done.

Present day esoteric work can also include a mystic marriage - sometimes this is carefully orchestrated, at other times it occurs spontaneously. The poet W. B. Yeats underwent two mystic marriages with Maud Gonne as part of their involvement with the Order of the Golden Dawn. The synastry between their charts perfectly expresses the 'can't live with him, can't live without her' dilemma their life reflected. Although Yeats fell in love with Maud at first sight, calling her a goddess, and continued to love her all his life, Maud steadfastly refused his proposals of marriage and married someone else. In the synastry between them, Maud's Sagittarian Sun opposes Yeat's Gemini Sun conjunct Uranus. Her Moon conjunction to Uranus widely conjuncts Yeat's Sun and the opposition is squared by Maud's nodal axis, forming a Grand Cross. Both recalled past lives together.

In a shared experience some ten years after they met, Yeats dreamt she kissed him for the first time, and Maud that a great spirit took her to a throng of spirits, amongst whom was Yeats. The great spirit put her hand into Yeats' and told her that they were married. When Maud related the dream to Yeats, she told him that it could never be because there was someone else.

A few days later, they did a silent meditation together. Maud found herself 'a great stone statue through which passed flame'. Yeats became 'a flame mounting up and through and looking out of the eyes of a great stone Minerva'. To both of them, this was confirmation of their mystic marriage at a mental and spiritual level. But Maud refused to consummate the union physically, saying she had an abhorrence of physical contact.

After another ten years had passed, they were exploring sexual magick on the astral plane - a kind of out-of-the-body tantric sex - when they once again experienced a renewing of their mystic vows. From the reports, the two do not seem to have been in physical proximity at the time. Yeats consciously invoked two red and green globes, a symbol of sexuality, uniting together. As a result, he experienced a 'great mingling' with Maud. That same night, Maud wrote to him recounting an experience in which she assumed a mothlike form. Yeats appeared as a great serpent, becoming one with Maud. Yeats wrote to Maud: 'I think today I could let you marry another ... for I know the spiritual union between us will outlive this life, even if we never see each other in this world again'. Eventually, Maud having married again, Yeats did marry. But it was to Maud that he wrote:

'Others because you did not keep
The deep sworn vow have been friends of mine
The triangle plays out to the end'.

It was also to Maud that Yeats stated: 'Too long a sacrifice can make a stone of the heart'.[6] There may come a time when mystic marriages have to end to open the way for something new.

There is however a different kind of mystic marriage to be made, one between the inner male and female that each soul carries with it - one of the specific challenges that the Capricorn/Cancer axis faces but which can be beneficial for any sign. Once this union is made, it brings inner wholeness. The soul can then go into relationship having connected to all the qualities of a perfect partner within itself and is no longer compelled to look 'out there' for someone to make it feel whole. The soul feels that it has something to offer a partner rather than having to fulfil its own needs. Relationships take on a new meaning when made from this state of inner completion. Projections cease and the soul can internalise personal qualities as 'mine'.

As a stage on the way to this inner marriage, a soul may find a perfect partner 'out there', a soulmate who reflects back all the unrecognised qualities of its own soul. Somewhere within that relationship, the soul has to recognise and own those qualities. At this moment, a wise soulmate steps back and allows the partner to make the inner integration knowing the relationship will be enhanced. This integration can be helped by visualisation.

Making the Inner Marriage
Choosing a time when you are sure there will be no distractions or interruptions, settle yourself comfortably in a chair. Take a few moments to focus your thoughts on the intention of the visualisation. Breathe gently, letting any tension flow away on the out-breath and breathing in a sense of peace and relaxation on the in-breath. When you have established a comfortable rhythm of breathing, slowly lower and raise your eyelids ten times letting your everyday concerns slip away as you do so. You will feel

waves of relaxation pulsing down your body. Then close your eyes and look up to the point between and slightly above your eyebrows.

When you are ready, picture yourself standing before the entrance to a vast temple. Before you are huge walls with their high, ornate gates. These are the gates to the inner courtyard. Slowly these gates open. A temple servant beckons you in.

The temple servant conducts you to a chamber in the inner courtyard. In this chamber a bath has been prepared. Servants bathe, dry and perfume you, and dress you in new robes to prepare you for your marriage.

When you are ready, the servant takes you to the offering chamber. Here you can make an offering to ensure a successful inner marriage. Whatever is most appropriate for you to offer up is on the altar before you.

Now the servant takes you to the bridal chamber to await your partner in this inner marriage. Behind thin, gauzy curtains your marriage bed awaits. When the servant withdraws from the room, your partner comes to you. This will be a total merging, a marriage on all levels. Allow your inner partner to come into your heart, to merge with you. To become one being. (Take as long as you need for this process).

It is now time to leave the bridal chamber. The temple servant comes to conduct you to the doors leading back to the outside world. As you step out of the gates, know that you are whole within yourself. You have integrated your masculine and feminine energies. No longer will you need to look outside yourself for your other half, it is within you.

As you stand outside the temple, picture yourself surrounded and protected by a ball of white light. Then take time to slowly bring your attention back to your physical body. Breathe a little more deeply, move your hands and feet. Gradually bring your attention back into the room, and then get up slowly. Standing with your feet on the floor, picture a grounding cord going from your feet deep down into the earth to hold you gently in incarnation. Then move around to become fully alert and back in everyday reality.

Note: If you find that the inner partner who appears is someone known to you in your day-to-day life, check out most carefully whether this is really your true inner partner. Projection, wishful thinking, past life events, or someone else's intense desire can affect who you see. Do not make the inner marriage unless you are sure. If you go ahead and make the marriage with someone who is in your life now, be sure to say: 'For as long as is appropriate'. It can be a powerful unifying force bringing the two of you together on all levels, and may be just what your relationship needs, but then, it may not be what you need. Be discriminating and ask for confirmation. If there is any doubt, wait until another day.

Making the mystic marriage helps you to become a whole person, as does fully living out the potential of your birth chart and the synastry embodied within close partnerships. To be fully whole you need to take back any projections, free yourself from old vows, have realistic expectations and allow yourself to practise love. Being whole leads to healthy relationships. In a healthy relationship each person takes responsibility for his or her own self and the feelings they have, but they also bring mutual, and unconditional, love and support to the partnership, which they nurture and cherish. When relationships are lived at this level, karma no longer operates. Souls can evolve together out of choice.

Chart Sources

Charlotte Bronte: Loretta Proctor and the Bronte Society. Time of birth was not recorded.

Elizabeth Barrett-Browning: *Profiles of Women* Lois Rodden.

Robert Browning: Birth Certificate via The Astrological Association.

Prince Charles: The Astrological Association.

Diana, Princess of Wales: The Astrological Association. A full discussion of the birthtimes given for Diana is contained in *The Mountain Astrologer* Dec/Jan 1997-98 pp32 ff.

Emily Dickinson: *Profiles of Women* Lois Rodden.

Lenin and the tsar: The Astrological Association.

Maud Gonne: Mary K.Greer and The Astrological Association. (Time has been rectified.)

Kenneth Halliwell: John Lahr - no birth time available.

Joe Orton: John Lahr - no birth time available.

Camilla Parker-Bowles: The Astrological Association.

Queen Victoria: Lois Rodden.

Roger Waters: Private source.

W.B. Yeats: Mary K.Greer and The Astrological Association. Time as noted by the family.

Client data has been withheld for confidentiality.

END NOTES

Introduction
1. *Homeric Hymns* Charles Boer translation, Spring Publications Inc, Dallas, 1993 pp 69- 70.

Chapter 1 - Karma and Relationships
1. *Many Mansions* Gina Cerminara. American Library, New York, 1988 p.123.
2. *Whole Heartedness Healing our Heartbreaks* Chuck Spezzano. Hodder and Stoughton, London, 2000 p.17.
3. *Soul Mates* Thomas Moore. Element, Shaftesbury, England, 1994 p.59.
4. *The Way of Karma* Judy Hall. Thorsons, London, 2001.

Chapter 2 - Kindred Spirits
1. *The Psychology of Romantic Love* Robert A. Johnston. Penguin, London 1986.
2. *Soul Mates* Thomas Moore p.59.
3. *Whole Heartedness* Chuck Spezzano.

Chapter 3 - Individual Expectations
1. *Successful But Something Missing* Ben Renshaw. Rider, London, 2000 p.111.
2. *Hands Acoss Time: The Soulmate Enigma*, Judy Hall. Findhorn Press, Scotland and *Successful But Something Missing* Ben Renshaw p.132.
3. *Hands Across Time* Judy Hall p.66.
4. *Women's Letters* Michelle Lovric. Michael O'Mara Books, London, 1998 p21.
5. See *The Hades Moon* Judy Hall. Samuel Weiser, Maine, 1998 pp.53ff for more details of the Bronte family.
6. *Elizabeth Barrett Browning* Margaret Forster. Chatto and Windus, London 1988 p.160.
7. ibid p.161 ff.
8. *Initiation* Elizabeth Haich. Mandala Books, London 1985.
9. Translated by a guide in Egypt.
10. *Hades Moon*, Judy Hall pp165ff.
11. *Astrology Karma and Transformation*, Steven Arroyo. CRCS, Vancouver, 1978.

12. ibid p.140.
13. *Women's Letters* Michelle Lovric p.7.
14. *Queen of the Night* Haydn Paul, Element Books, Shaftesbury, 1989 p.26. Later published as *The Astrological Moon* Samuel Weiser, Maine 1998.
15. *Dark Eros - The Imagination of Sadism* Thomas Moore. Spring Publictions, Connecticut, 1994. p.51.
16. ibid p.186.
17. ibid p.192.
18. *Saturn: A New Look at an Old Devil* Liz Greene. Samuel Weiser, Maine, 1976.
19. *Illusions* Richard Bach. Pan, London, 1979, p.65.
20. *Men Who Hate Women and the Women Who Love Them* Dr Susan Forward.Bantam Books, New York, NY, 1989 p113.
21. *The Hades Moon* Judy Hall.
22. *The Moon and the Virgin* Nor Hall. The Women's Press, London, 1980.
23. *Men Who Hate Women and the Women Who Love Them* Dr Susan Forward p. 43.

Chapter 4 - The Relationship Houses
1. *The Twelve Houses* Howard Sasportas. The Aquarian Press, Wellingborough, Northants. 1985.
2. *The Psychology of Romantic Love* Robert A Johnson.
3. ibid.
4. Debbie Shapiro, nee Boater, article in *Metamorphosis*, Autumn 1984.

Chapter 5 - The Karma of Interaspects
1. *Being Intimate* John and Kris Amodeo. Arkana, New York, 1986 p.108.
2. *Astrology Karma and Transformation* Steven Arroyo, p.162.
3. ibid p140.

Chapter 6 - Nodal Connections
1. *Astrology of Self Discovery* Tracy Marks. CCS, Reno, 1985 p.96.
2. ibid .
3. *Patterns of the Past* Judy Hall. The Wessex Astrologer, Bournemouth, England, 2000, pp. 184ff.
4. *Hands Across Time* Judy Hall pp. 73ff.
5. *Prick Up Your Ears* John Lahr, Penguin, London, 1978.
6. ibid.

7. ibid.
8. ibid
9. ibid.
10. ibid.
11. ibid.
12. ibid.
13. ibid.
14. ibid.
15. ibid.
16. ibid.
17. ibid.
18. ibid
19. ibid.
20. ibid.
21. ibid.
22. ibid.

Chapter 7
1. *The Hades Moon* Judy Hall p.81ff.
2. *Astrology, Karma And Transformation* Stephen Arroyo.
3. *Men Who Hate Women* Dr Susan Forward.
4. *The Chosen Child* Dr Patricia Love with Jo Robinson. Piatkus, London, 1990 p.8.

Chapter 8 - Adult Relationships
1. *Many Mansions* Gina Cerminara p.123
2. Reading 1436 quoted in *Edgar Cayce on Remembering Your Past Lives* Robert C. Smith. Aquarian press, Wellingborough 1990 p.43.
3. Source unknown.
4. *Hands Across Time* Judy Hall p.94.
5. *In the Light of Experience* David Icke,Thorsons London 1993.
6. *Many Mansions* Gina Cerminara.
7. *ibid* p.128.
8. *Whole Heartedness* Chuck Spezzano.
9. *Hands Across Time* Judy Hall p.157.
10. Note: Chuck Spezzano's book *Whole Heartedness* contains many exercises to find whole-heartedness.
11. Taken from *Hands Across Time* p.162ff.
12. *Relationships, Astrology and Karma* Pauline Stone. Harper Collins 1991 p.189.

Chapter 9 - What Do I See In You?

1. *How Love Works* Steve and Shaaron Biddulph. HarperCollins, London 2000.
2. C.G. Jung *Letters* vol.2 Edited and translated by Gerhard Adler with Aniela Jaffe. R.F.C.Hull Bollingen Series XCV, Princeton University Press, Princeton, 1973 p.27.
3. *Hands Across Time* Judy Hall p.142ff.
4. ibid pp.143ff.

Chapter 10 - Soulmates

1. *Plato's Symposium* Penguin, London, 1951 p.62.
2. For a more detailed discussion see *Hands Across Time*.
3. *The Astrology of Self Discovery*, Tracy Marks pp 95ff.
4. *Elizabeth Barrett Browning* Margaret Forster. Chatto and Windus, London, 1988, p.160.
5. *Principles of Past Life Therapy* Judy Hall p.42.
6. See *Hands Across Time* and Mary K Greer *Women of the Golden Dawn* Park Street Press, Rochester, 1995 for more details of this relationship.

Bibliography

ADLER, GERHARD AND JAFFE, ANIELA (trans) C.G. Jung *Letters* Vol.2. R.F.C.Hull, Bollingen Series XCV, Princeton University Press, Princeton, 1973 p.27.

AMODEO, JOHN AND CHRIS *Being Intimate* Arkana, NY, 1986.

ARROYO, STEPHEN *Astrology, Karma and Transformation* CRCS, Vancouver, 1978.

BACH, RICHARD *Illusions*, Pan, London, 1979.

BIDDULPH, STEVE AND SHAARON, *How Love Works* HarperCollins, London, 2000.

BOER, CHARLES (trans) *Homeric Hymns*, Spring Publications, Dallas, 1993.

CERMINARA, GINA *Many Mansions* New American Library, New York, 1988.

CERMINARA, GINA *Many Lives, Many Loves* De Vorss, Marina del Rey, CA, 1981.

ELLMAN, RICHARD *Yeats - the Man and his Masks* Penguin, London, 1979.

FORSTER, MARGARET *Elizabeth Barrett Browning* Chatto and Windus, London, 1988.

FORWARD, DR SUSAN *Men Who Hate Women and the Women Who Love Them*, Bantam Books, New York, 1989.

GREENE, LIZ *A New Look at an Old Devil*, Weiser, Maine, 1976.

GREER, MARY K. *Women of the Golden Dawn* Park Street Press, Rochester, 1996.

HAICH, ELIZABETH *Initiation* London, Mandala Books, 1985.

HALL, JUDY *Hands Across Time: The Soulmate Enigma* Findhorn Press, Forres, Scotland, 1997.

HALL, JUDY *Deja Who: A New Look at Past Lives* Findhorn Press, Forres, Scotland, 1998.

HALL, JUDY *The Hades Moon: Pluto in Aspect to the Moon* Samuel Weiser, Maine, 1997.

HALL, JUDY *Past Life Therapy* Thorsons, London, 1996.

HALL, JUDY *The Way of Reincarnation* Thorsons, London, 2000.

HALL, JUDY *The Way of Karma* Thorsons, London, 2001.

HALL, JUDY *Patterns of the Past* Wessex Astrologer, Bournemouth, 2000.

HALL, NOR *The Moon and the Virgin*, The Women's Press, London, 1980.

JEFFARES, A. NORMAN *W.B. Yeats: Man and Poet* Kyle Cathie, London, 1996.

JEFFARES, A. NORMAN *W.B. Yeats: A Vision* Arena, London, 1990.

JOHNSTON, ROBERT A. *The Psychology of Romantic Love* Penguin, London, 1986.

LAHR, JOHN *Prick Up Your Ears* Penguin, London, 1978.

LOVE, PATRICIA AND ROBINSON, JO *The Chosen Child* Piatkus, London, 1999.

LOVRIC, MICHELLE *Women's Letters* Michael O'Mara Books, London, 1998.

MARKS, TRACEY *The Astrology of Self Discovery* CCS Reno, NV, 1985.

MOORE, THOMAS *Soul Mates* Element, Shaftesbury, 1994.

MOORE, THOMAS *Dark Eros: The Imagination of Sadism* Spring Publications, Connecticut, 1994.

PAUL, HAYDN *Queen of the Night* Element Books, Shaftesbury, 1989. Republished as *The Astrological Moon*, Samuel Weiser, Maine, 1998.

PLATO *Symposium* Penguin, London, 1951.

RENSHAW, BEN *Successful But Something Missing* Rider, London, 2000.

RENSHAW, BEN *Together But Something Missing* Rider, London, 2001.

RODDEN, LOIS M. *Profiles of Women Astro-Data I* 1996 Edition.

SASPORTAS, HOWARD *The Twelve Houses* The Aquarian Press, Wellingborough, Northants. 1985.

SMITH, ROBERT C. *Edgar Cayce on Remembering Your Past Lives* Aquarian Press, Wellingborough, 1990.

SPEZZANO, CHUCK *Whole Heartedness* Hodder and Stoughton, London, 2000.

STONE, PAULINE *Relationships, Astrology and Karma* Aquarian Press, London, 1991.

YEATS, W.B. *Memoirs* MacMillan, London, 1972.

YEATS, W.B. *Autobiographies* MacMillan, London, 1980.

COPYRIGHT PERMISSION

Grateful thanks to John Lahr permission to quote from *Prick Up Your Ears* by John Lahr, published by Penguin, London, 1978.

ASTROLOGICAL SCHOOLS AND ORGANISATIONS

The Astrological Association
Lee Valley Technopark, Tottenham Hale, London N17 9LN.
Tel: 0208 880 4848, Fax: 0208 880 4849,
email: astrological.association@zetnet.co.uk.
website: www.astrologer.com/aanet
The AA publishes a bi-monthly Journal and runs an annual conference which is attended by astrologers from all over the world. Its main objectives are to facilitate the exchange of information within the astrological community, and promote the good name of astrology in general.

The Astrological Lodge of London
50, Gloucester Place, London W1H 4EA
The Astrological Lodge holds regular classes in London. It supports all branches of astrology, whilst encouraging the study and understanding of the philosophical, historical and symbolic aspects of astrology. Its magazine, The Astrological Quarterly, is free to members.

British Association for Vedic Astrology
1, Greenwood Close, Romsey, Hants. SO51 7QT
Tel: 01794 524178
email: bava@btinternet.com
website: www.bava.org
BAVA runs regular classes in London, and an annual conference which attracts speakers from all over the world.

British Astrological and Psychic Society
Robert Denholm House, Bletchingly Road, Nutfield Surrey, RH1 4HW
Tel: 0906 4700827
email: baps@tlpplc.com
website: www.bapsoc.co.uk
BAPS runs certificate courses in astrology, tarot and palmistry. It also provides a register of members, with details of local courses and discussion nights.

The Centre for Psychological Astrology (CPA)
Box 1815, London WC1N 3XX
Tel: 0208 749 2330
email cpalondon@aol.com
website: www.astrologer.com
Director: Liz Greene PhD, DFAstrolS, Dip Analyt Psych. The CPA is the outstanding centre in the world for the study of astrology in relationship to depth psychology. It runs regular courses and seminars in London and occasional additional seminars in Zurich. The 3-year Diploma programme, based at Regent's College in London, is also open to members of the public.

The Company of Astrologers
PO Box 3001, London, N1 1LY
Tel: 01227 362427
email: admin@coa.org.uk
website:: www/hubcom.com/coa
The Company is the home of divinatory astrology. It runs certificate courses as well as seminars and an annual conference.

The English Huber School of Astrological Counselling
PO Box 118, Knutsford, Cheshire, WA16 8TG
Tel/Fax: 01565 651131
email: huberschool@btinternet.com
website: www.ncsa.es/eschuber.sch
The English Huber School provides correspondence courses and workshops for all levels of astrology.

The Faculty of Astrological Studies
BM7470, London WC1N 3XX
Tel: 07000 790143
Fax: 01689 603537
email: info@astrology.org.uk
website: www.astrology.org.uk
The Faculty provides tuition at all levels of astrology, through home study courses, evening classes in London, seminar tapes and annual summer schools in Oxford.

The London School of Astrology
BCM Planets
London
WC1 3XX
Tel: 07002 33 44 55
email: admin@londonschoolofastrology.co.uk
website: www.londonschoolofastrology.co.uk
Started by Sue Tompkins, the LSA provides courses suitable for all levels, leading to certificate and diploma qualifications. Weekly and monthly lectures and workshops are held in London

The Mayo School
Alvana Gardens, Tregavethan, Truro, Cornwall, TR4 9EN
Tel: 01872 560048
email: jackie.h@virgin.net
website: www.astrology-world.com/mayo
Founded by Jeff Mayo, the school offers correspondence courses at certificate and diploma level and issues a list of their qualified consultants who have gained the diploma.

INDEX